ORGAN REGISTRATION
IN THEORY AND PRACTICE

ORGAN REGISTRATION

IN THEORY AND PRACTICE

BY

E. HAROLD GEER

J. FISCHER & BRO.
Harristown Road
Glen Rock, New Jersey

© 1957 by E. Harold Geer

Library of Congress Catalog Card Number: 56-5845

Printed in the United States of America

Kirby Lithographic Company, Inc.
409 Twelfth Street, Southwest
Washington 24, D. C.

Varityped by

Jones Composition Company, Inc.
930 F Street, Northwest
Washington 4, D. C.

TO MY

ORGAN STUDENTS

In appreciation of their patient,
though involuntary, participation
in the development of the theories
discussed in this book

PREFACE

One of the finest compliments ever paid to my teaching came from my daughter. While attending graduate school she once wrote: "Mr. W. is the same kind of teacher as you, Pop: he very firmly believes that a student should not only be told how to do something, but WHY it should be done that way." The importance of this came to me early in my career. So, in guiding the choice of registration I sought to explain *why* certain combinations were more effective than others, basing my reasoning inevitably on the physical nature of the tones combined, in so far as that was known. Gradually I evolved a theory of registration, which is set forth in this book.

However, that theory could not take definitive shape until I had more detailed scientific information than Helmholtz provided. When Dayton C. Miller's *The Science of Musical Sounds* became available I studied it eagerly, but the analyses of organ tone which it contained were completely inadequate to my purpose. When asked about other data, Dr. Miller graciously regretted that no analyses had been made beyond those reported in his book.

This situation led me to seek the assistance of the Department of Physics of Vassar College, where I was organist, in order that we might make our own analyses. Thanks to the hospitality and cooperation of that department, and to generous grants from research funds of the College for the purchase of additional equipment, I was able to carry on a series of experiments which, owing to schedule limitations, extended over many years. In the mean time physicists in other parts of the country who had more technical knowledge than I possessed, and more time for research, were doing valuable work along the same line. In this book, however, I am using only my own analyses because they were all made under the same conditions, and thus they afford a more valid comparison of the characteristics of different stops; moreover, they cover a wider range of organ tone than any published analyses. To the types which were available on our own campus were added others, which were kindly loaned by Austin Organs, Inc. These are represented by Graphs xvi, xx, xxi, and xxii.

My greatest personal debt is to Dr. Paul A. Northrop, who was responsible for the selection and installation of the equipment, and was my constant collaborator and adviser in making and interpreting the analyses. For further advice concerning the presentation of technical material I am indebted to Dr. Harvey Fletcher, and to my daughter, Dr. Ednah H. Geer.

I wish to express my gratitude to the many persons who read the first draft of this book and encouraged me with their interest. Helpful suggestions were received from Dr. George S. Dickinson, Mr. George E. Henry, and particularly from Mr. Edward B. Gammons who studied the entire manuscript, and whose constructive criticism was invaluable.

My indebtedness extends across the Atlantic to Monsieur Alexandre Cellier, for permission to quote from his *L'Orgue moderne*, and to Monsieur Flor Peeters, who graciously consented to the presentation of a different interpretation of the last page of his 'Élégie', and, together with his publisher, granted permission to reproduce that part of the music. My special thanks go to Professor Dr. Hans Klotz, who not only granted permission to use his book, *Über die Orgelkunst...*, as a source for certain specifications, but took the trouble to review the material in question, giving me the benefit of his latest study. Again, I cannot adequately thank Dr. M. A. Vente who, in response to my request to take specifications from his *Bouwstoffen...*, added valuable information — above all, sending me the newly discovered specifications of Sweelinck's large organ.

I am indebted to Mr. David Walsh of The Baldwin Piano Company, New York, for an explanation of swell pedal compensation for discrepancies in the aural response to different frequencies, quoted on page 19. Permission to quote or reproduce copyright material is acknowledged in the footnotes. I wish here to express my sincere thanks to the following publishers who have granted such permission:

Bärenreiter-Verlag, Kassel.
Bell Telephone Laboratories, New York.
A. & C. Black, Ltd., London.
VEB Breitkopf & Härtel Musikverlag, Leipzig.
Librairie E. Droz, Geneva.
Elkan-Vogel Company, Philadelphia; agents for Durand & Cie., and
    J. Hamelle & Cie., Paris.
Librairie Fischbacher, Paris.
J. Fischer & Bro., New York.
Henry Lemoine & Cie., Paris.
Macdonald and Company, Ltd., London.
The Macmillan Company, New York.
H. J. Paris, Amsterdam.
C. F. Peters Corporation, New York.
Éditions Musicales de la Schola Cantorum, Paris.
B. Schott's Söhne, Mainz.

Lastly I wish to record my deep gratitude to my daughter for drawing the graphs shown on pages 50-55, and to my wife for innumerable services, including the proofreading of the copy and of the master sheets.

North Sandwich, New Hampshire   E. HAROLD GEER
August 29, 1955

CONTENTS

PART V: PRACTICAL SUGGESTIONS

TABLES AND FIGURES

MUSICAL EXAMPLES

INTRODUCTION
CRITERIA

Lionel Dauriac[1] likens the awakening of musical intelligence in an individual to the process of learning to talk. The child learns (1) by hearing the speech of others, to the point of familiarity; (2) by his own experimentation, at first aimless, then imitative; and (3) by trying to express his own ideas. The parallel in the development of the musical intelligence of an individual is obvious. Still more impressive is the working of this process in a group of contemporaneous composers, and even extended through a series of generations.

The artistic activities of any individual begin with what is familiar. What he has heard is intelligible to him, and so determines his taste. His first efforts are to reproduce what he enjoys, to imitate what is familiar. Later he craves self expression, and departs from the beaten track in search of new paths, leading to unknown beauties and wider horizons. These excursions may be the result of an inner urge demanding expression; or of an imagination reaching beyond the range of experience; or of an adventurous spirit which demands something new and exciting; or a study of the terrain, as it were — investigating the theoretical possibilities of new procedures; or perhaps merely ennui — a vague dissatisfaction with familiar effects, and a desire for something, anything, different.

Such motives have led composers to introduce innovations which have affected the development of musical style. The significant fact is that the work of each period is founded on what has preceded — it is the outgrowth of what is familiar; and each age makes its own contribution to the process of evolution, adding new resources, perhaps introducing a new trend or modifying the direction of an old one, passing on to its heirs a richer and more varied art, all of which becomes familiar to the new generation and furnishes the basis of still further development.

In this process the theoretician has an important place. He studies the work of former composers, explaining the principles which have guided them, deducing formulae and codifying the details of their practices in statements which are unfortunately called rules. He also adds his original contribution, working out theories based on his analysis of the literature and his own scientific investigations.

Unpopular as the theoretician is among students who resent the restrictions of his so-called rules, and among composers who wish to discard all convention, his work is extremely valuable:

[1]Bibliography 142, pp. 101 ff.

1. It tends to preserve the continuity of the development of musical expression, keeping it consistent with the natural processes of evolution and psychological experience.

2. It contributes toward a more complete understanding, and a more just appraisal of existing musical literature.

3. It provides a vocabulary for the young composer, without which he would be handicapped in his self-expression.

4. It enables the student to learn from the experience of others what he would otherwise have to learn, more laboriously and perhaps more awkwardly, from his own experiments.

5. It establishes a standard of comparison which is valuable in assisting the young composer to criticise and perfect his own product.

The organist, whose registration is also a creative process, is without such advantages. The real theorist in this field has not yet appeared.[2] The player is largely dependent on his own intuition and taste, which are determined by his particular environment — by what happens to be familiar to him, personally. In certain centers, such as Paris and London, where there is ample opportunity for the interchange of ideas, and where there has been a constant teacher-pupil succession, a fairly consistent tradition has been handed down from one generation to another.

This tradition is promulgated and modified by the same sequence of familiarity, imitation, experiment, and individual expression, which affects the development of procedures in composition. The contribution of the theorist, however, is lacking. On the one hand the organist's connection with the past is tenuous and fallible. Records of past practices are meager and often difficult to interpret. Until a few years ago the average organist was largely dependent on casual references in historical and biographical works. Even with the added material brought to light by recent research the information is incomplete, and much of it is unavailable in English. So the organist inherits a vague tradition, affected to an unknown degree by local conditions and accidental influence.

The extent to which even the best organists have been guided by what was familiar in their generation is illustrated by the registrations suggested by such recent editors as Guilmant, Bonnet, Bossi, and even Straube, in their collections of sixteenth, seventeenth, and eighteenth century music.[3] In some instances their indications not only modernize, but actually denature the music. Straube, whose modernization never

[2]Everett E. Truette, in his book on *Organ Registration* (Bibl. 130), included a brief discussion of the analysis of tone qualities, but he did not derive a theory of registration from the facts presented. George Ashdown Audsley's monumental work, *The Art of Organ Building* (Bibl. 56), is suggestive, but he was primarily concerned with the tonal design of the organ and made no applications directly helpful to the organist.

[3]Bibl. 181, 182, 168, 170, 199.

reached the point of vandalism, made complete amends in his *Alte Meister, neue Folge.*[4] Bonnet also, in his later collections, showed a more sensitive understanding of the early music.[5]

The organist's independent experiments are guided almost wholly by intuition, his individual taste, and perhaps that of his public. The results are sometimes amazing, particularly in this country where the force of tradition is comparatively weak, and where the average listener has had, until recently, little opportunity to become familiar with organ music which goes deeper than a sensuous stimulus. Here, a few years ago, the prevailing taste was for music which could be absorbed with the least effort — pretty tunes presented in prettier colors.

Organists of the early part of this century were quite willing to satisfy that demand — in fact, their own taste was often determined by similar conditions. So organ builders were encouraged to devote their ingenuity to the invention of more varied and astonishing colors, and to the development of a more efficient mechanism with which to control them. Many organs of that period were primarily aggregations of solo stops, completely lacking any real ensemble. The tonal scheme was dominated by the eight foot pitch, and power was provided by heavy diapasons and loud reeds. With the advent of the cinema organ shortly thereafter the degeneration was complete.

This was the result of a vicious circle in which organists and builders catered to the popular taste, and thereby contributed to its perpetuation and further deterioration. There were, of course, exceptions — men who were guided by their own convictions and ideals, whose roots were in the best traditions of the past, and who reached out to a height from which they could see beyond their immediate environment.

George Ashdown Audsley was an architect, whose chief interest was the reform of organ building. His tonal designs were the result of profound study and technical knowledge, a sensitive ear, and freedom from both the shackles of convention and the lure of sensationalism. We have progressed far beyond his ideas, but he was a prophet in his time.

Lynnwood Farnam was a skillful organist whose uncompromising ideals led him to familiarize his public with the most significant available music. He commanded attention because of his impeccable execution, his refined taste, his subtle sense of color, and his unerring instinct for tone combination. His influence, together with that of others of lesser talent, almost transformed the taste of the American amateur of organ music in the decade which preceded his death. People began to appreci-

[4] Bibl. 200.
[5] Bibl. 167, 169.

ate the organ idiom, and to acquire a sense of ensemble and of synthetic color.

Further strides toward ensemble-consciousness have been made under the leadership of recent progressive organ designers and the organists who have cooperated with them. As our ears have become more accustomed to the sound of high pitches we have become less aware of them as such, and more ready to relate them to the lower pitches whose partials they reinforce. Combinations which, a few years ago, would have been condemned as screechy are now accepted as normal. Indeed, our taste demands them, and the registration of a generation ago is now considered dull and heavy. So far has the pendulum swung away from our conceptions at the beginning of the century that we now have, in place of the domination of the eight-foot pitch, what might facetiously be called the domination of the two-foot pitch.

In the confusion of such rapidly changing fashion we may well inquire into the validity of our criteria. Since taste is largely a matter of habit and familiarity, which can be arbitrarily controlled, it is subject to the influence of propaganda, fads, inertia and indolence on the part of both performers and listeners, and various other forces which coexist in the realm of art. How is the public, how indeed are the organists, to judge between good and bad? Obviously there is need of a more definite criterion. We shall seek it, or at least a guide and standard of comparison, in a *theory* of registration.

A theory of tone combination must logically be based on the nature of the tones employed. This brings us at once into the field of acoustics — a science which, although it dates from the time of Pythagoras, is still young. Probably the most significant achievement, for our special purpose, was the discovery of the physical nature of tone quality, corroborated by the experiments conducted by Helmholtz in the middle of the nineteenth century.[6] His equipment was inadequate, and some of his data must be corrected in the light of recent experiments with more precise instruments, but his explanation of tone quality is still sound and forms the basis of all modern investigations, including those which have led to the amazing improvement of the radio and the phonograph.

Helmholtz' analyses were made with the aid of resonators tuned to respond to the several partials of the tones tested. More accurate measurements were made by the late Dayton C. Miller, who used an instrument which he called a 'phonodeik'.[7] He photographed the wave form and separated it into its component parts, which were then accurately meas-

[6] Helmholtz' theory and the phenomena mentioned in the ensuing paragraphs are explained in Chapters I and II.

[7] These experiments are reported in Bibl. 28.

ured and recorded. The analyses reported in Chapter II of this book were made with an electric wave analyser. The sound was picked up by a microphone and amplified; the instrument was then tuned to each partial in turn, registering the pressure of its vibration in millevolts.

Work along these lines has only just begun. The problem is complicated by (1) the extreme difficulty of eliminating the effect of external standing waves; (2) the interference (in the case of an open pipe) between the wave originating at the mouth and the one originating at the end of the pipe; (3) the ever-varying acoustical environment which affects the listener, but cannot be taken into account in making analyses; and (4) the imperfectly understood factors of the response of the ear and the interpretation of the brain.

In view of these facts our analyses cannot be considered final or exact. Nevertheless, they give a sufficiently clear picture of the nature of various qualities to provide a reasonable basis for our theory of registration.

In the development of this theory and its application to the various situations encountered by the organist, many specific problems are examined. Since extensive quotations are impossible these examples are, in so far as practicable, taken from standard works which are generally accessible. An index of the compositions cited or studied will be found at the end of the volume.

This discussion is presented in five main sections:

  I. Preliminary scientific and technical information.
 II. The application of the acoustical information to the selection and combination of stops.
III. The application of the theory of tone combination to the interpretation of actual music.
 IV. Consideration of media, including a sketch of the history of tonal design and registration practices.
  V. Practical suggestions.

Part I

SCIENTIFIC AND TECHNICAL INFORMATION

CHAPTER ONE

ACOUSTICS

The Physical Nature of Sound

A musical tone is the aural perception of regularly alternating compression and rarefaction of the air. These alternations are called *waves*, partly because their behavior is analogous to that of waves in water. In fact, the vibrations which they produce can, by means of an oscillograph or oscilloscope, be translated into visible linear waves. It is, therefore, valid as well as convenient to use wave terminology, referring to the point of greatest compression as the *crest*, and the point of greatest rarefaction as the *trough* of the wave.

The specific location of a given point on the wave curve (representing the position in the compression-rarefaction cycle) is the *phase* of the wave at that instant. The term is also loosely used to suggest the direction of the displacement — whether compression or rarefaction, whether above or below the mean level of the linear wave.

We recognize three characteristics of a tone: *pitch*, *loudness* or *intensity*, and *quality* or *timbre*. Psychologists find a fourth characteristic, *volume*, which they conceive of as representing quantity as distinct from intensity of tone. Whatever significance this may have is a matter of perception, and will be explained after the discussion of the physical properties of tone.

The *frequency* with which the point of greatest compression (or any other point on the wave cycle) strikes the ear drum is heard as pitch. Thus, when we hear middle C (c^1)[1] at the present standard of pitch, the points of greatest compression are striking the ear 261.6 times a second. When we hear the A next above (a^1), the corresponding points reach the ear 440 times a second. Scientists normally identify pitch by this frequency, or rather (which is the same thing) by the frequency of the original vibrations. This is advantageous because it represents the actual physical phenomenon, it defines the smallest variations in pitch, and it is not subject to change in standard. When they have occasion to mention a pitch by name, their standard is the so-called *philosophical pitch*, where the frequency of every C is a power of two (16, 32, 64,

[1]We shall use the organ builders' pitch terminology, as shown below:

CC——BB C——B c^1——b^1 c^2——b^2 c^3——b^3 c^4 etc.

9

128, etc.).   This is arithmetically convenient, and it approximates the present standard.

Since absolute pitch corresponds to absolute frequency, relative pitch corresponds to relative frequency, and intervals correspond to frequency ratios.   When an octave is sounded, the frequency of the upper pitch is exactly twice that of the lower pitch.   This exact doubling of the fre-quency, so that (assuming phase correspondence) every wave crest of the lower pitch coincides with every alternate crest of the upper pitch, gives a sense of tonal identity, and we call the two pitches by the same name.

TABLE 1

INTERVALS AND FREQUENCY RATIOS

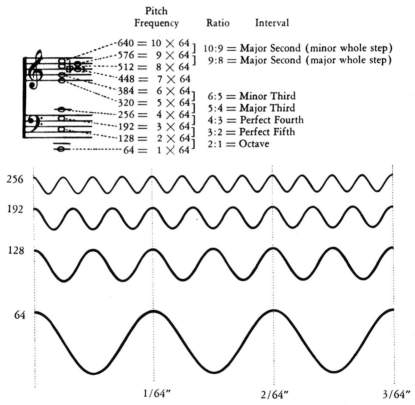

	Pitch Frequency	Ratio	Interval
	640 = 10 × 64	10:9 =	Major Second (minor whole step)
	576 = 9 × 64	9:8 =	Major Second (major whole step)
	512 = 8 × 64		
	448 = 7 × 64		
	384 = 6 × 64	6:5 =	Minor Third
	320 = 5 × 64	5:4 =	Major Third
	256 = 4 × 64	4:3 =	Perfect Fourth
	192 = 3 × 64	3:2 =	Perfect Fifth
	128 = 2 × 64	2:1 =	Octave
	64 = 1 × 64		

Figure 1. Linear waves showing frequency ratios. The waves show periodic compression (above the axis) and rarefaction (below the axis). The distance from left to right shows time lapse. For the frequencies given at the left of the figure, the vertical dotted lines are spaced 1/64 second apart.

Again, when we hear an interval of a pure fifth, there are three waves of the upper pitch for every two waves of the lower pitch.

Thus the octave is produced by a frequency ratio of 2:1; the perfect fifth by a ratio of 3:2. Continuing from there, the ratio of the perfect fourth is 4:3; the major third, 5:4; the minor third, 6:5; the major second, 9:8 (major whole step), or 10:9 (minor whole step). These ratios of course apply to acoustically pure intervals, which are only approximated by equal temperament.[2] See Table 1 and Figure 1.

The length of a sound wave (the distance which separates corresponding points on successive waves) is inversely proportional to its frequency. For example, the frequency of the lowest tone of an eight-foot rank is 65.4. That means that the wave crests are so spaced that they pass a given point at the rate of 65.4 per second. Assuming that they are travelling at a speed of 1132 feet per second,[3] the wave crests are $\frac{1132}{65.4}$ feet apart. The wave length, then, is $\frac{1132}{65.4}$ (= 17.3) feet. Again, the highest tone of the same rank has a frequency of 2093. Its wave length, then, is $\frac{1132}{2093}$ feet, or about 6.49 inches. Similarly the wave length of the lowest tone of a thirty-two foot rank can be computed to be about 69.19 feet, and that of the highest tone of a two-foot rank about 1.62 inches.

The sensation of loudness depends on the actual amount of displacement of the ear membrane, responding directly to the variation in air pressure. This is determined by the amount of energy received from the source (varying as its square root), and corresponds to the amplitude of the vibration. Thus, in order of cause and effect, the amount of energy determines the amount of variation in air pressure (the amount of compression and rarefaction), which acts upon the ear drum and is interpreted by the brain as loudness.

The unit of measurement of pressure variation is the *barye*,[4] the value of which may best be understood by comparison with more familiar measurements. Everyone knows that a barometer measures variations in atmospheric pressure in inches of mercury displacement. Organists are aware that the air pressure in an organ chest is measured in inches of water displacement. In these terms the minute value of the barye may be expressed as follows:

A barye equals about one-millionth of the normal atmospheric pressure. If we descend ten feet in an elevator the atmospheric pressure is in-

[2] See page 81, footnote 26.

[3] This is the approximate speed of sound under normal auditorium conditions — a temperature of 70° with some degree of humidity.

[4] Defined as one dyne per square centimeter.

creased by about 360 baryes.[5]

Again, a barye equals about 0.0004 of an inch of water displacement. Air pressure of four inches (a pressure frequently used in organs) is equivalent to about ten thousand baryes.

The response of the ear to pressure variation (like its response to frequency) is logarithmic. This means that the amount of pressure variation (so also the amount of energy) must be increased by a certain *proportion* in order to effect a specific increase in loudness (just as the frequency must be increased by a certain proportion in order to raise the pitch by a specific interval). In other words, the energy must be *multiplied* in order to *add* loudness.

Intensity may be considered the physical analogue of loudness. It can be measured in units of energy or of pressure variation, but because of the large range of numerical values, and because of its relation to loudness, a logarithmic scale is adopted for physical intensity also.

Variations in intensity and loudness are measured in *decibels* (db), or tenths of a *bel*. A bel is the amount of increase in intensity which is effected by multiplying the amount of energy by ten. A decibel, then, is the amount of increase in intensity effected by multiplying the amount of energy by the tenth root of ten (approximately 1.2589). Generally speaking this is about the smallest change which the ear can detect.

The quantitative relation among the factors of energy, pressure variation, and intensity are summed up in Table 2.

Absolute loudness is related to the threshold of hearing.[6] The scale of absolute *intensity* takes for its zero level 0.0002 barye (determined by the threshold of hearing at a frequency of 1,000 cycles per second).[7]

It would appear that the student of registration would be primarily concerned with the third characteristic of musical tones, which we call timbre. The investigations of Helmholtz, referred to in the Introduction, showed that what we hear as timbre is the effect of the simultaneous sounding of various discrete pitches. For example, when a violinist or a pianist plays a note, the string not only vibrates as a whole, producing its fundamental pitch, but it also vibrates in halves, producing the pitch an

[5]These comparisons are suggested by Sir James Jeans in Bibl. 18, p. 218. He uses the term *bar*, which in present usage means 1,000 baryes.

[6]See pp. 15-16.

[7]Intensity levels, in accordance with the equivalents shown in Table 2, are as follows:

0.0002	barye	=	0 db
0.002	barye	=	20 db
0.02	barye	=	40 db
0.2	barye	=	60 db
2	baryes	=	80 db
20	baryes	=	100 db
200	baryes	=	120 db

TABLE 2

QUANTITATIVE RELATION OF
ENERGY, PRESSURE VARIATION, AND INTENSITY

IF THE ENERGY IS MULTIPLIED BY	THEN THE PRESSURE VARIATION IS MULTIPLIED BY	AND THE INTENSITY IS INCREASED BY
* 1.2589	° 1.22	§ 1 db
10	3.162	10 db
100	10	20 db
1,000	31.623	30 db
10,000	100	40 db
100,000	316.228	50 db
1,000,000	1,000	60 db
10,000,000	3,162.278	70 db
100,000,000	10,000	80 db
1,000,000,000	31,622.777	90 db
10,000,000,000	100,000	100 db
100,000,000,000	316,227.766	110 db
1,000,000,000,000	1,000,000	120 db

* Energy coefficient § Ten times logarithm of energy coefficient
° Square root of energy coefficient

octave above the fundamental; it vibrates in thirds, producing the pitch a twelfth above the fundamental, and so on.[8] These various pitches, caused by the fractional vibrations of the string, are called *partials* of the tone of the string. Since the tone as we hear it is the effect of the sounding of *all* the included pitches, the fundamental itself is only a part of the tone, and it is called the first partial. The octave, with double the frequency, is the second partial; the twelfth, with three times the fundamental frequency, is the third partial; and so on. These facts are too familiar to call for extensive explanation. The first ten partials of CC are given in Table 1.

Any given timbre is the effect of the particular partials which the tone contains, and their relative loudness. For example, the tone of a fat flute is composed almost wholly of the fundamental pitch; a diapason normally has a large number of partials, tapering in intensity above the octave; a thin string has a relatively weak fundamental with stronger upper partials. In the next chapter will be found graphs showing the analyses of some typical organ stops.

These essential facts, first stated in Ohm's Law of Acoustics (1843), were developed by Helmholtz in his epoch-making work, *Die Lehre von*

[8] Actually these proportions are not quite exact, owing to the imperfect elasticity of strings.

der Tonempfindungen . . . (1862),[9] but the amazing number of partials included in familiar qualities, and the important contribution of very high partials to these qualities, have only recently been discovered. It is now known that a series of partials, each one of which is inaudible by itself, may unite to produce an audible tone.[10] It follows that high partials which are too weak or too high to be heard individually may actually affect the tone quality. This is one reason such a high frequency range is necessary for fidelity in phonographic and radio reproduction. It also has its bearing on organ registration.

This reduction of tone quality to its constituent elements is of the utmost importance to our theory of tone combination. Since timbre is the result of the synthesis of different pitches of various intensities, it follows that a combination of timbres is in reality a combination of combinations of pitches. Any stop combination, therefore, is nothing but a complex combination of single pitches, and the whole problem of registration resolves itself into a study of pitches. The basic principles are of the utmost simplicity, but their application is exceedingly involved.[11]

The Response of the Ear

The foregoing has to do with the actual, physical nature of sound. It does not follow that it shows exactly what we hear. The response of the ear varies greatly with the frequency and intensity of the stimulus.

Since pitch is the mind's interpretation of vibration frequency, the range of pitch might be supposed to be infinite. Such, however, is not the case. Few persons can hear a pure tone as low as 32' C, which has a frequency of sixteen vibrations per second. The highest frequency which a human being can hear is in the neighborhood of 20,000 vibrations per second, which is about e♭[7] — just above the top note of a one-foot rank on the organ. Beyond these limitations the vibration, if perceived at all, is felt rather than heard.

There are also limits to the intensity of vibrations which can be heard. If they are too feeble they make no impression; if they are too strong they produce a sensation of discomfort. The lower limits of perceptible in-

---

[9] Bibl. 16.

[10] "It is interesting to note here that the threshold data show that 10 pure tones, which are below the threshold when sounded separately, will combine to give a tone which can be heard. When the components are all in the high pitch range and all equally loud, each component may be from 6 to 8 db below the threshold and the combination will still be audible." — Harvey Fletcher and W. A. Munson, Bibl. 15, p. 93.

[11] In this explanation of the phenomenon of partials it is obvious that the word "pitch" has referred to simple, discrete pitches, which are the irreducible elements of timbre. In order to avoid ambiguity it will be understood, as we continue, that all reference to frequency or pitch, unless it is otherwise specified or implied by the context, assumes pure tones or single partials of a complex tone.

tensity vary greatly with the pitch. For example, the softest audible pure tone at middle C is about 22 db more intense (physically) than one which can be heard at f^4 (the point of maximum sensitivity of the ear). It requires 158 times the energy to produce it, and the pressure change is about 12.6 times as great. Again, the softest audible pure tone at 8' C (CC) is still more intense by 28 db. Its pressure variation is more than 25 times as great as that required at middle C, and is produced by 631 times the energy.[12]

The minimum intensity which will produce an audible pure tone is called the *threshold of hearing*; the maximum which can be heard without discomfort is called the *threshold of feeling*, or the *threshold of pain*. Figure 2 shows these thresholds for the various audible frequencies, the lowest curve indicating the minimum audible intensities for all pitches, and the uppermost curve indicating the threshold of feeling.

It will be seen from the foregoing that the region of the greatest sensitivity of the ear — that is, where tones of the smallest intensity can be heard — lies in the top octave of a four foot rank. Thus it is beyond the highest normal fundamental pitch of the organ keyboard.

Since a tone at 8' C can barely be heard when it is 28 db more intense than the softest audible tone at middle C, it is evident that if the intensity of middle C be raised 28 db to equal that of the softest audible 8' C, it will sound much louder than the low C. Therefore loudness (which is perceptual) is not equivalent to intensity (which is physical).

The curves in Figure 2 show for different pitches throughout the audible range, the physical intensities of tones which sound equally loud. These *loudness levels* are ten loudness decibels, or *phons*, apart, and are plotted on a scale representing intensity decibels. Phons are defined by the intensity decibels at a frequency of 1,000 cycles per second.[13] The significance of these data is shown by the following comparison.

If the lowest and highest keys of an organ manual are sounding pure tones of normal (8') pitch, of equal physical intensity, the relative loudness of the two tones (expressed in decibels, or phons, above the threshold) will be approximately as stated below:

When low C is barely audible,   the loudness of high C is 48 db
When the loudness of low C is 30 db, the loudness of high C is 65 db

[12]Measured on the graph in Figure 2. Jeans, Bibl. 18, p. 220, shows an extensive series of comparisons. Since he uses round number approximations, there are some discrepancies between his pressure and energy values, but the general picture is valid and significant.

[13]The arbitrary assignment of a frequency of 1,000 cycles per second as the point where physical and aural decibels correspond is a matter of convenience. It is also a region where the loudness levels are flatter than anywhere else in the normal range of music.

When the loudness of low C is   60 db, the loudness of high C is 77 db
When the loudness of low C is   90 db, the loudness of high C is 94 db
When the loudness of low C is 120 db, high C is 10 db above the audible limit

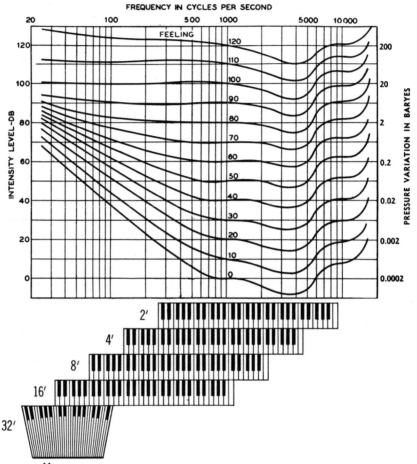

Figure 2.[14] Area of hearing, showing loudness levels in relation to frequency and
to the pitches of the organ keyboards.

The findings on which these estimates are based are subject to correction in later experiments, but the essential fact will remain that,
within the normal range of music, higher tones are louder in proportion to
their physical intensity than lower tones. From this it follows that a tone
which contains many upper partials is louder in proportion to its physical
intensity than a tone of the same pitch and same intensity which contains

[14]The graph of the area of hearing is reproduced from the *Bell System Technical Mono-
graph* B-756 (= Bibl. 15) through the courtesy of Bell Telephone Laboratories.

few upper partials. This relation between loudness and timbre has been the subject of direct experiment, with convincing results.[15] Its application to our theory of registration is of primary importance.

Early in this chapter it was mentioned that psychologists recognize volume as an attribute of tone, representing quantity as distinct from intensity. A similar conception is suggested by such common expressions as "a fat diapason", or "a tubby tone". Psychological experiments in the study of this quality indicate that low tones are more "voluminous" than high tones.

Although the author is neither a physicist nor a psychologist, he ventures to suggest that this sense of volume may be the result of the discrepancy between the physical intensity and the aural loudness of low tones. Greater intensity means greater pressure variation. If the variation becomes sufficiently violent, it produces a disagreeable sensation instead of a sound. Is it not inevitable that a very soft tone produced by a pressure variation of 25 millebaryes (CC) should give a different impression from that of an equally soft tone produced by a pressure variation of only one millebarye (c^1)? In fact, when we hear low pedal tones, giving the impression of volume, there is often more sense of feeling than of hearing.[16] We have only to extend this reasoning to higher pitches, where the sensation is too small to be so easily identified, to find a possible explanation of what the psychologists call volume. Whether or not this explanation is valid, the facts from which it is derived have an important bearing on our theory of registration.

A phenomenon which is related to the impression of volume is the effect of *masking*. Any tone tends to obscure other tones near to it, or to its partials, in pitch. More effective masking is produced by low tones, by loud tones, and by pure tones (which, if loud, produce aural partials[17]). Thus a loud low tone may affect the audibility of nearly all pitches above it. Moreover, tones which are near together in pitch do not make their full individual contributions to the loudness of the combination; the louder they each are, the farther apart must they be in order to avoid dynamic impairment.[18]

Audible Increments

The foregoing has to do with the absolute audibility of various pitches and intensities; but we are also concerned with discrimination, based

[15] Bibl. 12, pp. 61-63.

[16] Fletcher reports that laboratory experiments show that "for frequencies as low as 30 cycles [about 16' C] the auditory sensations are very indistinct... The hearing and feeling sensations are difficult to distinguish." — Bibl. 13, p. 161.

[17] See p. 20.

[18] Bibl. 11, p. 289. See also Bibl. 14, pp. 153 ff.

on a comparative perception of tones. We not only need to hear the sounds, but we must be able to recognize differences in pitch, and to perceive changes in intensity.

Many experiments have been conducted to discover the smallest variation in pitch which can be detected at various frequency levels. According to Shower and Biddulph[19] it requires a change of about a semitone at 8' C for the average listener to hear a difference in pitch between two pure tones. Ascending the scale, pitch discrimination becomes more acute — rapidly at first (the sensitivity doubling with each octave), then more and more gradually, until at the very top of an eight-foot rank the ear can detect a difference of only one twenty-fifth of a semitone. Experiments indicate only a slight falling off in pitch sensitivity above that.

These records show the differences "at which the observer could just detect a variation."[20] They do not show what intervals or pitches can be *recognized*. They are not, therefore, wholly valid from the musical standpoint. It means nothing, in listening to music, to be able to hear that two pitches are different, unless one can also hear their relationship. Since it is obviously impossible to recognize a difference which cannot be heard, the lack of pitch discrimination in the lower range has musical significance. It does not follow, however, that the detected differences above the range of an eight-foot stop indicate that that range is particularly favorable for musical delineation. On the contrary, the difficulty of identifying pitches and intervals in a high range is a common experience.[21] For our purpose we can accept the findings of the psychologist, Robert Morris Ogden, who places the point of greatest pitch sensitivity at c^3, with a falling off in both directions.[22]

Not only is the ear more sensitive to pitch differences at relatively high frequencies than in a lower range, but it perceives the high pitches more promptly. Complete data are not available, but Seashore reports that c^2 can be heard in less than half the time required for tenor C (two octaves below).[23]

For the sensitivity of the ear to changes in intensity we will return to Figure 2. Here we find that the lines representing loudness levels are farthest apart between the frequencies of 800 and 4,000, or approximately between g^2 and b^4. This shows that in this range a specific change of

[19] Bibl. 42, p. 275-87.

[20] Bibl. 42, p. 279.

[21] This fact is conceded by certain acousticians. See Bibl. 9, p. 47, and Bibl. 25, p.93.

[22] Bibl. 34, pp. 74-5.

[23] Bibl. 40, p. 62.

loudness involves thè greatest change in physical intensity; or, conversely, a specific change in intensity produces the least change in loudness.[24]

This is exemplified by the operation of certain electronic instruments in which the swell pedal controls the amount of electrical energy which is applied to the tone. Let us assume that the dynamics are so adjusted that when the swell pedal is 'closed' the lowest and highest tones of the eight-foot rank are each 40 db above the threshold of hearing. Then if the swell pedal is 'opened' to the point where the loudness of low C is increased 40 db (to 80 db above the threshold), high C will be only 14 db louder (54 db above the threshold). A similar comparison of the eight-foot and two-foot ranks at tenor C shows that when the loudness of the eight-foot tone is increased 40 db, the two-foot tone becomes only 24 db louder.[25]

Again, experiments have shown that the ear can detect the smallest change in physical intensity between the frequencies of 1,000 and 6,000 (between b^2 and $f\sharp^5$), with a maximum sensitivity at around 4,000 cycles (b^4).[26] Thus between b^2 and b^4 the smallest change in intensity can be heard, *and* a given change in intensity produces the smallest change in loudness. It follows that in this region (which corresponds roughly to the top two octaves of a four foot stop) the ear is most sensitive to dynamic changes. Accordingly it is in this region that dynamic changes are most effective.

Not only do the impression of loudness, the sensitivity to dynamic changes, and pitch discrimination vary with the frequency, but the perception of pitch is somewhat affected by loudness. Within the normal range of organ music the tendency is for pure tones to sound lower as the intensity is increased. This effect centers in the octave below middle C, with a maximum at G. At that point, if the loudness of a pure tone is increased from 40 db to 100 db above the threshold of hearing, the audible pitch will drop about two and a half semitones.[27]

This fact is not very significant to the organist for the following reasons: (1) the effect is negligible outside the range from GG to g^1; (2) it is corrected by the simultaneous sounding of other pitches; (3) it

[24]This is borne out by direct experiment. B. A. Kingsbury reports: "It was found that if the amplitudes of pure tones are increased in equal ratios the loudness of low frequency tones increases much more rapidly than that of high frequency tones." – Bibl. 21, p. 588.

[25]Some manufacturers of electronic instruments provide compensation in the design of their swell pedals. One manufacturer writes: "The essential feature is a simple high-pass filter in the expression control circuit which places the control arm only slightly in effect at the lowest frequencies and gradually more in effect as the frequencies increase."

[26]Bibl. 38, p. 212.

[27]Bibl. 12, p. 65.

is therefore nullified by the presence of a good proportion of   upper partials; and (4) it will be avoided by following the principles of registration set forth in later chapters. It does present an additional handicap to pure tones in that range, and has practical importance in the case of electronic instruments in which almost pure tones are susceptible of great amplification.

The fact that increased loudness tends to *raise* the pitch impression of tones above 3,500 cycles (about a^4) may exaggerate the screechiness of very high ranks which are not absorbed in the ensemble.[28]

Aural Additions

Before leaving the subject of sound perception we will pause for a brief consideration of what the ear adds to the tone. It must not be supposed, however, that the effects which we are about to describe exist only in the ear. They are believed to be produced by the asymmetry of the vibrating body, and will be found in any asymmetrical vibrator — that is, one which offers more resistance in one direction than in the other. Under such conditions some of these tones can be picked up by a microphone. These added tones fall in two categories:

1. The ear adds to a single pitch other pitches whose frequencies are multiples of the frequency of the principal tone. In other words, the ear adds partials beyond those which exist, or even where none exist, in the original tone. This is the result of overloading. The added partials are not heard in tones of low intensity, and their number and prominence increase as the intensity becomes greater.

2. When two tones are sounded simultaneously the ear adds tones whose frequencies equal the *difference* between the frequencies of the given tones, and the differences between their multiples (partials); it also adds tones whose frequencies are the *sums* of the frequencies of the principal tones and their partials.

Of these added pitches the *difference tones* (commonly called *resultants*, although that term may also apply to *summation* tones) are by far the most important to the organist. The hearer is not conscious of the aurally added multiples and sums of the frequencies. They are always above, and frequently correspond to actual partials of the principal tones or of the difference tones. When they do not they are lost in the superstructure of actual and aural partials. The difference tones, on the other hand, are outside the range of partials and are heard as separate pitches.

The production of difference tones is analogous to the effect of

[28]Bibl. 9, p. 48.

hearing two clocks ticking at different speeds. At regular intervals the ticking coincides and sounds like one, louder tick. Then they gradually get farther apart until they exactly alternate. From that stage they gradually come closer together again as they approach the next point of coincidence. The frequency of these points of coincidence (or approximate coincidence) is equal to the difference between the frequencies of the tickings of the two clocks. If one is ticking four times a second and the other four and a quarter times a second (seventeen times in four seconds) they will coincide once in four seconds.[29]

The same phenomenon occurs in sound vibrations. Whenever two tones of different pitch are sounded at the same time, the crests of their waves (that is, the points of greatest compression of the air) coincide — precisely or approximately — and reinforce each other at regular intervals. Midway between these points the crest of one wave coincides with the trough of the other, so that there is mutual interference, the two waves tending to cancel each other. The frequency of this periodic reinforcement is equal to the difference between the vibration frequencies of the two tones.

If the frequency difference is small — say, not more than eight per second — the periodic reinforcements are heard as *beats*. The tone seems louder at each coincidence, and softer at the intermediate points. But if, for example, A (220) and e[1] (330) are sounded simultaneously, their waves reinforce each other 110 times a second. This rapid cycle of reinforcement and interference produces the effect of a third tone whose frequency is 110, whose pitch is AA. If other tones are added

TABLE 3

RESULTANTS

	330	440	550	660	770	880	440	550	660	770	880
	−220	−330	−440	−550	−660	−770	−220	−330	−440	−550	−660
	=110	=110	=110	=110	=110	=110	=220	=220	=220	=220	=220

Combined Difference Tones

550	660	770	880	660	770	880	770	880	880
−220	−330	−440	−550	−220	−330	−440	−220	−330	−220
=330	=330	=330	=330	=440	=440	=440	=550	=550	=660

[29]Coincidence is assumed for the sake of simplicity. The general effect is the same if the coincidence is only approximate.

with the same frequency difference—a^1 (440), c$\sharp^2$ (550), e^2 (660), etc.—each new tone reinforces the resultant, so that it becomes more and more prominent. This effect is shown in Table 3.

Wider intervals produce higher resultants, so that the total effect of combining this series of tones is a series of resultants which are all partials of AA (110). Of course the resultants above AA coincide with tones actually sounded, so that their presence is not detected by the ear, but they contribute to the whole structure which produces and enriches the low resultant, AA (110).[30]

This phenomenon was unconsciously used by organists and organ builders long before the nature of the effect was recognized. Although probably discovered by the violinist, Giuseppe Tartini, in 1714, the earliest known published discussion of resultants was by a German organist, Georg A. Sorge, in 1745.[31] Their significance in tonal design was convincingly demonstrated by the French organ builder, Cavaillé-Coll, in the last century.[32] A more precise study has been made with recent electrical apparatus, using filters and controlled vibrations.[33]

A striking experiment, conducted in the Bell Telephone Laboratories, is reported by John Mills. Ten pure tones, with frequencies of 100, 200, 300, . . . 1,000, were sounded with equal intensity. The listener heard only the pitch of the lowest frequency. "Eliminating the 100-cycle fundamental produced no noticeable effect. In fact if any five consecutive frequencies were present the pitch was always judged to be 100 cycles."[34]

It is obvious that if the component pitches are represented by complex tones (each of which contains its own series of partials), resultants corresponding to the differences between the frequencies of the upper partials will also be produced, acting as upper partials to the principal difference tone and giving it the character of a complex tone.

The most familiar practical application of the difference tone principle is found in the resultant or "acoustic" thirty-two foot pedal stop, often found on organs of moderate size. The significance of the phenomenon, however, is far wider, and it must not be neglected in our theory of registration.

---

[30]The use of the difference tone principle at supersonic frequencies figures prominently in radio transmission and reception, and in the electrical production of audible tones.

[31]Bibl. 27, pp. 39-40.

[32]See Bibl. 159, pp. 176-7.

[33]The Bell Telephone Company has made some very instructive phonograph records which show the effect on the tone quality of various instruments when certain high or low frequencies are filtered out.

[34]Bibl. 30, p. 113.

The Acoustical Environment

We now have before us the essential facts concerning the physical nature of sound and its aural perception. It remains for us to discover what happens to the sound on its way from its source to the ear.[35]

Let us imagine a projectile fired into the air and exploding a great distance from the ground. At the moment of the explosion a violent sound wave is sent out in all directions. Disregarding such disturbing factors as wind and variation in the density and humidity of the air, the wave will be, at any given instant, in the form of a perfect sphere, whose center is the point of the explosion and whose radius is the distance which the sound has traveled since the explosion. The original energy (less losses en route) is distributed over the entire surface of the sphere. Since the area of the surface of a sphere is four times the square of the radius multiplied by π, it follows that the area over which the energy is distributed varies as the square of the distance from its source; accordingly the amount of energy received at any point is inversely proportional to the square of the distance.

Applying this to specific values, we see that the amount of energy at a distance of fifty feet from the source would be nine times as great as at a distance of 150 feet, and the intensity of the sound would be nearly ten (9.5424) decibels greater. If the sound had a definite frequency, and if we imagine a listener suspended in mid air, the difference in *loudness* would depend on the pitch. For CC the difference would be about twice as great as for middle C, and about two and a half times as great as for c^3. At higher pitches the variation would be much less.[36]

Reflection and Absorption

When the wave meets the ground its progress is interrupted. Part of the energy is reflected back and either disappears into space or strikes the surfaces of hills, trees, buildings, and other obstacles and is reflected and re-reflected in various directions. Part of the energy is absorbed by the ground and other surfaces which it encounters. Actually we never hear sounds which come to us in the simple fashion described in the foregoing paragraphs; everything which meets our ears has been modified by *reflection, absorption,* and *resonance.*

All the sound which is projected into a room is reflected or absorbed by its walls, architectural details, furniture, and occupants. The proportion of the amounts absorbed and reflected depends on the material which

[35] For a clear and readable discussion of auditorium acoustics see James Jeans, *Science and Music* (Bibl. 18), Chap. VI.

[36] Cf. pp. 18-19.

the sound encounters.   Hard, rigid, smooth surfaces absorb very little; draperies and acoustic products absorb a considerable proportion of the sound, and an audience even more.   No substance, however, is completely absorbent, and nothing is absolutely nonabsorbent.   So everything which the sound meets absorbs some of it and reflects the rest, sending it on to the next obstruction.   A listener hears the sound which comes directly from the source (as in the case of the explosion in the air), and in addition he hears it indirectly, as it is reflected and re-reflected from every object in the room.   If a single reflection is more prominent than the others it comes as a distinct echo.   In most cases, however, there are so many reflecting surfaces, and their locations cause such various delays in the arrival of the sound reflected from them, that there is a continuous *reverberation* until the sound is absorbed to the point of inaudibility.   If there could be an enclosure in which there was absolutely no absorption, and no resistance to the propagation of the sound wave, a sound once projected into the enclosure would continue forever.

In auditoriums the delay in the arrival of the sound reflected from the nearer surfaces is so slight as to be negligible.   It is heard at practically the same time as the sound coming directly from the source, so that it reinforces even the shortest tones of the music.   These reflections add considerably to the energy imparted to the ear.   Portions of the sound which, in free space, would go in other directions are deflected so that they come to the listener.   In a room of moderate size the reflected sounds come from all directions, often giving the impression that the room is actually filled with sound.

In large auditoriums it takes the sound so long to travel to and from the more distant reflecting surfaces that the total reinforcement is perceptibly delayed.   On long tones the effect is cumulative until the initial sound is absorbed, while short tones lose the advantage of these tardy reflections.   Instead, the reflected short tones coincide with the direct reception of later tones, causing confusion and impairing the clarity of detail.   This explains the fact that organ music often sounds better in the back of the room where the principal reflections arrive almost simultaneously, and the delayed reflections, being secondary, are weaker.   This advantage diminishes with increased reverberation and surface complexity.

Different materials vary greatly in their absorptive characteristics, and in all cases the proportion of absorption is different for different pitches.   These variations are exemplified by the results of measurements made by Wallace Sabine of the absorption characteristics of (1) the tile used in the arches of the West Point Chapel, (2) acoustic tile developed by Raphael Guastivino, (3) five-eighths inch pine paneling on studding fourteen inches apart, and (4) a seated audience.[37]   Table 4 shows the percentage of increment to the tones CC and c^1 resulting from three reflections, and from ten reflections, from these materials.

TABLE 4

INCREMENT FROM REFLECTIONS

From specific materials

MATERIAL	NUMBER OF REFLECTIONS	ADDITION TO CC (IN PERCENT)	ADDITION TO c^1 (IN PERCENT)	PERCENT BY WHICH ADDITION TO CC EXCEEDS ADDITION TO c^1
West Point Tile	3	292	289	1
	10	928	908	2.4
Acoustic Tile	3	263	233	13
	10	707	526	35
Paneling	3	263	238	10.8
	10	707	551	28.3
Audience	3	126.5	12.3	928
	10	167	12.3	1256

From these data we see that the absorption of the higher frequencies exceeds that of the lower, and the disparity is usually greater with the more absorbent materials.[38]   So the high pitches receive less reinforcement from reflection than the low tones, and the proportionate loss of high frequencies is greater in dead rooms, where the surfaces absorb much of the sound.

In this discussion no account has been taken of the phase of the sound waves. It has been assumed that sound added to sound would produce more sound. Such is not always the case. If, for example, the the crest of a reflected wave reaches the ear simultaneously with the trough of the direct wave, they tend to counteract each other; while if the direct and reflected waves arrive in similar phase, they reinforce each other. In general, however, the waves come from many reflecting surfaces at various phase stages; the phase relation also varies with the different partials; moreover the average listener hears with two ears, for which the interference pattern is not the same. So from the practical standpoint these effects balance out, and the question of phase can be disregarded.[39]

[37] Bibl. 39, pp. 208, 207, 227.

[38] There is sometimes a peak of absorption in the neighborhood of c^3, but such variations in detail may be ignored for our purpose. See Bibl. 18, p. 196.

[39] Bibl. 44, p. 139.

It is interesting to observe also that differences in phase have no appreciable effect on the perception on tone quality. Timbre is the result of the relative intensity of the partials, regardless of phase.[40]

So much for reflection and absorption; now what happens when something comes between the source of sound and the listener? Here it may be helpful to observe the phenomena of light, since one essential difference between sound and light lies in the length and frequency of the waves.

An opaque obstruction before a source of light casts a definite shadow; an observer located in that shadow cannot see the light. On the other hand, if an obstruction impervious to sound comes between the source and a listener, he hears the sound as coming from the edge of the obstruction. It appears that light travels only in a straight line, whereas the path of sound can turn. Once clear of the obstruction sound spreads out in all directions. Actually the difference is relative. Short waves do not bend as much as long waves; the shorter they are, the more they keep to a straight line. This is analogous to the behavior of water waves. When small waves meet an obstruction they break up and disappear; but large waves pass around the obstruction.

Light waves are so extremely short that they continue practically in a straight line, so that the shadow cast by an obstruction is clearly defined. The waves of even the highest sounds are from 30,000 to 50,000 times as long as light waves, and they bend around obstructions somewhat; but there *is* a *sound shadow*, the depth of which depends upon the wave length, and therefore on the frequency. An obstruction may interfere with high sounds to a considerable extent, but the effect of the shadow on low frequencies is negligible.

Resonance

Finally, the character of a sound is further modified by resonance – the transmission of vibrations from one sonorous body to another. Such transmission may be through contact or direct connection, or it may be through the medium of the sound wave traveling through the air.

The piano furnishes an obvious example of the first type of transmission. The vibration of the string is communicated through the bridge to the soundboard. This board, being elastic and responding to a wide range of frequencies, vibrates under the stimulus of the strings, and its large surface transmits the vibrations to the air.[41] The soundboard also

[40]Confirmation of this fact is frequently encountered: Bibl. 18, p. 249; 25, p. 103; 30, pp. 262-4; 10, p. 47. H. W. Homer gives a very interesting demonstration, showing the effects of varying phases on the wave form, which are not aurally distinguishable. Bibl. 66, pp. 84-5, and Figs. 43, 44.

[41]This is more fully explained in the next chapter.

communicates the vibrations through the bridge to all other strings of the instrument. Thus when the dampers are released by the damper pedal, so that all strings are free, vibrations are induced in those strings whose frequencies or partial frequencies approximately coincide with the frequency of the tone played, or any of its partials. The fullness of tone which results is familiar to everyone.

Other examples of resonance through direct contact occur in organ pipes, and will be explained in the next chapter. Common instances of resonance through the medium of sound waves in the air are the vibrations of loose window panes, curtain rods, ornaments, and other objects, when a tone is sounded which is near their natural frequency. Such vibrations are usually too feeble in themselves to make any perceptible contribution to the tone. What we hear is really a rattle caused by the vibrating object striking against something else.

There are, however, two examples of this sort of resonance which do affect the sound and complicate the acoustical characteristics of auditoriums. The first is the inducement of *standing waves*[42] in a confined space. Often the air in a room or in an alcove can be made to vibrate (in the same manner as the air in an organ pipe) with frequencies determined by the size and proportions of the enclosure. If a tone is sounded which coincides with one of these frequencies, standing waves are set up which reinforce the original tone. It is largely to compensate for such unpredictable resonance that organs must be re-regulated after they are in place, no matter how carefully they have been voiced at the factory.

The other example of resonance induced by sound waves in the air is the vibration of wood paneling. The soundboard of a piano and the body of a violin receive the vibrations from the strings, communicated directly through the bridge, and then give them out to the air. Wood paneling, on the other hand, receives its vibrations from the air; it takes energy from the air instead of giving it out to the air. Its elasticity cushions the impact, weakens the reflection, and partially absorbs the vibrations which coincide with its natural frequency. That frequency depends on the density of the wood, the thickness of the panels, and the spacing of the studding.[43] Such resonance tends to compensate for the greater surface absorption of high frequencies, thus reducing the distortion which normally occurs in sound reflections.[44]

[42]Again the reader is referred to the next chapter for a more complete explanation of the phenomenon referred to.

[43]Bibl. 39, p. 207.

[44]The most erratic of the external influences which modify the tone is standing wave resonance. A number of years ago an electronic thirty-two foot octave was added to the organ in Skinner Recital Hall at Vassar College. The first three partials were provided. When these were uniformly adjusted throughout the octave the scale proved to be very uneven, both in loudness and in quality. For the final adjustment three expert listeners were placed in different parts of the auditorium, and the regulation was determined by their combined, but discrepant, judgments.

This very sketchy presentation of some of the problems of auditorium acoustics suggests the extreme complexity of the conditions which modify the sound between its emission at the source and its reception by the ear. In Chapter V the subject is more fully discussed in connection with its practical application to organ registration.

Summary

The acoustical phenomena on which our theory of registration will be based, and which must be considered in its application, may be summarized as follows:

The characteristics of a musical tone are pitch, loudness, and timbre. Pitch is the aural interpretation of frequency of vibration; loudness is the aural interpretation of amplitude of vibration; timbre is the aural interpretation of complexity of vibration — the combination of vibrations of various frequencies and amplitudes. Tone combination is therefore to be conceived of as a complex combination of pitches.

The ear does not respond equally to all frequencies. In general it is more sensitive to high pitches than to low. In the upper range it can hear vibrations of smaller intensity, it can perceive smaller changes in intensity, and tones sound louder in proportion to their physical intensity, than in the lower range. The disparity between physical intensity and audible loudness at low pitches gives a sense of volume which, when exaggerated, may become disagreeable. Extreme volume impairs the audibility of other tones, especially those of higher pitch. Again, the aural sensitivity to pitch relationships is greatest at comparatively high frequencies.

In addition to these inequalities of perception, the ear further modifies the effect of the sound by the addition of combination tones or resultants, the most important of which are those whose frequencies are the arithmetical differences between the frequencies of the principal tones and of their upper partials. Under certain conditions such difference tones actually control the pitch impression.

The sound is also modified by certain external influences imposed upon it in transit. These modifications are due to reflection, absorption, obstruction, and resonance. They are all discriminatory with respect to pitch, tending, with the exception of certain resonances, to reduce the relative strength of the higher frequencies. The total result is an increase in loudness due to reflection (since absorption merely prevents reflection), and an alteration of the tone quality, due to the selective characteristics of absorption. Sometimes standing wave resonance reinforces certain tones. The effect of obstruction is slight in the average auditorium, except as it results from a faultily designed organ chamber. Controlled by swell shades, it is used for the dynamic modification of the organ tone.

Although all acoustical phenomena are subject to immutable laws, some of which are known and many of which have been the subject of extensive laboratory investigation, their ramifications are so complex that it would be quite impracticable for the organist to attempt to apply them in detail. The main facts will furnish the basis of our theory of registration, and the ear will guide in working out details. It is not too soon to urge, as will be done repeatedly in this book, the continual, discriminating, unprejudiced aural appraisal of all tonal effects.

CHAPTER TWO

THE ORGAN AS A SOURCE OF SOUND

Inducement of Sound Waves

In the preceding chapter our study of the nature of sound, its transmission and perception, took no account of the source. We observed the vibrations from the moment of the projection of the sound wave to its reception by the ear and perception by the mind, but we did not concern ourselves with how the vibrations were originally induced. In this chapter we shall discuss the organ as a source of sound, observing the manner in which its pipes produce tones and noting the characteristics of the tones thus produced. Since we are primarily concerned with the aural effects we must content ourselves with a minimum of technical explanation, leaving the reader to consult more specialized treatises for the details of pipe design and voicing.

It will be well to recall at the outset that the disturbance of the air which the ear interprets as sound consists of regular alternations of compression and rarefaction. The source of sound is the projector of such a wave. To produce sound it must cause such alternating compression and rarefaction of the air.

Compression is produced by the action of two opposing forces. If force is applied in one direction it meets the resistance of inertia, rigidity, or confinement in a limited space. Since inertia is proportionate to mass, the amount of resistance offered by a fluid substance, such as air or water, depends on the area over which the force is applied. One does not, for example, propel a canoe with a broom stick, but with the broad side of a paddle.

A vibrating string or tuning fork acts on such a small area that it produces very little compression of the air, and its tone is inaudible at a short distance; but if the vibrations are communicated directly to a soundboard, its larger surface meets the resistance of a greater mass of air and produces more effective waves of compression and rarefaction.[1] Thus the efficiency of all stringed instruments depends on the reinforcement of soundboards.[2]

Standing Waves

In wind instruments the compression and rarefaction are actually effected within the body of the instrument. The energy is confined within

[1] Of course the greater resistance demands more energy, but that is irrelevant at this point.

[2] Cf. Bibl. 41, Vol. II, pp. 516-17.

its walls, producing pressure variation which is communicated directly to the atmosphere through the open end(s). So wind instruments are (barring electrical sources of sound) the most efficient of all musical instruments, and are capable of producing the loudest sustained tones. The vibration of the air within the instrument or pipe is in the form of longitudinal *standing* or *stationary waves.*

A standing wave is one which oscillates in a limited space. It is thus distinguished from a traveling wave which progresses outward from a source. If a stone is dropped into a pool of water, waves travel out in all directions; but if a pan of water is disturbed, a wave oscillates back and forth with a frequency which is dependent on the size of the pan. The latter is a standing wave.

The phenomenon of longitudinal waves is the same, regardless of the vibrating medium, but we are concerned only with a vibrating column of air. We must bear in mind that air is very resilient; its density tends to remain constant under equal atmospheric conditions. If any local force alters the density, it returns to its normal condition as soon as the force is removed, the momentum of its particles carrying it a little too far, thus setting up temporary oscillation.

Since the walls of a pipe limit transverse motion, the free vibrations of a column of air move in a longitudinal direction. The individual particles all oscillate toward and away from the ends of the pipe. If both ends are open the in and out motion at the two ends is synchronized. As a result of this accordion-like action there is no motion or *displacement* of the particles at the center, and the greatest amount of motion occurs at the open ends. There is, then, a *displacement node* at the center, and a *displacement antinode* at each end.

At the same time the convergent motion from the ends toward the center, and the divergent motion from the center toward the ends, bring about the greatest compression and rarefaction at the center. At the ends, on the other hand, atmospheric conditions are approximated and there is the minimum change of density. So the center is a *pressure antinode* and the ends are *pressure nodes.* It is important, therefore, in speaking of nodes and antinodes, to specify whether reference is to displacement or pressure. Writers are not always explicit and confusion sometimes results.

Figure 3 represents the progress of the air particles in an open pipe through sixteen stages of a wave cycle. The horizontal lines in the first pipe show the positions of the selected particles when they are at rest; those in the second pipe show the positions of the same particles one-sixteenth of a cycle later; successive stages of the vibration cycle are shown in the following pipes until the original condition is repeated.

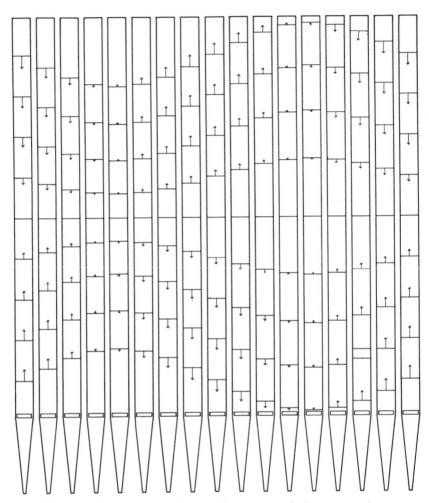

Figure 3. Sixteen stages of a standing wave cycle in an open pipe.

The arrows indicate the direction of the motion of the particles, and the lengths of the arrows show the distance which the respective particles will travel in the next sixteenth of a cycle.[3] Thus the lengths of the arrows correspond roughly to the velocities of the particles at each stage – except at the points of extreme displacement, where the direction is reversed. At such points the velocity is, of course, momentarily nil.

Where the standing wave meets the atmosphere it produces an alternating push and pull which sends out impulses in the form of spherical

[3]It should be noted, however, that these distances are greatly exaggerated in the drawing.

traveling waves of compression and rarefaction. The time which elapses between one push and the next determines the frequency, and the distance from one resulting compression to the next is the wave length.

To understand the relation between the wave length and the length of an open pipe, we may imagine the continuation of the standing wave through a series of open pipes placed end to end, as shown in Figure 4. There will be a displacement node at the middle of each, but the pressure phase will change with each successive pipe. When there is the maximum compression at the middle of the first pipe there will be the maximum rarefaction at the middle of the second, the maximum compression in the third, and so on. Thus it is evident that the wave length, which is the distance from one maximum compression to the next, is twice the length of one pipe which is open at both ends.

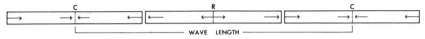

Figure 4. Series of open pipes, showing the relation of the wave length to the length of the pipe.

C = Compression   R = Rarefaction

The effect of placing two open pipes end to end is actually realized by making a small hole near the middle of the pipe, at the location of its displacement node. This connection with the atmosphere produces an open end effect and causes a displacement antinode at that point. The result is that the wave length of the tone produced by the pipe is reduced by half (the entire wave with two displacement nodes being included in the pipe), and the frequency is accordingly doubled. The pipe speaks an octave higher than it would without the hole.[4] Such pipes are called *harmonic*. This term applies to any vibration in which an upper partial assumes the role of fundamental.

If an open pipe should be cut off and completely closed at the displacement node, the node would remain. There would be no connection with the atmosphere at that point, and the stopper would prevent any motion of the air particles there. Such an alteration, therefore, would cause no change in the wave length or the pitch, although the actual length of the pipe would have been reduced by half.

There are, therefore, three kinds of pipes enclosing vibrating columns of air: the open pipe (which may be considered normal) is approximately half as long as the wave length; the stopped pipe is approximately a quarter as long as the wave length, and produces a tone an octave lower than an open pipe of the same length; the harmonic pipe, with a hole near its middle, is approximately as long as the wave length, and produces a

[4] Actually the pitch is favored also by other details of the design and voicing of the pipe.

tone an octave higher than a normal open pipe of the same length. The qualification "approximately" is due to open end correction, which will be explained later.[5]

All such standing waves are induced by the action of some other vibrating body. In the brass instruments of the orchestra they are produced by the vibration of the lips of the player. In reed instruments, such as the clarinet and oboe, a flexible reed is substituted for the lips. In organ pipes the design is adapted to an artificial wind supply with mechanical control. There are two methods of setting the air in vibration, according to which the pipes are called *flue pipes* or *reed pipes*.

Flue Pipes

Flue pipes, which comprise more than three quarters of the tonal equipment of the average organ, are sounded in the same manner as a flageolet, a recorder, or an ordinary whistle. Such instruments have been in use many hundreds of years, but the process whereby the air was set in vibration remained a mystery until the present century. In the early 1850's it was discovered that a sheet of air impinging on the edge of an obstruction would produce a tone, even without an attendant pipe. The present edge tone theory of the sounding of flue pipes and instruments of the flute type is largely due to the studies of Hensen and Wachsmuth at the beginning of this century.[6] It has been further developed and refined as a result of more recent experiments and observation of the behavior of air currents made visible by smoke. The following is an attempt at a nontechnical explanation of the phenomenon.[7]

If a stream of air passes an obstruction friction retards the speed of the air which is in contact with the obstruction, while the other side of the stream flows past. Thus the stream is bent in the direction of the obstruction. If the air is forced between two obstructions (i.e., through a slit) the friction of each tends to bend the air stream in its direction. Since their directions are opposite, the tendency is to split the air stream and produce a partial vacuum between the separating parts. What actually happens is that the two opposing forces take turns, and the stream is bent alternately one way and the other. Each bend starts the formation of an eddy which is prevented from maturing by the suction of the stream as it bends back in the opposite direction. If the edge of a thin object comes between the extreme positions of the fluctuating air

[5]See page 36.

[6]See Bibl. 37, p. 167, and Bibl. 27, p. 62.

[7]For a fuller description of the edge tone phenomena, see Bibl. 36, pp. 30-46; also Bibl. 48, pp. 115-17.

stream, the eddies become completely formed and alternate on the two sides of the edge, somewhat as suggested in Figure 5.

The result of this action is a tone, the frequency of which depends on the speed of the air stream and the distance from the slit (through which the air is forced) to the interposed edge. If the speed of the stream is increased, the eddies also move more rapidly and strike the edge with greater frequency. If the edge is removed farther from the slit, it takes longer for the eddies to cover the distance, and their frequency is reduced.

Normally the entire space between the slit and the edge is occupied by the generation of one pair of eddies (one complete vibration cycle), but there is a limit to the distance which can be thus covered at a given velocity. If the edge is removed beyond that distance two pairs of eddies are formed in place of one, the frequency is doubled, and the pitch becomes an octave higher.

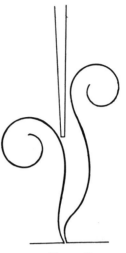

Figure 5.
Edge Tone Eddies

The instrument is then speaking its second partial. If the edge is moved beyond the next critical point, the phenomenon is repeated, and the third partial is heard.

In a flue pipe the air is forced through the slit between the *lower lip* and the *languid* (called the *cap* and *block*, respectively, in the case of a wood pipe), and the *upper lip* serves as the edge (see Fig. 6). When the air stream is directed outward, the suction force pulls the particles of air within the pipe *away* from the displacement node; the resulting rarefaction assists the reversal of the air stream, which is then directed inward, driving the particles *toward* the node. In an open pipe this impulse is transmitted through the pipe, but before it reaches the center node the air stream is again reversed, pulling in the opposite direction. So while the air particles in the upper half of the pipe are moving toward the open end, those in the lower half are returning toward the mouth. The resiliency of the air causes the upper particles to start back just as the

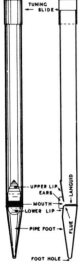

Figure 6.[8]
Flue Pipe

[8]Reproduced from Bonavia-Hunt and Homer, *The Organ Reed*, by kind permission of the publisher, J. Fischer & Bro.

air stream at the mouth again starts inward. Thus reciprocal vibrations are set up in the two halves of the pipe, with periodic compression and rarefaction centered at the displacement node. In a stopped pipe the impulse is reflected from the stopped end, producing a displacement node at that point; so no reciprocal vibration is set up.

Thus the tone of a flue pipe is produced by two coupled vibrations: the transverse vibration of the sheet of air at the mouth, and the longitudinal vibration of the column of air in the pipe. Ideally the natural frequencies of the two should be related; practically there is considerable latitude, for the more massive vibrations of the air in the pipe force the edge tone into resonance. If the speed of the air stream be increased (by increasing the pressure) the pitch is only slightly affected until the frequency of the edge tone becomes so great that it causes the air column in the pipe to vibrate in sections, jumping to the next higher partial. The pipe is then said to be *overblown*.[9]

End Correction and Scale

In Chapter I we learned that the wave length of the lowest note of an eight-foot rank was about 17'4". This pitch is normally produced, however, by an open pipe about eight feet long, which would theoretically give a tone with a sixteen-foot wave length. The discrepancy is due to the momentum of the air which carries the oscillation of the particles beyond the end of the pipe. The effect is much greater at the mouth of the pipe, due to the reduced opening, and to the force of the vibrating air stream which is added to the momentum of the particles within the pipe. The amount of *end correction* necessary for an open cylindrical pipe is about .6 times the radius at the open end, and about 2.7 times the radius at the mouth, making a total correction of about 3.3 times the radius.[10] Thus the wave length of an eight-foot pipe (actually 7' 10") which is six inches in diameter would be computed as follows: 2(7' 10" + 3.3 x 3") ≅ 17' 4".

The vibrations just described are nearly always accompanied by fractional vibrations which sound upper partials, as observed in Chapter I. The number and relative strength of these partials depend on many details of scale (the ratio of the diameter to the length), material, design, and voicing.

It is well known that large scales inhibit, and small scales encourage, the development of upper partials. The open end correction for fractional

---

[9]It is possible, however, so to voice a pipe that a clear harmonic cannot be produced by overblowing.

[10]This is the correction as usually given. Actually the mouth correction depends also on the area of the mouth and the air consumption. See Bibl. 17, pp. 22-26.

vibrations is less than for the fundamental, so that the upper partials, having proportionately shorter wave lengths, tend to be sharp. They are not, therefore, exact fractions of the whole, and they do not coincide with the natural partials of the tone.[11] Since the correction is approximately proportionate to the diameter of the pipe, the discrepancy is much less in pipes of small scale, and the reinforcement of the upper partials in such pipes is, accordingly, more effective.

There are other factors which also encourage the higher development of upper partials in slender pipes: It has been found that a pipe does not provide natural resonance to pitches whose wave lengths are less than four times its diameter.[12] Thus the scale of the pipe determines the highest partial which can have this natural reinforcement. However, it has been demonstrated that higher partials exist, and are essential to the tone quality.[13] They are presumably due to the edge tone, and perhaps to forcing the resonance. In this connection it is interesting to note that the pitch of the edge tone of a flute is nearest the fundamental, that of a diapason is nearest the second partial, and that of a string is nearest the third partial.[14]

We may assume that the upper partials are further encouraged in a slender pipe by the mere fact that thin bodies are more flexible, and break up more easily into fractional vibrations.

We have seen that the end of a stopped pipe is always at a displacement node, because there is no connection with the outside air at that point, and the air particles meet an impassable obstruction. It is obvious that if a wave length be divided by two or by any even number, there must be an antinode where the complete wave has a node. The stopper therefore prevents the division of the vibration into even fractions; so a stopped pipe gives only the odd partials (Figure 7). If it is overblown it speaks not the octave, but the twelfth — the third partial; beyond that it speaks the fifth partial. This fact can be demonstrated by blowing a stopped pipe with the mouth. Analysis shows the presence of very weak even partials, which may be assumed to come from the edge tone.

Pipe Materials

The characteristics of the tone of a pipe do not result solely from the behavior of the air itself. The walls of the pipe have a great influence on the partials, depending on their weight, rigidity, resilience, conduc-

[11] "It is a property of a sounding system to quench those overtones which are not truly harmonic to the fundamental." — Richardson, Bibl. 36, p. 26.

[12] Bibl. 1.

[13] Bibl. 5, p. 35.

[14] Bibl. 17, p. 42. Cf. Analyses on pp. 50-55.

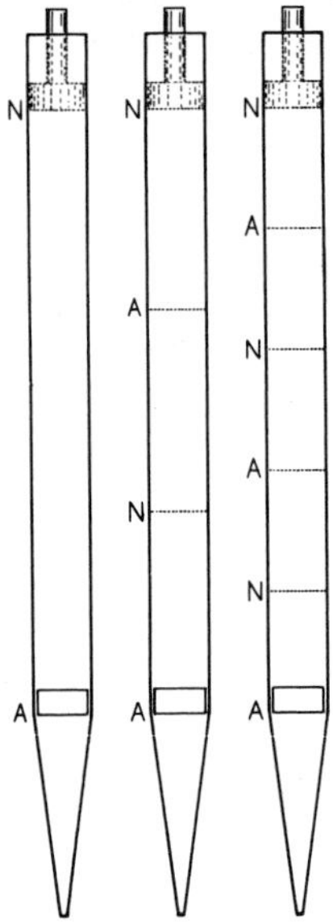

Funda- Third Fifth
mental Partial Partial

Figure 7. Partials of a stopped pipe.

N = Node   A = Antinode

tivity, and interior surface. Heavy and rigid walls resist the vibrations of the air, preventing the flexibility which encourages breaking up into fractional vibrations. Resilience assists such flexibility and provides reinforcing resonance for the high frequencies. The contribution of such resonance is often called the *formant* of the pipe. The quality of conductivity tends to distribute the formant throughout the pipe and to transmit the vibrations through the walls to the surrounding air. It also affects the natural frequency of the material on which the formant depends. The smoothness and hardness of the interior surface influence the ratio of absorption and reflection of the higher partials.

Metal pipes are usually made of an alloy of lead and tin, which goes by the name of *pipe metal*. Lead is very heavy and nonresilient; tin is relatively light, very resilient, and about twice as efficient as a sound conductor. By balancing these two constituents the desired characteristics can be secured. If the proportion of tin is as great as forty-five percent, spots appear in the metal, which become smaller and ·closer together as the amount of tin is increased until there is so little lead that the pipes look silvery. Pipe metal which contains the right proportion to produce spots is called *spotted metal*. For metal flutes a large proportion of lead is commonly used. Until comparatively recently metal which was twenty-five or thirty percent tin was considered right for diapasons, but spotted metal has increased in favor as the value of the upper partials in the diapason chorus has become more appreciated. The old continental builders used as high as ninety percent tin for small pipes and for display pipes — even large diapasons. American builders have used such a proportion for their fine strings.

The tone of wood pipes is apt to be poor in upper partials. Wood is resilient and resonant to high frequencies, but the interior surface is absorbent, and the walls of the pipes are thick and fairly rigid. Moreover, wood pipes are usually larger in scale than metal pipes.

Reed Pipes

A reed pipe differs from a flue pipe in the following essential features: (1) a metal reed takes the place of the vibrating sheet of air; (2) the air actually passes through the pipe; and (3) the energy is applied at the closed end, the pressure antinode, of the pipe. Like the flue pipe it is a coupled system, the tone being the result of the combined vibrations of the reed and the column of air. In this case, however, the frequency of the reed dominates the pitch.

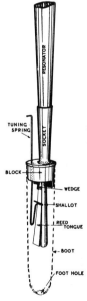

Figure 8. [15]
Reed Pipe

The sound producing section (shown in Figure 8) consists of a *beating reed* and *shallot* which are tightly held in a lead casting called the *block*, and enclosed in a *boot* to which air is admitted through a hole in the *toe*. The shallot is a brass tube which serves as a downward extension of the pipe. It is closed at the lower end and ground flat on one side. A hole in the flat side leads through into the pipe, and is the only escape for the air in the boot. The brass *tongue*, which is slightly curved, rests on the flat side of the shallot, covering the hole. A sliding wire spring presses firmly on the tongue to control the length of the vibrating portion, for the purpose of tuning and regulating.

The operation of the reed is this: When compressed air is admitted to the boot a small portion of it escapes under the curved end of the tongue, through the shallot into the pipe. The force of this rush of air at once draws the tongue flat against the shallot, closing the hole and interrupting the escape

[15]Reproduced from Bonavia-Hunt and Homer, *The Organ Reed*, by kind permission of the publisher, J. Fischer & Bro.

of the air.[16]   The elasticity of the tongue now pulls it away from the
shallot, allowing space for more air to escape.   This starts another
cycle which is repeated regularly as long as the air pressure is maintained in the boot.

This process results in two coupled vibrations: (1) The tongue vibrates, producing a tone with an excessive number of partials, some of
which are inharmonic (not multiples of the fundamental frequency).   (2) A
series of puffs of air is admitted to the pipe through the shallot.   These
little puffs give regularly repeated impulses to the particles of air in the
lower end of the pipe, each impulse producing momentary compression
and pushing the air toward the upper, open end of the pipe.   When the
opening in the shallot is closed the air continues upward by momentum,
causing rarefaction at the lower end until the next puff is admitted.   This
alternation of compression and rarefaction sets up a standing wave in the
pipe which projects impulses into the outside air.   The air column in the
pipe, which is often called the *resonator*, reinforces only the harmonic
frequencies, so that the inharmonic partials of the reed practically
disappear.

Since the lower end of the pipe is a pressure antinode (and therefore a
displacement node), it functions as a stopped pipe.   So cylindrical reed
pipes, such as the Clarinet, favor the odd partials, as explained in
connection with stopped flue pipes.   Conical pipes, however, even though
stopped, produce the complete series of partials, like an open pipe of
the same length.   A simple, descriptive explanation of this fact is impossible, but it can be demonstrated experimentally and mathematically.
Because of this phenomenon reed pipes are normally conical, the cylindrical form being used only when special qualities are desired.

As in the case of a flue pipe, it is advantageous that the natural frequencies of the reed and the pipe nearly coincide.   There is, however, a
certain amount of permissive latitude which is used for tone regulating.
To lengthen the vibrating portion of the tongue increases its flexibility
and the amplitude of its vibrations.   This results in a higher development
of upper partials and greater power.   The pitch, which is thus lowered,
can be adjusted by tuning the pipe.   It is thus possible, within limits, to
make a reed pipe louder and more brilliant, or softer and more smooth.   To
alter the loudness without changing the quality, however, requires a
modification of the curve of the tongue, which can be done only by a
skilled voicer.

Reed pipes are very sensitive.   The curve of the tongue must be so
perfectly graduated that throughout its entire speaking length it will roll

[16]H. W. Homer, who reports a very interesting study of the behavior of reeds and their
sound waves, found that the tongue does not quite touch the shallot, but the opening is
effectively closed. Bibl. 66, p. 60.

down smoothly on the shallot, without striking at any point. The smallest flat spot on the tongue, a speck of dust, or even corrosion caused by handling with moist fingers or by blowing with the mouth, will cause an unpleasant tone.

Effect of Temperature

The velocity of sound, which depends on the speed of molecular motion and is practically the same for standing and traveling waves, varies with the temperature, increasing about one percent with each rise of ten degrees Fahrenheit. Moreover, as the speed of sound in water vapor is about thirty percent greater than in dry air, the presence of moisture in the air makes sound travel faster. Thus, since the frequency of a sound wave of a given length is proportional to the velocity of sound, the pitch of a pipe (the frequency of its standing wave) rises with the temperature and also, slightly, with humidity. [17]

We have seen that in flue pipes the frequency is dominated by the column of air, while in reed pipes the reed is the controlling factor. So the effect of temperature on reed pipes is negligible, and any temperature change will produce a noticeable discrepancy between the reed and flue pipes. A change of thirty degrees will make a difference of about a quarter of a step, and less than five degrees will produce two beats a second at a^1. For this reason care must be taken to tune an organ at the same temperature at which it will be played. In cold weather churches which are not kept warm during the week should be heated the day before the organ is to be used, so that the temperature will be normal and stable throughout the entire chamber. It follows that the swell boxes should always be left open unless the entire organ is under effective automatic temperature control. In modern installations this matter is usually taken care of automatically, but it is advisable to acquire habits which meet every contingency.

Speech Characteristics

Timbre is not the only characteristic of the tone of a pipe which the organist must take into consideration in his registration. Ignoring the obvious question of loudness, other characteristics to study are promptness of speech, positiveness of speech, and tonal efficiency.

In all sound producing instruments low tones tend to be logy. This is because the weight necessary to produce slow vibrations provides considerable enertia for the initial energy to overcome. In most instruments compensating force can be supplied by the performer. This is true

[17]See p. 11, and Bibl. 41, Vol. II, p. 543.

of all orchestral instruments, while the percussion of the piano and the sudden release of the harpsichord strings inevitably make a practically instantaneous attack. However, it takes time to set up vibrations in a column of air, and the length of the delay in a flue pipe depends largely on the mass of air involved. Experiments have shown that, for the pipes in any one set, "the time required to reach steady speech ... is, to a first approximation, proportional to the frequency."[18] This means that, with any given stop, it will take twice as long for tenor C to speak as for middle C. Likewise a four-foot stop will speak in a quarter of the time required for a similar sixteen-foot stop.

The greater promptness of high tones is enhanced by the ear itself; for laboratory tests have shown that high frequencies are more quickly heard than low frequencies.[19]

Again, since the delay in the speech of a pipe depends partly on the mass of air to be set in motion, a stopped pipe speaks more promptly than an open pipe producing the same pitch; and pipes of large scale (other things being equal) require more time than small scale pipes.[20]

The initial speech of a pipe is also affected by various details of design and voicing. For example, a slender string pipe, voiced to secure an abnormal proportion of upper partials, tends to speak its second partial instead of the fundamental. This is avoided by placing a *bridge* or *beard* in front of the mouth to prevent the formation of multiple eddies in the air stream. Still the tone is slightly unstable, and a little time is required to develop the full fundamental speech of the pipe.

Similarly a harmonic pipe, which sounds its second partial, speaks with some initial uncertainty. This may be due to the fact that the natural pitch of the pipe is an octave lower. Possibly there is some additional delay because of the long standing wave which must be generated.

There is a pronounced difference in speech between a flue and a reed pipe. In the former the motive power of the air stream is applied at the displacement antinode, where the greatest amount of motion is involved and the minimum of resistance is encountered. The communication of this impulse through the pipe is gradual, so that the tone begins with a crescendo. In small pipes this is imperceptible, but it is always present.

The tone of a reed pipe, on the other hand, begins with what amounts almost to an explosion. It is dominated by the reed, which attains its full vibration almost instantaneously, and the puff of air which starts the standing wave in the pipe has the positive energy of the compressed air

[18] Bibl. 32, p. 154.
[19] Bibl. 13, p. 153.
[20] Bibl. 32, p. 152.

in the boot, and meets the positive resistance of the small shallot at the displacement node of the vibration. So the attack of the reed is more prompt and more solid than that of the flue pipe. Experiments show that not only is the full speech of a reed pipe attained in from one-half to one-fifth of the time required for a flue pipe of the same pitch, but the length of the transient state is negligible.[21]

A similar difference is felt in the continuation of the tone. The vibration of a reed pipe not only starts suddenly, but it is maintained by a series of explosive puffs, accompanied by the dominating vibration of the metal tongue. The minimum amount of air is consumed, and there is no waste energy.[22] On the other hand, the flexible air stream of the flue pipe exercises an elastic push and pull which meets very little resistance from the air in the pipe. The fluid coupling produces a less aggressive tone, and the rush of wasted air is often not quite inaudible.

These effects, subtle and sometimes imperceptible though they are, actually influence the general impression. Like the refinements of a meticulous touch, they are perceived without being detected.

Classification of Organ Stops

The separation of organ stops into the reed and flue categories forms the basic classification of the tonal resources of the instrument. In spite of the wide range of timbre within each group, there is a definite tonal differentiation between the two types. Within each of these main divisions there is further grouping according to quality and function. The complete classification is given below:

Flue Tone	Reed Tone
Diapasons	Chorus reeds
Flutes { Open flutes / Gedeckts	Solo reeds
Strings	

The literal meaning of *diapason* is "through all", and from this etymological source various usages have been derived. The complete phrase which defined its original signification was: ἡ διὰ πασῶν χορδῶν συμφωνία (the concord through all the strings). This concord (the range of the lyre) was the interval of an octave. Thus scores of old

[21]Bibl. 32, p. 152.

[22]The suddenness of the action of the tongue in admitting air to the shallot is shown in Bibl. 66, Fig. 35. The derivation of these curves is described in Part II, Chap. IV, of this work.

music sometimes contain such expressions as: "canon in the diapason", meaning a canon in the octave.

In organ nomenclature the word was originally applied to a stop running "through all" the notes of the keyboard, having a pipe for each key. If it was a set of open pipes it was the *open diapason*; if the pipes were stopped it was the *stopped diapason*.

The tone produced by an open diapason is the most characteristic of the entire instrument. It forms the basis of the organ ensemble, and it is quite unlike any sound which can be produced by any other instrument. Today the word diapason is generally restricted to this particular type of tone. The designation "open" is usually omitted as superfluous, and the label "stopped diapason", thus rendered contradictory, has given place to the German and French names, *gedeckt* and *bourdon*. [23]

The *flute* stops are those whose quality bears some resemblance to that of the orchestral flute. Strictly this designation should apply only to open and harmonic pipes, of which the latter provide the closest imitation of the orchestral instrument. The peculiar timbre of the stopped pipe, with its emphasis on the odd partials, justifies a separate category, which is called *gedeckt* (covered). It is impracticable, however, to maintain this distinction consistently. Often the same set will contain stopped pipes in the lower, open pipes in the middle, and harmonic pipes in the upper part of its range. The double-length pipes rarely extend below f^1, and space limitations frequently necessitate the use of stopped pipes for the lowest octave — a substitution which is not objectionable in a soft rank. In such cases the stop is classified according to its most characteristic range.

Stops of the *Rohrflöte* class offer another complication, for they are partially stopped, the stoppers being equipped with small "chimneys", These chimneys add their own frequency to the tone, usually reinforcing the fifth or sixth partial. Since they emphasize odd partials or their multiples, their quality still belongs to the gedeckt class.

The *Quintadena* is a gedeckt stop in which the pipes are overblown so that the third partial is clearly audible. The peculiar nasal quality which results has caused some confusion in its classification, but on the basis of the component partials there is no question.

The tone of the *string* stops is supposed to resemble that of stringed instruments, and many of them take their names from the particular instruments which they are intended to imitate, such as *Viola* , *Viola da Gamba*, *'Cello*, etc. The quality is rather thin, having a weak fundamen-

---

[23]Stopped Diapasons are sometimes included in modern specifications when it is intended to imitate the old stops of that name, which were of large scale with low mouth, voiced on light wind, producing an unforced, colorful tone.

tal and an abnormal development of upper partials. There is, however, a wide range from the placid tone of the classic *Salicional* to the cutting quality of the slender *violes* which were popular in this country in the second and third decades of this century.

Acoustically the flutes and strings are at opposite poles, and the diapasons hold a middle ground. The flutes have the minimum of upper partials and the strings the maximum, while the upper partials of the diapasons, though profusely represented, are less prominent than those of the strings. It is obvious, then, that the lines between these categories cannot be precisely drawn. There is more difference between a fluty diapason and a stringy diapason than there is between the former and a hard flute, or between the latter and a mild string. A *Geigen* is usually classed as a diapason, while the *Dulciana* is placed among the strings; yet if the boxes are adjusted to make them equal in loudness, their qualities will be found to be very similar.

The classification of reed stops is functional, and there is considerable overlapping. The stops which are normally used in ensemble combinations are called *chorus reeds*, and those which are chiefly valuable as solo stops are called *solo reeds*. Of course, any stop which is not actually disagreeable can be used for a solo; and many stops which are ordinarily used alone may occasionally be effective in combination. In general the chorus reeds are analogous to the brass of the orchestra, and the solo reeds to the wood wind. This analogy is shown in the names of the stops, such as *Trumpet, Trombone, Posaune,* and *Oboe, Clarinet, English Horn,* etc. The *French Horn,* which occupies a rather anomalous position in the orchestra, is distinctly a solo stop; moreover the round type of *Tuba,* in spite of its resemblance to its orchestral prototype, does not mix with the ensemble and must function as a solo stop.

Pitch Classification

The foregoing classification is entirely independent of pitch. In each group (excepting the solo reeds) may be found stops of eight-, four-, sixteen-, and even thirty-two foot pitch, while flue qualities are represented also at two-foot and other pitches. It is doubtless superfluous to observe that the pitch names are derived from the lengths of the open pipes which will produce the lowest tones of the respective ranks. In addition to such specific pitch identification, flue stops fall into two general pitch categories: *foundation* and *mutation*.

Etymologically speaking, *mutation* stops are those which "change" the pitch characteristic. They produce tones which are not octave duplications of the fundamental, and so sound not merely higher or lower, but different. A clear definition in artificial terms is this: A mutation stop is one which sounds a pitch of a different *name* from that of the key which is played. Any stop whose pitch is identified by a number which is neither a power of two, nor two divided by a power of two, is a mutation stop.[24]

All other flue stops may be classed as *foundation stops*. There is, however, some ambiguity in the use of this term. Some think of it as applying to stops of diapason quality — a view which is difficult to justify on either historical or practical grounds. The most common use of the term in registration indications is found in French music; so it would seem reasonable to adopt the definition which that use implies.

Each department of the French organ is customarily divided, the pipes being placed on two separate chests. One division contains the *jeux de fond* (foundation stops), and the other the *jeux de combinaison* (combination stops). The first group commonly includes all sixteen-, eight-, and four-foot flue stops, and the second group, all stops above four-foot pitch, all mutations, mixtures, and reeds. Since the division is for practical purposes it is not strictly determined by a literal definition. Sometimes a two-foot stop and even a twelfth or *Nasard*, and perhaps an *Oboe*, may be included in the foundation section. Again, four-foot stops are sometimes found among the *jeux de combinaison*.[25] In general, unless we are using the term in contradistinction from mutation stops, we shall define foundation stops as flue stops of sixteen-, eight-, and four-foot pitch.

Pitch classification also includes combinations of ranks of different pitches responding to a single register. A *mixture* or *compound stop* may be defined as a stop which controls two or more ranks of pipes whose tones duplicate partials of the reference fundamental. Its purpose is to emphasize certain overtone pitches so as to modify the balance and to brighten, enrich, or color the ensemble.[26] Mixtures differ in the number of ranks, the pitch range which they cover, the number and distribution of the breaks, the intervals included, the spacing of the ranks, and the tone quality of the pipes of which they are composed.

Modern mixtures usually comprise from three to six ranks. Larger mixtures are occasionally found, but it is more common to provide greater variety and flexibility by dividing the mixture work into different groups of varied composition. For example, the Great often contains a fairly full mixture (*Mixture, Fourniture, Plein Jeu*) which in general contributes to the ensemble centering in the eight-foot fundamental, and a smaller, high

[24] A mathematician might say: "identified by a number which is not an integral power of two, including zero and negative exponents." This obviously does not apply to old organs whose lowest notes were FFF or GGG, and whose fundamental pitches were therefore described as 12', 6', etc.

[25] See pp. 299-300.

[26] See Chapter VII.

mixture (*Scharf*, *Cymbal*) which contributes rather to the four-foot tone. Some organs contain also a mixture which corresponds to partials of the sixteen-foot series. These chorus mixtures are usually composed of successive octave- and fifth-sounding ranks. They are relatively higher in the bass than in the upper part of the keyboard, breaking back from time to time as they ascend. The higher the mixture, the more it must break back in order to prevent screechiness in the treble, and to avoid the use of impracticably small pipes. The effect of this procedure is to add high pitches in the lower range where they are needed, and to enrich the upper range which is naturally more telling.[27] The composition of these mixtures is by no means uniform, but the following (expressed in intervals above the eight-foot fundamental) may perhaps be considered typical:

Mixture: 15-19-22-26-29, breaking back to 1-5-8-12-15[28]

Scharf: 26-29-33-36, breaking back to 8-12-15-19

Some mixtures, such as the *Cornet* and *Sesquialtera*[29] contain a *Tierce* (seventeenth); and occasionally the *Septième* (flat twenty-seventh) is also added in a group called *Harmonics*. The insertion of these ranks naturally reduces the pitch span of the mixture unless the number of ranks is increased. Often such mixtures simply provide successive partials of the eight foot series, and run through without break — as in the typical Cornet ([1]-8-12-15-17). Occasionally, however, for a special effect, ranks will be skipped (giving greater prominence to the individual tones[30]) as in a *Carillon* (12-17-22).

Chorus mixtures belong to the diapason ensemble and are usually of diapason or Geigen quality. Dulciana pipes are often used for soft mixtures, such as the *Echo* or *Dolce Cornet*. Gemshorn mixtures are a valuable but neglected resource. String mixtures invaded the romantic String Organ of thirty years ago, and are sometimes found in echo divisions. The classic Cornet and Sesquialtera and the Carillon are normally composed of flute pipes.

Analysis of Tone Qualities

For detailed information concerning the construction, classification, timbre, and other characteristics of specific stops, the reader is referred

[27] See pp. 63ff, 95.

[28] Sometimes the fifth, which belongs to the sixteen-foot series, appears near the middle of the keyboard. In such cases care should be taken to avoid the use of the mixture when the sixteen-foot resultant is unpleasant.

[29] A curious name applied to a two-rank mixture sounding the 12th and the 17th, and by extension to larger overtone groups including these ranks. The word (*sesquialter* [Latin] = once and a half) means the interval of a fifth, and originally designated the octave and 12th sounding ranks. Possibly the 'every other' sense of *alter* suggested its application to the third and fifth partials. See Bibl. 125, p. 251.

[30] See p. 84.

to the various dictionaries of organ stops and other technical works. It will be useful, however, to have before us some hitherto unpublished analyses of the tones of certain typical pipes. As explained in the Introduction, these analyses cannot be accepted as literally and quantitatively exact. It is impossible to make unqualified statements concerning the precise proportions of the ingredients of any timbre, because of complications which may be partially illustrated by the problem of a single diapason pipe:

Let us analyze the tone of this pipe at the mouth, at the end of the pipe, at a point equidistant from the mouth and the end, at a more distant point directly in line from the end of the pipe (along the axis), and at various other points in the environment. For the present we will imagine that we have eliminated all reflected waves. We will find only approximate agreement between the analyses at the mouth and at the end of the pipe. At a point equidistant from the mouth and the end the odd partials arrive from the two sources in the same phase and are reinforced, while the even partials arrive in opposite phase and are partially canceled. At points along the axis all partials arrive out of phase and tend to be canceled. The interference pattern at other points depends on the relative distances from the two sources.[31]

In addition to the two principal sources there is probably some slight communication through the walls of the pipe. All these waves strike the walls of the chamber and other obstructions, and are reflected, causing still further interference complications as they meet the waves coming directly from the sources and other reflected waves. In actual performance there is further interference from the waves coming from other pipes. Moreover, some of the high pitches are absorbed or lost in meeting obstacles. Certain pitches are reinforced by standing waves in the room.

The ear tends to magnify the upper pitches, and it adds its own partials and combination tones. Certain pitches are masked by other tones. Also, the two ears do not receive the same stimuli — but this tends to compensate for the irregular effects of the acoustical environment.

Hopeless as these complications appear, the fact remains that the different stops of an organ do produce characteristic and recognizable timbres which can be identified by listeners in various parts of the auditorium. The differences heard correspond to differences at the source, which are measured in the analyses. So, in spite of the inevitable lack of precision and the impossibility of computing the effects of the environment and the auditory perception, the findings present a practically valid picture of the comparative content of various qualities.

[31]Bibl. 33. It should be noted, however, that analyses of reed pipes show a greater proportionate intensity of upper partials along the axis.

The usual method of presenting such data is to plot the intensities as ordinates against the pitches or frequencies as abscissas. For our purpose a more pictorial method of representation has been chosen. The pitches are shown on a vertical scale, and the lengths of the horizontal lines correspond to the relative intensities of the respective partials. The lowest line represents the fundamental; the second line, the second partial; the third line, the third partial; etc.

We have chosen to plot the actual readings of the wave analyzer, which show the physical intensities as defined in terms of pressure variation. Some acousticians, because of the logarithmic response of the ear, plot the logarithms of the readings, or their actual decibel values. Such a method, however, shows *levels* of intensity or loudness, but indicates nothing concerning proportionate loudness.

The ideal method would seem to be to show the analyses in *loudness units* (LU). These units for the quantitative measurement of loudness, derived by Harvey Fletcher,[32] provide a valid scale for proportionate loudness. However, their application would involve the assumption of data which could only be valid for a tone having a specific frequency and reaching the ear with a specific intensity. A comparison of LU values with pressure equivalents indicates that the pressure readings give a reasonably accurate impression of the characteristics of the different tone qualities, approaching the loudness proportions much more closely than the decibel values.

The measurements for the accompanying graphs are determined in the following manner: The readings for each pipe are reduced to proportionate values which total 100, so that each partial is represented as a percent of the total tone. In plotting, the same linear units are used for all diagrams; thus the graphs show the proportionate ingredients of the different qualities, but do not indicate differences in the loudness of the pipes analyzed. The vertical values are logarithmic, showing pitch intervals, not frequency differences.[33]

These graphs appear on the following pages.

[32]Bibl. 11.

[33]The method of making these analyses is described in Appendix I.

I. DIAPASON 1

II. DIAPASON 2

III. GEMSHORN 1

IV. GEMSHORN 2

V. DULCIANA I   VI. DULCIANA 2

VII. SALICIONAL   VIII. VIOLA DA GAMBA   IX. VIOLE
                                              D'ORCHESTRE

X. WOOD FLUTE (LARGE SCALE)

XI WOOD FLUTE (SMALL SCALE)

XII. METAL FLUTE

XIII. METAL HARMONIC FLUTE

XIV.   WOOD   GEDECKT

XV.   ROHRFLÖTE

XVI.   TRIANGULAR   FLUTE

XVII.   QUINTADENA

XVIII. TRUMPET

XIX. HARMONIC TRUMPET

XX. TROMPETTE
(AUSTIN)

XXI. TROMPETTE
(CAVAILLÉ-COLL)

XXII. BOMBARDE

XXIII. OBOE   XXIV. CONTRAFAGOTTO   XXV. ENGLISH HORN
(NONIMITATIVE)

XXVI. CLARINET   XXVII. FRENCH HORN

Special Effects

There are certain special tonal effects, not included in any of the classifications already given, which must be mentioned before this discussion is concluded. The most important is the effect of vibrato.

Stops of the *céleste* type employ two (rarely three) ranks of pipes which are slightly out of tune with each other; thus they produce beats, as described in Chapter I.[34] The effect is a sort of undulation, similar to the natural vibrato of a singer. Usually one rank is in tune with the rest of the organ and is available as a separate stop; the other rank is tuned a little sharp, or (occasionally, when the tone is soft) flat. The pitch impression is the mean between the two frequencies.[35]

String stops are best suited to this purpose because the wide distribution of partials produces beats of various frequencies, and because of the lack of emphasis on any one pitch. The effect is analogous to that of a group of violinists playing with a vibrato which naturally cannot be synchronized. The types with which we are most familiar in this country are: the keen *Viole Céleste*, which is very thin and provides the maximum of shimmer in the upper range, and which exists at various dynamic levels; the broad and telling *'Cello Céleste* (or *Gamba Céleste*[36]), which is the strongest of those in common use; the mild *Salicional Céleste* (commonly called simply *Voix Céleste*); the delicate *Dulciana Céleste* (usually named *Unda Maris*); and the colorful *Gemshorn Céleste*, a soft version of which has become popular under the name *Kleiner Erzähler*. The French *Voix Céleste* is composed of ranks which are of almost Geigen quality; the effect is somewhat similar to that of a broad Salicional Céleste, but even broader and more refined.

Flute stops, with their large proportion of fundamental, produce a more violent, single beat. *Flute Célestes*, therefore, must be soft, and are effectively located in echo divisions. The most satisfactory type of flute for this purpose is the *Spitzflöte*, because of its comparatively high development of upper partials.

A mechanical means of creating a vibrato is the familiar *tremolo*. This device causes a periodic fluctuation of wind pressure, resulting in an alternation of greater and less intensity in the tone, and a slight variation in pitch (caused by the variation in the velocity of the air stream).

This chapter would not be complete without some mention of percussion stops, although they are essentially foreign to organ tone, and they cannot contribute to the ensemble. The primary characteristic of the

[34]P. 21.

[35]Bibl. 44, p. 139.

[36]The author objects to the term 'Gamba Céleste' on etymological grounds.

organ is the immutable continuity of its tone. It is this which necessitates such extreme care in the mixing of combinations, and which affords
such satisfaction in a perfectly realized ensemble. But the tone of percussion instruments diminishes so rapidly that its effect on the ensemble
is of very limited duration — unless its initial intensity is quite out of
proportion.

The source of percussion tone, as commonly heard in the organ, is a
body of sonorous metal, set in vibration by the blow of a hammer. The
metal is usually in the form of a tube, as in the case of *Chimes*, or of a
bar, as in the *Celesta* or *Harp*. In both cases inharmonic partials are
produced.

Chimes are, of course, intended to imitate bells. A perfectly tuned
bell gives the following partials:

The *strike tone*, or fundamental

The *hum tone*, an octave below the strike tone

The *tierce*, a minor third above the strike tone

The *fifth*, a perfect fifth above the strike tone

The *nominal*, an octave above the strike tone

A major third and a perfect fifth above the nominal

The last two partials, without names, are very weak, and are not accurately tuned. The other partials are all concordant, though the minor
tierce is inharmonic.

Tubular chimes (such as are usually found in the organ) give, at best,
imperfect approximations of the tone of bells. Accurate tuning of their
partials is impossible. The vibration of the column of air within the tube
exerts some influence, but the tone is dominated by the much greater
mass of the metal tube. Electronic reproduction of the tone of bells is
satisfactory to the extent that the tuning and relative strength of the bell
partials are realized.

Celesta bars are provided with resonators, proportioned and tuned to
reinforce the harmonic partials. Their size is sufficient to modify to a
considerable degree the delicate tone of the metal bars. When used in
combination, the Celesta affects only the attack. After the initial stroke,
its vibrations are too feeble to be heard with even the softest pipe tones.

Summary

Having, in the first chapter, inquired into the nature and behavior of
sound waves, we have undertaken in this chapter to examine the function
of organ pipes in the projection of such waves, the characteristics of the
resulting waves, and the conditions which determine those characteristics.

We have found that the alternation of compression and rarefaction of the air, which is sound, actually exists in the pipe in the form of a standing wave. Such waves consist in the oscillation of the particles of air, producing a general accordion-like contraction and expansion in the air column.[37] A displacement antinode (pressure node) occurs where there is direct contact with the atmosphere — at the open ends, and at the hole in the side of a harmonic pipe. A displacement node (pressure antinode) occurs where contact with the atmosphere is the most remote — midway between the displacement antinodes of an open pipe, and at the closed end of a stopped pipe. Since adjacent antinodes are always opposite in phase, the complete wave length is twice the distance from one antinode to the next. So the normal open flue pipe contains about half of the complete wave; a stopped nontapering pipe contains about a quarter of the wave; and a harmonic pipe contains approximately the whole wave.

Coexistent with the fundamental vibration are fractional vibrations which produce upper partials. Open pipes have a continuous series of partials in varying number, ranging from the almost pure tone of the flutes, through the rich diapasons, to the highly complex strings, with their abnormal development of upper partials and weak fundamentals. The proportion of upper partials in the tone of stopped pipes is meager, with an almost complete absence of the even partials.

The longitudinal vibrations in the pipes are induced by concurrent transverse vibrations which are actuated by the compressed air in the wind chest. In flue pipes the auxiliary vibrator is a sheet of air which, meeting a thin obstruction, produces an edge tone. The tone produced by these coupled vibrations is dominated by the standing wave in the pipe, whose frequency is proportionate to the speed of sound and so dependent on the temperature. In reed pipes the vibrations are induced by a vibrating brass tongue. This reed largely controls the frequency of the vibrations and gives a peculiarly positive attack. The pipe serves as a resonator, selectively reinforcing the partials and so modifying the quality. It behaves as a stopped pipe, favoring the odd partials if cylindrical, but including the complete series if conical.

Not only is the attack of a reed pipe quicker than that of a flue pipe, but all low tones, being produced by larger vibrating bodies, are slower of speech than high tones. Uncertain attacks are also noticed in harmonic pipes and in strings which have an abnormally weak fundamental.

Stops are classified according to their construction, quality, function, and fundamental pitch. The terms *foundation* and *mutation* serve primarily to distinguish the unison and octave pitches from those which are not

---

[37] The simile applies of course only to an open pipe, since only half of the accordion motion is included in a stopped pipe.

octave duplications of the fundamental. As used by the French, however, the foundation group normally includes only the flue stops of sixteen-, eight-, and four-foot pitch.

Following this general discussion a detailed analysis of representative tone qualities was presented. It was explained that exact quantitative values cannot be determined, but the general picture of the content of each tone is sufficiently characteristic to serve as a guide in applying the principles which we are about to formulate.

We now have in mind the essential information concerning the nature of sound in general and the special tonal characteristics of the organ. This is the foundation on which we will construct our theory of registration.

Part II

APPLICATION OF THE
TECHNICAL INFORMATION
IN PART I TO
TONE COMBINATION

CHAPTER THREE
AUDIBILITY
Absolute Audibility and Loudness

In spite of the riddle canons of the fifteenth century and the 'twelve tone technique' of the twentieth, music must be considered an aural art. Aestheticians may argue about the legitimacy of crab canons and other devices which cannot be heard, but what really matters is the effect on the listener.

The same principle applies to the theories which we are about to present. It is futile to study acoustical phenomena and calculate their logical application to organ registration unless the result is satisfying to a sensitive ear. For this reason we have not confined our inquiry to the external physical behavior of sound, but have also investigated its aural perception. More than that, we shall continually insist that the ear is the final arbiter.

Having accepted as a fundamental principle the preëminence of aural considerations, the obvious starting point in the development of our theory is the problem of audibility. This includes (1) the actual existence of an aural impression — what can be heard; (2) the intensity of the aural impression — the sense of loudness; and (3) the clarity of the aural impression — the ease of discrimination among tones.

If we refer to the acoustical findings reported in Chapter I, we see that all these perceptions are greatly affected by pitch: (1) There is aural response to the weakest stimuli in the vicinity of f^4. (2) The greatest sense of loudness in proportion to the stimulus is in the same region. (3) The greatest sensitivity to dynamic changes is between b^2 and b^4, and the clearest pitch impressions are between c^2 and g^3. All of these regions of maximum sensitivity are well above the normal range of organ music, except the last, which is in the upper part of that range.

It would appear, therefore, that the greater part of the music which we hear lay in a range which imposed a rather startling acoustical handicap. That would be true if the media of performance produced only pure tones of fundamental pitch; but nearly all instruments and voices, excepting those of high pitch, provide an extensive series of upper partials which compensate for the aural deficiencies of the fundamental pitches. In organ music the amount of such compensation can be controlled by the performer's registration, subject, of course, to the limitations of his instrument.

To add these compensating upper pitches the organist has recourse to two methods:

1. The selection of stops which contain a large proportion of high

63

partials, such as strings, bright diapasons, and reeds. This is the method of the *choice* of timbre.

2. The use of a combination which includes stops of high fundamental pitch — four-foot and two-foot stops, mutations, and mixtures. This is the method of the *synthetic composition* of timbre.[1]

The entire study of registration is concerned with the employment and combination of these two processes. The fundamental nature of the problems may be illustrated by a few simple examples:

The 'Fantaisie in D flat' by Saint-Saëns ends with the cadence shown in Example 1. If we were to play this on an eight-foot flute or gedeckt

Example 1. Saint-Saëns: Fantaisie in D flat[2]

(stops which produce a nearly pure fundamental tone), the tones would be scarcely distinguishable. To compensate for the low pitch the composer indicated the use of eight- and four-foot stops, in accordance with the second method noted above. If, however, we add a four-foot flute to our pure fundamental, the effect is only slightly improved.

If we select eight- and four-foot stops of Geigen quality (combining methods two and one), the cadence is clearly heard, but it sounds higher than notated.[3] On the other hand, if we use a single keen string (employing the first method), the progression is heard clearly, and the pitch impression is consistent with the music. Such stops, with their present perfection of speech, were not known to Saint-Saëns.

Now let us compare the softest available high flute tone with a very soft low flute tone. If the two tones are approximately equal in audibility the lower tone will seem much heavier, because of the far greater energy which it gives out. At the same time it will be vague in pitch. Again, compare a chord in the middle of the keyboard played on the softest string with the same chord played on the softest flute. If the swells can be adjusted so that the two are equally audible, the string will

---

[1] These methods are mutually complementary. According to Helmholtz, "the ear has no decisive test by which it can in all cases distinguish between the effect of a motion of the air caused by several different musical tones arising from different sources, and that caused by the musical tone of a single sounding body." — Bibl. 16, pp. 25-6.

[2] Permission for reprint granted by Durand & Cie., Paris, France, copyright owners; Elkan-Vogel Co., Inc., Philadelphia, Penna., agents.

[3] The matter of pitch fidelity will be more fully discussed later; for the present we will merely observe that the addition of an audible higher pitch tends to transpose the pitch impression.

be found much more delicate and refined, because its upper partials are in a range where the ear is more sensitive, and the same degree of loudness is produced with much less energy.[4]

A similar comparison, at a higher dynamic level, may be made between a Grossflöte and a diapason of equal loudness. The amount of energy required to make the almost pure tone of the Grossflöte sound loud causes a more violent disturbance, and produces the effect which we call "fat" or "boomy", and which the psychologists call voluminous.

For an extreme test of this kind we must resort to amplification. We find it in certain electronic instruments, which competent observers agree are least effective in their fortissimo. If we amplify the fundamental pitch so that it sounds as loud as a full combination on a large organ, the tone is very unpleasant. The same difference is felt, to a lesser degree, between the fortissimo of a loudly voiced small organ with few stops of high pitch, and an equally loud ensemble produced on a larger organ by combining many more ranks and including a greater proportion and better distribution of upper pitches.

All of these experiments confirm the implications of laboratory findings that high pitches are essential to dynamic efficiency — the production of the desired degree of loudness with economy of energy, producing the minimum pressure variation and the least violent agitation of the ear drum.

Organists are sometimes accused of playing too loudly when what they are really doing is using combinations which are dynamically inefficient, so that an entirely suitable degree of loudness causes undue fatigue to the listener.[5] Other organists underestimate the dynamic efficiency of high ranks and make them too conspicuous. Other things being equal it is desirable that all loud effects be secured with the minimum release of energy; but this does not justify the indiscriminate use of high pitches. Dynamic efficiency is only one of many considerations which must enter into the planning of the organist's registration.

The value of high pitches is being increasingly recognized by American organists and builders. A comparison of recent instruments with former installations shows a smaller proportion of eight-foot stops, a larger number of mutations and mixtures, fewer heavy flutes, more brilliant voicing of the diapasons and reeds, and a larger number of four-foot reeds. The importance of these developments will be more and more evident as we continue our study.

---

[4]This is one reason why the softest stops on the organ usually are strings.

[5]The question of balance with other media of performance will be discussed in Chap. XIII.

Dynamic Changes

Since dynamic efficiency depends on the use of high pitches it naturally follows that they have an equally important function in changing
the level of loudness. For the sake of simplicity we will confine our
discussion to increasing loudness; obviously the same principles, conversely applied, are valid for dynamic reductions.

The relation of pitch level to loudness level is shown in the sense
of crescendo which is felt in ascending passages of music. This relation is so inescapable that, unless an abnormal effect is intended, an
increase in loudness is usually accompanied by a rise in pitch. The
parallel in registration is obvious: the most effective means of adding
power is to add high pitches or to increase their intensity. In this way
the increase is made in the range where the ear is most sensitive to
dynamic changes; moreover the greater proportion of upper pitches increases the dynamic efficiency of the ensemble.

Occasionally a composer may indicate a crescendo in a descending
passage of music. Similarly it is possible and sometimes effective to
devise a louder registration without increasing the proportion of upper
pitches (or at least, of upper ranks). Such a procedure is dynamically
less potent, and its use implies that the dynamic consideration is secondary. The result is increased volume, giving the impression of bigness
rather than intensity.

Normally, then, dynamic increase will be accompanied by an increase
in the proportion of upper pitches in the ensemble. The methods of producing such a change are: (1) the addition of stops of high fundamental
pitch;   (2) the addition of stops with a large proportion of upper partials; and (3) the opening of the swell box.

The first method is too obvious to require extended comment. We
need only call attention to the necessity of maintaining a suitable proportion, both in the increase and in the relation of the upper pitches to the
ensemble, and of keeping the tone quality consistent with the other
requirements of the music.

Similar observations apply to the second method. Its use in soft
combinations is exemplified by the addition of a soft diapason, or perhaps
a string[6] or a soft reed to soft flutes. In larger combinations the effect
is usually produced by the addition of chorus reeds.

The third method, enlarging the proportion of upper pitches by the
use of the swell pedal, is illustrated in the following example: Let
us assume that we are playing on the Great with the Swell coupled.
Eight- and four-foot stops are drawn on the Great, with perhaps   the

[6]Cf. pp. 74-6, 77.

Twelfth and Fifteenth if they are not too prominent. On the Swell we
have a brilliant ensemble with reeds and mixtures, containing a much
larger proportion of high pitches than the Great combination. As we
open the swell box, the brilliant quality of the Swell emerges more and
more, increasing the proportion of upper pitches in the whole ensemble.
The crescendo gives not merely more of the same thing; it provides increasing dynamic efficiency by bringing the most effective range more
and more into prominence. But there is more to it than that:

Let us try the effect of the swell pedal on a tone in the top octave
of a four-foot rank; then compare that with the effect on a tone in the
lowest octave of an eight- or sixteen-foot flute or gedeckt. We will
find the loudness of the high tone affected far more than that of the
low tone. Now let us make a similar comparison of the effect of the
swell pedal on a string and a flute, when a chord is played in the middle
of the keyboard. We will hear much more change in the case of the
string. Again, if we compare the effect on a full Swell combination,
with and without reeds and mixtures, we will note a similar advantage
in the inclusion of the upper pitches.

The greater effectiveness of the swell pedal when there is a large
proportion of high frequencies is due not only to the greater sensitivity of the ear to intensity changes in the upper pitch range, but also
to the physical effect of the swell box. As we observed in Chapter I,[7]
obstructions impede the transmission of short waves much more effectively than that of long waves. So the closed swell box filters out a
large proportion of the higher partials, and even of the fundamentals
of the smaller pipes. As the shades open the transmission of these high
pitches in less and less impeded, and they emerge with increasing
prominence. Hence the impression of the crescendo is amplified by the
increased proportion of upper pitches, in a manner analogous to the effect
of opening the swell shades when playing on the Great with the Swell
coupled.

The selective efficiency of the swell shades results in complications
for the organist in the operation of the swell pedals. If the parts played
on two manuals differ greatly in range or in timbre, there will be a corresponding discrepancy in the effectiveness of the two swells. In order to
compensate for this discrepancy the manipulation of the swell pedals
must be guided by an attentive ear.

The obstruction offered to short waves by partially open swell shades
has not been sufficiently appreciated by organ builders. The value of
the open Great has been recognized, and much has been said about the
"bloom of the diapasons"; but it also preserves as much as possible

[7] P. 26.

the natural dynamic efficiency of the individual stops and of the ensemble. The transmission of the upper partials is somewhat impaired by the presence of swell shades, even if open at right angles, and it is important to provide the absolute maximum of opening in order that the short waves may be obstructed as little as possible.

Clarity

As the impression of loudness depends on absolute audibility, so clarity depends on comparative audibility, or pitch discrimination, for which we found the maximum aural sensitivity around c^3. In that region both melodic and harmonic intervals are clearly distinguishable when played on a flute stop. As we descend toward the lower part of the keyboard, however, the pitch impression becomes increasingly vague. Example 1 involved this problem of clarity fully as much as absolute audibility.   The same remedy meets both requirements: Add upper pitches, either as separate stops (tending to alter the pitch impression) or by selecting qualities which contain a large proportion of upper partials. Thus a melody or a chord in the lower range is much clearer when played on a string or reed stop than when played on a diapason or flute.

Example 2. Rheinberger: First Sonata — ii. Andante

Example 3. Vierne: Lied[8]

Experimenting with the excerpts given in Examples 1-3, we find that the Saint-Saëns example and the last phrase of the Rheinberger are most satisfactory when played on a string, but the Vierne melody sounds clearer if played on a reed.[9] What is the reason for this?

Referring to the analyses in Chapter II we note that the fundamental of a string is usually small, and the abnormal prominence of certain

[8]From 24 Pièces en style libre. Permission for reprint granted by Durand & Cie., Paris, France, copyright owners; Elkan-Vogel Co., Inc., Philadelphia, Penna., agents.

[9]Good voicing is assumed in both cases, so that there will be no objectionable uncertainty of speech.

upper partials tends to weaken the stability of the pitch impression. A
reed may have an even wider range of partials, but the fundamental is
normally the strongest, and the others are more evenly proportioned,
tending to reinforce the fundamental pitch impression. Moreover, the
tonal efficiency of the reed, even in such exotic stops as the English
Horn, lends emphasis to the fundamental pitch.

Now we know from the experiments of Shower and Biddulph[10]   that
below c^2 the ear's ability to distinguish pitches is approximately proportional to the arithmetical difference in frequency. Thus, in Example
4, the tones of the triad CC-EE-GG are separated by only sixteen vibrations per second; they are as close together as C-D-E, or c^1-$c\sharp^1$-d^1.
When sounded simultaneously, tones in such close proximity tend to

Example 4. Equivalent Pitch Separations

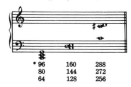

*96	160	288
80	144	272
64	128	256

*For simplicity, the "philosophical pitch" and pure intonation are assumed.

mask one another, and give a sense of crowding. In the lower range
this feeling is aggravated by the greater amount of energy in proportion
to the audible loudness. This proximity is less noticeable in a keen
string than in a reed because the fundamental of the string is so weak,
and the abnormal proportion of the upper partials has the effect of increasing the amount of frequency separation. The lower pitch impression prevails, but the fundamental is a smaller proportion of the tone
than in the case of the reed.

For melodic purposes, however, the predominance of the fundamental
is advantageous in any range. The effect of a melody depends on the
aural comparison of the successive pitches. The perception of such
pitch relationships is facilitated by emphasis on the actual pitches

Example 5. Vierne: Arabesque[11]

[10]Bibl. 42, p. 286.

[11]From *24 Pièces en style libre.* Permission for reprint granted by Durand & Cie.,
Paris, France, copyright owners; Elkan-Vogel Co., Inc., Philadelphia, Penna., agents.

compared. So a reed is more effective for a single melody than a string; likewise a flute, within its easily audible range, provides a clearer melodic line than a string. This can be demonstrated by comparing the effect of a flute and a string in playing the phrase quoted in Example 5.

Combining Stops

In explaining the application of the facts of audibility to registration we have, for the sake of simplicity, dealt largely with the effects of single stops of various timbres and pitches. The extension of these principles to apply to stop combinations is quite obvious if we assume that the effect of a combination of qualities or pitches is the sum of its individual, separate elements. That is, each element contributes its own characteristics in proportion to its audible intensity.[12] The addition of higher pitches gives greater power and clarity according to their nearness to the region of greatest sensitivity. The addition of lower pitches reduces the dynamic efficiency of the combination and obscures the pitch perception, according to their distance from the region of maximum sensitivity.

Translated into practical terms, each stop will make its contribution, on the one side or the other, according to its pitch and the relative prominence of its partials. So, in the normal range of organ music:

1. The addition of four-foot and two-foot stops, mutations, and mixtures tends to make a combination louder and more clearly audible.

2. The addition of sixteen-foot stops tends to make a combination heavy in proportion to its loudness, vague in pitch, and thick in texture.

3. The addition of a string to a diapason or flute of the same pitch increases pitch definition and reduces muddiness in the lower range; in the upper range it reduces clarity.

4. The addition of a flute to a diapason or string of the same pitch tends to make the lower range thick and vague, and clarifies the upper range.

These statements are very crude and self-evident, but by their very obviousness they may serve to suggest the method of meeting more complicated problems.

It must be borne in mind that in all this present discussion we are concerned only with the quality of audibility, as it manifests itself in absolute and comparative loudness and in clarity. In order to arrive at a clear understanding of the relation between acoustics and registration, we need to consider separately the different aspects of the subject.

---

[12]It must be understood that we are not speaking quantitatively. Exact computations are impracticable; but, since we are concerned with relative values rather than exact proportions, the principles we have deduced are valid from the practical standpoint.

The complete solution must reconcile all the different requirements of the music, of which audibility is only the first.

Factors of Blend

The hearing of synchronous tones involves not only comparative audibility (as suggested above), but separate audibility. This we will study from the standpoint of its converse, blend—which we will define as the absence of separate audibility. It is the fusion of different pitches or qualities so that they give the effect of a single sound. The factors which contribute to blend, then, are those which inhibit separate audibility. We will recognize three: (1) coincidence of partials; (2) interspacing of partials; (3) a normal balance of component pitches.

To illustrate the first factor, let us assume that two diapason tones are sounding an octave apart. Each partial of the upper tone coincides with a partial of the lower tone. This mutuality of partials deprives the upper tone of some of its individuality and tends to keep it from being separately heard. Example 6, A; also Figure 1.[13]

Example 6. Coincidence of Partials

A		B		C		D	
1100	1100	1100					1100
990		990	990	990	990	990	
880	880	880					
			825				
770		770		770		770	
660	660	660	660				660
550		550		550		550	
			495				
440	440	440					
330		330	330	330	330	330	
220	220	220					220
			165				
110		110		110		110	

Now if we choose two tones a perfect fifth apart, every second partial of the upper tone will coincide with every third partial of the lower tone. There is less mutuality of partials; half of the upper tone is foreign to the lower tone. So the upper tone retains more of its individuality, and the blend is less complete than in the case of the octave. Example 6, B, and Figure 1.

If we use for our illustration a Quintadena, or a gedeckt in which the upper partials are fairly well developed, we secure a different result. In such a tone the even partials are negligible, so we will sound two tones a twelfth apart (Example 6, C). Again, as in the case of the octave sounded on a diapason, each partial of the upper tone duplicates a

[13]P. 10.

partial of the lower tone; but the fusion is less perfect because of the
smaller number of coincident partials, their relative weakness, and
their wider pitch spacing.[14]   On the other hand, if we sound an octave
on the gedeckt there are no significant common partials. Any sense of
fusion in this case results from the fact that the upper tone supplies some
of the missing partials of the lower tone. Such fusion is very slight,
and is dependent on the second and third factors (the interspacing of
partials and the normal balance of component pitches), possibly reinforced by the coincidence of aural partials.[15] Example 6, D.

The effect of the second factor, the interspacing of partials, is less
obvious than the first, but it is an unmistakable fact of aural experience
and is not difficult to explain. In the case of two tones having common
partials, separate audibility is inhibited by the identity of the duplicated
components.   In the case of two tones whose partials do not coincide
but are closely interspaced, separate audibility is reduced by the blurring
of the distinguishing elements. This is due partly to masking and partly
to the complexity of the tonal structure. The result may be compared to
a halftone reproduction in which the finely spaced dots give the illusion
of solid shading. Close spacing of low pitched tones produces a thick
texture, but when the closely spaced pitches are represented by the
delicate partials of complex qualities, the result is a refined richness
which sounds homogeneous rather than crowded. This seems to provide
the most satisfactory explanation of the shimmer of the high divided
strings of the orchestra, and the rich cohesion of a multitional organ
ensemble.

Returning to Example 6, the blend of the diapason fifth at B is assisted by the interspacing of the noncoinciding partials. In the case
of the octave on the gedeckt at D, however, the more distant spacing
has little fusing effect.

The third factor contributing to blend, which we have called a normal
balance of component pitches, at once brings up the question of how
such a normal balance is to be determined. We may assume that such
a balance exists in the series of partials of a natural, unforced, musical
tone. We may take as our starting point Helmholtz' statement that "in all
natural tones which are suited for musical purposes, the higher partials
decrease in force as they rise in pitch."[16]

It would appear natural that the amplitude of a whole vibration should
be greater than that of a fractional vibration; also that the amplitudes

[14]But if a gedeckt is combined with a *soft* twelfth of gedeckt or Rohrflöte quality, the
combination is hardly distinguishable from a Quintadena.

[15]See p. 20.

[16]Bibl. 16, p. 57.

of the larger fractional vibrations should be greater than those of the smaller ones. In other words, proceeding in numerical order, the successive partials would naturally become weaker until the point of inaudibility was reached.

We may define a normal balance of component pitches, therefore, as one in which no pitch is conspicuously out of line with a generally tapering series. The taper may be abrupt, as in a flute, or very gradual, as in a Trumpet; it may be continuous, or interrupted; but it will be fairly consistent. An examination of the analyses in Chapter II shows that the only stops which do not conform to this description are those whose qualities may be considered somewhat abnormal, due to certain prominent partials.

This conception is admirably illustrated by an experiment performed by Karl Rudolph Koenig — a German-born acoustician who worked in Paris, of whom Dayton C. Miller said: "he probably did more to develop the science of sound than any other one man."[17] The experiment was as follows:[18]

Fourteen tuning forks were tuned to produce the first fourteen partials of the pitch sounded by the lowest fork of the series. These were successively set in vibration by a violin bow, beginning with the highest and proceeding in order down to the second partial. Then, after a slight delay, the fundamental was sounded. Immediately the separate pitches disappeared, absorbed in the fundamental, producing a rich tone, altogether different from the pure tone of a single tuning fork.

Since the tones of the individual forks were practically devoid of upper partials, there were no coincident or interspaced partials to produce this fusion. The effect resulted solely from the perfect proportion of the of the component pitches. The order in which the forks were sounded, allowing the longest time for the highest pitch to die away and progressively less as the fundamental was approached, produced the regular tapering of the partials which we have described as normal.

Any marked deviation from such a normal proportion tends toward separate audibility. If the deviation is sufficient the result is a definite lack of blend. If a single pitch thus emerges from the normal line, a sensitive listener will be conscious of that particular tone. If more than one pitch, or a group of pitches are out of proportion, the result is an exotic quality. It is to such irregularities that the Orchestral Oboe and even the Clarinet owe their characteristic timbre.

[17]Bibl. 27, p. 91.
[18]Described by Audsley in Bibl. 56, Vol. I, p. 411.

Combining Tones of Equal Pitch

Now let us examine specific tone combinations in the light of our study of the factors of blend. It must be understood before we proceed that we are not discussing euphony or desirability, but the bare fact of blend, defined as the fusion of different elements into a single sound impression. The question of the degree of fusion which is suited to a given situation will be taken up later.

First we will try the effect of combining two tones of the same pitch. Here we find that the degree of blend depends on the degree of similarity of the timbres of the two tones. If the two tones are identical all the partials will coincide, and their proportion will remain the same as in a single tone. The blend, then, is complete. Such a combination, however, provides the conditions for the maximum amount of interference, so it is not dynamically effective. This is one reason for the avoidance of exact duplications in all good organs.

If the qualities of the two tones are similar, most of the partials will coincide and their proportion will not be greatly affected. The blend of such a combination is approximately complete. Examples are: two diapasons, two flutes or a flute and a gedeckt, two strings. The same applies, to a slightly less degree, to a mild diapason combined with a flute or a gedeckt; to a rich diapason combined with a moderate string; and to a string combined with a bright reed.

If, on the other hand, we combine opposite timbres, such as a flute and a keen string, the tones do not fuse well. This fact, which is apparent to a sensitive listener, may be explained as follows:

If we study the analyses of the Viole d'Orchestre and the large scale Wood Flute, given in Chapter II,[19] we notice that the string has prominent partials which are well above the range of the highest components of the flute. Obviously, in this range there can be neither coincidence nor interspacing of partials. These high partials could be absorbed in the combination only in case they contributed to a normal proportion of component pitches.

Again, it is evident that the very large fundamental of the flute is completely out of line with the general contour of the string. This tone will inevitably assert itself unless the upper partials can taper naturally from it.

To show the characteristics of the combination we give in Figure 9 a theoretical analysis of the tone of the two stops sounding together, assuming equal intensity. In this graph we see that the lower partials of the combination establish a very abrupt taper (line 1), from which

[19]Graphs IX and X.

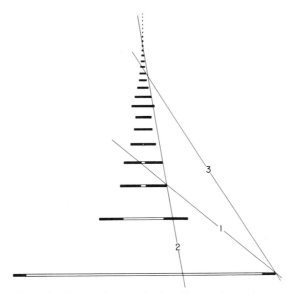

Figure 9. Composite graph of a flute and a string.
White portions of the horizontal lines show the
analysis of a large scale wood flute; black portions show the analysis of a Viole d'Orchestre.

the upper partials stand apart. The high partials, on the other hand,
form a very gradual taper (line 2), from which the fundamental protrudes
conspicuously.   Any attempt to show a taper which will include both
the fundamental and the high partials (line 3) reveals a gap in the
middle, where the intensities of the partials are too small to participate
in the general contour.

So we have a prominent and characteristic upper section, whose relative intensity is magnified by the sensitivity of the ear, and at the same
time a big, assertive fundamental which demands attention.   Between
these two there is insufficient intermediate tone to effect a satisfactory
connection.[20]

From these observations we may make the following important deductions:

1. A tone which contains a large proportion of fundamental, such as
a flute or a round diapason, tends to make its own pitch separately
audible.

2. An exotic quality tends to be prominent.

3. A gap in the development of partials tends to keep the upper
pitches separate from the lower.

[20] Again the reader is reminded that any reasoning based on a quantitative interpretation of our analyses is inexact, but the approximation is sufficiently close to assure the
validity of our conclusions.

All of these tendencies are relative, depending on the comparative audible intensities of the factors involved. Pitches which, if prominent, stick out unpleasantly may, if subdued, serve a perfectly normal purpose or, at most, lend a slightly exotic color. This is exemplified in the combination of a flute and a string which we have just studied. If the string is relatively soft, it will serve to reinforce the weak partials of the flute and be absorbed by it. If the flute is relatively soft, it will serve to compensate for the weak fundamental of the string. The incompatibility of such opposite qualities is most evident when the loudness of the tones is approximately equal. Since the effect is dependent on aural intensity, it is affected by pitch. Thus a combination of an eight-foot flute and an eight-foot string may (if the flute is not too heavy) be satisfactory as a modified string in the lower part of the keyboard, where the flute is almost inaudible; it may sound like a slightly colored flute in the upper range, where the flute is clearly audible and overbalances the string; but the same combination may refuse to blend in the middle of the keyboard, where neither dominates the other.

Combining Tones of Different Pitch

Now let us consider the combination of two tones of different pitches. For the present we have in mind the use of different stops, and will assume that the pitches are related.

If the two tones are alike in quality, the degree of blend will be somewhat in proportion to the harmonic development — the number of partials included in each tone. For example, if both are pure tones there can be no common partials, except the multiple frequencies which the ear adds. There is, therefore, little blend from the coincidence or the interspacing of partials, and the upper tone can lose its identity only if its frequency is a multiple of that of the lower one, and if it is sufficiently soft to be absorbed, serving as an upper partial of the lower tone.

On the other hand, if both tones are rich in partials blend is encouraged by three conditions: (1) the coincidence of many partials; (2) the interspacing of noncoinciding partials; and   (3) the relative weakness of the upper fundamental, which prevents it from unduly distorting the normal gradation of component pitches.

If the two tones differ in quality as well as in pitch, the effect depends so much on their relative loudness that generalization is difficult. Assuming that the upper tone is no louder than the lower one, a complex tone above a simple tone tends to be absorbed, the amount of absorption depending on the pitch relation of the two tones, their relative aural intensity, and the degree of prominence of the high partials. This tendency is favored by the following conditions: (1) Since the fundamental of the lower tone is much more intense than any other single pitch in the combination, it tends to mask the upper frequencies. (2) Some or all of the partials of the upper tone add to the lower tone partials which are weak or lacking in its structure. (3) No single upper pitch is emphasized to compete with the fundamental of the lower tone. Thus, in combining a four-foot string with an eight-foot gedeckt, the string supplies the even partials which the gedeckt (almost) lacks, giving a bright richness which sounds homogeneous. But if the upper partials of the string are too intense, the blend is impaired.

A simple tone above a complex tone of equal or less loudness tends to be distinctly audible. If, for example, we combine a four-foot flute with an eight-foot string, all the partials of the flute coincide with with partials of the string, but the partials which they reinforce are prominent in the string itself; so the flute exaggerates an already abnormal proportion. Moreover the strong fundamental of the flute gives special emphasis to its own pitch. The resulting tone is exotic, perhaps harsh, with an assertive four-foot pitch, whose prominence depends on the proportion of the various partials.

It must be emphasized that these statements concerning the blending of flutes and strings at different pitches assume that the flute is not softer than the string in the range in which the combination is played. Because of the poor response of the ear to low frequencies, the loudness of a flute varies greatly with its pitch. So in the lower part of the keyboard a four-foot string will assert itself above an eight-foot flute, leaving the latter vague and isolated. Likewise in the lower range a four-foot flute is weak, and adds only a slightly exotic character to an eight-foot string. As we ascend the keyboard, the four-foot string merges more and more with the eight-foot flute, and the four-foot flute (combined with an eight-foot string) becomes more and more prominent.

The blend between the flute and string depends also on the number of tones sounding. In single tones the flute is more apt to be subordinate to the string, whether above or below. In chords the tendency of the string tones to blend with one another prevents the assertion of their individual pitches. So the four-foot string provides a rich superstructure for the eight-foot flute or gedeckt, while the four-foot flute asserts its own pitches above the thin mesh of the eight-foot string tones.

Complex Combinations

In this explanation of the results of combining different timbres the opposite qualities of flute and string have been used, in order to show by extreme examples the respective tendencies of simple and complex tones at unison and at higher and lower pitches. The extent to which these tendencies are realized in a given situation depends on the conditions which we have discussed, and also on the amount of disparity between the tones which are combined. For example, we have found a heavy flute and a brilliant string incompatible at the same pitch, but a light flute and a mild string often combine acceptably.

Also, for the sake of clarity, we have studied the simplest situations, involving the combination of only two stops. It is obvious that larger and more varied combinations create much more complex problems. The understanding of these complexities will be facilitated if we remember that each stop functions in its environment in accordance with the principles which we have discovered. The degree to which each stop influences the total effect depends on its relative audible intensity. To that degree the principles stated on page 75 are valid for larger combinations, and may be repeated here in more specific, concrete terms:

1. A flute always tends to emphasize its particular pitch. An eight-foot flute (unless it replaces a diapason with an even stronger fundamental) increases the domination of the eight-foot pitch and reduces the dynamic efficiency of the combination. Similarly a four-foot or two-foot flute tends to single out its own pitch. Where the maximum degree of cohesion is desired we must not be conscious of separate pitches. That end will be best served by omitting all flutes from the combination.[21] The same applies to fluty diapasons and round, smooth reeds.

2. A keen or coarse eight-foot string, an Orchestral Oboe, or any other exotic timbre, tends to assert its individuality and so interferes with complete tonal fusion. A four-foot string is more easily absorbed. This is partly because four-foot stops are usually milder, but it is also true that a higher complex tone merges better with the ensemble.[22]

If a painter finds that he has put too much blue into his green he can correct it by increasing the proportion of yellow. Can the organist in the same way compensate for an excessive proportion of flute by adding string tone? The answer is found in Figure 9. This picture is very different from the graph of a diapason in Chapter II.[23] The painter is using prime colors, but the organist is not using pure tones. He is

[21]It is suggested that the inexperienced or skeptical organist compare a full flue chorus on the Swell, including all the soft flutes (usually present at four pitches), with the same combination without the flutes. If the Swell has a complete ensemble of other qualities, the sensitive listener cannot fail to observe the more perfect cohesion when the flutes are omitted.

[22]In planning specifications it has been found advantageous to assign a mild English Horn to the Choir at four-foot pitch. Experiment showed that, although its abnormal series of partials refused to blend with other stops at eight-foot pitch, it had combinational value at four-foot pitch. The lost eight-foot octave being outside the characteristic range of the English Horn, the higher pitch did not impair its usefulness as a solo stop, while it enabled it to serve in the ensemble.

[23]Graphs I and II.

obliged to compensate for one abnormality with another, and the compensation can never be exact. In large combinations the effect of an undesirable timbre may be reduced to a negligible quantity, and it may even be so balanced that its contribution is, on the whole, useful. From the standpoint of blend, however, the inclusion of extreme qualities is almost always detrimental.

If an electronic instrument could provide a hundred pure partials for each note of the keyboard, all in perfect tune with the fundamental, and each one separately controlled with minute gradations of intensity throughout a wide dynamic range, the organist could mix his colors as the painter does. The tonal possibilities of such an instrument are beyond the imagination, but of course its mechanical and mental complexities would exceed the limits of practicability.

Conditions Which Affect Separate Audibility

This discussion of the factors of blend has dealt largely with the combination of timbres at the same and different pitches. There are other conditions which affect separate audibility which must be noted before we leave the subject.

1. In general, the higher ranks are more distinguishable in the lower than in the upper part of the keyboard. In the lower range there is the greatest discrepancy in the aural response to different pitches, as to both dynamic and pitch perception. If mixtures are used, this condition is magnified by the fact that they corroborate higher partials in the lower part of the keyboard, breaking back from time to time as the fundamental pitch rises.

2. Corollary to the preceding paragraph, wide pitch spacing favors separate audibility. It provides fewer coincident partials, less interspacing of partials, less masking, and greater discrepancy in aural response. However, the mere fact of pitch isolation is probably the strongest factor in encouraging mental tone separation.

3. The separate pitches of a combination are most audible when single notes are sounded. A sensitive ear can often detect the third partial in a single tone of a gedeckt, or the second partial in a diapason. Combinations of stops of various pitches are quite transparent in the playing of a single melody. This separateness is largely lost with the addition of a second voice, and the ensemble becomes more and more fused as the number of voices increases, or the spacing becomes more compact. Then the separate pitches are lost in the close texture of the music.

The practical significance of this observation is that care should be taken in the use of high pitches, prominent mutations, and sixteen-foot stops, when playing a single melody. The upper pitches should be so proportioned that they will be absorbed in the fundamental, unless separate audibility is specifically desired. Sixteen-foot stops should either be omitted or else made sufficiently loud to give the impression of intentional octaves. A soft sixteen-foot tone adds a vague undertone which detracts from the clarity of the melody without any compensating advantage.

4. In chords or polyphony the octave pitches are more audible than the mutation pitches. Because of the equivalence of octaves the addition of four-foot, two-foot, and sixteen-foot stops merely duplicates the notes played, in these other ranges. If all the pitches were played on an eight-foot stop, the result would be heard as an extension of the pitch span of the music. But when a twelfth or a seventeenth is added it brings in tones which, as fundamental pitches, are incompatible with the music. The mind is therefore forced to hear the mutation pitches as partials of the fundamental tones, modifying their quality, and reinforcing their pitch with the resultants which they produce. Their presence also fills in the gaps in the harmonic series, and so tends to refer the octave pitches also to the fundamental, thus reducing *their* separate audibility.[24]

Corollary to this is the fact that upper octave pitches brighten the tone, while mutation pitches contribute color. The former transpose the tones to a more clearly audible range, without affecting their tonality. One hears the same thing higher. Mutation pitches, on the other hand, refer the whole impression to the fundamental, modifying the timbre by altering the proportion of the artificial partials.[25]

5. A tone which is out of tune is not absorbed in the ensemble. None of its partials coincide (except fortuitously) with any of the partials of the correct pitch. There can therefore be neither coincidence of partials nor any contribution to a normal proportion of component pitches, as factors of blend. Even the possible effect of interspacing partials is vitiated by the fact that out-of-tune partials clash with nearby partials, rather than occupying vacant spaces; and their discrepancies are emphasized by the beats which they produce.

For this reason it is of the utmost importance that the upper ranks of the organ be in perfect tune. Much of the prejudice against mixtures is due to the fact that they are rarely properly tuned. As a result they not only are not absorbed in the ensemble, but they are discordant.

In addition to conditions which are the responsibility of the organ tuner, there are three common examples of out-of-tune tones which call

---

[24]Cf. p. 87.

[25]Cf. pp. 167-8. Obviously the octave pitches in "brightening the tone" are modifying the timbre in that direction, but the listener does not relate the change so clearly to the fundamental.

for discretion in registration: borrowed mutations, stops of the celeste category, and chimes.

Borrowed mutations are out of tune because they are taken from the tempered scale.[26] The twelfth or Nasard and the Larigot are too low, and the seventeenth (Tierce) and Septième are too high. In certain combinations a borrowed Nasard may be bent into place by what organ tuners know as 'pulling' — the tendency of frequencies which almost coincide to come together, through the influence of resonance. The discrepancies produced by the borrowed Tierce and Septième, however, are much greater. Such stops are usable only for short, staccato notes, where they add an element of piquancy, while the ear does not have time to appreciate their harmonic incompatibility.

The effect of a céleste is dependent on the approximate balance of two tones, one of which is out of tune. We learned in Chapter II[27] that the pitch impression is the mean between the two. If one of the pitches is reinforced by the addition of fairly loud unison stops, the pitch impression is shifted in that direction, and the out-of-tune rank is more at variance with the prevailing impression. Instead of the mutual action of

---

[26]It is assumed that the reader is familiar with the significance of equal temperament as a practical means of performing music on a keyboard instrument having only twelve tones within the octave. Complete flexibility is attained by making the tones exactly equidistant, which only approximates the true pitches. Detailed explanation may be found in any standard reference work.

Considerations of economy and space have led many American organ builders to borrow certain mutations from ranks of foundation pitch, with the result that tempered intervals are substituted for pure tuning. Table 5 shows the frequencies of the natural and tempered overtone ranks for a[1] (= 440), and the number of beats which each tempered mutation would cause.

TABLE 5

Comparison of Natural and Tempered Overtone Ranks

Showing beats produced by tempered mutations

	PITCH	NATURAL FREQUENCY	TEMPERED FREQUENCY	NUMBER OF BEATS PER SECOND
Fundamental	8'	440	440	0
Octave	4'	880	880	0
Twelfth (Nasard)	2 2/3'	1320	1318.5	1.5
Fifteenth	2'	1760	1760	0
Seventeenth (Tierce)	1 3/5'	2200	2217.5	17.5
Nineteenth (Larigot)	1 1/3'	2640	2637	3
Twenty-first (Septième)	1 1/7'	3080	3136	56
Twenty-second	1'	3520	3520	0

[27]P. 56.

two pitches, one dominates and the other sounds more out of tune.   An eight-foot stop added to a céleste must not be too loud, and its fundamental should not be too strong.

A string céleste can be combined with a soft sixteen-foot stop without making the hearer too conscious of its out-of-tune character.   A sixteen-foot flute has few partials to clash with the out-of-tune rank, and a gedeckt almost none.   Even a sixteen-foot string does not single out any one pitch to disturb the balance of the vibrato.   If, on the other hand, a flute céleste be combined with a sixteen-foot string, one rank emphasizes an already prominent partial of the string, and the other rank clashes.

In the same way, any stop or combination which includes an audible higher pitch — even a Quintadena — makes a string céleste sound out of tune.   This is particularly true of a four-foot flute, which strongly reinforces the second partial of one rank of the céleste and stresses the beats at that pitch, which are twice as rapid as those of the fundamental.

The frequency with which distinguished organists disregard the facts presented in the foregoing paragraphs tempts one to quote Widor's favorite comment: "Organists never listen to themselves."[28] More specific is the observation of Alexandre Cellier. Concerning the four-foot flute he says: "Its combination with the strings alone is antipathetic, and with the Voix Céleste impossible, for this eight-foot stop . . . would form with the four-foot stop a false octave." Elsewhere, having described the beats of the Voix Céleste, he comments: "This dissonance renders the stop unsuitable to combine with four-foot stops, reeds, and mixtures."[29]

It is to be recommended, therefore, that a céleste *never* be used in any combination which includes stops of higher pitch, with the possible exception of a light four-foot string which fuses perfectly with the normal rank of the céleste.

The tone of chimes stands apart partly because of its percussive attack, and partly because of the inharmonic partials. If the partials are perfectly tuned (which is seldom the case) the discrepancy comes not from their being out of tune, but from the juxtaposition of the minor tierce of the chimes with the major harmonic tierce. The more prominent these conflicting partials are, the more distinctly, and perhaps the more disagreeably, does the tone of the chimes remain separate. They are not suited to combination with any other stops, and care must be exercised in selecting their accompaniment. The problem is to avoid audible pitches and strong partials which are near the inharmonic partials of the chimes. The relation between the chime melody and the accompanying

[28]"Les organistes ne s'écoutent jamais." — Bibl. 159, p. 182 (160, p. 143). This comment is familiar to all who ever studied with Widor.

[29]Bibl. 68, pp. 64, 29; quoted with the kind permission of the author.

parts is, of course, determined by the composer, but the clash can be minimized by using fairly simple qualities below the offending partials, and avoiding emphasis on any pitch in the region in which they fall. But chimes are most effective when played alone, unaccompanied, and *of course* in single notes.

The tremolo is occasionally useful as a fusing agent. The periodic variations in loudness and pitch reduce the clarity of the individual tones which compose the ensemble, thus impairing their separate audibility and encouraging the integration of the tonal mass. The unsteadiness and indefiniteness tend to obscure pitch discrepancies. For example, with the aid of a tremolo a tempered twelfth may be absorbed in the ensemble and make its normal color contribution. It also promotes cohesion in combinations which include a céleste. The added stops clash less clearly with the out-of-tune rank of the céleste and, because of the vibrato which the tremolo imparts, become more like the céleste. On the other hand, a tremolo with a céleste alone simply results in two vibratos which do not agree.

In all these cases the tremolo serves only to conceal or mitigate defects. Often, indeed, the tremolo itself should be regarded as an added defect. Like all devices for compensation it does not offer an ideal solution, and it should be resorted to only when it provides a value, not otherwise attainable, which outweighs the total defect.

Summary

Now we have before us the essential facts about what we can hear — absolutely, quantitatively, comparatively, and separately. We have observed that, because of the greater sensitivity of the ear to sound impressions in the upper pitch range, dynamic efficiency and clarity of perception require the inclusion of high pitches, either as fundamentals of upper ranks, or as partials of the chosen qualities, or both. Under normal conditions this inclusion of high pitches is necessary for all music in the lower range of the keyboard, for music in which the spacing is close, and for loud music. Upper pitches also play an important part in dynamic changes, either by the operation of stops or through the control of the swell shades.

We proceeded to the study of blend, which we defined as the absence of separate audibility. We found three contributing factors: coincidence of partials, interspacing of partials, and a normal balance of component pitches. Applying these tests to specific combinations we learned the following:

1. Two tones of the same pitch blend in approximate proportion to their similarity.

2. Two tones of similar quality but different in pitch blend in approximate proportion to their complexity.

3. The blend of two tones differing in both pitch and quality depends on the range, the relative loudness, and the degree of disparity in their overtone composition. In general, a simple tone fuses with a lower complex tone better in the lower part of the keyboard than in the upper, while the reverse is true of a complex tone above a simple tone. In part playing a complex tone tends to lose its individuality whether it is above or below the simple tone.

Applying these findings to larger combinations, we learned that simple tones always tend to emphasize their own pitch. If low, they add weight and thickness at the expense of clarity and dynamic efficiency; if high, they add clarity but tend to remain separate from the ensemble. We found extremely complex and exotic tones quarreling with their neighbors and penetrating the ensemble, but less assertive at four-foot pitch.

Other facts noted are: (1) Wide pitch separation inhibits blend; (2) the separate tones of a combination are most audible when single notes are sounded; (3) in part playing, octave pitches are more audible than mutation pitches; and (4) tones which are out of tune do not merge with the ensemble. Because of the last, particular care must be exercised in the use of borrowed mutations and celestes.

Throughout this discussion we have had in mind combinations of stops, but in principle it makes no difference whether the different pitches are sounded by different ranks or by different keys. So the observations made and the conclusions drawn apply equally to the tones combined in chords and polyphony. Naturally there are the added complications that the pitch relationships are less simple and that each note of a chord may include several ranks of different pitches. All this adds up to a threefold ramification of the pitch structure: Several keys are played at the same time; each key sounds several pipes of various pitches; and each pipe has its own series of partials. This does not involve any different principles, but merely adds complexity to the application of the principles already determined.

In studying the blend of the different tones of a chord or a polyphonic ensemble we will be dealing with purely relative values. Perfect fusion is rendered impossible by the discrepancies of equal temperament, by the relative loudness of the different tones, and by the fact that the different pitches do not represent a series of partials. Of course, however, complete fusion would make it impossible to hear the details of the music. This leads us to the question of the optimum degree of blend, which is the subject of the next chapter.

CHAPTER FOUR
THE OPTIMUM DEGREE OF BLEND
Criterion of the Desirability of Blend

It is natural to think of blend as a desideratum and the absence of blend as a defect. Such an assumption is due to the confusion of blend with euphony. In determining the optimum degree of blend we must remember that it means simply the absence of separate audibility of simultaneous sounds. With this in view our criterion is obvious: Blend is desirable when and to the extent that the synchronized different pitches of the music are mutually dependent; a lack of blend is desirable when and to the extent that certain pitches have independent significance. Such a statement seems too self-evident — it is even tautological; but by very reason of the simplicity and obviousness of this principle its application to specific conditions is unmistakable. The problem is to recognize the degree of independence of the various tonal elements in the music.

The considerations involved fall naturally into two groups: (1) those which concern the blending of the elements which compose the tonal ensemble, i.e., the stop combination; and (2) those which concern the blending of the different voices — the elements which compose the musical texture.

Blend in Stop Combinations

It would seem obvious that, as a general rule, when we play a note or a group of notes, we do not expect to be conscious of other pitches than those played. We expect each note to give a single impression. To this end the normal stop combination will produce an intrinsically cohesive sound, centering in the fundamental pitch. Octave ranks will be made prominent when we wish to duplicate the pitch impression at octaves; mutation ranks may be emphasized when the music invites exotic coloring. These are abnormal requirements for interpretative purposes.

Normally, then, in designing a tonal ensemble, the blending of its elements *is* a desideratum. Applying the discoveries of the last chapter, we will avoid extreme qualities, such as loud flutes and keen or coarse strings, and we will build our ensemble of tones which are not too far from the center of the tonal spectrum. Within these limits there will be an ample opportunity for interesting variety of color, unless the resources of the instrument are meager. The subtle shades of timbre offered separately by the individual stops are greatly multiplied by combinations of even two or three qualities, while the addition of different pitches and the construction of larger ensembles afford still greater possibilities.

Throughout this study it will be borne in mind that it concerns not only the combination of the fundamental pitches of various stops, but also the combination of the discrete pitches which compose the timbres of the individual stops. It must also be remembered that special qualities for interpretative purposes are not now under consideration; at present we are discussing normal combinations.

In combining stops of the same pitch we may say categorically that blend is always desirable. Our chief concern will be to avoid too great disparity in the character of the tones which we combine.[1] It is sometimes possible to unite an extreme quality with its acoustical neighbor, but it is usually preferable, if the interpretation calls for such a quality, to use a single stop. In general, the most effective blend results from combinations which do not include either loud flutes or stops with an abnormal development of partials.

The foregoing applies not only to eight-foot stops but to combinations at any one pitch. The problem of such combinations at other than eight-foot pitch, however, is modified by the complexity of the ensemble, the relationship of each stop to the fundamental, and by the fact that in most organs the more extreme qualities are found only at eight-foot pitch.

In combining stops of different pitches blend is usually desirable; the introduction of any unabsorbed pitches will be dictated by considerations of texture and interpretation which will be discussed later. In selecting the stops to be included we will be guided by the findings of the last chapter. Loud flutes, round diapasons, and smooth reeds will be avoided as much as possible; if they are used at all, care will be taken to balance them with ample and well distributed upper work. Even soft flutes will be used with discretion. Loud strings and other assertive qualities will also be avoided, except that they may occasionally be useful at four-foot pitch to compensate for the lack of sufficient octave diapason and reed tone.

Balance of Pitches

The mere elimination of undesirable elements is comparatively simple. The real problem in composing an ensemble is to effect an ideal balance of pitches. In order to do this we must know the contribution which each pitch will make to the total effect.

The strength of the fundamental rank should be sufficient to control the ensemble, so that the upper work will be heard as quality only. (We

_____
[1]See pp. 74-5.

shall see later that this aural impression may be produced with an eight-foot tone of small physical intensity.) On the other hand it must not be so strong as to prevent the upper work from making its contribution to the clarity and dynamic efficiency of the tone. Just what the proportion should be depends on the pitch of the fundamental, the composition of the ensemble, and the character of the music.

In the lower part of the keyboard the fundamental tone has all the handicaps and defects which we have found characteristic of low frequencies. It tends to sound heavy, logy, and vague. In that range, therefore, it is usually best to use the minimum amount of fundamental tone which will control the pitch impression. In the upper range a larger proportion of fundamental is desirable. As we come into the range of greater aural sensitivity the fundamental pitch itself becomes more effective, and a greater proportion is needed to absorb the upper ranks and prevent them from being screechy.[2]

The function of the fundamental, however, is served not only by stops of eight-foot pitch. The experiments described in Chapters I and III[3] show how a perfectly balanced series of overtone pitches contributes to the fundamental tone. The following experiments at the console are very revealing — assuming an organ with fairly well balanced upper work and an eight-foot diapasion which is not too heavy:

Play a full chord on the Great, using Diapason 8', Octave, and Fifteenth. Now add the Twelfth and play the same chord. One hears not an added upper pitch, but a reinforcement of the fundamental. This is a practical demonstration of the fact that mutation pitches lose their identity in part playing.[4]

Now play the same chord, using Diapason 8', Twelfth, and Fifteenth, possibly including a mixture. Then add the Octave and compare the effect. Again the fundamental is reinforced, in spite of the tendency of octave stops to be heard separately. This is because the Octave fills a vacancy in the total superstructure, effecting a nearer approach to the normal balance of component pitches.

The importance of the role of the four-foot pitch in ensemble combinations has only recently been appreciated by organists and organ builders. We now understand that the strength of the Octave should be almost, if not quite, as great as that of the Diapason 8', and that the four-foot chorus reed should be even louder than the eight-foot. Indeed, it is

[2]The breaking back of mixtures effects this gradual shifting of the balance of pitches. Indeed, individual single stops are so voiced that the proportion of fundamental increases as the pitch becomes higher.

[3]Pp. 22, 73.

[4]See p. 80.

often effective to use the Octave in combinations which do not contain
an eight-foot diapasion, and the Clarion should usually be added (in
dynamically graduated combinations) before the Trumpet 8'. A loud eight-
foot reed should almost never be used in an ensemble combination without a corresponding four-foot reed, or ample brilliant mixtures. If the
eight-foot reed is smooth its insistent fundamental overemphasizes the
eight-foot pitch; if it is brilliant it is better absorbed, but such reeds are
rarely free from exaggerated upper partials which make them prominent.
Such qualities, as we have observed, are more readily assimilated at
four-foot pitch. On the other hand, the addition of a brilliant four-foot
reed to the eight-foot provides a wide distribution of strong partials
which lend both intensity and cohesion to the ensemble.

To demonstrate the contribution of the upper ranks of pipes to the
fundamental, Aristide Cavaillé-Coll, the great French organ builder of
the nineteenth century, constructed an instrument which he called an
Enregistreur Harmonique (harmonic recorder). Its operation is thus described by Widor: "This *Enregistreur* of thirty-two pipes can sound,
successively or simultaneously, the first thirty-two partials of low A of
an eight-foot rank. . . . If, beginning at the top, you gradually set in
vibration all the pipes of the instrument, this synthetic A will increase
proportionately until it becomes thirty-two times as strong as the tone
given by the lowest pipe itself.[5] If you sound all thirty-two pipes at
once, you hear a single fundamental tone of unparalleled vitality and
perfect intonation."[6]

This demonstration differs from the experiment of Koenig, described in
the last chapter,[7] in the following important respects: (1) The upper
pitches are produced by organ pipes with complex tones, so that many
resultant partials are added. (2) The tones produced by the pipes are
positive and continuous, so that a definite resultant is heard as soon as
two pipes are sounding. (3) The upper tones are louder in proportion to
the fundamental than in the case of the tuning forks.

The facts which we have been discussing are of the utmost value to
the organist. They enable him to give vitality to his ensemble, and to
avoid the indefiniteness and fatiguing heaviness which result from too
much fundamental. This does not mean that such prominence should be
given to the upper pitches that the fundamental is lost and the tone

---

[5] This is not intended to be mathematically exact.

[6] From Widor, *Technique de l'orchestre moderne*, published by Henry Lemoine et Cie.,
Paris; by kind permission of the publishers. Bibl. 159, pp. 176-7.

[7] See p. 73.

becomes thin and screechy.[8] Reformers are inclined to exaggerate, and some organists, revolting against the dull and feeble registration which prevailed in this country during the first part of this century, have cultivated an abnormal taste for high pitches. Such organists need particularly to be warned against using an excessive proportion of high ranks above the middle of the keyboard, where less compensation is needed and stridency can easily result. Particular stress should be laid on the importance of four-foot and other intermediate pitches, which are essential to cohesion.

In general, then, the upper ranks are indispensable in the composition of an effective ensemble, but for normal purposes they should be heard as tone quality, and not as added pitches.

Sixteen-foot Manual Stops

If the ensemble is to be so designed as to give a single pitch impression to which all ranks contribute, what is the function of the sixteen-foot stops? They lie outside the tonal structure; only their even partials belong to the eight-foot series. They obtrude their own fundamental tone, which tends to usurp the place of the normal fundamental, bringing some of the ensemble under its own domination. The tone ceases to give a single pitch impression, it loses homogeneity, and the audible lower pitch introduces all the defects which are inherent in low frequencies.

Under most conditions the inclusion of sixteen-foot manual stops is a blemish. They provide richness at the expense of clarity, and are justified only when and to the extent that that is desirable. For that purpose the quality of the sixteen-foot tone should have a wide distribution of upper partials and a relatively weak fundamental. Then the partials will mingle with those of the eight-foot fundamental, enriching the texture. The added sixteen-foot pitch, if sufficiently soft, will not be separately heard in chords of three or more tones.

Unfortunately, considerations of economy and space have led to the customary selection of a gedeckt or bourdon as the first, and often the only soft sixteen-foot stop. Lacking the even partials, it has nothing in common with the rest of the ensemble, and the acoustical deficiencies of its pitch tend further to keep it separate. Although its tone is vague, it possesses considerable volume, making the texture thick, rather than rich, and producing a heavy effect. Sometimes, in their large specifications, builders have gone to the opposite extreme, including a thin

[8]One of the designers of the Chapel organ at Harvard University, Edward B. Gammons, commented: "While a true baroque organ may be built today, you need have no fear that its tone need be harsh, irregular, or unpleasant." Bibl. 82, pp. 123-4.

sixteen-foot string on one or more manuals. This avoids the heaviness of the gedeckt, but its incisive quality is obtrusive. Such a stop can be absorbed only by an ensemble which is extremely complex.[9]

The stops which can best serve at sixteen-foot pitch in a cohesive ensemble are a Dulciana, a Gemshorn, a Quintaten, a broad Salicional, a Geigen, and a light reed. In full combinations the sixteen-foot pitch can be effectively represented by a bright Trumpet or a small diapason, if the texture of the music permits.

Synthetic Tone Quality

We have been discussing the relation of various pitches and pitch-proportions to the composition of a unified ensemble, centering in the fundamental. Within the limits imposed by that conception we can devise an almost inexhaustible variety of combinations, capable of meeting the normal interpretative requirements of organ music. If, as you sit at the console of a large organ, you test one stop after another, you will find as many different qualities as there are ranks of pipes, ranging from the almost pure tone of the flute to the highly complex tone of the Viole d'Orchestre and the exotic timbre of the English Horn. Yet each pipe (with the exception of the Quintadena) gives the clear impression of its fundamental. In the synthetic production of tone qualities a vastly wider range is possible without losing the central pitch impression. This is a normal condition of legitimate interpretation.

On the other hand, composers sometimes indicate registration which causes separate pitches to be heard, or which weakens the domination of the fundamental. Furthermore, the interpreter may occasionally feel justified in employing varying degrees of pitch separation and even quasi-transposition. These possibilities will be discussed in later pages.

In concluding this discussion of stop combinations let us, by way of example, apply the principles evolved to the composition of a rich, solid, refined ensemble:

Richness is imparted by a wide spread of many pitches, so spaced and balanced that they form a fine tonal mesh, no single element of which is conspicuous. Ranks of many fundamental pitches, including mutations, will be used which, by their evenly graded proportion, will contribute to the fundamental impression. We will select qualities with an extensive but nicely tapered series of partials, avoiding on the one hand stops with a large proportion of fundamental, and on the other those with an excessive or erratic development of upper partials.

For solidity the tone must be both instantaneous and definite. This necessitates an ample proportion of high pitches, lying near the region

[9] See p. 76.

of greatest aural sensitivity. At the same time the overlapping partials must be so proportioned that the effect is one of concentration rather than diffusion. Stops must be chosen which give a clean attack; strings will be avoided, and reeds will probably be included — their number and strength depending on the desired loudness of the total ensemble.

Refinement is produced by the avoidance of qualities which are not perfectly absorbed, and by the omission of small stops which make no perceptible contribution to the tone. Such stops add warmth at the expense of clarity.

In concrete terms, the qualities of richness, solidity, and refinement can best be combined by the use of diapason ranks of many different pitches. Single pitches will not be duplicated any more than is necessary to effect a perfect balance. The addition of bright eight- and four-foot reeds will increase the loudness and solidity. The addition of more eight- and four-foot diapason tone will impair the refinement and richness more than it will increase the loudness. More high pitches will add clarity and loudness rather than solidity, and will likewise reduce the refinement and richness. The use of a light sixteen-foot diapason or a bright sixteen-foot reed will add richness at the expense of refinement and (except in the upper range) of solidity.

Relation between Blend and Texture

While it is usually desirable that the elements of a tonal ensemble be blended so as to give a single impression, it is obvious that the elements of a harmonic or polyphonic ensemble — that is, the voices or parts — must be more or less separately audible, according to the character of the music. In general, the optimum degree of blend among the parts will depend on the texture, varying in inverse proportion to the independent significance of the different pitches.

In polyphonic music the interest centers in the movement of the individual voices. In order that the listener may hear each melody clearly they must be separately audible. There must be a lack of blend among them.

In harmonic music the interest in individual voices is largely subservient to the total impression. Here the voices should merge into a unified ensemble.

It is obvious that a solo voice must be distinctly audible. Whatever the texture of the accompaniment, the principal melody must remain separate.

But no music is polyphonic to the exclusion of any consideration of ensemble; nor is harmonic music ever completely devoid of the element of voice leading. Moreover it seldom happens that the accompaniment to a solo is absolutely complete in itself. Both melodic and harmonic elements are always present, but in widely varying proportions. These conditions determine the degree of cohesion which the registration should provide. The realization of the right degree of cohesion involves the application of the fact that tones of different pitches blend in approximate proportion to the number and diffusion of their component pitch elements. This holds not only for the natural partials of the individual pipes, but for the artificial reinforcement of these partials by high pitched stops.

Since music which is essentially harmonic calls for a high degree of cohesion, it should be played with a wide distribution of pitches, none of which are given prominence. There should be enough fundamental to control the pitch impression and make the music intelligible, without calling too much attention to the individual voices. The combination may include strings which are not too extreme, provided those of eight-foot pitch are balanced by similar four-foot stops. If the dynamic level warrants the inclusion of reeds they should be bright, and should stress the four-foot, rather than the eight-foot pitch. Light or bright sixteen-foot stops may be included if the range permits. Flutes, round diapasons, and smooth reeds should be avoided.

If there is enough interest in the voice leading to affect the registration, there should be more emphasis on individual pitches. A slight reinforcement of the fundamental will assist the separate audibility of all parts, although the upper voice is always in a favorable position. Emphasis on the upper octave pitches (four- and two-foot) tends to bring out the upper voice. The high tones belonging to the lower voices are more or less covered by the upper voices, but an added octave to the top voice has an extreme position, and stands clear of the rest of the ensemble. Conversely, the addition of a distinctly audible sixteen-foot tone tends to emphasize the lower voice.

Balance of Harmonic and Polyphonic Interest

The more melodic interest the music provides, the more clearly audible should be the individual voices, and therefore the more the registration should emphasize one pitch, usually the fundamental, either by increasing the proportion of eight-foot tone, or by adjusting the balance, or both. Music in which the proportion of harmonic and polyphonic interest is approximately equal calls for a delicate adjustment of the factors of cohesion and separate audibility. The spread of the component pitches will be limited, or compensation in the lower ranks will be provided — but too much fundamental will defeat the purpose, since it will reduce the absolute audibility of the tones and cover the detail with volume and thick texture. Strings should be avoided, since they tend to fuse all pitch elements. Reeds also should be sparingly used. Bright reeds at eight- and four-foot pitch, which blend with the ensemble, induce blend also among the voices, reducing their independent clarity; heavy reeds do not blend with the ensemble, and they thicken the texture; all reeds, because of their aggressive tone, tend to impair the smoothness of the melodic line.

The music of Bach is, of course, the supreme example of the even balance of polyphonic and harmonic elements. It was not only the product of his time, but it was perfectly adapted to his instruments. It is from a desire to duplicate his effects that organs have recently been built to Baroque specifications. We must not assume, however, that the realization of that ideal is assured by the inclusion of many high ranks. Upper pitches which are too prominent confuse the polyphony.[10] The ideal is not audible high pitches but synthetic fundamental. Such an ensemble provides singleness of intonation and blending of parts, both of which are necessary for a perfect interpretation of the eighteenth century harmonic polyphony.[11]

The practical means of attaining this ideal may be summarized thus: (1) the avoidance of extreme qualities; (2) the avoidance of sixteen-foot and of *prominent* two-foot pitches; (3) the inclusion of an ample range and rich mixture of upper work, so balanced as to reinforce the fundamental impression. The foundation of such an ensemble may be the eight- and four-foot diapasons, other elements being added as needed for power, color, cohesion, *et cetera.*

This discussion has assumed a homogeneous ensemble, played from one keyboard, so that no voice would be singled out from the others. By this method it is not possible to show the crossing of parts, which occasionally occurs in polyphonic music. Such overlapping may, when feasible, be made audible by playing on separate manuals, using combinations which differ slightly in their make-up, but are sufficiently similar to preserve the consistency of the ensemble. The practicability of this procedure is limited by the resources of the instrument and the technical problems involved.

[10]The author had a startling demonstration of this fact while testing a fine new instrument which contained a wealth of upper work. Coming to the thrilling six-four chord in Bach's 'Fantasia in G minor' (measure 36), the left hand figure proved to be practically inaudible. The proportion and range of the upper pitches were such that the greater part of the tones sounded by the left hand were lost in the chord above.

[11]Thus Sumner, describing Schnitger's bright-toned principal chorus of moderate power, with a quiet eight-foot rank, characterized it as "contrapuntal tone par excellence." Bibl. 128, p. 88.

Polyphonic Texture

Music in which polyphonic interest predominates calls for a maximum of separate audibility. For this the individual clarity afforded by giving prominence to the fundamental is not sufficient; it requires the more effective nonblending element of contrast in timbre. Such contrast necessitates the use of separate keyboards; hence three is the practical limit to the number of voices, and the trio is the characteristic example of such music.

Such compositions are usually light. Melodic interest is dependent on either movement or emotional expressiveness, both of which imply an elasticity which is inconsistent with weight or force. Moreover, the conditions which produce effective power impair the separate audibility which such music needs. A continuous forte is agreeable only when it is produced by a combination of stops of various pitches, and such combinations, having much in common, tend to blend with one another.

The most perfect separation is effected by the use of single stops of contrasting timbre. The stops should have enough fundamental to give a clear pitch impression in the range employed.[12] Reeds are usually better than strings; flutes are effective in a high range. A combination of eight- and four-foot flutes is more fluent than an eight-foot flute alone, and it can be used in a lower range. It emphasizes two distinct pitches and remains separate from a characteristic unison quality. It is important to use only one flute at each pitch; duplication sounds heavy and tends to produce interference, impairing the purity of the tone. Diapasons are sometimes usable, but they are less characteristic, and more inclined to merge with the other parts. Small complex combinations are satisfactory, particularly for fluent melodies, provided there is enough fundamental, or balanced mutation, to preserve the pitch impression — and that may sometimes be transposed. In fact, any single stop may be shaded or colored by the addition of other elements which are sufficiently absorbed to avoid confusion. A delightful effect, particularly suited to gracefully ornamented soprano melodies, is produced by combining one or two delicate mutations with one or two soft flutes. If the unison is omitted the pitch is less definite, but the motion is clear.

Trios which demand a considerable degree of vitality in the tone necessitate a compromise. Loud single stops are intolerable for any length of time. Complex combinations, which dynamic intensity requires, partake of the ensemble nature, and cannot be perfectly isolated. Some individuality can be given to the parts by differentiation in the composition of the ensembles. For example, a combination using mainly octave

---

[12]See pp. 69-70.

pitches (perhaps only a Diapason 8' and an Octave) may be used against one which is rich in mutations. Again, a diapason ensemble may be used against a flute ensemble, with mutations. For a louder effect it may be necessary to include reeds in one combination and mixture work in the other. The louder the combinations, the less satisfactory the effect will be; so it is wise to keep trios as light as the musical demands permit.

Having found suitable contrasting qualities for the different voices, we have to assign them to the different parts. Assuming that the musical material is similar, the deciding factor will be the range. The lower the pitch, the more upper partials will be needed for clear audibility; the higher the pitch, the more satisfactory are simple tones. Moreover, as-suming equal audibility, contrasting tones remain more separate if the simple tone is above the complex tone. Both of these considerations favor assigning the tone which contains more upper work (strings, reeds, mutations, etc.) to the lower voice, and the one which has a larger pro-portion of fundamental (flutes, fewer high ranks, etc.) to the upper voice. To compensate for any disregard of this principle it is necessary to in-crease the loudness of the lower part, or to find a more distinctive, per-haps exotic, quality. If the disparity in pitch range is small, however, a slight adjustment of the swell pedals may make the combinations inter-changeable. Indeed, such an interchange for repetitions, or at suitable division points, is often an effective means of variety.

These observations apply to the two manual parts of a trio; the pedal part usually serves as a bass for the other two, differing from them in material as well as in function. For this reason its quality should be less distinctive. It can well hold a middle ground between the other two, having enough richness to give pitch definition, but lacking the as-sertiveness which would divert the attention of the listener from the upper melodies. In the comparatively rare cases where the three voices are all similar, the middle voice may be distinguished by a more exotic quality (perhaps a Clarinet, or an English Horn), while the lower voice is rich in partials in more normal proportion. If the two upper parts are fairly close together in range, the middle part may have fewer partials than the other two, thus providing contrast between adjacent voices.

Solo and Accompaniment

The registration of a solo and accompaniment also calls for separate audibility. The principles governing the registration of trios will apply here, modified by the following considerations: (1) The solo must be not only separate, but prominent; it must command the primary attention of the listener. (2) The registration of the accompaniment will be determined by its own material and texture, and its relation to the solo.

It is not sufficient that the solo be louder than its accompaniment. To render it sufficiently prominent by dynamic contrast alone would fatigue the listener, would limit the expressive dynamic range of the solo voice, and might necessitate too great subordination of the accompaniment. In order that the solo may easily maintain the dominant role which belongs to it, all of the following conditions must be met: (1) It must be given a quality which will not blend with accompaniment, so that it will inevitably be isolated from the ensemble. (2) It must be more clearly audible than the accompaniment, so that the listener will not have to choose which part will receive his special attention. (3) Its fundamental pitch must be unequivocal, so that the contour of the melody will be clearly drawn.

The first condition is met by the application of the principles discussed under polyphony, which need not be repeated here.

The second condition requires that the solo contain enough high frequencies (in the region of greater aural sensitivity) of sufficient intensity to make it stand out from the accompaniment. In the lower and middle range stops must be chosen which are rich in upper partials, or higher ranks must be added. Flutes are effective in the upper part of the keyboard, provided the accompaniment is soft and contrasted. A flute may be used against a wide spread of strings, even though their partials extend into a more favorable range, because of the extreme lack of blend — the single pitch of the flute stands out from the mass of diffused pitches.

The desirability of making the solo more easily audible than the accompaniment does not imply that the accompaniment should be faint. The balance will depend on the nature of the accompaniment and its relation to the whole. If it is only a background it must be heard as such, completely subordinate to the solo; if it has organic interest, its features must be heard in proportion to their significance.

The third condition, like the first, calls for concentration of the pitch impression. This is best provided by a single characteristic stop, modified at most by one or two well absorbed additions. Mutations may be included if their color is wanted. It will be remembered that tones of different pitches are most clearly audible in a single voice, so special care is needed in planning a solo combination to avoid the inclusion of audible pitches, other than the fundamental, unless a quasi-transposition of the melody is desired. Competing pitches disperse the solo voice, making it less distinct, increasing its tendency to blend with the accompaniment, and impairing the integrity of the melodic impression. In general, then, upper pitches added to a solo stop should be very delicate, and a sixteen-foot tone will be avoided altogether, except as suggested in the following paragraph.

It is perfectly legitimate to have a melody intentionally duplicated at the octave. In that case each of the melody tones should meet the conditions imposed above on a single solo voice. In this connection it should be noted that the addition of a second solo voice, whether duplicating the principal melody or adding another, affects the dynamic balance between the solo and the accompaniment. When contrasting qualities are used, the ear hears not a balance of voices, but a balance of qualities.

Thus, in the 'Adagio' of Mendelssohn's *Second Sonata*, the entrance of a new melody in measure 32 necessitates the partial closing of the swell which controls the solo voice, in order that the accompaniment may not be overbalanced. The swell will open again in the following measure, when the lower melody drops into the accompaniment. [13]

Our insistence on keeping the solo separate from the accompaniment has presupposed that each was complete in itself—the solo as a melody and the accompaniment as an ensemble. Such absolute independence rarely exists. Excepting plainsong and some folk tunes, there are few melodies which do not imply some kind of harmonic or polyphonic support; and it is rare that accompaniments are entirely satisfying without the melodies with which they are associated. The independence of solo and accompaniment is relative, varying from a maximum degree to a condition of almost complete interdependence, where the solo is an essential part of the ensemble.

As in the case of polyphony, the registration must be adjusted to this variable degree of independence, effecting a blend between the solo and accompaniment in proportion to the contribution which each makes to the other. When each is almost complete in itself, the maximum lack of blend will be sought. Adjustment for intermediate conditions will follow the principles already outlined. The registration for solos which are an essential part of the ensemble calls for a different procedure:

The typical example of this sort of solo treatment is the bringing out of a theme in a polyphonic ensemble, as in the development of a fugue. This is not a solo against an accompaniment, but a part of the ensemble which is more important than the other voices. The theme should not be isolated, but thrown into relief, preserving the integrity of the general ensemble. To this end the voice which carries the theme should include

---

[13] The introduction of a new color for the entrance of the upper voice is not to be recommended. It is the upper voice that continues. If it remains in the new color, the rest of the movement is inconsistent with what has preceded; if it is transferred back to the first quality, there is an unfortunate break in the continuity of the melody.

the same or a similar ensemble — usually done by coupling the combination on which the other parts are played to the manual which plays the theme. This manual will add an imperfectly blending element, but not a contrasting quality. This addition should emphasize the unison pitch, specifically or synthetically. Unless it is in the upper voice, the tone will need to be intensified by the inclusion of well-absorbed upper pitches.

Use of the Voix Céleste

Before concluding this study of the relation of blend to texture, something should be added concerning the use of the Voix Céleste, whose out-of-tune characteristic, inimical to blend, makes it useful, within limits, for purposes of isolation. A melody played on a string céleste retains its individuality against almost any properly balanced combination with a meager string content. Moreover the string céleste is more versatile in range than any other labial stop. The large proportion of upper partials gives it a quality which penetrates the ensemble even in the lower part of the keyboard. Its weak fundamental prevents heaviness, while the discrepancy in tuning widens the pitch impression and compensates for the thinness which is characteristic of single strings. This compensation is effective even in the upper range, although the higher tones have less pitch discrepancy and are more readily assimilated by ensemble, so they necessitate greater contrast in the accompanying combination. The fundamental impression of the céleste is also favored by the fact that the beats of the upper partials are so rapid (twice, three times, etc., the frequency of the fundamental beats) that they are not recognized, and the ear relates the whole effect to the fundamental pitch.

When used in more than one voice the ambiguous pitch of the céleste enhances the tendency, inherent in string tones, to amalgamate. The use of a céleste, therefore, greatly obscures the voice leading, and should always be avoided in polyphony. In a purely harmonic texture, where the interest centers in chord color, the use of a céleste is most suitable. Extended over a wide pitch range, perhaps by means of octave couplers, a string céleste provides a maximum interfusion of partials in one vast, finely-woven fabric of sound. A similar, but more ethereal effect is produced by such quiet célestes as the Unda Maris. A flute céleste gives the sobbing of two irreconcilable fundamentals. Its tone is too vague and out of tune to be used for single voices, and it lacks the upper partials necessary for cohesion. Its usefulness is confined to music of an extreme romantic character. Like the Vox Humana, its effectiveness on occasion must be admitted, but is in proportion to the infrequency of its use.

The adaptability of the Voix Céleste to various situations, as well as its romantic appeal, has led to its abuse by many organists. Others, on the other hand, have reacted so strongly that they oppose its use altogether. The author recommends a middle ground, using it when no other solution seems equally effective, but making such uses comparatively rare. It is like a confection which may be delicious in moderation, but is unwholesome and unpalatable as a chief source of nourishment.

Functions of the Pedals

In this study of the relation of blend to texture no mention has been made of the pedals, except as representing the lowest voice of a polyphonic ensemble. The pedal section is usually thought of as providing the bass, and it is assumed that, like the contrabass of the orchestra, it will sound an octave below the notated pitch. For that purpose the tonal ensemble of the pedal department is built on a sixteen-foot fundamental, all the ranks bearing the same relation to that pitch that those of the manual ensemble bear to the eight-foot pitch. The use of the pedal keyboard, however, is not so limited. It serves three distinct functions: (1) to extend the range of the manuals; (2) to supplement the reach of the hands; and (3) to provide a separate, independent voice.

The first function is related to the second. Since the organ fortunately lacks anything analogous to the damper pedal of the piano, the number and range of independent tones which can be sounded at one time is restricted. Moreover, for reasons which we have seen, the spacing of the voices is wider, and passage work is less effective, at the lower pitches. So the limit of practicability for the manual keyboards is five octaves, and to extend this range a separate keyboard is provided, played with the feet.

In this function the pedals are a part of the ensemble, and the registration should be determined by the same principles which control the manual combinations. It should provide a quality similar to that of the manuals, but based on a sixteen-foot fundamental and adapted to the lower pitch. The nature of this adaptation depends on the texture of the music. If the pedals are playing the lowest voice of a polyphonic ensemble, a considerable proportion of the fundamental tone should be synthetic, in order to avoid heaviness and vagueness which would impair the clarity of the melodic movement. If the pedal part is the foundation of a harmonic superstructure, a greater proportion of fundamental is effective — but there must be enough upper work to join it to the manual ensemble. As these textural elements are combined in different proportions, the registration should, of course, be correspondingly adjusted. [14]

It is rare that the pedals serve this first function exclusively; such instances as exist are more likely to be found in the works of composers who are not organists. Polyphony is not effective below the manual range, and when the texture is harmonic the use of the manual to pedal coupler is usually assumed.

In the second function the pedals are again a part of the ensemble, and their registration is governed by the same principles. Here, however, the fundamental is normally at eight-foot pitch. There is no reason to differentiate the pedal combination from that of the manuals beyond compensating for the lower pitch. The use of manual to pedal couplers is normal and usually necessary on American organs. Pedal stops belonging to the eight-foot series of partials may be added, care being taken to avoid unduly enlarging the fundamental or overbalancing the upper voices.

Should sixteen-foot stops be included? This is equivalent to adding the contrabasses to the 'cellos of the orchestra, or to playing the bass in octaves on the piano. It combines the first and second functions of the pedals, extending both the range of the keyboard and the grasp of the hands. As a general rule, if the pedal part is simply the lowest voice of a polyphonic ensemble, on a par with the other voices, the sixteen-foot tone should be omitted. [15] On the other hand, if the pedal part serves also as a bass to support the ensemble, it may need the added stability which the sixteen-foot affords. Since absolute polyphony (a combination of melodies with no regard for the effect of the ensemble as a whole) is rare, the bass usually has this added function which favors the use of the sixteen-foot pitch. If the composer has indicated a separate pedal part it may be assumed, in the absence of contrary evidence, that a sixteen-foot pedal is intended. The amount of sixteen-foot tone to be used depends on the balance between the melodic and foundation functions served by the pedal part.

In its third function — to provide a separate, independent voice — the pedals are treated exactly like the manuals; the only difference is that the pedals usually play the lowest voice. The influence of this fact on the choice of stops has already been fully discussed.

On the other hand, the pedals do not always play the lowest part. We shall see in Chapters X and XI that the organs of the Renaissance and

[14] Always in discussing the procedures adapted to extreme conditions it is assumed that the coexistence of diverse elements in the music calls for a combination in similar proportions of the tonal characteristics suited to each.

[15] This situation frequently occurs when the organist chooses to play on the pedal keyboard a melody which the composer has included in the manual part.

Baroque periods (except in Italy and England) usually had pedal stops specifically intended for the cantus firmus – even in the soprano. The idea that the pedal is a bass keyboard belongs to the era of harmonic music. Fortunately it is now becoming more versatile again. For example, it is quite usual to play Brahms's setting of 'Schmücke dich, o liebe Seele' as a trio, assigning the melody to the feet with a four-foot solo stop, while the accompanying counterpoints are played on suitably differentiated manual combinations. In this type of treatment the left hand plays the lowest voice, and its combination is influenced by the relative importance of the bass function, as suggested above for the pedal part. For example, in Bach's transcription from his Cantata 93, 'Wer nur den lieben Gott lässt walten' (Sechs Choräle, No. 3), the left hand part is the original basso continuo, and its combination may suitably include a sixteen-foot stop. Few modern organs contain the pedal stops needed for the upper voices, so the organist is obliged to use the resources of the manual divisions, coupled to the pedals.

Unfortunately the appointments of the pedal sections of many American organs are dictated by considerations of economy and routine, rather than of artistic effect. Wood pipes prevail, giving an almost pure tone which will not merge in the ensemble.[16] The individual ranks lack pitch definition and incline to be boomy. If several stops are combined, the energy is increased without an effective increase in loudness. It is impossible to build up a complex tonal ensemble; the lower ranks are lost in vague volume, while the higher ones are heard as separate pitches. Many organs include rather strong sixteen- and eight-foot strings which afford some compensation by adding pitch definition, but do not unite with the tone of the wood pipes to build an ensemble. If the strings are substituted for the heavier stops, they may fail to provide enough fundamental to support the superstructure, or they may be too assertive. Some organs have metal pipes at only eight-foot and perhaps four-foot pitch. Such stops help to clarify the pedal tone, but they do not define the sixteen-foot pitch.

The only satisfactory ensemble for the pedals, as for the manuals, is produced by combining many pitches, and avoiding extreme qualities. This is not possible unless the builder provides modestly scaled *metal* diapasons for all the principal pitches of the sixteen-foot harmonic series. If such ranks are properly balanced, they will give a solid sixteen-foot foundation which will blend with the ensemble, and will not weary the ear. Lacking these resources, the organist must effect a compromise, the nature of which will depend on the character of the music.

[16]There are exceptions to this characterization of the tone of wood pipes. Some builders have made beautiful sixteen-foot strings of wood.

If he is obliged to use a sixteen-foot tone which gives too much fundamental, it should usually be on the soft side. Unless it is supporting a
massive ensemble, it is better that the foundation be inadequate, rather
than oppressive. An excessive proportion of string tone (if available)
may be the lesser evil. In that case the upper ensemble should be as
rich in partials as the character of the music will permit. If the pedal
reeds are good — not too loud, and neither raucous nor round — they will
often provide the best substitute for the ideal diapason ensemble. Normally the big wood diapason and its eight- and four-foot counterparts, if
used at all, will be the last pedal stops to add.

Summary

The study of the optimum degree of blend has led us along devious
paths and has involved the exploration of many byways. A complete
résumé of these wanderings would be neither practicable nor profitable.
They all proceed from the fundamental assumption that pitch elements,
whether ingredients of a single tone or voices in a polyphonic or harmonic
ensemble, should be separately heard in proportion to their individual
significance. We observed that each tone should normally give a single
impression, the components of its timbre being fused into one sound. The
degree of blend desired in combinations of different tones, however, depends on the texture. Melodies should be sufficiently isolated to be
heard as melodies; chords should be so integrated as to be heard as
units; solos should be separated from their accompaniments and brought
into prominence.

The realization of these conditions is the result of a complex application of all the facts concerning blend which were presented in the last
chapter. The coexistence of the different elements of texture in various
proportions requires complete flexibility of treatment, with due regard to
the relative importance of each element. The ramifications of the problem
are bewildering to the organist who does not have a complete understanding of each factor and its relation to the whole.

Obviously the solutions cannot be determined purely on the basis of
theory. Our study of acoustical principles will serve to direct the attention of the listener to effects which might otherwise be unnoticed or
imperfectly appreciated, but experiment must be guided by the imagination, and the judgment of the trained, sensitive ear is final.

CHAPTER FIVE

PRODUCTION, PERCEPTION, PERPETUATION, AND PROPAGATION

Attack and Release

The effective beginning of a tone is the perception of its complete and characteristic vibration. After the attack of the key the air is admitted to the pipe, a standing wave is set up in the pipe, and a traveling wave carries its impulses to the membrane of the ear, the response of which is interpreted by the brain. This sequence of events causes a slight delay between the initial attack and the aural perception, the amount of which varies with conditions.

The time required for the air to be admitted to the pipe depends on the mechanical efficiency of the organ. The delay is usually greater for the larger pipes, because of the larger valves controlling a greater volume of air.

The delay in setting up vibrations within the pipes depends on their size and construction.[1] Variations in speech can be minimized but not elininated by skillful voicing.

The time required for the traveling wave to reach the ear is practically the same for all tones, and can, therefore, be ignored except as it is affected by the acoustical pattern of the auditorium.

The time required for the aural perception of tones varies with the pitch and the intensity.[2] It is less for high frequencies than for low, and less for loud than for soft tones.

There is also a delay between the release of the key and the perception of the cessation of the tone. The amount of delay depends on some of the same conditions which affect the attack, and is approximately equal to the initial delay. On some organs the valves may close more promptly than they open, and in most pipes (particularly large ones) the vibrations cease more promptly than they start.

The greater delay in the sounding of low tones is not peculiar to the organ. The proverb, "Large bodies move slowly," states a general physical tendency which can be overcome only by increased energy. The relative slowness of lower tones (produced by the vibration of greater masses) is universal. A coloratura singer is a soprano. Compare the agility of the trumpet and the tuba, of the violin and the double bass, or even the highest and lowest strings of a violin or a 'cello. The bassoon,

[1]See pp. 41-3.
[2]See pp. 18, 42.

although slower than the oboe, is abnormally agile for its pitch, and from this fact it derives its value in suggesting humor. Such agility is not associated with low pitches, and when it is heard it seems incongruous. The effect is enhanced by the characteristic reed attack which is possessed by all orchestral reed and brass instruments. [3]

The discrepancies in the promptness of speech of pipes of different sizes and design, and in the response of the ear to different frequencies, must be taken into account in planning the registration. It is obvious that if prompt and slow pipes, and high and low frequencies, are included in the same combination, the more delayed responses will cause tardy additions to the tone, and so impair the precision of attack. In the lower part of the keyboard it is impossible to avoid this altogether, but it can be reduced to a minimum by choosing for the low tones pipes with relatively prompt speech and not too much fundamental. Broad strings are preferable to heavy diapasons, since the delayed fundamental is not so large. The nearest approach to a perfect synchronization of all elements results from a balanced ensemble of many ranks of diapason pipes, with the avoidance of both heaviness and excessive slowness in the unison rank. Flutes may be included for the higher pitches if they are not too prominent.

Although it is always desirable that the perception of simultaneous movements exactly coincide, this synchronization is most important when the temporal relation of the parts is essential. Obviously the different ranks which compose the ensemble should be heard together, and all vertical textural relations (chords and simultaneously moving melodies) demand perfect coincidence. This can only be achieved by promptness in the sounding and hearing of the tones. [4]

Such promptness is of the utmost importance in rapid or detached playing. Short tones should be heard as nearly instantaneously as possible. They should be produced by pipes whose speech is prompt and definite, and should include a good proportion of pitches in the range of quick hearing. Fortunately composers are conscious of the slow production and perception of low tones and avoid rapid passages and short staccato in that range. [5] When they do occur it is necessary to make compensation

---

[3] This attack is characteristic of beating reeds. The vibration of a free reed, which oscillates freely in a frame, begins more gradually than that of a flue pipe. Such reeds are used in the harmonium and in the American cabinet organ.

[4] To test the promptness of any stop or combination, play a single note or chord with the shortest possible staccato and compare the effect with the same note or chord prolonged. By increasing the length of the staccato sound until the effect is identical with the prolonged tone, the time required for full speech can be determined.

[5] The many exceptions in the works of Bach indicate (1) that the ensemble of his instruments was so balanced that an effective composite tone could be produced by the use

in the registration, even at the expense of fidelity to the notated pitch. Often such quasi-transposition is consistent with the mood of such compositions.[6]

Particularly inept, in registration for short notes, is the use of effects which require time for their apprehension. For example, a céleste or a tremolo should never be used for tones which do not allow time to hear the beats on which their distinctive impression depends. Moreover, the false and indefinite intonation of the one, and the unstable wind pressure of the other, destroy the clarity which is essential to the easy perception of quick sounds.

Detached playing calls for clarity of release as well as of attack; but this does not offer an added problem, for the conditions which produce a prompt attack will also provide a quick release. On the other hand, the discrepancy between the promptness of the attack and the release in large pipes presents a difficulty in legato playing. A perfect legato involves the exact coincidence of the cessation of one tone and the beginning of the next. This can be effected by the synchronization of the release of one key and the attack of the next only if the pipes respond with equal promptness to the attack and the release of the key. The greater delay in the attack, which is noticeable in large pipes, necessitates actual overlapping in the touch in order to secure a legato effect. Complete compensation by building up an ensemble of smaller pipes is not always desirable from the standpoint of interpretation. The meticulous organist, therefore, adjusts the timing of his touch to produce the desired effect.[7]

Duration

Within limits, the prolongation of any sound tends to intensify its effect. In nonabsorbent rooms an increase in power is produced by

---

of high ranks, and (2) that he did not play his music so fast as many modern performers imagine. The latter conclusion is supported by the fact that the heavy action of the old organs made rapid playing in the lower part of the keyboard practically impossible. This statement has been disputed on the assumption that Bach's manuals were used uncoupled. Certainly the use of couplers was much less common than now, but we shall see in Chapter XI that in the late Baroque organ, subsidiary manuals were designed to supplement the ensemble of the principal manual. Cf. the quotation from Schweitzer on p. 267, fn. 36; also Sumner's statement concerning Schnitger's organs: "The depth of touch of the different manuals varied between 3/4 in. and 2/3 in. and for the chief manual (Hauptwerk) was often so great as to be uncomfortable for modern methods of playing." – Bibl. 128, p. 87.

[6]See Chap. VII.

[7]The habit of doing this causes trouble when an organist first plays an electronic instrument in which the attack of even the low tones is almost perfectly instantaneous. He finds himself overlapping the tones, producing a disagreeable barking effect.

reflection.   Moreover, the listener fails to notice, in a sound of short duration, characteristics which are more and more impressed on his attention as the sound continues.

How many pupils of Widor remember him, sitting at the console of the little organ in his apartment on the rue des Saints Pères, with its large French doors opening onto the court, explaining the effect of prolonged sound somewhat as follows: "If I were to open these windows in the middle of the night and play a single, short chord on full organ, no one would notice it; but if I should sustain a chord indefinitely on the softest stop, soon all the neighbors would be putting their heads out of their windows to see what was the matter."

This fact, so picturesquely illustrated by the great maître, holds for continuous sound in general.   The effect is most felt when there is the greatest degree of continuity in all the characteristics of the sound; it is lessened by any change of pitch, loudness, texture, or timbre, and by interruptions caused by rests or detached playing.   So it is more strongly felt in long notes than in short, in slow movement than in quick, in legato than in detached playing.   Observe in Example 7, quoted from the last movement of Widor's *Seventh Symphony*, how clearly the melody, even in

Example 7. Widor: Seventh Symphony — vi. Finale [8]

*Swell, with reeds (closed)

the lower voice, is heard against the detached chords, without being brought out on another manual.   Another illustration is in the fugal section of the finale of Franck's *Grande Pièce Symphonique*, beginning at the forty-fifth measure of the movement.   Here the detached inner parts throw the soprano and bass into clear relief.

Widor applied this principle to phrasing and rhythmic interpretation. Thus he wished the 'Toccata' from his *Fifth Symphony* to be played as shown in Example 8, with agogic stress on each accent. [9]

These considerations have an important bearing on various phases of registration.   Obviously they affect the balance of the parts of the ensemble.   For example, a long pedal point becomes obtrusive if it is as loud as

[8]Permission to reprint these excerpts from Widor's Seventh and Fifth Symphonies is granted by J. Hamelle & Cie., Paris, France, copyright owners; Elkan-Vogel Co., Inc., Philadelphia, Penna., agents.

[9]In his later years Widor exaggerated the agogic principle so that rhythmic coherence was impaired. However, if not allowed to disturb the steady flow of the movement, this procedure adds greatly to the vitality and intelligibility of the piece.

Example 8. Widor: Fifth Symphony — v. Toccata[8]

the moving parts. On most organs it is necessary to omit the Great to Pedal coupler for the pedal points in such situations as occur in Bach's 'Toccata in F', 'Fantasia in G minor', and 'Prelude in A minor', adding it when the pedal has melodic significance. But the interrupted pedal point in the 'Prelude in F minor' does not need to be subdued; on the contrary, the interrupting figure must be clearly heard.

Often short, detached, or isolated notes require a more prominent registration. For example, the organist who plays the pedal part of the 'Adagio' in Bach's *Toccata, Adagio, and Fugue in C* with a *pizzicato* effect will use a heavier combination than he who plays it only slightly detached, perhaps slurring the upward skips. [10] Again, when the limitations of the instrument or mechanical difficulties prevent an ideal balance, notes may be shortened to compensate for stops which are too loud or heavy, and vice versa.

Music which involves continuity of sound, particularly if the movement is slow, requires special care in the aesthetic appraisal of the tone combination. The listener becomes conscious of everything. Qualities which can be tolerated in detached or rapid playing are found disagreeable. Loud tones with too much fundamental, as well as harsh, screechy combinations, should be avoided. The dynamic balance must be nicely adjusted, and the tonal ensemble perfectly blended. Combinations which sound out of tune, such as tempered mutations or upper pitches used with a céleste, are particularly objectionable. Special attention should be given to the sensuous appeal and the interpretative value of the tone quality.

Although in general these are requirements of all good registration, they may be relatively less important in rapid movements, and in music in which the tone and texture are not very continuous. In such cases other considerations, such as clarity, variety, interpretation, etc., may justify some modification of these demands. This applies particularly to the balance and blend of the tonal ensemble. It requires time to hear the individual ranks of a combination or to be conscious of pitches which

[10]Widor usually detached descending octaves in a low range and connected ascending octaves, in order that the length of tone might compensate for the slowness of the lower pitch.

are overemphasized, even in a single voice.[11] This fact makes it
possible, when notes are short, to secure vitality, clarity, and quick
attack, by including stops which would be unduly prominent if the tones
were prolonged.

What is true of long notes and slow movement is even more important
in continuous playing over a period of time. Especially fatiguing is the
prolonged use of voluminous or dynamically inefficient qualities. The
ineffectual bombardment of too much fundamental, particularly in the
lower half of the keyboard, causes strain which becomes increasingly
disagreeable as it persists.

Not only are defects aggravated by continuation, but effects which are
delightful for a short time eventually become fatiguing. Anything which
forces itself on the attention of the listener, or which requires his concentration, cannot be long continued without fatigue. The prolonged use
of loud or brilliant combinations, of colorful effects such as the célestes,
or of exotic qualities, wearies the listener. Also long pianissimo passages, or the continued use of a dull, uninteresting quality, makes tiring
demands on the attention of the listener. Indeed there is a limit to the
enjoyment of any effect — but the most durable combinations are those
which avoid extremes of all kinds.[12]

Three Fortissimo Movements

Before quitting the subject of duration of sound it may be profitable to
compare from this point of view the following movements, all of which
call for a loud registration, and could be effectively played without any
change of combination: Bach, 'Gravement', from the *Fantasia in G major*;
Mendelssohn, 'Allegro assai vivace', from the *Sonata in F minor*, Number
1; Widor, 'Toccata', from the *Symphony in F minor*, Number 5.

The section from the Bach Fantasia is a rare example of prolonged
uniformity of texture. The five voices continue without interruption for

---

[11]This may be demonstrated, using a mixture which contains the 12th, 15th, and 17th,
and preferably also the octave, but not a unison rank. If a scale in the lowest octave is
played very slowly, the progression is heard as a succession of chords; but if the scale is
played rapidly, the listener is no longer conscious of the upper pitches, but hears rather
the resultant fundamentals, which are not sounded by any rank.

[12]Of course the piano and the string quartet are essentially monochromatic (or at best,
oligochromatic), and they can hold the attention of an audience throughout an entire program; but they possess compensating characteristics, such as greater dynamic flexibility
and the capability of extremely rapid movement without loss of clarity. Moreover the
usable fundamental pitch range of the piano exceeds that of the organ, and the extreme
tones of the string quartet are more versatile. Still it must be admitted that the appeal of
the string quartet is largely dependent on an appreciation of the texture, content, and development of the music, and the refinement of its interpretation, while the piano affords
variety through the great flexibility of its idiom, and the enormous range of textural devices often superimposed on music of slight substance — an indictment which is equally
applicable to much organ registration.

five minutes, and the pitch range is very restricted.[13] One hears a perpetual mass of sound, unfolding the logical development of an imposing musical edifice. The effect is magnificent if the organist is judicious in his registration. The rather restrained movement of the inner voices must be as clearly audible as possible; at the same time the combination should be designed to cause the minimum of fatigue, in spite of the fact that it will approach fortissimo. Screechiness and harshness must be avoided, as well as too much fundamental. The most satisfactory combination is the rich ensemble, previously described, composed of many pitches centering in, but not dominated by the fundamental. Prominent high pitches and loud reeds should be absolutely excluded.

The Mendelssohn movement, on the other hand, affords much relief in its continual motion, wide pitch range, and textural variety. It begins with a surging wave of sound which grows from two to nine parts in the first measure, and recedes in the second. This design, with many modifications, is characteristic of the movement; but it gives way, from time to time, to such procedures as the punctuated two-part arpeggios against a steady bass progression, beginning with measure 27, and the fluent two-part movement above a pedal point, beginning in measure 96. The variety and rapid movement permit the use of an unusual number of high ranks and prominent octave pitches. The texture is predominently harmonic, and when an inner voice is important it is given ample space. The high pitches lend clarity to the melodic movement, and the rapid and wide changes of pitch prevent the fatigue which they might otherwise cause. They are needed for the low notes, and their transposing tendency is not objectionable; as the chords pile up they are lost in the ensemble (except for the top voice, which needs to be prominent), while in other passages they fill in and compensate for the thin spacing of the music. At the same time, the fundamental should not be slighted; it is needed to define the melodies. Reeds should be excluded if possible, as they would interfere with the fluency which is essential. If the organ lacks the flue stops necessary to give brilliance, a *four-foot* reed may possibly be included.

The Widor Toccata lacks the variety of texture, the wide pitch range and long sweeps which afford relief from perpetual sound in the Mendelssohn movement, but it provides interruption in the staccato of the toccata figure (which the composer did not wish to be incessant[14]) and in the detached chords, and change in the occasional pompous entrance of the pedal. All of these features call for a clear, positive attack and

[13]Bach did not do that sort of thing after he reached maturity.
[14]See p. 106 and Ex. 8.

release.   The range of the manual part is too high to allow a large proportion of high ranks, and the pedal part demands a solid pitch impression.   The use of reeds is inescapable.   The manual combination will include as much upper work as the reeds will absorb — no more — to add sprightliness to the solidity of the reeds.   The pedal theme requires a telling fundamental; its tone must be dominated by reeds.

So we find considerations of texture and duration dictating very different registration for these three pieces.   The combination chosen for the Mendelssohn and Widor movements would be fatiguing if applied to the Bach.   The spread of foundation pitches used for the Mendelssohn finale would confuse the compact polyphony of the Bach movement, and their decentralized ensemble would fail to provide the solidity which the five-part writing requires.   Again, the aggressiveness of the reeds used in the Widor Toccata would destroy the fluency of the Mendelssohn finale; and the compact ensemble assigned to the Fantasia would lack the agility and clarity which the lively excursions of the Mendelssohn music require, and which can only be provided by audible high pitches.   Finally, neither of the combinations suggested for the first two pieces would provide the vitality of tone and attack which the detached style of the Toccata demands, and their small proportion of fundamental would make them sound thin in the range which prevails in that movement.

These three works have been chosen as typical examples, illustrating the application of the principles we have been outlining.   We have not yet examined all the factors which must enter into our registration calculations; others will be brought out as we study the music itself and its setting.   Moreover there still remains one section of our technical information which has not been applied to the problem of tone combination. We have discussed this problem from the standpoint of the nature of the tones themselves and their relation to one another, and of the aural response, but practically nothing has yet been said about the influence of the acoustical environment on the registration.

Influence of Auditorium Characteristics

What the listener actually hears in an auditorium depends not only on the sound which the organist produces, but also on the form and dimensions of the room, and the absorbent qualities of its walls and other surfaces.

We know from what was said in Chapter I[15] that below c^2 the relative loudness of lower tones diminishes as the distance from the source increases; but above c^2 the distance has little effect on the balance which

[15]p. 23.

the ear hears.   This means that, disregarding external influences, the listener in the back seat would hear relatively less of the sixteen-foot pedal than one in the front seat; but they would hear practically the same quality of ensemble in the middle and upper part of the manual keyboard.

Actually such a condition could only exist out-of-doors in a large open space.   In an auditorium the lower pitches are more reinforced by reflection and less affected by obstructions.   This tends to compensate for the discrepancy in loudness which would result from distance alone.   The degree of compensation depends on the ratio of the acoustical reinforcement of the lower frequencies to the weakening due to distance — both taken in comparison with the higher pitches.   The principal factors involved are as follows:

1. The distance from the organ to the majority of the auditors.

2. The number of effective reflections received by the listener.   This depends on the size and shape of the auditorium and all its architectural details, on the location of the organ and the audience in relation to the reflecting surfaces, on the absorbent characteristics of the surfaces, and on the length of the notes.   If a sound has to travel a considerable distance before being reflected, and again between reflections, the total effect is delayed and weakened by the extra distance.   Under these conditions compensation for the distortion of balance due to distance is much greater for prolonged tones than for short ones, and further depends on

3. The absorption coefficients of the surfaces for various frequencies. The extreme complexity of these influences is indicated by the computations reported in Chapter I.[16]   It is evident from Sabine's findings that the compensating reinforcement of the sixteen-foot pedal varies with the character of the reflecting surfaces, and is relatively greatly enhanced (through the deadening of the higher pitches) by the presence of an audience.   These conditions also affect the quality of the ensemble and the cohesion of its ingredients.

4. The presence of obstacles which obstruct the paths of the direct sound wave and of its reflections.   Transept corners, pillars, arches, screens, and other architectural features, cast sound shadows which discriminate in favor of low pitches.

Experiments in the Vassar College Chapel

The significance of these considerations and the complexity of the problem are shown by a few simple experiments conducted in the Vassar College Chapel.   This is a rather spacious, absorbent auditorium in

[16]Pp. 24-5.

which the reflecting surfaces are a considerable distance apart. The nave and transepts are each 58 feet wide, and shallow in proportion. The nave is less than 40 feet long, with a gallery extending beyond; the transepts are only 16 feet deep, and the chancel (?) only 14, with an added semicircular apse about 33 feet in diameter. The peak of the (approximately) 45° ceiling is about 56 feet above the floor. Above the eight-foot oak-paneled wainscoting the walls are plastered on stone; the window surface is relatively large. The ceiling is supported by an intricate design of oak beams and arches. Its surface — which is greater than the entire area of the walls — is covered with celotex. The platform and aisles are carpeted, and the pews are cushioned.

It is obvious that these conditions provide considerable loss from distance, with little reinforcement from reflection — particularly for the high frequencies. Reflection from the floor is inhibited by the carpet and upholstering, even when the room is empty. The ceiling supports interfere with the short waves, and those which get by suffer considerable absorption by the celotex. The only efficient reflecting surfaces are the walls, which are too far apart to be very effective. Thus we would expect, as we move toward the back of the room, to notice (1) a loss in over-all loudness, (2) a loss in brilliance due to the absorption of high frequencies, and (3) a certain amount of compensating reflection of low tones.

These expectations were fulfilled in tests in which chords were played on a brilliant Swell combination with a heavy pedal, having wood diapason tone at sixteen- and eight-foot pitch. The total loudness and proportion of high partials decreased considerably as the listeners went back in the nave. The relative loudness of the pedal varied with the pitch, depending on standing wave resonance. In general it became proportionately weaker with increased distance, showing that the reflections favoring low frequencies were not sufficient to compensate for the loudness loss. At GGG the balance was about the same in the front and back of the room, but the attack of the pedal was slower in the rear, showing that the reinforcement traveled farther, or was due to resonance which required time to be set up. The latter was the more important factor. Standing just inside the transept this tone became strikingly prominent. Computation showed that the width of the transept was approximately five times the wave length of the second partial of this sixteen-foot pipe, or the fundamental of the eight-foot.

Listening from the center of the long narthex, with doors open only at the ends, the pedal was relatively louder than in the nave — illustrating the fact that the longer waves pass around obstructions with less loss than the shorter waves. Outside the building, in line with the open doors, the effect of the discriminating reflections was lost, and the upper partials made practically their full contribution to the ensemble. At the same time the pedal, lacking acoustical reinforcement, was much weaker; at a short distance from the building it became inaudible. This discrepancy was observed to be less when the tone came through a side door, which it reached by a circuitous route.

The characteristics of this rather unsatisfactory auditorium have been described at some length because we can learn much from the observation of one type of acoustical problem, and a study of the modifications which different conditions would make. If the reflecting surfaces of this room had been nearer to one another, and so related to the source that the reflections would be directed to near surfaces, the number of effective reflections would have been greater. These would have increased the relative loudness of the pedal; they would also have further reinforced the manual tone, but at the expense of the proportion of high partials. Had the reflecting surfaces been less absorbent, the loss in loudness and quality heard in the back of the room would have been less. Indeed a remarkable improvement is observed when the cushions are removed from the seats and the room is empty. In general, the greater the amount of reverberation in a room (thus the smaller the proportion of the total effect produced by the direct sound), the less discrepancy there is between near and far seats, and the more the absorbent characteristics of the reflecting surfaces determine the balance and quality which the listener hears.

Adjustment of the Registration to the Auditorium

It is evident that in most auditoriums what the audience hears differs in loudness, balance, quality, and timing, from what the player himself hears. Moreover, listeners in different parts of the room do not hear the same thing. The organist is obliged to adapt his registration to these conditions, seeking to provide the best possible effect for the majority of the listeners. He will be concerned with absolute loudness, the balance between different parts of his instrument, the balance between different pitches, and the selection and composition of tone quality. In a fairly large, absorbent room like the Vassar College Chapel, he may need to use a louder registration than his own ear would dictate; on the other hand, in a reverberant or small room he must guard against fatiguing his listeners with too much power. In the Vassar College Chapel the organist needs to bear in mind that the pedal sounds relatively weaker to his audience – although the discrepancy is slight; but in a reverberant room (unless the discrimination against high frequencies is abnormally small) he must keep his pedal on the soft side – particularly when it plays long notes. The balance between different parts of the organ depends on their location and the direction of the swell shade openings. A department which speaks more directly into the organist's ear must be made disproportionately loud, in order that the balance may be right to the audience; converse compensation must be made for any section which is more advantageously placed from the standpoint of the listener.

In adjusting the registration to the acoustical environment the adaptation of the tone quality is perhaps the most perplexing problem. The organist, being nearer to his instrument than his auditors, hears an effect which is more largely dominated by the sound coming directly from the source, while the tone which comes to the listener is modified to a greater degree by such influences as have been described in the foregoing paragraphs. The organist should be thoroughly familiar with the acoustical characteristics of his auditorium, so that he can anticipate the nature and extent of its influence on the tone, and compensate for it in his registration. An exhaustive discussion of the problem is obviously impossible, but the general tendencies of reverberant and absorbent rooms, and the effective adaptation of the registration to their characteristics, can be briefly noted.

We know that all surfaces absorb more of the high than of the low frequencies. The variation is not always consistent with the change of frequency, but these irregularities have little practical significance, except in the case of paneling,[17] and of plaster on lath, which has absorption peaks at the lower end of an eight-foot, and the upper end of a four-foot rank, and also around c^2 or c^3.[18] Solid masonry, on the other hand, has a very low absorption coefficient, which increases very gradually with higher frequencies.

A reverberant church with stone walls, therefore, reinforces all pitches with comparatively little discrimination against the high frequencies, but such discrimination increases with the prolongation of the tones until the reverberation period has elapsed.[19] This means that the organist can plan his registration approximately according to his own ear, slightly exaggerating the proportion of upper pitches. In balancing contrasting qualities, the more complex tone should be a trifle on the loud side, to compensate for the greater absorption of the upper partials which are so large a proportion of its tone. In ensemble combinations too much fundamental should be avoided: the lower pitches, being more affected by reverberation, become heavy in slow movement, and in fluent polyphony their overlapping confuses the voice leading. The presence of an

[17]See pp. 24-5.
[18]See Bibl. 18, p. 196
[19]See Table 4, p. 25.

audience greatly increases the absorption of high frequencies, but unless the people occupy a relatively large area a stone or brick interior demands little compensation for the loss of upper partials.

Such an auditorium is flattering to both the organist and his instrument. It multiplies the sound, so that the listener hears loudness without forcing; by preserving the proportion of upper partials it provides the maximum of dynamic efficiency; the reinforcement of almost the entire range of partials produces the greatest possible cohesion in the ensemble, resulting in an integrated, complex tone in which individual defects in balance are minimized. Moreover, the slight confusion due to reverberation conceals imperfections in the registration as well as in the execution. The mitigation of faults and amelioration of over-prominent partials are not merely a boon to the careless and a compensation for a poor instrument; the absorption of high pitches and their reduced proportion on long notes make it possible to enjoy the advantage of brilliant upper work without unpleasantness.

In a very large and reverberant auditorium special care must be taken to keep the fundamental of the pedal as light as possible, relying on mutations and mixtures to give the illusion of sixteen-foot tone. The time-lag for low notes (which distance would render almost inaudible, except for the reinforcement of reflections) is very disturbing. [20]

Surfaces which have a peak of absorption around c^2 or c^3 (such as plaster on lath, and possibly certain paneling) call for special care in the upper part of the treble staff. In that range mutations, or even the third partial of a Quintadena, may become disagreeably prominent.

A dead room — one which lacks reverberation — presents the most difficult problem. In it the upper partials are lost through absorption, and the lower pitches are exaggerated unless weakened by distance. The organist needs to compensate for this distortion by adding more upper work, but finds that the resulting combination lacks cohesion. The individual ranks, deprived of their natural complement of harmonics, do not fuse satisfactorily. All defects in the voicing of individual stops, in the balance of the different elements of the ensemble, and in the execution, are clearly audible. Moreover, the presence of an audience makes conditions worse. A completely satisfactory solution is often impossible. It is dependent on the perfect design and meticulous voicing of the instrument, and on the consummate taste, skill, and ingenuity of the performer.

---

[20] In a choral performance in the Cathedral of Saint John the Divine, New York, a listener seated well back in the nave actually heard the bass one beat behind the upper voices — in a slow tempo.

Appraisal of Registration

Ideally the tonal design of the organ, its location and layout, and the scaling and voicing of the pipes, should be adapted to the acoustics of the room. Actually builders, if competent, are seldom allowed the freedom to produce the best results. Indeed, it is impossible to foresee all the conditions which will be revealed after the instrument is in place, and the correction of errors is expensive and time-consuming, when not actually impossible. But, granted a satisfactory installation, the organist appraises his effects by ear, and so he must be able to allow for the differences between what he hears and what comes to the audience. It is hoped that the foregoing paragraphs may be helpful, but at best they can only be suggestive. It is impossible to know all the conditions or to compute their effects. The organist must master the acoustical problem of his auditorium by intelligent, exhaustive, attentive, and open-minded experimentation.

The methods of testing will be developed and perfected by experience. In general, one must listen from different parts of the auditorium to the actual and relative loudness of various combinations; to the balance between different divisions of the organ with a large variety of combinations; to the balance of the various pitches in the tonal ensemble, and of the different voices which make up the musical texture; to the tone quality of the individual stops and combinations in various parts of their range; to the dynamic and qualitative effect of the swell shades; to the effect of reflected sound on the perception of details; etc., etc. Every phase of the problem of performance must be studied from the standpoint of the listener.

If possible, the player should secure the assistance of another organist, so that he can listen to the effects himself and form his judgments from his own hearing. He should listen to predetermined combinations, or at least he should know what stops are included, and should know the exact adjustment of the swell pedals. Tests should be made with chords of various kinds and with passages of music in various styles. Often he will wish to try out the registration which he contemplates using for specific compositions. In appraising the results of these experiments it is necessary to make allowance for the acoustical effect of the expected audience.

It is also desirable to get the judgment of a critical listener, whose reaction may not agree with that of the performer. Moreover, an organist should always welcome intelligent and constructive comments on his public performance, reporting the actual effect under recital or service conditions. He can also profit by listening analytically to the

performances of other organists, with view to applying what he learns
to his own playing.

Of course the complexities of auditorium acoustics are not the exclusive problem of the organist. Pianists, violinists, singers, conductors —
all bring forth sounds which are subject to the same laws of propagation.
The study is more important to the organist, however, because the tones
of his instrument are capable of unlimited and invariable prolongation,
which produces the maximum accumulation of reflections, with the maximum distortion. The effect of reverberation on the tone of a piano is
merely to delay its inevitable, sudden diminuendo; even the tone of the
orchestra is limited in its continuous duration by the breath and bow of
the players, the possibilities of prolongation being less at loud levels.
Only the organist can enjoy the full benefit, and must suffer the full
penalty, of the accrual of reflected sound. Moreover, no other performer
can do so much to compensate for, or to take advantage of these effects
of environment — assuming that the organ itself provides the necessary
tonal material.

But the organist cannot completely overcome fundamental defects in
the installation. Architects, unfortunately, are prone to consider the
organ incidental to their preconceived design, and to minimize the importance of the protestations of organists and organ builders. Tone which
must pass through a meager opening and turn at least one corner, is
killed before it can reach the listener. Sometimes it is stifled by an
absorbent screen, or even draperies! An organ should be given ample
space and stand out in the open, speaking directly into the auditorium
with no impediments to distort the tone. Assuming ecclesiastical architecture, an ideal placement is on the choir screen, as in certain English
cathedrals, or in the gallery at the rear of the nave, as in French
churches. In concert halls and churches without chancels the best
location is directly in front of the listeners, set against a hard reflecting
wall, and as much in the open as possible.

Conclusion

This completes our discussion of the theory of tone combination. We
have studied it from the standpoints of both absolute and comparative
audibility, applying the principles which we have deduced from our
knowledge of the nature and behavior of sound. We are now ready for the
final application of the theory which we have developed to the actual
interpretation of the music.

Part III

APPLICATION OF THE THEORY OF TONE COMBINATION TO MUSICAL INTERPRETATION

CHAPTER SIX

THE NATURE OF THE MATERIAL

Taste in Registration

All that has been presented in the foregoing chapters has had to do with the development of a technique of registration. We have sought to discover how to present the musical material so that the listener will actually hear what the composer set down. This, like an accurate execution of the notes of the score, is a first essential of adequate performance, but it has little value except as a means of interpreting to the listener the musical and spiritual values of the composition.

This leads us to debatable ground. The subjective character of music invites wide divergence of interpretation, and seems to give license to various whims of personal taste. For example, the writer once heard a distinguished organist play Bach's so-called 'Cathedral Fugue' in the spirit of a string quartet, using the Voix Céleste. It gave to the music a luscious, romantic flavor, appealing to those who lack a taste for the unyielding organ tone and an appreciation of architectural design in music.

The brilliant nineteenth century English organist, William T. Best, was perhaps the first organist to be known primarily for his concert performances rather than his church connections.[1] He presided at the great concert organ in St. George's Hall, Liverpool, built by Henry Willis in 1855. Best edited a more than complete collection of Bach's organ works, with phrasing and registration designed to appeal to Victorian ears. A notable example is the 'Toccata in F'; for the beginning canon he suggested eight- and four-foot flutes for the right hand and an Oboe for the left. It makes a charming trio!

Why do these examples shock us? Are we not dealing with matters of taste in which each individual has a right to his own preference? Certainly, in an age when freedom of utterance is stressed and nonconformity is the norm, we cannot appeal to tradition. When a student in a Registration class insisted that she considered the French Horn ideal for the performance of one of Bach's little *manualiter* chorale settings, it was (as was doubtless her intention!) a challenge to the ingenuity of the instructor. He could not counter with the statement that it was in poor taste, or that Bach had no such stop on his organs: he was obliged to find some reason, based on the music itself, for rejecting the French Horn and preferring some other registration.

[1]Ignoring Abt Vogler. See p. 288.

121

Yet we cannot proceed purely on the basis of logic and the application of scientific laws. Registration is necessarily affected by personal taste. As the registration practices of organists improve, their own taste and that of their pupils and auditors will develop. In the mean time we can present the principles of good registration, which may serve to guide and correct the practices of the inexperienced and conscientious organist.

The Function of Registration

At the outset let us lay down the universal law which must govern all interpretative registration: *The function of registration is to enhance what is inherent in the music, and to make it clear to the listener. Like all means of interpretation, it should be suggested by the music, not superimposed on the music.*

In some cases it may be contended that the music is not sufficiently appealing without the addition of color interest. When that is true the answer is simple: Don't play it. Some claim that the public cannot enjoy the works of Bach, Buxtehude, and other such composers, unless they are decorated up – sugar-coated, as it were. Let the organist who plays to such a public present first the shorter and more obvious compositions of these masters in a strictly legitimate interpretation, gradually leading his hearers to an appreciation of the larger works. It is better to develop slowly a taste for the real Bach than to win immediate popularity for a denatured Bach.

In order to "enhance what is inherent in the music" the interpreter must, obviously, have a complete understanding of the work which he is presenting. He must study the material, the mood, the formal structure, the style, the historical and local setting of the music, the characteristics of the composer, and the type of instrument for which he wrote. These considerations will determine, subject to some adaptations to the conditions under which the music is to be performed, the character of the registration.

Adjustment of the Registration to the Musical Material

In the first place, then, the registration must at all times be suited to the material of the music. When, therefore, there is a change in the character of the material, there will be a corresponding change in the registration. The relation of the new combination to the old will be taken up in connection with the discussion of formal structure, but the organist must make whatever adjustment is necessary to present the musical matter effectively. Does it follow, conversely, that when there is no change in the character of the material the registration should remain the same? The purist may say: "Yes; to change the registration when there is no change in material is to superimpose the registration on the music." Such an opinion is superficial. Our guiding principle has been stated: "The function of registration is to enhance what is inherent in the music, and to make it clear to the listener." In the application of this principle the musical material is only one of the elements to be taken into consideration.

It was pointed out in the last chapter[2] that the continued use of any quality becomes fatiguing. As the listener becomes fatigued his attention is dulled, so that he does not hear clearly what is inherent in the music. A suitable change, therefore, would serve the purpose stated above.

A composer often provides an exact repetition of a section of a composition. Unless the music means something more, or something different, the second time it is heard, the repetition is redundant (except from the standpoint of formal balance) and the whole effect is weakened. In order to give the repetition significance it is necessary to alter the manner of presentation. This may be done by adopting a different dynamic level through the adjustment of the swell shades, by altering the dynamic plan within the section, by changing the rhythmic interpretation, by employing a different registration, or by a combination of two or more of these methods. Sometimes it is not practicable to devise a registration which will show all the elements of the texture with equal clearness; then it may be possible on the repetition to change the emphasis, bringing out features which were previously in the background.

If the attention of the listener is to be held for an extended period of time without essential change of material or tone, there must be great interest in the texture and in the development of the musical ideas. If the music lacks these qualities, or the audience is incapable of appreciating them, the interpreter must provide some compensating interest. This need not, must not mean catering to vulgar taste or superimposing irrelevant decoration to make the music superficially attractive. Its sole purpose is to enable the hearer to listen more attentively and intelligently to music which has sufficient merit and vitality to reward the the effort. The procedure is obviously dangerous and easily abused; it must be followed with the utmost discretion.

Moreover, the variation of the registration when there is no essential change in the music must depend on the ability of the organist to find different combinations which are adapted to the presentation of the same material. The principle of suitability must not be violated.

[2]P. 108.

In Part II the relation of registration to the musical material was discussed from the standpoint of audibility. Since a clear hearing of the essential elements of the music is necessary for the understanding of any interpretation, the facts presented in the foregoing chapters are equally relevant here. It remains to show the relation of those more or less detached theoretical observations to more obviously musical values. A certain amount of repetition will be inevitable, but the context will lend new significance to the principles discussed, and they will be related to specific examples. They will be applied with reference to the following characteristics of the material: texture, continuity, pace, rhythm, and weight.

Adjustment of the Registration to the Texture

The horizontal and vertical elements in music, which constitute the warp and woof of musical texture, are woven into an infinite variety of patterns to which they contribute in ever-changing proportions. The kind of registration best suited to bring out these elements and its adjustment to their relative importance have been fully discussed in Chapter IV. There is no need to repeat the explanation of the methods used. The point to be stressed here is the importance of a just evaluation of these elements in the music at hand, with a careful planning of the registration so that the listener may hear them in proper balance.

The textural impression is also affected by the degree of continuity of the voices. Detached playing calls attention to the beginnings and ends of tones, and so emphasizes the vertical relation of those which are attacked or released at the same time. It tends to isolate the individual tones of a melody, and thus impairs the natural perception of the melodic movement. Just as the form of a continuous line is more obvious than that of a broken line, so the contour of a melody is more clearly heard when it is played legato. From the horizontal standpoint the individual notes are important only in relation to those which precede and follow; so it is their connection, rather than their individuality, which should be heard.

For horizontal clarity the registration should provide this same continuity and ease of comparison of successive pitches. It is more important to select a quality which will give a clear delineation of the pitch pattern than to provide instantaneous audibility. Indeed, anything which calls particular attention to the attack mars the fluency of the melody.[3]

As detached playing brings out the vertical element in the texture by separating the individual notes and chords, so the registration may serve

[3]For this reason the piano, harpsichord, etc., are inferior to the organ and other wind instruments, and bowed stringed instruments, for melodic purposes.

the same purpose by emphasizing the attack and release. To this end instantaneous audibility is essential, and the positive attack of the reeds is often advantageous. The fact that the organ is the only instrument which is incapable of exaggerating the attack by means of dynamic accent makes it the least satisfactory medium for the interpretation of music in which the vertical element predominates. It is partly for this reason that the most significant organ music is polyphonic, and that the instrument was almost wholly neglected by the great composers of the nineteenth century.

Effect of Pace on Registration

Music is a temporal art; unchanging sound is meaningless. Synchronous effects have little significance except through comparison with what precedes and follows. So sounds have limited duration, and the shifting of pitches and pitch combinations is related to the passage of time. The rate of motion – the frequency of change – is a most important consideration in musical interpretation, which is reflected in the registration.

If the pace is rapid the listener is less conscious of the individual sounds than of the movement itself. The registration should accordingly be designed to facilitate the apprehension of melodic movement or chord changes. Instantaneous audibility and clarity are essential. Any tone which is slow or indefinite, or which for any reason requires time or effort for the complete hearing of all its properties – pitch, loudness, quality, or attack – impedes the perception of the movement, which is the most important feature of the music. Likewise very characteristic qualities invite the listener's attention to the individual tones, and so compete with the main interest of the music. Too much loudness also tends to retard the movement.[4]

The easy perception of motion is equally important in listening to music which depends for its effect on proportionate duration – either the use of characteristic rhythmic patterns, or rhythmic variation or flexibility. Whatever may be the specific devices, the appreciation of relative time values, like that of rapid movement, involves the instantaneous recognition of pitch changes. The registration requirements are the same, with some allowance for long notes.

If the pace is slow, relatively more attention is given to the quality of individual tones and combinations. The listener has time to perceive synchronous effects, and the element of motion is less evident. Fluency in the registration is accordingly less important, but the lack of motional interest calls for compensating immediate interest in the vertical aspect of the music and/or in the timbre of the tones.

[4]See p. 128.

Why have solo violinists chosen to transpose the celebrated 'Air' from Bach's *Suite in D,* so as to play it entirely on the G string? It is because the rich timbre of the G string, warmed by vibrato, possesses sensuous beauty and possibilities of intensification which the upper strings cannot match, and which greatly enhance the appeal and interest of the long tones which are characteristic of the melody.[5] For contrast one may imagine it played by a flute. The tone of that instrument, with its prompt, effortless emission, and the prominence of the fundamental and octave pitches in a range of clear audibility, is ideal for fluent melodies; but the paucity of upper partials renders it insipid for long tones, unless they serve purely as a background. Orchestra composers take advantage of the natural agility of the flute, while assigning slow melodies to the more colorful oboe or English horn, or especially to the strings, which add the warmth and intensity of undulation to their rich complement of upper partials.

So in organ registration, slow movement demands the added tonal interest provided by complexity. In the case of single melodies this will usually be achieved by the selection of individual stops having many partials, rather than by combinations of stops of different pitches, since the separate ingredients of synthetic qualities are more audible in prolonged tones. For this reason reeds are usually the most effective solo stops; strings are sometimes possible with judicious reinforcement of their fundamental. Occasionally prolonged tones may benefit by the effect of undulation produced by a Voix Céleste, or perhaps even a tremolo. These add a quasi-temporal element which tends to compensate for the lack of melodic motion. At the same time slow movement requires special attention to the durability of the tone quality. Vibrato, exotic timbre, and too much volume become fatiguing on long notes, and call for extreme caution.

A few examples will serve to illustrate the application of these principles.

Examples of Quick Movement

In the last movement of Widor's *Symphonie Gothique,* the first variation presents the plainsong against a fluent melody (to which a second counterpoint is later added) for which a single eight-foot flute is indicated. In general, these melodies lie in the region of easy pitch recognition, so that their contour and movement are most effectively shown by the pure, prompt, unforced tones of the flute.

[5]When played by a group of violins, as originally intended, the unsynchronized vibrato of the several players widens the pitch and compensates for the thinness which is characteristic of single strings in the upper range.

Vierne specified eight- and four-foot flutes for the scherzo of his *First Symphony*, and eight-, four-, and two-foot flutes for that of his *Second Symphony*. The difference is due to the texture: the single line of the first scherzo is clearer without the addition of the third pitch; in the second, the melodic line is relatively unimportant, but a wide spread of closely interspaced but separate pitches is desired. When, in the second scherzo, he wishes to bring out a single voice, he reinforces the fundamental by the addition of eight-foot tone and a mutation. In both movements the pace is lively and the pitch relatively high, making flutes the ideal medium. In the second scherzo, passing mention may be made of the addition of strings for the pedal melody beginning on page 24. Upper partials are needed for audibility, and strings, being more fluid than reeds, are better suited to this freely flowing melody.

The scherzo from Widor's *Fourth Symphony* resembles the one from Vierne's *First Symphony* in the significance of melodic motion, the prevailing staccato, and the registration for eight- and four-foot flutes. In this case it is not so much the contour of the melodic line which is important as the effect of rapid movement over a considerable range. The impression of sprightliness, which is enhanced by the detached playing, is even more vivid in the Widor movement because of the more continuous motion, the liveliness of two simultaneous voices, and the frequent melodic skips. It suffers, however, from heaviness and indefiniteness in places where the flutes are carried below their effective range.

An even more striking example of the agility and responsiveness of high flutes occurs in the scherzo of Guilmant's *Fifth Sonata*. The last episode is a brief fugal development of the theme in the upper and middle part of the keyboard, for which the composer has specified the use of eight- and two-foot flutes only. The paucity of upper partials and the wide spacing of these two pitches keep the tones almost completely separate, so that the listener hears a duplication of the material in the most sensitive range. This would result in confusion of the polyphony had not the composer employed every means – rhythm, spacing, phrasing, etc. – of keeping the texture transparent. It is one of the sprightliest and merriest passages in organ literature.

The advantage of using flutes in these movements can be demonstrated by experimenting with other combinations. We will find that diapasons and reeds impair the fluency by giving more emphasis to individual tones, while the weak fundamental of strings does not give a clear impression of the melodic motion. The addition of delicate mutations would not be objectionable, and would even be advantageous in a lower range, but in the higher range the greatest clarity is produced by the simple, separately audible tones of the flute. For the effect of exotic timbres in diverting the listener's attention from the movement itself, the scherzo from Vierne's *Second Symphony* might be played on an Orchestral Oboe, or an English Horn, or an ensemble combination in which mutation pitches are prominent. The grotesque result shows by exaggeration the danger of assigning too much interest to the tone quality when the most important characteristic of the material is fluency.

It is noteworthy that all these examples of lively movement are light. In general loudness is inimical to agility, because of the amount of energy required. Of course not all lively music is soft, but the combination of quick movement and loudness gives an impression of vigor, rather than fluency, unless the loudness is produced by small, high pitched pipes. Only at high frequencies can tones sound loud without the application of considerable energy. The registration suggested for the last movement of Mendelssohn's *First Sonata*, with a good proportion of audible high flue ranks, meets these requirements.[6] Similar considerations will govern the registration of such works as Bach's 'Prelude and Fugue in G', his 'Toccata, [Adagio,] and Fugue in C', and his chorale prelude on 'In dir ist Freude'; and such later examples as Saint-Saëns' 'Fantaisie in E flat', and the third movement of Widor's *Symphonie Gothique*, for which mixtures are specifically indicated. For the most part these examples do not call for a real fortissimo, and should be played without the use of loud reeds. Reeds are specified for the final 'Allegro' section of the last movement of Widor's *Symphonie Gothique* because the high pitch requires concentration in the fundamental, and the vitality of the reeds is needed to give clarity to the rapid motion. The popular Widor 'Toccata' falls in a different category. Its lively notes do not constitute an essentially rapid movement, but rather a superficial excitation imposed on a moderate movement. All the elements combine to give an impression of vigor.

The appreciation of synchronous effects requires time; so a rapid pace emphasizes the linear aspect of music. As a general rule, quick movements either present one or two melodies against a contrasting background, or are polyphonic in texture. In the foregoing examples we have sought to show the essential movement by melodic clarity, or, in the case of staccato material, by clarity of speech. The interpretation of music which moves slowly, however, involves both horizontal and vertical relations. To illustrate the considerations involved we shall present two types of examples: (1) slow solo melodies, and (2) slowly moving polyphony or harmony.

[6]See p. 109.

Slow Solo Melodies

Slow melodies are found in innumerable chorale preludes and in cantabile movements of various styles. We will begin with Bach's setting of
'Herzlich tut mich verlangen'. Let us play the melody on the following
stops in turn — always with a suitably balanced accompaniment: flute
(open or harmonic), diapason, string, Trumpet or other chorus reed (with
and without tremolo), Clarinet, French Horn, imitative English Horn or
Orchestral Oboe, Voix Céleste. We will try to appraise these stops from
the standpoint of the most effective presentation of the melody itself,
excluding from our consideration as far as possible matters of taste,
historical tradition, and mood.

We will find the flute tedious and uninteresting in proportion to the
lack of movement; the occasional ornamentation is more effective than
the longer notes. If we should transpose the melody up an octave, to
eliminate the handicap of the lower pitch, there would be a slight improvement from the melodic standpoint also. The more complex tone of
the diapason is a great improvement, but it does not contribute greatly to
the interest of the long notes, and it has some tendency to blend with the
accompaniment. The string does not lack interest, but it lacks the fundamental needed for melodic clarity, and its abnormal proportion of partials
tends to weary the listener. A good chorus reed provides a rich development of upper partials which holds the listener's interest through long
notes without surfeiting excess or abnormality. The undulation of a good
tremolo may add to the interest of the long notes for those whose taste is
not offended thereby. The Clarinet also has an effective complement of
partials, but its abnormal emphasis on the odd partials limits the length
of time for which it can be enjoyed. The French Horn is open to the
same objection as the flute, with certain modifications. It is more audible in the range of the melody, but the added volume is fatiguing, and in
some cases certain partials are prominent which lend interest to the tone
at the expense of durability. Much more exotic is the tone of the English
Horn or Orchestral Oboe, which becomes fatiguing on long notes and detracts from the natural appeal of the melody. The dual pitch of the Voix
Céleste compensates for the thinness of the string, and its undulation
adds interest to the long notes, but, like the tremolo, its effect is somewhat artificial and palls if used to excess.

Whatever quality may be chosen for the solo, the accompaniment should
neither absorb nor compete with it. On the other hand, it is more than a
background and should make its full contribution to the ensemble. Since
the harmony is incomplete without the solo, the contrast should not be
too great, but the solo should primarily be heard as a separate melody.

The accompanying combination should reveal both the vertical and
horizontal elements in the texture, care being taken to avoid thickness
in the relatively low range. If the melody is sung by a Trumpet the accompaniment might be played on a light diapason with a four-foot Gemshorn. The four-foot stop should not be separately heard; the homogeneity
of the texture should be reflected in the registration, and the melody
should be heard as the highest pitch.

Melodies at Different Pitch Levels

The observation above that prolonged flute tones are less objectionable at a high pitch invites further attention. This would seem to be related to the matter of volume. The upper tones are more durable·because
they are more easily heard, and the ear is attacked with less energy. It
may be that the actual pitch of the component partials is important, as
well as the complexity of their distribution. At any rate, it appears that
considerations of durability corroborate the requirements of audibility
that the proportion of fundamental be reduced as the pitch descends.
With this in mind let us compare the beginning of the second movement
of Widor's *Symphonie Gothique* with the middle section of Vierne's
'Clair de lune' from his *Pièces de Fantaisie*.

The flute registration which Widor specified is consistent with the
placid mood, and provides fluency for the occasional ornamentation.
Disregarding these considerations, it is still evident that the flute is a
more effective medium for this high melody than for the Bach chorale
which we have just discussed. Moreover, the substitution of a diapason,
a string, or a reed does not produce a happy effect. A smooth reed might
be acceptable for the single line, but when the second melody enters the
long notes would continue to claim the attention of the listener, to the
disadvantage of the more important, moving part. The flute does not
hold the interest in the sustained tones, and so leaves the hearer free to
listen to the movement of the other part. Even at this pitch the flute
emphasizes movement rather than duration.

In the passage from Vierne's 'Clair de lune' the composer's registration reveals the limitations of the organ which he had in mind. In order
to make the foundation stops of the Pédale and Positif audible by contrast, he assigns the manual part to the Voix Céleste of the Récit. This
he also couples to the pedal to give better definition to the tenor melody.
The Voix Céleste obscures the sixteenth-note undulation, not to mention
the loss of the tones which happen to be duplicated by the pedal. Apart
from expressive considerations (to be taken up later), this registration
cannot give the melody sufficient prominence without an objectionable
degree of volume; moreover, long notes in that pitch range demand a

larger proportion of upper partials. The audibility of the melody should therefore be effected by the avoidance of blend, not only by emphasizing the fundamental.

Let us substitute a complex manual combination with a light fundamental and a good distribution of upper pitches. The vagueness which the composer provided by the use of the Voix Céleste can be achieved by avoiding too much concentration in the ensemble. For the melody we will try, successively and in combination, a reed, a string, and a broad string céleste, such as a 'Cello Céleste. The reed stands out distinctly against the background of the accompaniment; its complex quality holds the attention of the listener, while its strong fundamental impression outlines the melody clearly. The string alone has insufficient fundamental; if it is not lost in the ensemble it is because of an abnormal quality which is not adapted to melodic delineation. If combined with a flute the result is not clear but heavy. The addition of a diapason would tend to merge the solo with the accompaniment. Combined with a reed, the string may serve (if the blend is satisfactory) to compensate for any overemphasis which the former might give to the fundamental.

The 'Cello Céleste, although vague in pitch, stresses the fundamental in relation to the upper pitches, and keeps the solo separate from the ensemble. The undulation added to the complex quality enhances the effect of the long notes and lends continuity to the melody. Comparing the effects of the céleste and the reed we find that the latter, because of its more exact pitch definition and stronger audible fundamental, outlines the melody more distinctly; at the same time its more positive attack and unyielding tone tend to emphasize the individual notes of the melody, rather than their connection. The slightly blurred intonation of the céleste gives less emphasis to the individual tones and helps the horizontal impression; it lends curve to the melody, which the reed makes sound almost angular. Moreover the céleste gives the impression of a dominant fundamental of relatively slight intensity, lacking the volume which might make the reed fatiguing. On the other hand, some listeners find the undulation of a céleste cloying. The relative durability of the two qualities at this pitch is largely a matter of individual reaction. In such cases it is not our purpose to arrive at positive conclusions, but rather to examine relative values on the basis of which the individual interpreter may establish his own preferences.

Why have we defended the use of a Voix Céleste in this passage by Vierne, but discouraged it for the Bach chorale setting? This is not altogether due to the difference between Baroque and romantic music. The plastic sweep of Vierne's melody calls for the smooth flow which a Voix Céleste provides. Moreover, the melody is all-important, and it does not form a part of the ensemble; the accompaniment is complete in itself and serves as a background for the melody. In the Bach chorale, on the other hand, the melody completes the ensemble, and the vertical relation of each tone is essential. Again, the difference in pitch is important, even though it is a matter of only an octave. The proportion of fundamental which is ideal for the chorale is a bit heavy in the range of the Vierne melody. But if the reed is more effective in the higher range, it is equally true that the céleste benefits by the lower pitch. As it is usually tuned its beats become more rapid as the pitch ascends, but not proportionately, so the actual pitch discrepancy between the ranks is less in the higher range. The tone of the céleste is, therefore, thinner in the region where more fundamental is needed; and the more rapid beats do not have the warmth of a natural vibrato.

Adjustments to different pitch levels are often necessary in different sections of the same piece, where the same melodic material is transposed to another range and assumes another relation to the accompaniment. In César Franck's 'Cantabile in B' the melody, first appearing in the upper voice, is effectively sung by a single reed, which may be fairly smooth if desired. The repetition in the tenor calls for a relatively reduced fundamental and an increase in the upper partials. If a brighter reed is substituted, it should seem a modification of the first, rather than a contrast to it. Often a string may advantageously be added to the original solo stop. A Voix Céleste is not effective here because of the essential vertical relations of the tones of the melody. Incidentally, the accompaniment combination will be changed for this repetition, both because it is above the melody and because of the increased importance of the horizontal element. Light eight- and four-foot flutes may suitably be included.

Other examples of such transpositions may be noted in Franck's 'Choral in A minor' and in the 'Adagio' of Mendelssohn's *Sonata in C minor*, Number 2. In the first instance, the soprano melody of the middle section is repeated in the tenor in the transition to the *reprise*; in the second, the melody alternates between the soprano and tenor during the first half of the movement. These melodies are more fluent than those previously referred to; the element of motion is important, but the pace is still relatively slow. In both cases a reed should be used for the soprano melody, while the tenor may be effectively sung by a 'Cello Céleste, which suits the plastic nature of the melody. In the Mendelssohn movement the continuity of the accompaniment prevents any change in it when the melody is shifted. The wide range necessitates a compromise. The eight- and four-foot flutes which, in the upper range, would be ideal for the continuously moving counterpoints, are ineffective in the lower part of the keyboard. Since, for the most part, the accompanying melodies remain above middle C, the requirements of the upper range will prevail, with the possible addition of a light string or mutation to assist the definition of the lower pitches. The change in texture in the seventh measure from the end necessitates an alteration in the registration, but some of the characteristics of the first combination should be retained if possible, in order that the new material may not seem too irrelevant.

The 'Allegretto' movement of Mendelssohn's *Sonata in B flat,* Number 4, presents a similar alternation of soprano and tenor melodies, complicated by the fact that the two are combined in the last section. Ideally this section should be played on three manuals, but the technical difficulties involved would probably result in a loss of fluency. The following procedure is suggested as a practical approximation of the ideal differentiation of the three voices: Play the accompaniment on the Choir, using eight- and four-foot flutes, possibly colored by a soft mutation. Play the soprano melody on the Swell Oboe, and the tenor melody on the Solo, using a more incisive solo stop. Both the Swell and Choir will be coupled to the Great, on which no stops are drawn. When the melody returns in the upper voice the right hand will play on the Great, the swell pedals being adjusted to favor the Swell reed. Two measures later, when the tenor melody enters again, the Swell box will be closed and the Choir partly open, so that the accompanying combination will dominate the right hand part. The reed will again be brought into prominence two measures later, with the return of the soprano melody. For the coda, the Solo must drop out, the F being sustained on the less obtrusive Swell, and the accompaniment returning to the Choir. On a three-manual organ the Great will have to be substituted for the Solo, the combination of the Swell and Choir being effected by the Swell to Choir coupler. The effectiveness of this solution depends on the resources of the instrument and on the skillful manipulation of the swell pedals.

Melodies with Varied Motion

The foregoing examples have included melodies in which the element of motion predominates, and others in which the quality of the individual tones commands the attention of the listener. It will be interesting to add two or three examples in which there is a wider range of note values, requiring a registration which provides both flexibility and prolonged interest.

In the 'Cantilene' from Widor's *Symphonie Romane* we find an extreme variation in the rate of movement. For this the composer has specified a Clarinet. Like its orchestral counterpart, this stop is the most fluent of the reeds.[7] If well voiced it gives less emphasis on the attack, and so produces a smoother legato than the other reeds. At the same time its odd-partials timbre sustains the interest through the long notes, and emphasizes the fundamental sufficiently for clear melodic delineation at a fairly high pitch. The fatigue which this quality might otherwise produce is prevented by the little melodic excursions in the music. The Clarinet is an ideal medium for this uniquely varied and plastic melody. On some organs a comparable effect may be produced synthetically, but any substitution must provide the same essential values — timbre-interest, clarity of outline, agility, and elasticity.[8]

The first section of Vierne's 'Clair de lune' presents a somewhat similar melody, but the composer's registration is much less happy. He assigns the melody to an eight-foot flute on the Grand Orgue (Great), to which is coupled the Récit (Swell) with eight-foot flute and string. Apparently he relies on the flute for fluency, and on the Récit for timbre-interest and dynamic control. But a combination of three eight-foot stops inevitably lacks clarity — not to mention fluency. The flute alone would have been preferable, in spite of the long notes. Here, as in the Widor movement just discussed, a Clarinet produces an excellent effect; or a flute or gedeckt with one or two very delicate mutations may be used.[9]

The melody of the same composer's 'Arabesque' from the set of 24 *Pièces en Style Libre* keeps moving more than the last two examples, and at the same time presents the utmost rhythmic flexibility. The suggested eight-foot flute is justified,[10] in spite of its vagueness on the lower notes, by the primary consideration of motion — both relative and actual. More partials can well be introduced if suitable stops are available. The composer's registration is specifically for a small instrument.

Harmonic Texture

In slowly moving polyphony and in music which is primarily harmonic, the synchronous relation of the voices is an essential, and sometimes the most important, part of the effect to which the registration must contribute. But interest in the vertical aspect of music cannot long be maintained without other engaging factors. In the music of Bach we find such

[7] The oboe of the orchestra is sprightly, but its tones sound more separate, and it is more frequently played detached in rapid passages.

[8] Attention may be drawn in passing to the second movement of this symphony, pages 14 & 15, where the composer has employed simultaneously the effects discussed on pages 130-31, assigning an eight-foot flute to the upper melody, and a combination including a string (a celeste might be used) to the pedal.

[9] The writer usually plays this on a Clarinet, adding a delicate Tierce in the third measure on page 28.

[10] Owing to an obvious typographical error it is not actually indicated in the first part.

passages as the beginning of the great 'Prelude in C minor',[11] the massive bridge leading to the fugue in the 'Toccata, Adagio, and Fugue in C', the two stupendous passages in the 'Fantasia in G minor', introduced by the then unprecedented attack on a six-four chord, and of course various chorale harmonizations. Similar fragments might be cited from the music of other composers. For more extended examples we have to go to less significant works. The lesser composers of the late nineteenth and early twentieth centuries wrote many pieces in the style of the French *Grand Chœur*, and the Voix Céleste slow movement became a convention. The registration of such material should provide a cohesive ensemble, varied to fit the style, rhythm, color, mood, etc., of the music, care being taken not to conceal any textural interest which may exist. We will examine a few typical examples.

The three passages cited from the works of Bach should all be played fortissimo, with a complete representation of harmonic pitches over a wide range. Cohesion will be provided by the complexity of the ensemble, and vitality by the large proportion of high ranks and partials. All soft eight- and four-foot stops and all flutes and strings may well be omitted, since they make no dynamic contribution, and they tend to impair the clarity of the combination. If the organ is large enough to allow some differentiation for these three examples, the following is recommended: A larger proportion of reeds should be used for the beginning of the 'Prelude in C minor', giving a more positive attack for the separated chords, and serving to prevent a too complete fusion of the right- and left-hand parts. The bridge leading to the 'Fugue in C' should, if possible, have less eight-foot reed than four-foot, and the sixteen-foot element will be provided largely by gross mutations; these lend richness and vitality without thickness. The passages in the 'Fantasia in G minor' should have a normal balance of eight- and four-foot reeds with a complete diapason ensemble, to combine solidity and brilliance with clarity for the moving inner parts. The spacing calls for sixteen-foot tone, but the ensemble must not be thick nor the tenor heavy.

An Extreme Example

Probably the most familiar example of long continued vertical texture is (or was until recently) de la Tombelle's 'Marche Pontificale'. Hackneyed though it is, this march serves as a typical example of purely harmonic writing in organ music. Not only does it contain the minimum of horizontal element, but its function as a march is served by a lack of rhythmic variety and a continual synchronization of the voice movements.

[11]Schirmer Edition, Vol. III, p. 34.

The registration must emphasize the same characteristics. The ensemble must be cohesive throughout, the balance of pitches varying according to the loudness, range, degree of legato, and the melodic importance of the upper voice. The principal theme being detached and strong in rhythm must have solid attacks and clean releases; reeds should be rather prominent, enriched by a large complement of absorbed diapason pitches. The range is high enough to bar too large a proportion of high ranks, and to permit a certain amount of definite sixteen-foot tone — preferably reeds — in the manual.

The first subordinate section presents the same material, less loud, legato, and an octave lower. The registration should preserve the style and enhance the contrast. The attack should emphasize the synchronized chords and persistent rhythm, in spite of the legato; the change in pitch should not be minimized, and the melody in the upper voice should be clear. This purpose will be served by a very reedy ensemble, completely absorbing the rich mixture work. The quality must be highly complex, with no audible separation of the upper ranks. The pitch scarcely admits the inclusion of sixteen-foot stops. Usually this section will be played on a full combination from the Swell and perhaps the Choir, including reeds, excluding flutes and sixteen-foot stops, and using only a light eight-foot diapason tone. The two long episodes afford opportunity to provide some relief from the prominence of the reeds. For these diapason tone at various pitches should prevail, with enough light reed tone to lend some vitality and incisiveness. The strong rhythm will be maintained by an almost obtrusive registration of the bass figure. Loud reeds will be introduced within a closed swell at the beginning of the crescendo leading to the return of the principal theme.

More space has been given to this march than its musical merit warrants because it is such a consistent example of almost unmitigated harmonic texture. At the same time, the organist who plays for academic processions is regretfully aware that no better slow march, from the practical standpoint, has been written for the organ. There is, to be sure, far superior march music which provides more horizontal interest, thereby weakening the rhythmic emphasis which is dependent on synchronous movement.

Harmonic Slow Movements

Harmonic texture also prevails in the typical slow movement of the cyclical works of the romantic composers. French organists, and others, discovered the rich cohesion and vibrancy of the Voix Céleste and found it peculiarly adapted to enhance the effect of lush chords in soft, slow compositions. From the 'Voix Céleste Andante' of Batiste to the symphonies and other works of Vierne, it has been the typical medium of romantic musings. It must be admitted that it is eminently suited to the material, and there is real beauty and emotional warmth in the best examples. For instance, the use of the Voix Céleste seems inevitable in the 'Adagio' from Vierne's *Symphony in D minor*, Number 1 — which so strongly suggests Bizet's *L'Arlésienne* music. It is as legitimate as Bizet's muted strings; if it were as infrequently used it would be in better repute. Moreover, we should bear in mind that the French Voix Céleste is less objectionable than the American type. [12]

To serve a similar purpose composers have sometimes suggested the use of the Vox Humana, as seen in the last movement of Franck's 'Fantaisie in C', and in the 'Adagio' of Widor's *Symphony in F minor*, Number 4. Incongruous as it may seem, the human and celestial voices fall in the same category, and are to a certain extent interchangeable! They both serve to lend immediate timbre-appeal to material which lacks horizontal textural interest. The Vox Humana is by nature less cohesive, but that difference is obscured by the conventional use of the tremolo. Still, if the voicing is good and the tremolo unobtrusive, it makes the melodic line clearer than the Voix Céleste. It is less adapted to wide spacing because of its more restricted partial content, and it is usually most effective in the middle of the keyboard. Compare from that standpoint the movements just cited with the slow movements of Widor's first, second, fifth, and sixth symphonies. Above all it should be remembered that the tone of the Vox Humana is one of the least durable of the sounds produced by organ pipes; it should never be heard for more than a phrase or two without interruption.

Variation in Texture

The appeal of a momentary effect, such as a chord or a timbre, is largely sensuous. There is no stimulus to mental activity until there is something new with which to compare the first sensation. Since mental participation is essential to prolonged interest, continued appeal is dependent on change — on a succession of different sounds. Music which is deficient in this horizontal quality soon becomes boring. If the texture is not polyphonic, horizontal interest may be provided by a single melodic line — either the upper tones of the harmonies, as in the Franck and Widor movements cited above, or a solo melody for which the harmonic texture provides an accompaniment, as in the slow movement of Franck's *Grande Pièce Symphonique*, and other examples already discussed.

Of course the distinction between harmonic and polyphonic texture is comparative. Chord progressions involve melodic motion in the individual

[12]See p. 56.

parts; but that is not enough to hold the interest of the listener for any length of time. · So composers vary the texture, introducing more movement in the inner parts from time to time, as we see in the first and last movements of Franck's 'Fantasie in C'. Probably one reason for the tedious effect of the Voix Céleste is that it obscures such bits of polyphony.

Still more important, as a means of avoiding the monotony which is characteristic of harmonic writing, is to limit its duration, confining it to relatively brief sections which are interspersed with more polyphonic passages. We will accordingly conclude this discussion of slow moving music by citing a few examples of this treatment, observing the relation of the harmonic passages to their environment.

The first statement of a theme which is to be treated in variations usually presents a simple harmonization of the melody, with nothing to distract the attention of the listener from his primary concern with becoming familiar with the subject of the variations. Of course chorale variations deal with material which is already familiar, but the first statement is like a hymn, and its registration may suggest the original function. Details vary, but the ensemble will be cohesive, showing the chords as units and at the same time outlining clearly the upper voice. For example, the harmonization of 'Vater unser im Himmelreich' in Mendelssohn's *Sonata in D minor,* Number 6, may be played on a rich combination of many pitches, *possibly* including a light sixteen-foot stop. The eight- and four-foot elements should be sufficient to make the tune clearly heard, and not be overbalanced by the higher ranks: but the low range will not permit a dominant eight-foot tone. Since the dynamic level should not exceed a mezzo forte, no reeds louder than an Oboe should be included. This suggested registration is influenced by the element of mysticism and reverence which is felt in both the music and the text. [13]

Aside from its place in the theme and variations form, the independent use of essentially harmonic texture is rare in the best organ music. Usually it is introduced to provide contrast to more polyphonic or melodic passages. In Franck's 'Cantabile in B' the phrases of the melody are separated by little scraps of harmonic writing. These serve as a frame to set off the graceful contours of the melodic picture. The registration should be neutral, showing the vertical relation of the voices without attracting undue attention. A single eight-foot diapason is ideal if it is warm and not heavy. If the voicing is not right the tone can be modified by not more than two, or possibly three, blending stops; but heaviness must be avoided.

[13] See Chap. VII.

An example of the alternation of different types of material, worked
into an effectively cumulative formal scheme, appears in Mendelssohn's
Sonata in F minor, Number 1. The first movement is fugal in character,
the development of the animated polyphonic material being interspersed
with phrases of the chorale, 'Was mein Gott will, das g'scheh allzeit'.
The hymn-like quality of the chorale is retained, and should govern the
registration. The richness of the ensemble may even be exaggerated in
order to provide a more definite contrast to the clarity of the animated
material. The author likes to include light, bright reeds, irradiated by
as much upper work as they will absorb, and restrained by the swell
pedal. With a little ingenuity the differentiation of the two kinds of
ensemble can be continued when the two types of material are heard
simultaneously. In the third entrance of the chorale the fugue theme
can be played by the feet, the pedal stops being silenced and the fugue
manual combination being coupled in. In the later entries it is possible
to play the two themes on different manuals, if the chorale is assigned
to the Choir keyboard and the fugue theme to the Great — although small
hands may require the assistance of the feet for the lowest voice. With
the entrance of the pedal cadenza the elements of both combinations must
be united and reinforced, to provide a rich, telling vertical ensemble, and
to lead into the climactic entrance over the tonic pedal point. There
more upper work should be added for the return of the animated polyphonic material. Incidentally, the occasional wide gap between the
pedal and manual parts needs to be filled in with sixteen-foot manual
tone, or even a suboctave coupler. During the pedal cadenza the manual
part may be duplicated by the left hand playing an octave lower on a
secondary manual. The modern organist does not need his left hand free
to preserve his balance!

Franck's 'Choral in A minor'

A similar procedure, with very different material and design, is found
in Franck's 'Choral in A minor'. In the first part of this piece activity
and lack of motion alternate; in the last section the two elements are
combined. The animated figure at the beginning calls primarily for a
clear perception of the movement; the combination should not be too
cohesive; the upper octave pitches may well be exposed by the sparing
use of mutations or their complete omission, and reeds should be avoided.
By contrast the slowly arpeggiated chords provide a vertical piling up of
tonal substance which requires a great mass of cohesive material. It
should be rich in reeds and diapasons of all pitches, although the close
spacing will not permit the use of heavy sixteen-foot stops.

With the entrance of the chorale the alternation of quick and slow movement continues on a softer plane. In general, the conditions which determine the registration are similar to those imposed by the use of chorale themes in the Mendelssohn movements already discussed. The ensemble will be cohesive, emphasizing the vertical aspect of the music without obscuring the soprano melody, and providing a definite contrast to the combinations used for the quicker movement which precedes and follows. There are distinct differences, however, which must be taken into consideration: Mendelssohn was using chorales which were familiar as hymn melodies; they are unison vocal music, existing and known independent of any accompanying harmonies. The composer's harmonization is subservient to the melodies; it is straightforward, calling for a normal balance of pitches — although their range and complexity vary with the general pitch level, dynamic intensity, and mood. Franck's theme, on the other hand, is not a hymn tune; it is an instrumental theme, apparently conceived coincidentally with the harmonies. The melodic and harmonic elements are mutually dependent, mutually contributory; if anything, the harmonies have the larger share in the musical expression. It is notable that when the same theme appears, fortissimo, at the end of the piece, the harmonization is the same. This peculiar vertical interest in the musical material should be matched by the timbre interest of the ensemble. Mutation pitches may be favored, the fundamental should be slight, and a gentle sixteen-foot string or Dulciana may be included. The last will contribute to the impression of mysticism, and will lend significance to the melodic movement of the bass at the cadences. Only flue stops should be used; the continuity of the sound should be perfect, and no single pitch should be stressed beyond what is necessary for the audibility of the soprano.

There are very few organs on which a perfectly satisfactory registration of the final statement of the chorale is possible. Ideally the right hand and pedal should have a full, rich, rather reedy, fortissimo ensemble, with enough sixteen-foot tone to bridge the gap in pitch. The left hand should emphasize its own line, with high pitches for audibility. It should contain much telling, but imperfectly blending tone, so that it will not be lost in the vertical tonal mass; at the same time some of the general ensemble should be included, as this part occasionally shares in the harmonies. The difficulties of the problem are (1) to find on one organ two ensembles which are suitably differentiated, and at the same time loud and brilliant enough to provide the necessary éclat for this climactic statement, and (2) to make the accompanying figure clearly audible without its attracting too much attention. It is more important for the listener to get the general effect than to recognize details, and the chorale is the main thing. To make it sufficiently imposing usually requires most of the effective resources of the organ, which necessitates playing the toccata figure on the same manual. By omitting octave couplers, depending on reeds for a considerable proportion of the richness, and avoiding high ranks which are separately audible, it is sometimes possible to make the left hand heard—but often it merely gives the impression of a slight commotion in the middle of the ensemble.

Rhythmic Stress

From time to time in the foregoing discussion mention has been made of the rhythmic effect of detached playing and its relation to the registration, and, per contra, the selection of stops and combinations suited to the smoothness of legato playing. This question of rhythmic emphasis and its relation to the interpretation of different styles merits brief separate consideration.

In general, rhythmic emphasis is a matter of energy. Almost all other media of performance—piano, stringed instruments, wind instruments, voice—produce dynamic stress by the application of energy. On the organ it is not possible to control momentary changes in the amount of energy applied to the tone, unless one of the values is zero; so the effect of accent can only be produced by a sudden release of energy after an interruption. The amount of stress depends on the effective amount of energy and the suddenness with which it is released. It is also affected by the length of silence preceding the attack, the duration of the tone or chord attacked, and the relation of the attack to the expected timing.

The last sentence needs to be elaborated and illustrated in order that its bearing on the registration may be fully realized. The effect of these factors on the impression of stress may be demonstrated by playing Example 9 on the organ, with careful attention to the note values and

Example 9. Agogic Stress

releases. The listener (preferably not the player) should compare the amount of stress given to the last tone by the different versions.

The application of these devices to the interpretation of music is almost too common to need illustration. The three repeated chords which often conclude a piece (e.g., the last movements of Franck's *Grande Pièce Symphonique* and Vierne's *Symphony in D minor*, Number 1) need a prolongation of the last rest, emphasizing the attack on the last chord by lengthening the silence and delaying the attack beyond the expected time — keeping the listener in suspense. The same device enhances the satisfaction of the arrival at the final tonic in a cadence, as at the end of Mendelssohn's *Sonata in F minor*, Number 1, and Vierne's *Symphony in E minor*, Number 2. The amount of delay depends, of course, on the character of the music; it should be almost imperceptible in the Mendelssohn movement, but considerable in the Vierne. In Saint-Saëns' 'Improvisation in A minor' the rhythmic drive is intended to be invariable; so he has notated out a relatively slow final cadence, and prolonged the last chord to more than four measures. A slightly different situation occurs when the final chord is anticipated, as in de la Tombelle's 'Marche Pontificale', or the 'Toccata' from Widor's *Fifth Symphony*. Here not only will the anticipation be slightly delayed, but it will be very definitely separated from the following chord, so as to emphasize the attack on the real final tonic. [14]

What has all this to do with registration? All these interpretative devices depend for their effect on the clear perception of the attack and release, and on the efficient continuation of the tone for its specified duration. They therefore provide additional evidence that definiteness of attack and release and dynamic efficiency are essential for rhythmic emphasis. This means, then, the use of high pitches, prompt speaking pipes, and reeds, whose selection, combination, and proportion depend on the amount of emphasis desired, and other characteristics of the music. Strings should almost never be.used, and flutes are effective only at a high pitch, and especially for light movements.

---

[14]One is tempted to go on and discuss the analogous functions of pedal points, dissonance, etc., but we have already digressed too far from our main subject.

We cannot refrain, however, from pausing to observe that organists and conductors often fail to realize that retards and other interpretative devices are matters of relativity. They derive their effect from their deviation from the expected. Either the assumption of a slower tempo or a long continued retard changes the standard of reference — the one abruptly, and the other gradually. Neither achieves the effect of emphasis, which is the more usual purpose of rhythmic and tempo variation. The interpreter who plays the last part of Bach's 'Passacaglia and Fugue' in a much slower tempo than the rest, or who introduces a gradual retard in a piece of a *moto perpetuo* or a fluent type, changes the character of the music. He defeats his own purpose by losing the sense of motion with which the altered tempo is to be compared, and thus destroys the essential emphasis of the final arrival on the tonic. Composers who abandon the quick motion of their lively movements for the last section or final cadence (See Mendelssohn, Sonatas 1 and 5; Widor, 'Toccata'; and many other examples) are psychologically right. When the lively motion is maintained to the very end, as in Bach's 'Fugue in C major' from the 'Toccata, Adagio, and Fugue', it indicates that the composer did not want the emphasis which a retard would give. Let us respect his intentions.

The application of the effects which we have been describing to the general rhythmic character of musical material is illustrated in the interpretation of the 'Toccata' from Widor's *Fifth Symphony*.[15] In this connection we will add two other examples: Saint-Saëns, 'Improvisation in A minor', and Widor, 'Moderato' from the *Symphony in A minor*, Number 7.

Saint-Saëns did not indicate detached playing, except by the implication of occasional slurs, but the material demands it. The attack on the first and third beats of each measure, with the stress of longer notes on the first, produces a very strong rhythmic effect, calling for clear, decisive registration. The first part may be played on the Swell eight- and four-foot reeds alone; any addition must not be allowed to disperse the pitch effect. When the pedal enters, a balanced selection of diapason ranks will be added to give more substance to the tone. The eighth-note passages will be played legato, and would naturally be assigned to a fluent flue combination. Not necessarily. The range is high, where the positive attack of the reeds is less pronounced; the audibility of the reed attack is less apparent in a single line; the speed is so great that the listener is not conscious of the individual attacks, but hears their contribution to the clarity of the rapid movement. A flue combination which would be agile and clear at this pace in the lower part of the range of these passages would tend to blend with other voices, impairing the distinctness of the two themes when they are combined. So the author prefers to play these sections on the reeds of a secondary manual, enlivened by a good distribution of flue ranks in which octave pitches are almost prominent. The sweeping arpeggios leading to cadential chords will, of course, be played on a full, brilliant combination, while the legato passages in quarter-note movement will use a lighter combination in which flues predominate.

In contrast to the persistent, exuberant rhythm of the work just discussed, the first movement of Widor's *Seventh Symphony* is characterized by a vigor and vitality of rhythmic substance, rare in organ literature. An adequate study of this amazing work cannot even be begun in these pages, but the interested organist will find it very rewarding.

The rhythmic effects are produced by skillful and ingenious phrasing, whereby every rhythmic stress receives a clean, separate attack, except for relatively long notes prefixed by a single sixteenth. Complete, clearcut, precise, positive attacks and releases are imperative, both in the execution and in the registration. The extreme energy of the rhythm must be evident in the performance of the theme whenever it occurs fortissimo. The indication "*fff*" suggests absolutely full organ, but

[15]See pp. 106-7, 109-10.

that should never be interpreted to mean all the stops. Strings, flutes, and other weak stops should be omitted. All the ingredients of the ensemble should be telling and prompt. There must be an ample proportion of reeds and absorbed high pitches for attack and efficiency, but at the same time enough fundamental and sixteen-foot tone should be included to give massiveness to the octave sections. This impression of weight (which will be taken up shortly) must not be allowed to impede the motion; rather it will increase the sense of energy because of the great mass to be moved. The organist must judge how much weight the motion will stand.

The variety of texture in which this motive figures calls for a very sensitive differentiation in the registration. Always the clarity of attack and release must be preserved, but in the lighter passages the reeds will play a smaller part, particularly when the characteristic rhythm is in single notes. The contrasting legato material needs a fluent combination composed largely of flue stops.

Fluency

This introduces the complementary consideration of the absence of rhythmic stress. So much has been said about the requirements of a smooth or cantabile style that we will merely summarize briefly what we already know, in order that it may appear in juxtaposition to the discussion of rhythmic emphasis.

The continuous flow from one tone to the next, which is essential for a natural melodic impression, and particularly for a cantabile style, requires the minimum of stress on the initial emission of the tone. Reeds should be used with caution. They are satisfactory for a single voice if not combined with more than one or two other stops; a light reed may be used for two independent voices. Flutes are particularly good at high pitches, and a Voix Céleste is often effective when the texture is not polyphonic.

For fluency, or rhythmic elasticity (which also depends on the easy perception of motion), stops with quick and uniform speech should be used. For the greatest clarity, unison and octave pitches should be prominent – particularly ranks in a range favoring easy pitch recognition. If a reed is used it should be light, and not combined with another stop of the same pitch. Discrepancy in attack, imperfect blend, and unnecessary volume – all tend to impede the movement. A four-foot flute will often lend fluency to a light reed for a single voice. For example, the delicate tracery of the 'Largo' from Bach's *Sonata in C*, Number 5, is revealed with delightful clarity if the right hand plays on eight- and four-foot flutes, and the left hand on a well-voiced, unimitative Oboe combined with a Harmonic Flute 4'.

Weight

The words "heavy" and "light" have been freely used in characterizing tonal impressions. The meaning is obvious, but we need to know just what it is that gives the sense of weight, and how different degrees of heaviness or lightness are produced. The impression of weight, or mass, is closely related to the sense of volume. In general it depends on the discrepancy between physical intensity and aural loudness, and is augmented by conditions which make that discrepancy more evident. More specifically, the impression of weight depends on the following:

1. Vibration frequency: Low pitches sound heavy; high pitches sound light.

2. Vibration amplitude: In the same pitch range, soft tones sound lighter (or less heavy) than loud tones.

3. Frequency difference, or pitch spacing: A sense of crowding increases the impression of weight, so that simultaneous tones which are close together sound heavier than those which are far apart. The effect of weight is more or less inversely proportional to the arithmetical difference between the frequencies of the adjacent tones; the same interval will, therefore, be much heavier in a low, than in a high range.

4. Continuity of vibration, or the length of the notes: The sense of weight is to a certain extent cumulative, so that, other things being equal, long notes are heavier than short notes.[16]

5. Promptness of perception: Anything which delays the recognition of all the qualities of a tone tends toward sluggishness, and thus increases the impression of heaviness. This applies both to the actual production of the tone and to its audition.

6. The nature of the attack: An explosive attack, giving the impression of energy, as well as a delayed attack, tends toward heaviness.

Applying these facts to the actual composition of an ensemble to produce a massive effect, such as would suggest majesty or dignity, we will adopt the following procedure: The balance of the ensemble will be kept relatively low, the higher pitches being adequately absorbed. The proportion of eight-foot tone will be relatively large, and the inclusion of sixteen-foot tone will increase the effect. The combination needs to be fairly loud; if the music is soft, a large combination in a closed swell box is more effective than a softer combination. The listener feels the energy, in spite of the reduction in loudness effected by the enclosure. Sixteen-foot stops may also serve to compensate for softness of tone. Reeds at low pitches help to give the impression of weight without vagueness. The sense of heaviness is also favored by the emphasis on

16See pp. 105-6.

the attack which results from detached playing, and the contribution of reeds to that emphasis; but the notes should not be shortened enough to lose the effect of duration.

The application of these methods to the registration of specific compositions has already been shown in the discussion of the beginning of Bach's 'Prelude in C minor' and the bridge in the 'Toccata, Adagio, and Fugue in C',[17] as well as de la Tombelle's 'Marche Pontificale'.[18] Although the matter of weight was not specifically mentioned, it is clear how it was provided for in the suggested registrations. It is often noticeable that a registration planned to fit one aspect of given musical material is equally adapted to meet other requirements, because of consistency, either natural or artistic, in the elements of the music. Let us glance at two or three other examples, observing them with special reference to the question of weight.

A comparison of the first and last movements of Widor's *Symphony in G minor*, Number 6, is instructive, particularly because of the apparent similarity of their material — big, detached chords, like spacing, and *fff* dynamic indication. But the one is in minor and the other in major. Moreover the last movement is much faster, and the element of motion is further emphasized by the prevailing quarter- and eighth-note values as against the half- and quarter-note values of the first movement. The last movement, therefore, should be registered for clarity — as much high pitch as possible without screechiness, ample eight-foot tone (since the range is high), and just enough sixteen-foot tone to bridge the gap between the manual and pedal parts. In the first movement the chords are long enough to give an impression of heaviness, which should be augmented in the registration. Upper pitches are still needed to produce a triple forte, but as much eight- and sixteen-foot tone should be included as the spacing will allow. The effect should be massive without being thick or clumsy. This will be accomplished by employing a large proportion of reed tone, with many pitches of diapasons for cohesion and richness. The same impression of weight at a softer level and lower pitch is demanded at the bottom of page 8. This requires a still larger proportion of reeds, at all pitches, played on a secondary manual and reduced to mezzo forte by the swell box.

In the first movement of Widor's *Symphonie Gothique* the composer attempts to suggest the lofty grandeur of a Gothic cathedral. The broad sweep of the architectural lines, as well as the sense of vastness and permanence, led him to develop his material with almost uninterrupted

[17]See pp. 134-5.
[18]See pp. 135-6.

continuity. He was obliged, therefore, to give the impression of massiveness without the advantage of weight of attack. This he accomplished with remarkable success by means of his close spacing, the relatively low pitch, and the indicated registration – foundation stops and reeds at sixteen-, eight-, and four-foot pitches, the moving part, in general, being brought out by the flues against the reeds. Because of the heavy voicing of the average American organ, it is very difficult for us to duplicate this effect. The reeds must usually be assisted by mixtures (which should not be definitely heard), and the proportion of sixteen-foot flues greatly reduced. A certain amount of weight will lend drive to the motion, by seeming to provide something to overcome; but it must not sound logy or unwieldy.

The most magnificent example in all literature is the great six-part setting of 'Aus tiefer Not schrei ich zu dir' in Bach's *Clavierübung*, Part III. Here the impression of weight is produced by the large number of voices and the resulting close spacing at a relatively low range. The polyphonic texture will not permit too heavy a registration, but the large number of upper ranks which are essential must be well absorbed. Ideally the cantus firmus should be played on the Solo Tuba by an assistant. This not only gives the melody the prominence which it ought to have, but it clarifies the polyphony by separating out one of the lower voices. Moreover it makes it possible to enhance the massive effect by providing a solid sixteen-foot pedal, perhaps even including a thirty-two-foot tone, which would be impossible if double pedaling were used. [19]

Lightness

Lightness, being the contrary of heaviness, obviously calls for the opposite registration procedure. It is favored by high pitches, lack of loudness, wide pitch spacing, short duration, promptness of perception, and a quick, natural attack. More specifically, it will be effected by the following methods:

The upper pitches will be not only present, but audible; so a cohesive ensemble will be avoided. High flutes, tending to emphasize their own pitch, are useful. Mutations should be used sparingly, mixtures rarely, and sixteen-foot tone almost never. Loud stops and combinations will be avoided. An open soft combination is lighter than a louder combination in a closed box. If it is necessary to increase the loudness, it is best done by adding high pitches. Staccato playing tends toward lightness if the notes are shortened as much as one-half. The prompt speech

[19] It is possible, though extremely difficult, for a single player with long fingers to duplicate this effect. It necessitates coupling the Solo at different pitches to the Swell and Choir manuals, whose own stops are silenced by their unison-release couplers.

which this requires again dictates the use of high ranks. The slow
response of strings and their lack of emphasis on any one pitch make
them unsuited to light effects. Wide spacing tends toward lightness,
both because of the lack of crowding and because of the aural separation
of the higher pitches. A combination of eight- and two-foot stops gives
a lighter impression than one of eight- and four-foot stops both because
the upper pitch is higher and because the tones are farther apart. Indeed,
the addition of a four-foot stop to the eight- and two-foot combination
would make it less light. Similarly, eight- and four-foot flutes are lighter
than eight- and four-foot diapasons, not only because they are softer, but
because of the separate audibility of the upper rank. These effects are
amply illustrated in the examples of quick movement already cited.[20]

Spacing

The spacing of the musical material is a characteristic of the texture
which must always enter into the interpreter's calculations. It is related
not only to the impression of weight, but to such other qualities as blend,
movement, timbre-interest, mood, and even, in some cases, such practical
considerations as technical limitations. It is the business of the organist to discover the real intention of the composer and bring that out in
his registration. If all the effects which are inherent in the musical
material are essential parts of the composer's conception, they should,
if possible, be faithfully matched in the registration. It sometimes
happens, however, that material which is designed for certain purposes
incidentally produces other effects which are unessential, or even undesirable. This is particularly true in the matter of spacing. In such
cases the registration should show the primary intention of the composer,
and at the same time minimize or compensate for the unessential effect.

In Bach's setting of 'Aus tiefer Not' and the first movement of Widor's
Symphonie Gothique, cited above, all the effects of the close spacing
are consistent with the meaning of the music, except that in the Bach
chorale care must be taken not to allow it to confuse the polyphony. On
the other hand, in the middle section of Brahms's chorale prelude on
'O Gott, du frommer Gott', close spacing at a relatively low pitch serves
purposes of blend, timbre-interest, and mood, but the effect of heaviness
should be avoided. Stops should be chosen which have relatively weak
fundamentals; a string may be added to a light diapason, or possibly a
soft reed may be used. No upper ranks should be heard, as any tendency
to raise the pitch impression would change the mood, and lessen the
contrast with the following phrase.

[20]See pp. 127-8.

Max Reger, particularly in his larger works, often increased the number of voices and thickened the texture in a vain effort to produce more tone. [21] He defeated his purpose, for the resulting heaviness and vagueness reduces the dynamic efficiency of the tone, and the effect is not telling, but depressing and fatiguing. In playing such passages the organist must compensate for the extravagance of the composer by reducing the lower pitches and adding a large proportion of upper ranks — even, if necessary, at the cost of fidelity to the notated pitch. In that way he will more nearly nearly realize the tonal increase which the composer intended.

Wide spacing is less likely to have results which are not a part of the composer's design. However, it serves two distinct purposes which must be differentiated in the registration: It may be intended to provide a wide pitch spread for a cohesive ensemble, or to separate the voices for the sake of clarity. The last section of the 'Invocation' from Reger's *Second Sonata* illustrates the first purpose. It is effectively played on an Unda Maris, whose upper partials serve to fill in the pitch gaps, while the céleste directs attention to the fundamental and shows the outline of the slowly moving voices. The chorale tune may be subtly emphasized by playing it on an adjacent manual (above), using a delicate flute, with a suboctave coupler to provide the octave pitches.

The use of wide spacing for clarity (as well as timbre and mood) is exemplified in the first movement of Franck's 'Fantaisie in C'. This effect should not be modified by any complicating pitches. Eight-foot diapason tone is right for the purpose, shaded by such additions as its voicing and the wide range of the music may require. This registration is more fully discussed under mood. [22] In the last movement of Widor's *Symphonie Gothique*, in the first variation, the two hands are widely separated much of the time, to provide the maximum of isolation and distinctness for each part. A more striking example is found in the same composer's *Symphonie Romane*, at the bottom of page 3. Using exaggeration to explain his purpose to his pupils, the composer suggested playing the left hand on a sixteen-foot Bourdon and the upper part on a four-foot flute!

An example of the simultaneous use of wide and close spacing occurs in the last section of the second movement of Widor's *Symphonie Gothique*. The purpose is to separate the solo so completely from the accompaniment that it will stand out prominently, even though played

---

[21] A notable example is in the final build-up of his monumental 'Fantasia and Fugue in D minor', Opus 135b, which Weigl characterizes as "the crown of Reger's organ works." — Bibl. 133, p. 68.

[22] See p. 163.

pianissimo. Strings are assigned to the lower parts, providing cohesion and avoiding heaviness. According to the composer's registration the pedal (eight-foot, of course) outlines the counter melody by adding a flute to the manual combination. A Gemshorn (not available on his organ) is better, providing enough fundamental for the purpose, but avoiding the vagueness and (at the end) thickness of the flute in that range. A single eight-foot flute is inevitable for the upper melody. At the very end, where a second high voice is added, it must become immediately softer.[23] If this cannot be done with a swell pedal, a similar, softer flute should be substituted if possible.

We often find wide gaps between the voices due to practical considerations, where the composer has assumed, presumably or specifically, compensation in the registration. Such a case in Mendelssohn's *Sonata in F minor*, Number 1, has already been cited.[24] In the last movement of Franck's *Grande Pièce Symphonique*, after the fugal section, the composer has specified the use of suboctave couplers. This is absolutely necessary to fill in the otherwise thin texture of what is intended to be an imposing statement of the theme. In the 'Lento' of Widor's *Symphony in A minor*, Number 7, he has specified the inclusion of a sixteen-foot stop on the manual because of the distance between the manual and pedal parts — or perhaps he provided the gap because he wanted the rich but unmixed tone quality which the sixteen-, eight-, and four-foot diapasons would give.

The Interpretation of the Composer's Intention

Some of the foregoing examples have shown that, in adapting our registration to the material of the music, we need to consider not only its characteristics, but its significance. "To enhance what in inherent in the music" involves not merely the clear and effective presentation of the notes which the composer wrote, but the realization of the composer's design. The organist must not only interpret, but supplement the composer's notation. Some of the principles involved have been illustrated by typical examples selected from works which are easily accessible to the reader. At best, these are only suggestive. The full realization of the intentions of the composer requires thorough musicianship, broad scholarship, profound study, and intuitive insight. The printed page cannot bring the reader to that goal; it can only point the way.

[23]Cf. p. 97.
[24]P. 139.

CHAPTER SEVEN
COLOR AND MOOD
Expressive Registration

Up to this point we have been dealing with physical phenomena. Starting with observable, measurable characteristics of sound, we developed a logical, practical procedure designed to present these characteristics to the listener with fidelity, revealed in proportion to their artistic significance. Even the texture, rhythm, and other features of the composer's material proved to be but ramifications of the essential physical behavior of sound; however skillfully and ingeniously employed, they are susceptible of analysis and rational interpretation through registration. It might almost seem that registration is a science rather than an art; that once we have discovered the nature of the musical fabric and the pattern of its weave, the method of illumination is more or less inevitable.

Some will contend, however, that the real substance of music lies beyond the range of the analyst's scrutiny, that all the resources of the various techniques of composition are merely the language of the musical literature, and have no significance beyond the effectiveness with which they express the composer's thought. Others, on the other hand, find real emotional satisfaction in following the logical development of a complex musical structure. The composers themselves are guided by similarly divergent aesthetic philosophies. The important thing for us, regardless of our personal prejudices, is to recognize and evaluate the different elements in the music which we are interpreting, and be guided by their proportionate contributions to the whole effect.

It is probably safe to assume that most composers have been moved by something more than the mere satisfaction of creation. They have sought to make an aesthetic and emotional appeal beyond the appreciation of design, technical skill, and finesse. These abstract functions are not susceptible of the detailed analysis which we have applied to the material which the composer has used. They cannot be resolved into specific acoustical effects which the registration must expose. They are the product of the imagination, and must be intuitively recognized. Nevertheless, they are interpreted through tones which, in their essence, have no characteristic other than frequency and intensity. In order to make effective use of our means of interpretations we need to understand the relationship between these elemental characteristics and the aesthetic purpose of the composer. Such an understanding is the aim of this chapter.

It is obvious that, however abstract may be the composer's conception, he himself is obliged to express it through the complex manipulation of these same elements of frequency and intensity. But, just as a complex combination of pitches is heard as tone quality, so the art of the composer produces an impression which is independent of any recognition of the mechanism employed. If, following the methods already developed, the registration is planned for the most effective presentation of the composer's material, it will naturally contribute to the aesthetic effect which the material is intended to make. The interpreter should go further, however, and seek to enhance that effect. This involves finding some relation between tone quality, per se, and the unreasoned impression of the music itself.

Functions of Tone Color

We have already noted the independent significance of tone quality in the last chapter, where it was suggested that timbre-interest be added to compensate for a paucity of motional or textural interest.[1] This timbre-interest we call color; the analogy to color in painting, as regards both function and effect, is very close. The word is also applied to vertical harmonic interest, which is another method of combining different pitches to produce various qualities. Acoustically and interpretatively, harmonic and tone color are identical, except for the elements of tendency and succession, which involve a horizontal conception. The desirability of fitting the tone color to the harmonic color has been mentioned in the discussion of Franck's 'Choral in A minor'.[2] Moreover, color may be used to bring out certain details of the material. For example, the use of a special timbre for a melody will not only serve to prevent it from blending with the accompanying parts, but its very color will attract the attention of the listener, and thus give the melody added prominence. This of course applies particularly to melodies with slight motional interest.[3]

In addition to these textural values, color has two independent functions: sensuous appeal, and the interpretation of mood.

Aesthetic Criteria

An adequate discussion of the purely aesthetic effect of color would lead us into the mazes of psychology and philosophy. The practical value of such a digression would be doubtful. This is, indeed, the phase of the problem of registration which is the least scientific, the most

[1] See pp. 125-6, 129, &c.
[2] P. 140.
[3] See p. 126.

controversial, and the most dependent on the caprices of individual taste. What is beautiful to one is ugly to another, and neither can be proven right or wrong. The harmonies of Wagner are trite to the devotee of contemporary idioms, but they would have sounded cacophonic to a sixteenth century musician. Similarly the subtle purity of Dufay is dull to the romanticist who finds in Wagner his supreme ideal of beauty. In organ registration, some persons find combinations beautifully clear and bright which others consider intolerably screechy; some revel in the luscious effects of a Vox Humana and other extravagant colors which are offensive to the taste of others. However confident we may be in the correctness of our own taste, we cannot deny to others the right to an entirely different idea of what is beautiful.

The nearest we can come to establishing a reliable standard is to find a concensus of the taste of a large number of musicians over a period of time. Those aesthetic values are highest of which the sensitive ear does not weary, and which satisfy the greatest number of connoisseurs over a long period of changing fashion. Thus we may rate Palestrina and Bach higher than Schumann because the music of the former composers, though not contemporary in spirit, is as much alive and as keenly enjoyed by musicians today as it was two or four centuries ago, while the music of Schumann, after only a hundred years, begins to sound obvious. So also the rich ensemble of diapason tones which was characteristic of the German organs of the time of Bach is still satisfying, and can be heard for a long time without undue fatigue. On the other hand, many who, thirty years ago, took delight in the lavish coloring of floating string sections and other attempts to convert the organ into an orchestra, which were then popular, now find such effects distasteful. Even when it was in vogue, such vivid coloring had a short span of effectiveness; it soon cloyed.

If we accept permanence and universality of appeal — the continued verdict of a large number and diversity of cultured listeners — as the most valid aesthetic criterion, how are we to appraise new effects? Obviously there can be no continued verdict concerning novelties. We can, however, make some deductions from the experience of the past. It appears that the qualities which give aesthetic satisfaction to the greatest number of persons over a long period of time are those which, in Chapter V,[4] we found to be the least fatiguing. The appeal of extreme qualities is limited, both in duration and in prevalence. Qualities which are most generally recognized as beautiful are characterized by moderation, ease of perception, naturalness of transition (absence of shock),

[4]P. 108

and balanced proportions. The last characteristic applies not merely to the composition of timbre, but to the overall interpretation of the music. Any departure from the norm should be balanced by a longer period of normality, or even a deviation in another direction. This equilibrium may be maintained in a specific composition, or it may be extended over a group, an entire program, or even a series of programs. This principle will be taken up again in the last chapter. Our present purpose is to show that preference for medial qualities is not to be interpreted as exclusive, or even deprecative, of the use of more extreme qualities. On the contrary, they have an important function if they do not assume too large a place in the total scheme. Intermediate colors should be usual; vivid colors should serve some special purpose.

How beautifully all this is exemplified in nature! Gorgeous sunsets are only occasional; the variegated colors of the autumn foliage last but a short time; bright colored flowers are found in relatively small patches — but the prevailing color of the landscape is a modest green, varied in shade and giving way, to a certain extent, to white in winter. If the latter tries the eyes, it is a physical, not an aesthetic fatigue. The sea is constantly changing, with an infinite variety of shades of blue and gray. The light may dazzle, but brilliant colors are relatively infrequent. The organist will do well to emulate nature, striving to achieve variety within a medial range; then when the music calls for special treatment, vivid coloring will be all the more effective because it is unusual.

Relation between Color and Mood

It is not possible completely to isolate the decorative from the emotional function of color. The former contributes to the latter. One may be greatly moved by sheer beauty, as in the contemplation of a sunset, or a flower. The stimulus, however, is more than sensory. The effect is greatly enhanced by the form of the clouds and the landscape below; or the shape and proportions of the flower, and its setting amid the green foliage. The appreciation of design is involved; but there is also a direct connection between color and mood.

The association of physical qualities of tone with analogous emotional qualities is illustrated by a parallelism in nomenclature. Such words as "somber" and "bright" apply equally to color and mood, and the qualities so described correspond. A somber timbre suggests a somber mood, or sadness; a bright timbre suggests a bright mood, or happiness. This association derives from the natural, spontaneous vocal expression of emotion.

Natural Expression of Emotion

If a child runs to his mother in excitement, she does not need to hear his words in order to know whether he is moved by joy or grief, or by fear or anger. Or if he is merely relating a story, she can tell from his tone of voice and inflection whether the incident is pleasant or sad, or humorous, or just interesting. The tonal characteristics by which the mother recognizes the mood of the child are composed of the same basic elements — selected frequencies of varying degrees of intensity — which constitute the raw material of music. The musical equivalent of the child's inflection is the expressive use of melody; his "tone of voice" is represented by the timbre of the musical tones and the synchronous effect of harmony — that is, by color. In order to reproduce in music this spontaneous vocal expression of mood, we need to know its component elements. To that end let us try to discover the physiological conditions which accompany the expression of different emotions.

Sadness is naturally accompanied by lassitude. One who feels merely sad does not use enough energy to raise his voice; he speaks in a low pitch with only moderate power. His cheeks are flabby, so that they absorb the higher partials, but not the lower ones. Part of the tone may pass through the nose, encouraging partials of medium pitch. So sadness and gloominess are expressed by audible low pitches which are fairly soft, and have a moderate development of upper partials.

If the feeling of sadness is more intense, more energy is expended. This results in a slight raising of the pitch, and a forcing of the tone, increasing and perhaps even exaggerating the upper partials. Moreover, there is a tenseness of the muscles which tightens the walls of the resonance cavities, so that there is less absorption of the upper partials. Intense sadness, then, is expressed by a medium or moderately low pitch, a fair degree of loudness, and a high development of partials.

On the other side of the emotional range, joy is accompanied by spontaneous energy, which is free from stiffness or forcing. The pitch goes up easily, retaining its natural partials. The muscles of the face are resilient but not tense, encouraging the lower partials, but not the extremely high ones. Joy is accordingly expressed by audible high tones which are fairly loud and not very complex.

If joy is accompanied by excitement, the amount of energy is increased, with a consequent tendency toward forcing, and more tenseness in the walls of the resonance cavities. All of this increases the proportion of upper partials. The addition of tonal complexity, then, as with the use of many mutations and high pitched reeds, would express more excitement.

Relation between Mood and Pitch

Thus we see that somberness is expressed by audible low pitches, and brightness by audible high pitches. Between these two extremes every shade of color can be provided, representing every degree of the emotional gamut, by following the pitch range. The parallel gradations of emotion and color coincide throughout the range; the identity of nomenclature does not always hold, but the equivalence of mood and color is continuous. Partials will, of course, be proportioned so as to intensify the essential pitch impression. In any range, greater intensity, excitement, or violence, is expressed by tonal complexity. The following examples, illustrating the expression of various specific moods through pitch and color, will show the significance and practical application of this correspondence.

Taking up first the composer's use of pitch and color, we will cite a few familiar examples from Handel's *The Messiah*. He chose a bass voice for 'The people that walked in darkness', usually leading the melody downward for the word "darkness", and upward for the word "light". On the other hand, the two joyful arias, 'Rejoice greatly' and 'I know that my Redeemer liveth', are assigned to the soprano. An alto sings 'He was despised and rejected', the rich complement of lower partials serving to enhance the somber effect of the relatively low range. The entire aria contains only a single note above bb^1. Then in the incomparable recitative and arioso, 'Thy rebuke hath broken his heart' (the most eloquent pages of the entire oratorio), the tenor voice, singing half an octave below the range of the alto aria, lends great intensity through the complexity of the tone, which contains a large proportion of high partials.

Passing on to the field of instrumental music, we note how the mood of funeral music is almost invariably set by low pitches; a later use of a higher range often suggests peace, personal qualities of the deceased, etc. The following may profitably be studied from this standpoint: 'Marcia funebre' from Beethoven's *Sinfonia eroica*; the 'Trauermusik' from the last act of Wagner's *Götterdämmerung*; and the funeral marches from Beethoven's *Sonata in A flat*, Opus 26, and Chopin's *Sonata in B flat minor*. The last movement of Beethoven's *Fifth Symphony* begins with an outburst of joy which is naturally expressed in high pitches, while the setting of Schiller's 'Ode to Joy' in the last movement of the *Ninth Symphony* goes so far as to tax the participating singers. In the 'Vorspiel' to Wagner's *Lohengrin* the beatific mysteries of Montsalvat and the holy Grail are introduced by a diffusion of high pitches.

The reader will immediately recall many examples which seem to contravene these principles. Obviously pitch is not the only means of suggesting mood, and other considerations may influence the range of the material; but the foregoing examples do demonstrate a relation between pitch and mood which, from the standpoint of color, is inescapable. Related to this effect of pitch range is the effect of pitch spacing. Tones which are close together produce lower difference tones than those which are farther apart. The difference tones may not be audible, but the mood follows their tendency. So close spacing tends to darken the color and the mood, while wide spacing tends toward brightness. The impression of weight also has an influence similar to the lower pitch. It is impossible to separate these factors from the absolute pitch element, but they all share in the total effect.

Somber Registration

Turning now to the field of organ music, we will examine a greater variety of examples, noting the composer's method of expressing his mood, and attempting to find a registration which will interpret it through color.

A striking example of somber color, confirmed by the composer's own registration, is Tournemire's 'Fioretto, Number 4', from *Sei Fioretti*. The exclusive use of sixteen-foot tone keeps the pitch low. Moreover the indicated stops are poor in upper partials, except the soft reed, which lends definition in the lowest range, but is removed for the second theme which lies higher.[5] It is obviously the intention of the composer to keep the pitch as low as possible, with emphasis on the fundamental, including only such upper partials as are necessary from the standpoint of audibility. On American organs his registration would be too heavy, but we should respect his primary purpose and avoid, if possible, the use of keen strings and upper ranks.

Similar in color, but more intense in mood, is the third movement, 'Crucifixion', of Dupré's *Symphonie-Passion*. The thirty-two foot pedal with an audible sixteen-foot tone (Violon), and the low-lying melody on the soft sixteen- and eight-foot reeds, suggest the extreme depth of gloom. When, in measure 12, an eight-foot manual combination is substituted,[6] the mood is continued by the closely spaced dissonant chords.

---

[5]Two printer's errors should be noted, unless they are corrected in later impressions: In measure 4 there should be a treble clef for the left hand. At measure 10 there should be a minus sign before "Bombarde".

[6]The registration suggested for American organs is not ideal. Most French Horns would sound clumsy, rather than sad.

Less gloomy, but still somber, is the first section of Franck's 'Prière in C sharp minor'. The prevailing pitch is slightly higher, but the spacing is close. Although only eight-foot stops are indicated, the quality is intended to be warm and rich. The American organist may wish, in order to avoid thickness, to add a few soft upper ranks and reduce the fundamental — but the upper pitches must be completely absorbed.

Franck's 'Pièce Héroïque' is similar in mood and range, but it has more vitality and intensity. These qualities are provided by the reeds and upper work of the Récit (Swell), which are under the control of the swell box. Even when the box opens, the sixteen-foot tone in the Grand Orgue (which has the tune) preserves the somberness of color and mood, at the same time allowing the "heroic" quality to emerge as the pitch rises and reeds are added to the Positif (Choir).

Vierne's 'Marche funèbre' from his *24 Pièces en style libre* specifies foundation stops and reeds of sixteen-, eight-, and four-foot pitch. The range is relatively low, and the prevailing five- and six-part chords provide close spacing. The mood is not only somber but intense, demanding a very complex ensemble. The "smothered fire" of the brilliant sixteen-, eight-, and four-foot reeds within a swell box is ideal, and it must not be covered by the diapasons. Mixtures and mutations may be added in so far as they contribute to the reed tone, but the pitch impression must not be raised. When such a concentrated, complex tone is released by the opening of the swell shades, the increase in intensity as well as dynamics gives poignant expression to the emotional development of the music.

We have observed in the foregoing examples that as the intensity of the mood has increased, the ensemble has included more upper pitches and proportionately less fundamental. The upper pitches have not been allowed to be heard, but have added complexity to the tone. Reeds have become more prominent, and four-foot reeds have been included. Upper ranks which stress their own pitch have been avoided, as intensity is a result of cohesive complexity.

Obviously there are degrees of intensity of mood, and the most poignant emotion is not necessarily expressed by loud tones. Herbert Howells, in his 'Psalm-Prelude, Number 3', suggests the "valley of the shadow of death" by low, soft tones. Since at that dynamic level upper ranks cannot be so completely absorbed, complexity must be provided by the voicing of individual stops, in order not to raise the pitch impression. Strings should be used; a Voix Céleste will avoid thinness and enhance the emotional effect. The quality of the melody should be slightly exotic, so that the listener hears it as something different. A Clarinet is admirable for the purpose, possibly warmed by the inclusion of the Voix

Céleste. A good English Horn would also be suitable. Where the texture thickens, on the second page (page 3), the Voix Céleste needs to be slightly reinforced – perhaps by a very light diapason or Geigen. On page 4 the element of confidence appears ("I will fear no evil"); the pitch rises and the registration should change.

In this piece by Howells the mood is conveyed by rhythmic and melodic means, and the minor mode, stressing the downward leaning of the sixth tone of the scale. In Honegger's 'Choral', beginning at the eighth measure, there is a similar intensity expressed more by synchronous effects – dissonance and harmonic color. This calls for greater cohesion among the voices and permits a smaller fundamental. The tone will be built on broad strings or a light Geigen. Soft upper work may contribute richness, but the pitch impression must be concentrated in the fundamental without any sense of heaviness. As the pitch rises, there must be more fundamental without loss of complexity.

Flor Peeters' 'Élégie' in memory of his mother begins in a mood of gloom and restrained intensity of emotion. The low pitch is accentuated by the fundamental emphasis of the Oboe and a Bourdon 16', enriched by eight- and four-foot strings. A lighter sixteen-foot stop could be substituted with advantage. The essential condition is a cohesive spread from sixteen- to four-foot, with the eight-foot tone dominant. The low pitch provides somberness, and the strings add some degree of intensity. As the movement develops the pitch rises, the number of parts is increased, keeping the spacing close, and the music becomes louder and more intense, reaching a very poignant fortissimo at the climax, from which it subsides to the original effect. In order to follow this development the tone quality must be kept complex and focused. Reeds will dominate the ensemble, amply enriched by absorbed upper work. The combination will include as much sixteen-foot tone as is possible without heaviness, but no flutes or large diapasons. The increase in intensity must be matched in the registration by increased complexity, loudness, and dynamic efficiency. The new mood of the coda will be taken up later.

Somberness and brightness, sadness and happiness, are opposite color and mood phases, represented respectively by low and high audible pitches. The organist, seeking to interpret the emotional quality of the music in his registration, will stress the particular pitch range which corresponds to the mood, adjusting the tonal complexity to the intensity of the mood expressed. But, since the composer's emotional vocabulary includes other elements, such as tonality, melodic contour, spacing, dissonance, external associations, etc., the organist will not merely nor necessarily present clearly the actual pitches which the composer has written; he may slight, or even alter the pitch emphasis to suit the total expression of the music. Obviously this is not an exact, purely logical process. The method has been illustrated in the discussion of music of a somber character; it will now be applied to various other degrees of the mood-color gamut.

Warm Color — Sentimental Mood

The next emotional level for us to consider is popularly called "expressive". Perhaps this inaccurate use of the word springs from the type of emotion which was most frequently expressed by composers of the romantic school, and from the implication of such directions as *espressivo*, and *con espressione*. It suggests a mood which is neither happy nor sad, but is by no means neutral. It lies between brightness and somberness, leaning rather toward the latter, but characterized more by fervor than by the emotional phase or direction. We might call it "tender". Its tonal characteristics are: medium pitch, not more than moderate loudness, a rich but normal development of partials, and elasticity. Since the upper pitches must be completely absorbed, they will in general be supplied by the voicing of individual stops, rather than by high ranks. Moreover, the aggressiveness of loud reeds and the crisp attack of small pipes should generally be avoided.

To meet these requirements strings are often effective, but they usually require some compensation for their meager fundamental. They may therefore be combined with other qualities, or their fundamental may be expanded by the Voix Céleste, which also enhances the "expressive" effect by its vibrato, imitating the natural vocal unsteadiness which is caused by emotion. A similar purpose is served by the tremolo (for those who do not find it offensive), which lends an emotional quality to the inflexible tone of reeds.

Since music of this type is usually rather slow, it will be profitable to review, from the standpoint of mood, the examples of slow movement discussed in the last chapter.[7] In general we will find that the qualities chosen to give timbre interest to the long tones possess the complexity needed to provide emotional intensity. In the interpretation of Bach's setting of 'Herzlich tut mich verlangen' the expressive requirements would be met by playing the solo on a Trumpet (with or without tremolo), a Clarinet, an English Horn, or a Voix Céleste. The preference for a Trumpet without tremolo still holds for the reasons previously given, and also because, since the music itself is free from exaggeration, its interpretation should accordingly be somewhat restrained. We will resist the

[7]Pp. 129-32.

temptation to increase the intensity of the accompaniment for the same reason, and also in order to keep it separate from, and subordinate to, the solo.

Our registration for the middle section of Vierne's 'Clair de lune'[8] makes use of the expressive characteristics of the 'Cello Céleste, and is justified by the fervor of the music. Our registration is preferable to that of the composer from the emotional standpoint as well as that of audibility. Vierne assigned his most eloquent quality to the accompaniment, which merely furnishes a background for the pedal tune; but the emotion in this section is concentrated in the melody, which should, accordingly, have the more expressive tone quality.

The use of the Voix Céleste for harmonic slow movements has been discussed from the textural standpoint,[9] but it is probable that composers chose it rather for expressive reasons. A notable example is the 'Adagio' from Widor's *Symphony in G minor*, Number 6. This music, which the composer admitted was conceived as for the orchestral strings, and which is expressed in a Wagnerian idiom, *demands* the Voix Céleste — shaded, perhaps, by a Geigen and other mild strings. The Vox Humana again falls in the same category, but since it derives much of its emotional effect from the peculiar throbbing which the tremolo lends to its unique quality, many organists prefer to find another method of expressing the desired mood. For example, a Gedeckt 8' combined with eight- and four-foot strings provides a suitable degree of complexity for the mood and pitch of the last movement of Franck's 'Fantaisie in C'. The music is too placid for the Vox Humana anyway.

As this "expressive" mood is shaded toward somberness, it may simply become darker, or it may become more intense. The darkening may be accomplished by merely lowering the pitch. Thus Tournemire's registration for his 'Fioretto, Number 6' (Quintaton 16', Bourdon 16', Salicional 8') is similar to that suggested above for Franck's 'Fantaisie in C', but since it is based on a sixteen-foot fundamental, the pitch level is lower, and the effect is more somber. A somewhat similar quality is called for in Karg-Elert's 'Harmonies du soir', page 2; but here the sixteen-foot tone is sub-fundamental, and the upper combination should be more complex.

Such complexity, enriching the ensemble with ranks of many pitches (including a light sixteen-foot) which, though absorbed in a single tonal impression, are not strongly concentrated in the fundamental, is one of the most effective means of darkening the color and mood without

[8]Pp. 131-2.
[9]Pp. 136-7.

causing undue heaviness. The combination suggested in the previous
chapter[10] for the chorale theme in Franck's 'Choral in A minor' serves
this purpose. A comparable effect is suggested by Flor Peeters for his
setting of 'Ick wil mi gaen vertroosten' (I will be comforted) – Number 8
of his *Orgelchoräle*. The Quintaton 16', soft Gamba 8', and Flauto
Dolce 4' provide a complex ensemble which is cohesive except for the
slight prominence of the four-foot flute, which serves to outline the
voice leading. The relatively high pitch might put this in a somewhat
bright category except for the tune, which is sung in the tenor range by
a Cromorne 8' and Dulciana 16'.

Brahms's second version of 'Herzlich tut mich verlangen' sets the mood
in the accompaniment, developing a motive borrowed from Bach's *Orgelbüchlein* setting of 'Ich ruf zu dir'. The low range of the material
dictates a complex tone without too much fundamental, while its fluency
requires the use of upper ranks rather than strings or reeds. Fidelity to
the fundamental pitch impression is essential to preserve the mood, and
moderation in the use of upper ranks is necessary, lest they become
obtrusive when the music rises above the middle of the keyboard, as in
measure 5 and corresponding places. These requirements suggest a well-
balanced ensemble, ranging from the fundamental to the Tierce. Against
this combination the melody stands out with a fairly smooth reed, which
may be varied for the repetition. The mood is preserved by the prevailing
moderately low pitch and the complexity of the tone quality. The change
in material at the end of measure 11 calls for an increased proportion of
fundamental. Here the sixteenth-note motion avoids the lower range,
and there is an implied imitation of the melody which, in measure 13,
becomes a reality.

Progressive intensity is often characteristic of the development of
compositions with strong emotional content. This is strikingly exemplified in Franck's 'Cantabile in B'. A detailed study of the composer's
use of various expressive devices – pitch, dynamics, melodic form,
tonality, harmonic color, dissonance – intriguing as it would be, would
delay us too long. We must content ourselves with noting the general
effect of this development on the registration. The registration suggested in the previous chapter[11] suits the almost placid beginning, but
contains enough complexity to make it adaptable to the subtle gradation
of mood, and susceptible of intensification by the swell shades. When
the melody is transferred to the tenor, the more complex timbre, formerly
suggested to compensate for the lower pitch, serves also to enhance its

[10]P. 140.
[11]Pp. 132, 138.

darkening effect on the mood. As the pitch rises and the boxes open, the quality becomes more intense. When, after the second phrase of the tenor melody, the right-hand part assumes more responsibility for the mood, its complexity should be accordingly increased, providing a plastic ensemble against which the focused intensity of the reed will stand out clearly. The material changes over the F♯ pedal point. The right-hand part, more static, more dependent on synchronous effects, needs, if possible, the restrained fire of enclosed reeds, which can be released at will; the left-hand part, with its quicker but restricted motion, needs greater flexibility, and should have a large proportion of flue stops, sufficiently incisive to cut through the ensemble. This piece presents an intricate registration problem, both from the interpretative and from the practical standpoint.

Registration for Placid Moods

We now come to the border line between somber and bright. We might think of the color as neutral, shading toward brightness or darkness as the mood leans toward contentment or pensiveness. The tonal expression will use clearly audible medium pitches, with a minimum of complexity. The partial content will depend on the actual pitch range and mood shades of the music. Flutes are suitable if easily heard; below their effective range more upper partials must be provided, but in order to preserve the impression of simplicity, the number of stops should be kept small.

For unalloyed placidity we will look at the beginning of Franck's 'Fantaisie in C'. The clarity of the lower tones requires a good proportion of upper partials, but they must not be sufficient to intensify the upper voice. A mellow but light diapason is ideal, but it may be necessary to add a small gedeckt to keep the upper tones from being thin, and a soft Oboe, or possibly a mild string, to lend definition to the bass. The wide spacing compensates for the resulting complexity (if it is not exaggerated), keeping the mood placid. The more fluent material of the canonic section calls for a change, even though the mood remains the same. The pedal line must be clearly audible; the left-hand part needs some four-foot tone (soft eight- and four-foot diapasons are good), both for fluency and to keep the lower pitch from darkening the mood; the melody is best sung by a smooth reed, which will remain separate and at the same time meet the requirements of pitch and mood. The return to the intensified repetition of the first material requires some ingenuity.

Brahms's second setting of 'O Welt, ich muss dich lassen' expresses a deeper placidness – contentment tinged with longing, suggested by the text. The registration for the principal phrases can be similar to that suggested for the beginning of the Franck 'Fantaisie' – a mild diapason, modified, if necessary, to provide a warm color without either thinness or heaviness. The lower pitch, the five-part writing, and close spacing unite to intensify the mood. The echoes should be less intense, but the low range of the second calls for mild strings, while the imitation of the melodic cadence (usually in the alto) can be brought out on an unobtrusive solo stop.[12]

Registration to Express Quiet Joy

On the other side, a placid mood often contains an element of brightness, suggesting quiet joy. This calls for clearly audible tones in the upper middle range. It is a region where flutes begin to be effective, and their simple tonal structure is admirably suited to express this mood. At the same time they serve to clarify the gentle fluency which often characterizes this sort of music. Unless the pitch range is high a four-foot flute must be included. For low tones the eight-foot element must be modified to avoid vagueness and heaviness. Often a Quintadena or a Gemshorn may be substituted for the eight-foot flute. The Quintadena, being an exaggerated gedeckt, is particularly useful for this purpose if it is not too nasal. Its small fundamental lacks the heaviness of flutes in the lower range, while the absence of even partials tends to keep it separate from the four-foot flute. The use of an eight-foot string is less satisfactory; the four-foot flute, instead of keeping completely separate, joins with the string to form an exotic quality which is neither placid nor bright.

The following examples illustrate the musical expression of this mood of quiet joy, and the adaptability of eight- and four-foot flute combinations to its interpretation. The registration is of course subject to modification as suggested in the foregoing paragraph, and also to meet the special requirements of the individual pieces. In studying these compositions in the light of our theory of the relation of pitch to mood, it should be noted that the sixteen-foot pedal is sparingly used; when it does occur it is separate from the ensemble, serving as a background (often a pedal point) against which the mood is pictured.

Brahms's collection of *Elf Choralvorspiele* contains two characteristic examples: (1) 'Es ist ein' Ros' entsprungen' combines gentle happiness with naïveté, perfectly interpreting the mediaeval Christmas text. The effect of eight- and four-foot flutes should be approached as closely as possible without vagueness. Where the melody occurs in the tenor, it should be brought out by a not too characteristic solo stop – probably a light reed. (2) A somewhat deeper joy is expressed in 'O wie selig seid

[12]Cf. p. 158.

ihr doch'. Here the four-foot flute should remain in evidence, but the spacing is too close, and the pitch too low, to use an eight-foot flute for the lower parts. The unison pitch may be provided by a Quintadena, or perhaps a Dulciana or other mild string, and possibly one or two delicate mutations may be added. In order to show the occasional crossing of parts, the tenor should be very slightly differentiated from the other voices, the bass being played by the feet. Then the sixteen-foot pedal which is called for at the end can be provided by adding the lower D. With the exercise of some ingenuity it is possible to play this setting on four different keyboards. In that case it is not necessary to hold to the flute registration, since transparency is provided by the individuality of the voices. Their differentiation, however, should be subtle, avoiding any impression of either complexity or heterogeneity.

Similar examples could be multiplied indefinitely. The 'Choral' from Widor's Easter *Symphonie Romane* is too obvious to call for comment. In Tournemire's 'Fioretto, Number 3', from his *Sei Fioretti*, the tranquil cheerfulness of the rather discursive flutes is interrupted from time to time by the introduction of vertical texture in the right hand, to which the composer has assigned the seemingly commonplace combination: Vox Humana, Voix Céleste, Gedeckt. The pitch is too high for warmth, and the exotic harmonies, together with the persistence of the contrasting flute, produce an effect of color rather than sentimentality.

A Complex Example

The last page of Flor Peeters' 'Élégie' in memory of his mother (quoted in Example 10) presents a more complex emotional situation. The anguish and gloom of the first three pages[13] give place to a sense of resignation, as he thinks of her present happy state. The persistent syncopated pedal point which has dominated the first part of the piece is now in the background, transferred to an inner voice; it soon subsides and finally ceases. Above it is heard the serene melody of the funeral antiphon, 'In paradisum', which is sung during the procession to the cemetery, after the Requiem Mass. The composer's registration, even making allowance for the brighter voicing of French and Belgian organs, does not convey the emotion which is unmistakably suggested in the music. The intensity of his tone color contradicts the implications of the high pitch and of the melody quoted, while the flute, to which the melody is later assigned in a lower pitch, is quite inarticulate in that range. The writer's registration follows:

The syncopated repeated notes are played on a Quintadena alone,

[13]See p. 159.

whose melancholy odd partials preserve the undercurrent of sadness
which the persistent rhythm suggests. For the pedal a Dulciana 16' is
used, avoiding the heaviness of the more common Bourdon. The pitch
and material of the upper parts suggest a single eight-foot flute. A

Example 10. Peeters: Élégie

harmonic flute would be effective, but since the composer's vision of his mother in paradise is tinged with sadness, we will choose a light Rohrflöte, whose odd-partials color lends subtle intensity to the tone. Gradually the vision is obscured by a sense of loss; the melody drops into the alto and is sung by the French Horn (if it is not too fat), whose added intensity is desirable from both the standpoint of audibility and that of mood. In the last phrase he sees his mother through a veil of quiet grief. The tenor melody may be given to a good Vox Humana *without* tremolo, the right hand playing on a very delicate Gemshorn or Spitzflöte.

Registration for Happy Moods

Having paused to discuss this work at some length because of the exceptional opportunity it provides for the interpretation of various shades of mood through registration, we will now continue our course through the emotional gamut. The increased brightness of flutes as they rise in pitch is illustrated in examples cited in Chapter VI:[14] The addition of a two-foot flute in the scherzo of Vierne's *Second Symphony* unites with the lively movement to produce a merry mood. Still gayer is the fugal episode in the scherzo of Guilmant's *Fifth Sonata*, where the two-foot flute is made conspicuous by the absence of four-foot tone; also the staccato playing not only lends vivacity, but it emphasizes the high tones which respond more quickly than the eight-foot rank.

Of course the happy moods expressed by high flutes lack vitality. They range from gentle joy to merriness and quiet gaiety, but they do not include jubilation. Here again the musical expression follows the natural vocal reaction. As the degree of happiness is suggested by the audible pitch, so the vitality of the emotion is represented by the degree of loudness. Its interpretation is limited by the loudness which can be attained without the upper pitches being absorbed. Fortissimo brightness is possible only when the fundamental pitches are high.

One of the happiest of Bach's chorale preludes is the setting of 'In dir ist Freude'. The texture, the lively movement throughout a wide range, and the reiterated 'joy' theme in the bass, unite to provide an interpretation of the word "Freude" which is easily vitiated by a dull or strident registration. The ensemble should be composed of eight-, four-, and two-foot diapasons, with the possible addition of a few four- and two-foot flutes, and one or two quint mixtures.[15] The amount of eight-foot and

[14]P. 127

[15]Mixtures having only octave- and fifth-sounding ranks (see p. 47). The inclusion of other ranks increases the cohesion, reduces the spacing, and impairs the effectiveness of the high pitches.

mutation tone should be barely sufficient to preserve the fundamental pitch and avoid confusion in the polyphony. In a word, the mood demands that the high tones be as audible as possible without violating the requirements of pitch fidelity, of the texture, and of euphony. Since the bass function of the pedal is secondary, it should share the mood of the ensemble by omitting the sixteen-foot tone and including a maximum of upper work. This is also advantageous for the imitation of the tneme in measures 7 and 24. The sixteen-foot tone may well be added to lend weight to the cantus firmus when it appears in the pedals, and to support the ensemble at cadences, where the bass function predominates.

The 'Fugue in C' from the 'Toccata, Adagio, and Fugue' is still gayer. The natural brightness of the prevailingly high range and lively movement is enhanced by a simple and transparent texture. Rapid figures in an obvious pattern are set in single lines, or at most in pairs of similarly moving voices, against a subordinated accompaniment, or in antiphonal imitation. The sense of easy animation and the merry mood call for audible high pitches. The registration will be similar to that of 'In dir ist Freude', but there is less danger of confusing the polyphony by insufficient fundamental, and on the other hand even greater care is required to avoid screechiness.

The toccata of the same work is similar in mood, but somewhat more serious. It is joyous, rather than gay. It calls for more vitality in the registration, and will tolerate less sense of pitch dispersion, although the upper ranks must be sufficiently audible to keep the mood bright. The 'joy' motive (see Example 11)[16] must always be prominent and fluent.

Example 11.   Bach: Toccata in C – 'Joy' motive

Toward the end of the movement reeds may be introduced for the cadences, but they should not be used for the animated material.

A comparison of the foregoing suggestions with those proposed for quick movement[17] shows again the consistency which exists among the various elements of music. The registration required to effect an easy perception of the rapid movement which contributes to the expression of a happy mood is similar to that which the mood itself dictates. The effect of the movement depends on the prompt speech of small pipes and the quick aural response to high frequencies; brightness of mood is suggested by the same conditions, but requires that the upper pitches be

[16]See Bibl. 156, Vol. II, p. 66.
[17]See pp. 126-8.

heard as such, and not absorbed in a lower fundamental. For this reason complex qualities, such as strings and reeds, are less desirable to express happiness. If the reeds are needed for solidity or loudness, implied by such conceptions as triumph or rejoicing, brightness can be secured only by the use of high fundamental pitches.

The composer's use of such means of effect, already noted in choral and orchestral music,[18] is exemplified by the last movements of Widor's *Symphony in G minor*, Number 6, and Franck's *Grande Pièce Symphonique*. The latter example merits study from the standpoint of the maintenance of the joyous mood throughout various textural changes. The pompous beginning is triumphant in its massive high sound, completely separate from the peripatetic pedal. In the fugal section the texture is kept transparent by wide spacing and by frequent interruption of the individual voices. In the following section, where the suboctave couplers are added, only the voice which carries the melody is continuous, and it is given ample space above and below. The accompanying parts are intermittent, and are detached when two voices are above the melody. Only as the climax approaches is the texture less sparse, and there the high range maintains the mood as the music becomes increasingly exuberant. For this movement the registration must sound the notated pitches with brilliancy and éclat. The upper ranks will be well absorbed to avoid screechiness, and reeds will be included except for the short polyphonic section.

Registration for Excited Moods

In the last example the reeds, by their rich array of partials focused in the fundamental, served to intensify the composer's pitches. If the loudness had been secured by the use of less perfectly absorbed high pitches, the effect would not have been joyous, but harsh. Again music follows the natural vocal expression of mood. The voice of an angry person is forced; the rise in pitch is due to increased energy more than to the adjustment of the vocal cords. Upper partials attain an abnormal prominence. So a harsh mood is expressed by fundamentals of medium pitch with loud reinforcement of upper partials. Mutation, rather than octave, pitches are stressed, since the latter would tend to brighten the tone. Rough reeds with exaggerated and perhaps inharmonic upper partials, mixtures, and mutations will produce the effect. If the fundamental range is high, the mood of such a combination becomes wild; if reeds are prominent, their intensity suggests viciousness. The use of such effects is usually restricted to music of a programmatic character. For example,

[18]See p. 156.

Alec Rowley's 'East Wind' bears the quotation from Joseph Conrad: "His weapon is a dagger carried under a black cloak when he goes out on his unlawful enterprises." This calls for a maximum proportion of high pitches; the fundamental will be relatively small, and the amount of reed tone will depend on whether the interpreter wishes to stress the viciousness of the "unlawful enterprises" or the terror which they instill.

Vague Qualities

In addition to the complete range of moods which can be suggested through registration there are many special color effects, which may or may not be associated with mood conceptions, outside the series just discussed. Their variety is limited only by the imagination and ingenuity of the composer and the organist. Any attempt to list or classify such effects would tend to limit, rather than extend, the interpreter's resources. We will, therefore, merely cite two or three examples of possible methods, intended to be suggestive, rather than definitive.

The expression of mood has been identified with actual audible pitches. On the other hand, the absence of clear pitch definition produces a characteristic effect which is vague, mysterious, ethereal, or radiant, according to the range of pitches used, and the method of avoiding clarity of pitch impression.

Low tones with a small proportion of upper partials are vague because they lie in a region of poor aural sensitivity. In general they suggest uncertainty or dullness, rather than mystery. The latter quality appears in the medium range, as in Flor Peeters' 'Mystieke Avond'.

A combination of different pitches represented by simple tones without fundamental domination produces vagueness through confusion. If the tones are soft, the impression is mysterious. There is also a suggestion of somberness, placidity, or brightness, according to the general pitch range. Karg-Elert was fond of such effects, specifying "16', 8', 4', & 2', *pp, misterioso.*" Widor indicated the use of a Bourdon 16' and a four-foot flute, without any eight-foot rank, in his *Fifth Symphony*, first movement, first variation, and in his *Symphonie Gothique*, at the beginning of the last movement. In the first instance, the four-foot tone serves to clarify the melodic movement, while the sixteen-foot tone introduces an element of vagueness; the second, interpreting the mood of 'Puer nobis nascitur' for the Christmas midnight Mass, combines mysticism (in the omission of the unison pitch) with quiet joy (suggested by the high flute). [19]

---

[19] It may well be asked why the composer did not write the music an octave lower, and specify eight- and two-foot flutes. On some organs that might produce the desired effect; but since the stops are designed with reference to an eight-foot fundamental, the tonal balance would usually be different. The eight- and two-foot flutes played an octave lower would probably give the impression of a lower fundamental, rather than an omitted fundamental. It is a subtle distinction.

The Quintadena, through the ambiguous pitch impression of almost equally audible fundamental and twelfth, produces a similar impression of vagueness or mystery. It may be effectively substituted for the gedeckt indicated for Flor Peeters' 'Mystieke Avond', mentioned above.

In these instances lack of pitch definition results from a combination of different audible tones; the effect is produced by pitch distribution. If we substitute highly complex tones for the relatively simple flutes, we secure a more refined vagueness through pitch diffusion. Instead of the confusion of many isolated tones, we have a fine mesh of overlapping partials. In both cases the domination of any one pitch is avoided by an even spread over a wide area, but the effect of the first is a scattering of the tonal elements, while that of the second is their amalgamation. The disappearance of the individual pitch elements provides a finer texture. This refined vagueness produces an ethereal impression, or one of diffused radiance, according to the intensity of the component elements. The effect is sometimes enhanced by the addition of céleste ranks at eight- and four-foot pitch.

Such an ethereal quality, produced by a Dulciana 16' and Unda Maris (Dulciana Céleste) with the superoctave coupler, is well suited to such material as is found in the final section of Franck's 'Choral in B minor', or the reprise of the second movement of his Grande Pièce Symphonique. The diffused radiance produced by the distribution of more intense complex tones is exemplified by the beginning of the 'Vorspiel' to Wagner's Lohengrin.[20] On the organ a comparable effect is secured by using keen strings at several pitches, or by adding sub- and superoctave couplers to a Voix Céleste. This latter effect is adaptable to various pitch areas, with corresponding expressive implications, extending from the rich warmth of the lower range to the refulgent glow of the higher frequencies. However, in spite of their inherent attractiveness as color, the application of these qualities in organ music is extremely limited. They are not suited to polyphony nor to any melodic material; they can only serve as a background, or for transient effects.

Exotic Color

Since the suggestion of mood depends on the aural perception of pitch, it has to do with octave pitches which tend to transpose the music into a different range, or with mutation pitches which are subordinate to the fundamental. On the other hand, the vague effects which we have just been observing result from the weakening of individual pitch impressions. There is still another color category in which pitches which have no

[20]See p. 156.

octave relationship with the fundamental are emphasized. These over-prominent mutations are not heard as transpositions; they produce an abnormal balance of component pitches which is heard as an exotic timbre.[21]

Examples of individual stops having such characteristics are the Quintadena, the Clarinet, the Orchestral Oboe and English Horn, the Vox Humana, etc. The organist who has a good selection of individual muta-tion stops at his disposal can produce an almost limitless variety of synthetic exotic color. For this purpose relatively simple qualities, such as the Rohrflöte, are most effective, as they single out clearly the partial to be stressed.

The use of such qualities, in spite of their erratic characteristics, should not be a matter of whim. Except for the occasional suitability of exotic combinations to give an archaic impression in the interpretation of early music,[22] abnormal colors should be suggested by analogous qualities in the music itself. In color as in all other matters, it is our business to "enhance what is inherent [or implicit] in the music." If the music itself is extravagant, we may be led to devise effects which are in questionable taste. This does not invalidate the principle, though it may lead us to question the validity of the music.

A Comparison of two Scherzos

In this connection it will be instructive to compare the registration of two scherzos which possess some superficial similarity: the scherzo from Widor's *Fourth Symphony*, and the 'Scherzetto in F sharp minor' from Vierne's *24 Pièces en style libre*. Both are lively, light, and, according to the composers' indications, played staccato; yet the registration should be quite different.

The first of these scherzos has already been discussed from the stand-point of motion.[23] Actually that is its principal, almost its only signifi-cant characteristic. The melodies disport themselves over a wide pitch area; there is no competing interest; the accompanying support, largely unnecessary because of the second melody, is kept at a minimum. In interpreting this work the organist should choose a registration which will give the greatest possible clarity and naturalness to this lively motion. The flutes specified by the composer are inevitable; any color added by mutations or complex timbres would be a blemish.[24]

[21]See pp. 73, 79.

[22]See Chaps. X & XI.

[23]See p. 127.

[24]Horatio Parker's 'Scherzino in E' from his collection of *Recital Pieces for the Organ* would provide a more striking comparison. We have substituted the Widor scherzo because of the inaccessibility of the other. If the reader happens to have the Parker scherzo available, it is suggested that he study it in this connection.

In Vierne's 'Scherzetto' the element of motion is essential, but not dominant. The movement is less continuous and smooth than that of the previous example; except for spurts it is made up largely of the rhythmic figure ♩♪♪ , and it is frequently interrupted by accents and cadences. The vertical interest is perhaps even stronger than the horizontal; the harmonies are piquant, chromatic, and frequently changing. The mood is whimsical, rather than gay. Audible four- and two-foot pitches are needed for melodic and motional clarity and for sprightliness, but the exotic harmonies call for mutations. Moreover the occasional lively phrases in the lower range and the closely spaced chords also require a synthetic fundamental, avoiding too much simple eight-foot tone.

The section beginning with measure 17 (and the corresponding section in the last part) invites heresy. Shall we at that point add a Gamba, and possibly another four-foot flute and mutation? It would suit the exotic harmonies and close spacing, but the slow speech of the string is not conducive to clarity. Perhaps the very fact of its inherent unsuitability would contribute to the whimsical, almost humorous effect. In any event, the string should not be used for the lighter texture, eight measures later.

The middle section of this scherzo is sometimes misunderstood; it is not intended to provide contrast, but relief. The movement continues unslackened; the mood is still whimsical; but sprightliness and energy give place to easy fluency. The characteristic rhythmic figure is re- tained, but is shifted so that the longer note is stressed, and the com- poser has indicated that the music be played legato. The texture is more polyphonic, and the chromatic harmony seems more incidental. The registration for this part should be modified in the direction of fluency, without introducing any contrast. The mutation element will be reduced, but not eliminated; the more exotic character of the first part will dis- appear.

If allowance is made for the limited resources of the instrument which Vierne had in mind, these suggestions will not be found inconsistent with his indications.

Summary

Having studied the principles involved in adapting the registration to the mood and other subjective qualities of the musical material, and applied these principles to various typical examples, we may now review the resources at our disposal and summarize their effects as we have observed them.

Since the expression of mood depends on audible pitch, flutes, which are the most isolated tones of the organ, are particularly useful within the limits of their audibility. However, they are easily heard only at high pitches, and their dynamic range is restricted. They are chiefly valuable, then, for bright moods not involving any suggestion of energy. At lower pitches their impression is vague, rather than somber. Diapasons are less isolated than flutes, but their octave pitches stand out enough to give brightness, and even quint mutations may contribute to a happy mood if the texture is not compact. The comparative dynamic efficiency of diapasons makes them adaptable to joyous and enthusiastic moods. In their lower range, however, as commonly voiced, their heaviness makes them dull, rather than somber. There is also too much energy in their tone to suggest vagueness, even though their low tones are indefinite in pitch.

String tone, with its weak fundamental and many relatively strong upper partials, is not sufficiently isolated to be effective in defining moods, except in the lower range. There, where the diapasons and flutes are heavy and indefinite, the strings give a clear pitch impression, suggesting a somber mood. For that purpose little should be added to them: other eight-foot flue stops tend to reduce the clarity of pitch definition, and the addition of higher ranks tends to brighten the tone. So the usefulness of strings is confined to quiet effects. In the middle range they may be added to other stops (in so far as they will blend) to produce a more complex quality and intensify the mood.

Reeds emphasize their fundamental pitch throughout their entire range, except that thin four-foot reeds may be absorbed in a complex ensemble. In the lower range they are more somber than strings, because of their stronger fundamental. Their dynamic efficiency lends vitality, and their complexity lends intensity, to the mood suggested by their fundamental pitch. They are therefore particularly valuable for expressing strong emotions. Also, their positive pitch definition renders them effective in suggesting the mood of a melody, especially when the range and dynamic requirements exceed the limitations of flutes.

Four- and two-foot stops, with their tendency to be heard as separate pitches, are effective in brightening the mood. This is a general statement which is subject to some qualification. It is always true of the highest octave stops of a combination; but the addition of a four-foot stop to a complex combination may, particularly if the texture is close, enrich, rather than brighten the tone.

Mutations, in spite of their high pitch, do not usually add brightness unless the texture is open. They are normally related to the fundamental pitch, providing color and intensifying the mood by increasing the complexity of the tone.

Quiet célestes, such as those of Dulciana, Gemshorn, or flute quality, tend toward vagueness because of their pitch discrepancy. String

célestes provide effective pitch definition for a single voice in the lower
and middle range. In a combination of many pitches, particularly with
sub- and superoctave couplers, their pitch definition is lost. The extensive distribution of several overlapping series of partials, and the
conflicting undulations caused by their various discrepant pitches, produce a fusion of tone spread over a wide area. No single pitch emerges
from the mass; but if the range is high, there is a shimmering glow which
is vaguely bright.

The reader may wonder why so many of the examples used in this
chapter have been taken from the works of nineteenth and twentieth century composers. Why have we not drawn from the much more stimulating
period of the Baroque? The answer is that the use of harmonic and tone
color as an essential means of expression was particularly characteristic
of the romantic school. Moreover, of the great composers who were identified with this development, Franck is the only one who made a significant contribution to the literature of the organ. The great bulk of the
organ music written in the last two hundred years has come from composers who have not been prominent in other fields. They have not been
pioneers in the evolution of musical styles, but have followed trails
blazed by others. Some, recognizing the supremacy of Bach and the incomparable fitness of his music to their medium, have sought to translate
his idiom into the vernacular; some have adopted the aesthetic ideals of
the romanticists, while others have experimented with the methods of the
modernists.

The fundamental premise that organ registration must interpret what is
inherent in the music, considered from the standpoint of mood, means not
only that the tone color must be consistent with the mood suggested by
the music, but that it must be adapted to the *method* by which the mood
is conveyed. If the composer has relied strongly on harmonic color for
his expression, as in the case of the chorale section of Franck's 'Choral
in A minor', or the 'Adagio' of Widor's *Sixth Symphony*, the organist's
first consideration is to match the harmonic effect with his tone color. If
the mood is expressed through the contour of the melody, as in the middle
sections of Franck's 'Chorals' in E and in A minor, or in the coloratura
chorale preludes of Bach, the most essential requirement of expressive
registration is to reveal the contour of the melody to the listener. If the
mood is expressed by the lively movement, as in most of the scherzos
which we have cited, or the interplay of the voices, as in Bach's 'In dir
ist Freude', then the primary concern of the organist is to assist the
auditor in hearing these particular qualities. If the mood is suggested by
the association of some melody, rhythm, or quality, these too should be
brought out by the registration — for example, the use of the melody of 'In

paradisum' in the coda of Flor Peeters' 'Élégie', and the quotation of 'Victimae paschali' in the 'Cantilène' of Widor's *Symphonie Romane*;[25] the dotted rhythm of a pastorale, or the martial implications of a fanfare.

But it is not sufficient to adapt the registration to the most important expressive characteristic of the music. This is a mistake made by organists of widely differing tastes. The romantically inclined may find a color which suits the mood of the composition which he is playing, but which obscures the voice-leading which has a significant share in the expression. The Baroque enthusiast, on the other hand, is prone to feel that he has made the music of Bach completely expressive by devising a registration which presents it clearly in every detail, even though it may emphasize pitches which are in conflict with the mood of the piece.

Expression in music is a complex process, involving the combination of many elements. Ideally the various means employed by the composer should be proportionately represented in the registration.[26] From the practical standpoint this is not always possible, but it is the goal toward which the interpreter should strive. The minimum requirement is that the registration be at least consistent with all the essential qualities of the music.

[25]Widor did not intend this quotation to be differentiated from the previous melody by any change of registration. An unobtrusive change of color, however, is not unsuitable, and it lends significance to the quotation – particularly to listeners who are not familiar with the Easter Sequence.

[26]This is more fully discussed under 'Relativity' at the end of Chapter IX. See pp. 219-21.

CHAPTER EIGHT
DESIGN

The Conception of the Whole

The preceding chapters have dealt with the stuff of which music is made. Although we have occasionally compared different materials and noticed their use in sequence and in contrast, we have not studied the way in which they are put together to form a complete whole. We have found methods of devising registration to reveal the more immediate characteristics of the music, but it remains for us to discover the relation of changes in registration to the development of the composition.

A work of art is conceived as a whole, and the details are planned to fit into the general scheme. However beautiful the material, however intriguing the details of its texture, it has meaning only in relation to the complete design. The performing artist, then, must envisage the whole work, planning his interpretation to reveal the unity of the composition, the relation of its parts, and the technical and aesthetic development of its structural elements. Since the design is realized in the manipulation of the material itself, the organist who perfectly adapts his registration to the material throughout will not go far astray in the larger interpretation. Nevertheless, there are questions of proportion and balance, of dynamic planes, of thematic outline and differentiation, of contrast and coherence, which must influence the presentation of the material.

In interpreting the composition as a whole it is of fundamental importance that the registration not only be consistent with, but serve to clarify, the design. The various structural elements will be revealed by adjustments in the loudness and character of the ensemble, in the balance of parts, in the tonal texture,[1] and in various other characteristics of the registration. The nature of such adjustments should, of course, always be suited to the material, and they should be proportioned to the importance of each structural feature.

In general, these structural elements fall into two categories, according as their appearance is concurrent or successive. The first type has primarily to do with the linear or horizontal aspect of texture, the mutual relation of simultaneous melodies, and the appearance of significant melodic material against an ensemble; it is particularly identified with the polyphonic idiom. The second is characterized by the division of music into sections, which are defined by points of arrival, departure, or

---

[1] We shall employ the term "tonal texture" to suggest the number and relation of combinations or qualities used simultaneously for different voices. It represents the fabric of timbres.

change, which serve to emphasize the vertical aspect of texture, and are particularly characteristic of the harmonic or homophonic idiom. These two types are inevitably combined, in widely varying proportions.

Horizontal Structural Elements

The horizontal details are subordinate to the overall design, but at the same time they form the material of which the whole is composed. We need to understand the interpretation of the details before we can fit them into the larger form. More specifically, we must make the listener hear the melodic themes in order for him to appreciate the structure as a whole. The method of accomplishing this is merely an application of the principles discussed in Chapters III, IV, and VI. The degree of prominence given to a melody depends on its importance in relation to the ensemble, and in relation to the form. Everything must be kept in just proportion, and the general development must not be obscured by too much attention to detail.

To bring out the horizontal structural elements it is particularly important to show clearly the beginning of a theme. Once the attention of the listener is attracted, he will more easily follow its continuation. The hearing of a theme is, therefore, assisted by a noticeable change in the quality or intensity of the tone when it enters. If it is in the soprano, a high pitch may be added; if it is in the lowest voice, the addition should strengthen the fundamental, or, more rarely, add sixteen-foot tone. A change of manual, providing either a suitable increase or a more prominent quality, is often desirable, particularly when the theme is in an inner voice. Sometimes a whole theme may thus be played as a quasi-solo; at other times, only the beginning of the theme will be brought out, and the other voices may follow to increase the general dynamic level. In this way a manual change may serve the dual purpose of calling attention to the melodic phrase and contributing to a general crescendo.

This procedure is admirably adapted to show the development of the middle section of the fugue of Bach's 'Prelude (Fantasia) and Fugue in C minor'.[2] Whether this middle part is to be regarded as the development of the second subject (with its countersubject) of a double fugue, or merely as an extended episode, is immaterial. It builds up consistently, by two stages, to a climactic half cadence which prepares, in true ternary form fashion, for the reprise. The latter is essentially identical with the exposition until the arrival of the pedal point which supports the

[2]Schirmer Edition, Vol. III, p. 24. This is one of two fine fugues which Bach composed in a frank ternary form. In this case the third part presents an almost exact repetition of the exposition. The so-called "Wedge Fugue" in E minor is even more striking. In it the entire first part is repeated, note for note, in the reprise.

final entry of the theme. The following interpretation assumes that the Swell is coupled to the Choir, and that both the Swell and Choir are coupled to the Great.

After the cadence to the first beat of measure 57, the author begins the episode (starting with the alto theme) on the Choir,[3] going over to the Swell in measure 60 (with b♮^{1} and e♮^{1}), where the higher pitch lightens the texture. The Great stops are canceled, so as to make the effect of the Choir available on an adjacent manual. Beginning in measure 62, the left hand plays on the Choir – for that is the theme, in spite of the alteration of the first two notes. The soprano is played on the Great (= Choir) beginning with the second note of measure 65; similarly the alto in measure 66. In the following measure the right hand is transferred to the Choir (without change of effect), after which a suitable Great combination is added. In measure 70 the left hand plays on the Great, the alto following in measure 71, and the soprano in measure 72. The best place to add the Great to Pedal coupler is with the G in measure 72. An inconspicuous addition of upper pitches within a closed box may be made on the f♯^{1} in measure 74, or, perhaps better, at the beginning of measure 75, where it will be covered by the coincidence of the soprano and alto.

In measure 78 the hands drop back to the Choir for the next stage of the build-up. As the first part was planned to bring out the eighth-note theme, the dynamic increases in this part can emphasize the chromatic theme.[4] In this case the Great will be coupled to the Pedal for the entry in measure 87; the tenor will go to the Great in the middle of measure 89; stops will be added to the Great at the moment of the alto entry in measure 92, the soprano transferring to the Great on the a♭^{2}; further reinforcements will be added in the partially closed Swell at the middle of measure 94, and in the Pedal for its entry in measure 97.

Sometimes, when it is not practicable to go to a louder manual or otherwise make an increase at the beginning of a theme, its entrance can be made more noticeable by lightening what immediately precedes. In the fugue just cited, the entrance of the theme in measure 24 will be clearer if four notes of the tenor, beginning with B♮, are played on a secondary manual. Similarly, in the fugue of the 'Fantasia and Fugue in G minor', measure 21, the eighth-notes in the alto may be detached, and the b♭^{1} and c^1 played on a secondary manual. This renders the imitation in the tenor more audible, and the entrance of the theme in the soprano more noticeable. A similar situation occurs in measure 79; but

[3]Theoretically the episode should begin on the Swell, but the contrast would be too great.

[4]Cf. the suggestion on p. 123 for the variation of a repetition.

this entrance, being in an inner voice, is bound to be lost if the interpreter's phrasing involves detaching the first note of the theme.

Solo Treatment of a Fugue Theme

The practice of bringing out the themes of fugues and other polyphonic compositions on a separate manual is too common to call for extended comment. The extent to which it is desirable is debatable. It is a question of relative values. Anything which can be done to assist the listener to hear any feature of the music is good, unless it is done at the expense of something more important. If the organist so emphasizes the details that the ensemble becomes disintegrated, or the fluency of the execution is impaired, or the essential progress of the music is lost, or the overall design is obscured, then he is sacrificing a greater good for a lesser; but if he can clarify the details without detracting, or diverting the attention of the listener, from the effect of the whole, it is all to the good.

Some organists like to begin a fugue on the Swell, playing succeeding entries on the Choir and Great in such a way as to effect a general crescendo during the exposition. Schweitzer, on the other hand, insists that Bach's fugues should *always* begin on the Great. Schweitzer is right in wishing to preserve the unity of the exposition; but we need not assume that all of Bach's fugues call for the same treatment, or that the use of the Great keyboard is essential. It is true that on practically all organs we must go to the Great for the solid tone needed for the fugues in F, F minor, and E flat; but the more florid themes, such as the one in A minor, and quiet themes, like that of the A major, may begin on a secondary manual if suitable stops are available. The combination should be adapted to the material and its treatment, but it matters not what keyboard is used. If, however, beginning on the Great prevents the listener from hearing the fourth entry in the 'Fugue in F minor', or in the 'Fugue in E flat', it is not so serious as it would be to spoil the effect of the entire exposition by using an unsuitable or inadequate combination. Moreover, if the fugue is begun on a secondary manual in order to show the successive entries more clearly, it is essential that they be marked by consistent additions, rather than contrast, so that the exposition will be a homogeneous unit.

The quasi-solo treatment of the theme is best suited to the subordinate sections of the fugue, for the following reasons: (1) The sequence of entries in the exposition is conventional; the listener knows what to expect and does not need to have the theme underlined. In the freer portions of the fugue the entrances are not definitely anticipated; it is advantageous to call attention to them. Moreover, it is psychologically effective to emphasize the recurrence of the invariable feature of the movement in a section of unrestricted development. (2) The variable tonal texture[5] forms a contrast to the more uniform texture of the exposition, which corresponds to the contrast between the free development of the musical material and the more systematic organization of the exposition. (3) Since the subordinate sections are usually softer and often use fewer voices, the mechanical separation of the theme is more practicable.

A rare example of the effectiveness of bringing out a theme in a principal section of a fugue occurs in the last part of the fugue of Bach's 'Prelude and Fugue in B minor'. This magnificent fugue gives somewhat the impression of a ternary form. The middle section is differentiated by the omission of the pedal, the lightening of the texture, the substitution of a new countersubject, and freedom of modulation. The third part is marked by the conspicuous appearance of the theme in its original key, the return of the first countersubject, and the simultaneous addition of a new countersubject which assumes the importance of a second principal theme. It is this new and arresting theme which may be underscored when it appears in an inner voice.

The mechanical accomplishment of this requires a large organ with complete coupler equipment, including couplers in reverse direction. The Great, Swell, and Solo will all be coupled to the Choir, and the Great, Choir, and Solo will all be coupled to the Swell, so that playing on either the Swell or the Choir will give the full ensemble plus the Solo. Each manual entry of the new theme can be played on one of these two manuals, and the pedal entry can include either the Solo or its own reeds. The Solo addition must stand out without violating the integrity of the ensemble; it will probably include eight- and four-foot reeds, plus various diapason ranks if they are available. If the Solo contains a good diapason chorus it may be possible to omit the Great to Swell and Great to Choir couplers. It is of course understood that the Solo combination is added only for the entries of the new theme, and will drop out at the conclusion of the theme. This procedure is rather complicated and difficult, but it is worth the trouble if suitable resources are available. If the console lacks the necessary couplers, the theme may be played on the Solo by an assistant, in addition to its inclusion in the ensemble.

Again, at the risk of redundancy, we would caution the ambitious organist against overelaboration and fussiness. Unless such procedures as we have suggested can be subordinated to the continuous flow and natural build-up of the music, a simple, straightforward presentation is to be preferred.

[5] See footnote 1, p. 177.

Differentiation of Themes

If two or more themes are associated, it is desirable, if practicable, to effect a differentiation in their registration, so as to keep them separate in the mind of the listener when they are heard simultaneously, and to identify them when they are heard successively. If there is a marked difference in the character of the themes, that itself will determine the differentiation. For example, in the last section of the fugue just discussed, the fragmentary and rhythmic character of the new theme calls for an assertive, reedy tone, which is unsuited to the steady, continuous movement of the principal theme.

If the character and range of the themes are similar, it is good to exaggerate their slight difference in the registration, or to add an arbitrary difference in the tone quality (within the limits of suitability), in order to preserve their individuality. In the case of canons, the only differences inherent in the music itself are the pitch of the voices and their relation to the ensemble.

Canons

If the canon is a part of a polyphonic ensemble, it may be a textural detail which is subordinate to the total effect. In that case, it is only necessary for the registration to make the voice-leading clearly audible. Examples of such canons are fugal stretti, the beginning of Bach's 'Toccata in F', the accompanying counterpoints of the *Orgelbüchlein* setting of 'In dulci jubilo', the fourth section of the last movement of Widor's *Symphonie Gothique*, etc. Again, the canon may be an essential feature of the design, demanding varying degrees of emphasis according to its relative importance.

The supreme example, of course, is Bach's set of *Canonic Variations on 'Vom Himmel hoch'*. [6] The first two variations are in three parts, and should be registered as trios. [7] Variation III requires a clear differentiation between the quality of the canon and that of the other manual parts, particularly because of the frequent crossing of the two inner voices. At the same time it must be admitted that a combination which is suited to the florid counterpoint is not ideal for the chorale melody in the soprano. The organist who has the knack of playing on two manuals with one hand can select a Swell combination for the florid alto part, and play the chorale melody on the Solo; the canonic imitation can be played on Choir stops, coupled to the Great, so that the left hand can occasionally assist

---

[6] Einige canonische Veränderungen über das Weihnachtslied: Vom Himmel hoch da komm ich her.

[7] See pp. 94-5.

the right in playing the florid melody. In Variation IV it is not possible
to do more than choose a combination for the left hand which will present
the two voices clearly.   The impracticability of differentiating the
voices of the canon is not regrettable, for a canon in augmentation soon
becomes too distant to be recognized.   The same procedure will be
adopted for Variation V, as soon as it ceases to be a trio – although it is
not impossible to play the tenor on the Great and the alto on the Choir.
When the imitation is transferred to the soprano, it is heard by its position.   The complexity of the last five measures defies any effort to bring
out the imitations.   The canons are a part of the texture; only to the most
attentive listener can they be made audible by choosing an ensemble
which will not blur the individual voices.

Many compositions whose texture is primarily harmonic include two
horizontal threads of canon.   Usually the melody is in the soprano, and
its imitation in a lower voice.   Although harmonic texture ordinarily calls
for a cohesive ensemble, there should be enough fundamental and octave
tone to give clarity to the upper voice, while the imitation will be brought
out by giving it a prominent, nonblending quality.   The degree of separation will depend on how complete the ensemble is without the imitating
voice.   Examples are found in Franck's 'Cantabile in B', at the reprise,
and in the second movement of his *Grande Pièce Symphonique*, beginning
at the eighth measure.   In the latter the melody is treated as a solo, and
the imitation can (with difficulty) be played on a contrasting solo stop.

In the canonic sections of 'Chant de May' by Jongen, the ensemble is
almost absolutely complete without the imitating voice.   The material
and range call for the lightness of eight- and four-foot flutes, and the
imitating voice can be assigned to a light, characteristic reed, or possibly even to a Voix Céleste.   The same composer's 'Choral in E'
presents a canon between the soprano and bass which continues throughout the composition.   Here the imitating voice serves as the bass of the
harmonies, and it should be distinguished by added intensity, rather than
contrast.   The same is true of Bach's *Orgelbüchlein* setting of 'Christus,
der uns selig macht', which falls in this same category, in spite of its
polyphonic texture.

Canons between lower voices are relatively infrequent, because of the
difficulty of making them heard. In Franck's 'Fantaisie in C', the second
section of the first movement presents a canon between the alto and
bass. However, the alto is the highest voice of the accompaniment, from
which the soprano melody is kept separate, both by spacing and by
registration.[8]   Bach's setting of 'Christe, du Lamm Gottes', in the

---

[8]See p. 163.

Orgelbüchlein, presents the melody in the tenor, imitated by the soprano. This canon is difficult to hear because it enters unobtrusively, and is concealed by moving counterpoints. The organist with an exceptional reach can keep the melodies separate by playing them on four different manuals. The average player will have to rely on a skillful differentiation of two manuals, and an increase to show each beginning of the chorale melody. The combination for the left hand should be designed for clear audibility and pitch definition in the tenor range, sufficiently complex to distinguish it from the right hand quality, but not too exotic to participate in the ensemble. The additions at the entrances of the canon can be made with stops, or with manual changes, or merely by slightly opening the respective swells.

Canon between Solo Voices

If the canon is between two solo voices heard against an accompaniment, the treatment is similar to that of a single solo melody. If possible, the two voices should be differentiated in timbre. If they are similar in range, such differentiation helps the listener to keep them distinct; if there is disparity in range (as in a canon in the octave), pitch considerations will dictate a difference in quality. In both cases the lower voice will have more upper partials than the upper voice, for reasons which have already been fully discussed.

There are eight canonic chorale settings in Bach's *Orgelbüchlein*, of which two have already been mentioned. For the other six Bach indicated the solo treatment of one or both of the melodies. The canon in the fifth in 'Hilf Gott, dass mirs gelinge', and the canon in the fourth in 'Liebster Jesu, wir sind hier', were intended to be played on the same manual. It is quite possible, and more effective, to play them on different manuals, the quality of the lower voice being somewhat more incisive than that of the upper voice. 'Erschienen ist der herrliche Tag' may have a fairly smooth reed for the soprano, while the pedals should use a bright Trumpet 8', probably with the addition of a Clarion 4'. The use of a sixteen-foot tone in the pedal is a matter of taste.

'Gott, durch deine Güte' (or, 'Gottes Sohn ist kommen') is one of the few compositions for which Bach provided registration indications. The Principal (Diapason) 8', which he suggested for the right hand, meets the requirements of separate audibility, so that the melody and the upper voice will be clear; the Trumpet 8' assigned to the pedal part provides the added upper partials needed in the tenor range. The addition of four-foot tone, and possibly a two-foot flute, to the right hand part will enhance the mobility of the alto, while preserving the domination of the soprano. It is not impossible to play the melody on a separate manual, but it is not worth sacrificing the fluency of the execution. The left hand part, which suggests a *basso continuo*, may include a light sixteen-foot stop.

The other two canons in the *Orgelbüchlein* seem to justify a complicated scheme to bring out the melodies as solos, but the technical difficulties are considerable. The following suggestions are offered to those who are able to follow them without impairing the fluency of the music:

Both voices of the canon in 'O Lamm Gottes, unschuldig' can be played with the feet, an octave lower than notated, using a four-foot solo stop. This will often be the best solution, but it has the following disadvantages: The individuality of the voices is lost in the third measure, and the skip at the beginning of the second phrase cannot be made legato. Another solution is this: Play the soprano on the Swell; play the alto melody on the Great, perhaps using a stop from the Solo; and play the bass on the Choir with unison-off and suboctave couplers, so that the notes are played an octave higher than written. Alto notes which cannot be played with the right hand, reaching down from the Swell, can be managed with the left.

The delightful double canon on 'In dulci jubilo' can be played in the manner first suggested for 'O Lamm Gottes'. There are two disadvantages to this procedure: (1) The disparity in range affects the balance: if the tenor melody is loud enough, the soprano melody will be too loud. (2) No use can be made of the swell pedals. This method has the advantage, however, of making it possible to differentiate between the two counterpoints. The author's solution is as follows: The accompanying parts are played on a Swell combination which is also coupled to the Choir; the upper melody is played on the Great, to which a suitable Solo stop is coupled. The upper counterpoint alternates between the Swell and Choir, according to the exigencies of the situation. If there is no suitable pedal reed, a Choir stop or combination can be coupled to the Pedal, while it is silenced on the Choir manual by the unison off; or the pedal tone can come from the Solo, and the Great from the Choir. Of course the last four notes, apparently assigned to the left foot, should be played on one of the accompanying manuals.

We have discussed canons as a part of the ensemble and as solos against an accompaniment. Obviously the relation of any melody, or pair of melodies, to the other parts is infinitely varied, and the registration should be adjusted accordingly.[9]

Successive Structural Elements – The Chorale

After this brief study of typical problems in the presentation of the

[9] Cf. p. 97.

horizontal elements of design, we turn to the question of successive units in the musical structure.

The simplest and most obvious example of sectional division is the chorale, which is a succession of phrases, each ending in a cadence. In spite of the apparently approved English practice of changing the combination for each new phrase of a hymn or chant, it is not artistically desirable to set off such small sections by varied registration. The continuity of the whole is lost; the chorale becomes fragmentary. Discreet dynamic changes are suitable, and these should be guided by the sectional character of the piece. Students planning their use of the swell pedal are advised first to establish the dynamic level of each phrase, in such proportions that the whole will be effective and consistent without any change within the phrase. Then detailed shading may be superimposed on the general dynamic scheme thus established. If for any reason a general crescendo is desirable, additions will, of course, be made at the beginnings of phrases.

The repetition of the first two (or, more rarely, three) phrases, which is characteristic of many chorales, invites a change of registration. [10] This is not merely because an unaltered restatement seems redundant, but because a change calls attention to the fact that the section is being repeated, and so serves to clarify the design. However, the material is the same, and the form is too small to be cut up into unrelated sections. There should be no contrast — merely a modification which varies the impression without disturbing the consistency of the whole. Often it is effective to play the repeated phrases at a lower dynamic level, returning to the original level for the continuation after the repetition. This gives the impression of resuming the course of the music after pausing to reconsider the first part — which is exactly what the design suggests. These changes may be effected by varying the selection of stops, by swell pedal adjustments, or by both.

These observations concerning the interpretation of a simple chorale apply equally to a chorale prelude which follows the phrase structure of the original melody. The dynamic shading effected by the swell pedals will be adapted to the respective predetermined levels of the individual phrases, although increased elaboration in the setting allows greater flexibility of interpretation. In general, changes of registration will not be introduced except for the repetition of the first section. If the melody is played on a solo stop, another stop of not too contrasting timbre may be substituted for the repetition, with or without a change of accompaniment. Often the continuity of the accompaniment makes it impracticable

[10] Cf. p. 123.

to modify it. If it remains unchanged, greater contrast can be introduced in the quality of the solo without destroying the unity of the composition.

This conformity of the chorale prelude to the phrase structure of the chorale itself is characteristic of most of the *Orgelbüchlein* settings, and many other short preludes and variations, as well as those of a coloratura type, from Sweelinck down to the present.

Interpolated Interludes

If the sections are extended by the interpolation of interludes between the phrases of the chorale, other considerations enter in. In large forms it is more important to avoid monotony, and the sections can be more clearly differentiated. At the same time the entrance of the chorale melody must always be recognizable as the return of the principal feature, and there must be no change in the general effect which is out of proportion to the change in the material. This may be clarified by a few examples.

Reger's setting of 'Vater unser im Himmelreich'[11] is a simple, expressive harmonization, each phrase of which is followed by an answering repetition, softer, an octave higher, and without pedal. These echo phrases separate the main phrases and lend variety to the whole. Continuity is secured by the consistent use of the two alternating combinations. At the same time dynamic progress is provided in each by an occasional subtle modification, which preserves the essential character of the ensemble, and the mutual relation of the two.

Such echo repetitions add length and variety, but they do not constitute an expansion of the form. The methods of separating or enlarging the sections identified with the respective phrases of the chorale vary from the splashy interludes of unrelated material, found in Bach's setting (presumably for congregational accompaniment!) of 'In dulci jubilo',[12] to the consistent working out of the so-called "Pachelbel form", in which each phrase is introduced by a miniature fugal exposition of its melody; from the independent sections of Buxtehude's chorale fantasias to continuous compositions, such as Bach's setting of 'Nun freut euch, lieben Christen g'mein'.

In Bach's 'In dulci jubilo', just mentioned, bravura material appears in alternation and in combination with the chorale, which is always differentiated by an increase in the number of voices, if not by the use of actual chords. It can be further marked by the use of the pedal, which

[11]Op. 67, No. 39.

[12]Bach-Gesellschaft Edition, Vol. XL, p. 74; Peters Edition, Vol. V, p. 103.

Bach indicated without assigning it to specific places.[13] No further
differentiation is necessary, but a richer combination, perhaps including
some sixteen-foot tone, may be used for the chorale phrases, and a
marked addition may be made for the final entry, thirteen measures before
the end.

Chorale Phrases Set Against a Continuous Movement

'Nun freut euch' provides neither the opportunity nor the necessity for
changing the registration, which will be dictated by the material, the
mood, and a suitable prominence of the cantus firmus. So short a movement should give a single impression. In the same category, though
vastly different in texture and mood, is the last part of Bach's setting of
'Komm, Gott, Schöpfer, heiliger Geist', from the set of *Achtzehn Choräle*.
This piece, with its continuous flow of brilliant counterpoints against
which the phrases of the chorale are enunciated by the pedals, is strongly
reminiscent of Pachelbel. Many of Bach's extended settings combine the
characteristics of this type with more or less imitation of the principal
melody. Often he developed long movements from motives taken, or
themes derived, from the first phrase of the chorale. The wide range of
style and texture is exemplified, on the one hand, by the second
Clavierübung setting of 'Allein Gott in der Höh sei Ehr', and on the
other by the large settings of the Kyries, the third of which is one of
the most glorious compositions ever written for the organ. Varying
degrees of sectionalism are found in these works, which will be proportionately reflected in the registration. The composition should be interpreted according to its form, independent of the chorale, the cantus
firmus being given due prominence as it enters against the development
of the polyphony.

The Chorale Fantasia

The Buxtehude type of chorale fantasia is completely sectional. Each
phrase in turn is elaborately developed, in toto and in fragments. The
problem in registration is to follow the development within each section,
differentiate it clearly from the other sections, according to its material,
and present it in its relation to the logic of the whole. An extreme
example of this type of chorale treatment is Buxtehude's setting of 'Nun
freut euch, lieben Christen g'mein' — an amazing composition (filling
twelve pages in the Spitta edition) which may be studied with interest and
profit, but cannot be discussed in the space which could legitimately be
allotted to it here.

[13]This involves the occasional addition of an essential bass to the harmonies, where
the left hand passage work is not suited to the pedals.

A remarkable adaptation of this process to a more continuous form is found in Bach's 'In dir ist Freude', which has already been studied from the standpoint of mood.[14] Bach seems to be so filled with the spirit of joy that he is unable to get beyond the first four notes of the tune before he breaks off into a roulade of delight. Not until the sixth attempt does he manage to state the first four measures. The next phrase starts off inverted, but is soon lost in a modulation to the relative minor, where the first section ends. He then begins again for the repeat, following the same procedure; but this time the second phrase remains right side up, and, after two starts, is completed in the pedals and followed by an extended cadence. Thus the first part, with its repetition, is made into a balanced binary form with contrasting cadences. The last part follows the choral exactly, although the florid material here invades the melody itself. It is repeated without alteration.

The registration should show the sectional structure and emphasize the complete phrase statements, at the same time, of course, conforming to the previously discussed requirements of mood. The writer begins on a secondary manual; the Great to Pedal is added for the entry in measure 7, and the hands play on the Great beginning with measure 9. We return to the secondary manual in measure 17 (after the E's), and the same procedure is followed again. Sixteen-foot stops are added to the pedal for the melody beginning in measure 34. In measure 39, after the cadence, we return to the secondary manual, as shown in Example 12, and drop the

Example 12. Bach: In dir ist Freude

sixteen-foot pedal. From measure 44 we again play on the Great, with the Great to Pedal coupler, adding sixteen-foot tone to the pedal at the octave skip in measure 46, or perhaps waiting until the last repetition of the pedal figure, in measure 49. Returning to the secondary manual again in measure 51, the same procedure is repeated, with perhaps added reinforcement for the final cadence. It will be obvious to the reader who has followed our methods thus far, how this plan brings out both the

[14]Pp. 167-8.

concurrent and successive elements of the design, while preserving throughout the mood of joy.

Closer to the Buxtehude form is Bach's setting of 'Ein' feste Burg ist unser Gott'. Special interest attaches to this piece because Bach's own registration of it has been preserved.[15] It is not usually practicable to follow it in detail, but it is instructive to note the relation of his scheme to the structure of the composition. He played the first twenty measures as a duet on two manuals. This section corresponds to the first two phrases of the chorale and their repetition. Note that Bach varies the treatment for the repetition by two interchanges: (1) The melody is transferred from the right hand to the left; (2) the first time, the melody of the first phrase is more ornamented than that of the second; the second time, the reverse is true. The fifth phrase (counting the repetition) is so disguised as to be scarcely recognizable. It functions as an interlude, and Bach made it subordinate by playing it on a softer manual. In measure 24 he returned to the original manuals (reinforced) for the sixth and seventh phrases, increasing the pedal (probably including reeds) for a telling statement of the melody. The eighth is the weakest phrase of the melody. Bach took advantage of this fact to introduce another interlude, playing around the tune with scraps of figuration. Accordingly he went over to the softer manual again in measure 33. Beginning at the end of measure 39 he returned to the principal manual, using full organ for the two statements of the last phrase.

The general scheme, as thus revealed, is as follows:

     I   II   III   IV   v   VI   VII   viii   IX   IX

This essential outline can be adapted to any organ of any size. On an instrument with ample resources the combinations can be varied to suit the material, and the melody, except in the subordinate sections, distinguished by characteristic registration — presumably including an eight-foot reed. Final reinforcements can be reserved for measure 48, which introduces the concluding statement of the last phrase. If the organ possesses a Solo to Choir coupler (and preferably a Great to Choir also), the melody itself can be brought out on the Solo reeds, divided between the two thumbs — an effect which Bach hardly anticipated, but which is in keeping with the exuberant spirit of the music. Moreover, we know that Bach was not bound by tradition in his own registration.

The So-called "Pachelbel Form"

Like the chorale fantasia, the so-called "Pachelbel form" of chorale

[15] Bach's registration is described by Albert Schweitzer in Bibl. 156, Vol. I, pp. 302-3, and by Harvey Grace, Bibl. 87, p. 196. Grace calls attention to Schweitzer's error in counting measures.

prelude also is divided into sections, corresponding to the phrases of
the chorale. In its strictest application, each section begins with a
fugal treatment of its line of the melody, leading to a complete statement
of the phrase. This may be considered a specific variety of chorale
fantasia, in which the procedure in each section follows a predetermined
scheme. The principle of *Vorimitation* ("imitation before" – that is, in
anticipation of the cantus firmus) is suggested in the settings of Schlick
(1512) and of Cavazzoni (1542). A nearer approach to the almost stereotyped plan of Pachelbel is found in the works of Titelouze, Scheidt, and
other composers of the early seventeenth century. In general, the
Pachelbel examples are distinguished by their frank major and minor
tonalities and the dominance of the cantus firmus. However, there is no
essential formal difference between his setting of 'Vater unser im
Himmelreich',[16] which is one of the most beautiful and characteristic
examples of his treatment, and the third verset of Titelouze's 'Sanctorum
meritis'.[17] Indeed, the older composer's handling of the melodic material
is more ingenious, and his polyphony is freer and smoother, embodying,
rather than accompanying, the cantus.

When the division between the sections of such compositions is clearly
defined, any change in registration will naturally take place at that point.
The chief practical difference, then, between this form and the Buxtehude
fantasia, is that there is less variation in the material of the different
sections. The form is a more consistent unit, and there is seldom any
call for contrast in the registration. The dynamic planes of the sections
may vary, and for this a change in combination may sometimes be suitable. Such changes should be planned, if possible, so as to call attention to the entrance of the new phrase elements. The method will depend
on the material, and the relative dynamics.

The simplest possible example of this problem is offered by Pachelbel's trio setting of 'Vom Himmel hoch da komm ich her'. Here there is
little call for dynamic variation, but the changes in thematic material
can be subtly brought out in the following manner: Select three contrasting manual qualities which are fluent and mutually balanced – e.g.,
(1) flutes 8' & 4', (2) Oboe, (3) Clarinet and flute 4'. Begin with the
most obvious combination; then with each new section change both
hands, starting the new material on the manual which was not used for
the preceding passage. This might be arranged thus:

First section: right hand, flutes; left hand, Oboe
Second section: left hand, Clarinet; right hand, Oboe

---

[16]Bibl. 191, p. 125; also Bibl. 192, Vol. III, p. 8, and Bibl. 199, p. 76.
[17]Bibl. 205, p. 77.

Third section: right hand, flutes; left hand, Oboe; right hand changes to
   Clarinet for the repeated sixteenth-notes
Fourth section: right hand, flutes; left hand, Clarinet

The antiphonal runs in the first section will be played as shown in
Example 13.[18] The use of a sixteen-foot pedal stop is optional. The

Example 13. Pachelbel: Vom Himmel hoch

author prefers a single eight-foot reed, as close to the bassoon quality
as possible.

Overlapping Sections

Sometimes continuity is provided at division points by means of dovetailing the material. Indeed, this is a very common procedure, not only
in various types of chorale preludes, but in all forms of music. In interpreting such pieces the organist's method should, as always, conform to
that of the composer. If it is desirable to change the combination at the
division points, the registration also should overlap, using the new
quality for the new material.

A beautiful modern example of such overlapping in a setting of the
Pachelbel type is Brahms's chorale prelude on 'Mein Jesu, der du mich'.
However, we have chosen to examine a much older work: the second
verset of Titelouze's 'Ave maris stella'.[19] This movement is in real
motet form, without cantus firmus. The successive sections develop in
turn the four phrases of the hymn melody, the new material always overlapping the old. The last section is extended to a length approximately
equaling that of the first three. The music implies a general crescendo
to the end, perhaps interrupted in the early part of the last section where

[18]Attention is called to the error in measure 5 in the Guilmant and Bonnet editions. The
measure is correct in Bibl. 191, 192, and 201.

[19]The most accessible source is Bibl. 168, p. 30. Bonnet's assignment of portions of
the bass to the pedal and his registration indications follow the suggestion of Guilmant
in Bibl. 205. Cf. p. 3. Note Bonnet's error in measure 6, where the alto should read as
follows:

the texture becomes lighter. Since Titelouze wrote four versets for a seven-stanza hymn, it may be assumed that they were intended for the odd stanzas. In that case, this verset would have been substituted for the third stanza, which is as follows:

Solve vincla reis,	Break the chains of prisoners,
profer lumen caecis:	Bring light to the blind:
mala nostra pelle,	Drive away our ills,
bona cuncta posce.	Ask for all good things.

One can almost imagine that the composer had the text in mind.[20]

The organist will of course ignore Guilmant's registration, which is utterly unsuited both to the spirit of the music and to its polyphonic texture. At the beginning, the tone should be placid in mood, quietly bright; the second phrase will be somewhat brighter; the third will add vitality; and the fourth, except for the lighter portion, will have both brightness and vitality, with added richness for the last seven measures, ending about forte. The ensemble must be transparent throughout, clearly revealing the details of the polyphony. The following scheme is suggested:

At the beginning, the Swell is coupled to the Great and to the Choir; the Swell and Choir are coupled to the Pedal; no Pedal stops are drawn. The first section is played on the Swell. At the end of measure 11 the alto entrance is played with the feet, continuing until the right hand is free to take it on the Choir. The succeeding soprano entrance is also played on the Choir, and the pedals provide the same combination for the bass entry. In measure 17 the tenor may be subtly brought out on the Great if suitable stops are available, but there must be a definite addition two measures later, when the third phrase enters in the same voice. The right hand goes to the Great on the second c^1 in measure 20, and the entire third section is played on the Great. The bass entry in measure 26 is played with the feet, the Great to Pedal having previously been substituted for the Choir to Pedal, and possibly some light eight- and four-foot pedal stops added. The Choir is now reinforced, so that it is brighter, and perhaps louder, than the Great. The fourth phrase of the melody, entering in the soprano in measure 29, is played on the Choir. The Pedal is probably reduced in the same measure, as its statement of the third phrase is concluded. In measure 31, the left hand goes to the Choir and the right hand (with the alto) to the Swell; the Great to Pedal

[20]This is corroborated by Gastoué: "Et il est intéressant de voir comment l'organiste de Rouen s'efforce à l'expression, dans ces *Magnificat*, en les écrivant 'comme si les paroles étaient prononcées,' en forme de motets diversifiés, tandis que les hymnes 'à la manière de M. Titelouze'—ainsi que s'exprime Gigault—affectionnent de traiter successivement chaque vers en exposition de fugue." —Bibl. 83, p. 80.

is removed not later than the middle of this measure. The left hand is transferred to the Swell on the c^1 in measure 32; it may return to the *closed* Choir in the following measure, or it may wait until measure 35, when the box should be open enough to make a distinct addition. The right hand follows at the end of measure 36.[21] The Choir is coupled to the Pedal for the bass entry in measure 38, and the Great to Pedal may perhaps be added in measure 41. The Choir to Great is added sometime before measure 44, at which time the left hand goes over to the Great. The alto follows at the end of measure 45, and the soprano on the last beat of measure 46. The Swell shades may be closed during the first beat of measure 50, and Swell mixtures added on the second beat, with which a crescendo can be effected to the end of the piece. Sixteen-foot Pedal stops may be added for the bass entry in measure 51, unless the organist has chosen to add them for the entry in measure 38, or the one in measure 41.

The details will vary with the individual organ and the taste of the organist, but the procedure just outlined suggests the manner in which the registration can show the overlapping of the sections, preserve the continuity, and contribute to the general effectiveness of the structure.

Transition Problems

This method of securing continuity at division points by introducing the new phrase in one voice while the others continue the preceding material, is characteristic of polyphony. In compositions in which the vertical textural element plays a more important part the overlapping is often limited to a single note or chord; or the connection may be made by the uninterrupted motion of one or more voices. This naturally reduces the opportunity for overlapping in the registration, sometimes necessitating a single change at a given point. The more continuous the music, the more difficult it is to determine the most effective procedure. The following general principles are almost universally valid:

1. Any noticeable addition must be made at the *beginning* of a musical unit. This often coincides with the accent of the measure.

2. Any noticeable reduction must be made at the *end* (with the release of the last note or chord) of a metrical unit. In a majority of cases this occurs *after* the accent of the measure.

3. A change involving a contrast of tone quality provides both a noticeable addition and a noticeable reduction, and should fulfill both

---

[21]Ideally the alto should wait until the f^1 in the succeeding measure, which would necessitate silencing the Great stops so that the Swell combination could be played from the Great keyboard. The Great combination would then be restored as soon as the alto transferred to the Choir.

conditions. In case the last note or chord of one unit coincides with the beginning of the next, the common note or chord should be played on *both* combinations.

In doubtful cases it is often helpful to think in orchestral terms. An addition to the tone is equivalent to the entrance of a new instrument; a reduction is equivalent to the dropping out of an instrument. Additions should be made, therefore, at points where it would be natural for an instrument to enter, and reductions should be made where it would be natural for an instrument to cease playing. After our study of entrances in polyphonic material, additions will not usually offer any difficulty; problems are more apt to occur in cases which involve a reduction, with or without a coincident addition. The nature of such problems and their solution may be shown in a study of two chorale preludes by Brahms.

In the second setting of 'O Welt, ich muss dich lassen', Opus 122, Number 11, the problems are concerned with the transitions to the echo cadences. The first two phrases are quite straightforward; we need only observe that in measure 7 the low AA should be played on the third manual, unless that manual is coupled to the second, since the following BB is a passing tone. In other cases the best procedure is not quite so evident. The tenor in measure 11, the alto in measures 15 and 16, and the alto and tenor at the end of the fifth phrase, all admit of different interpretations. The tenor in measure 11 seems to lead into the F; the alto in measures 15 and 16 leads into the c^1, the d^1 being a nonharmonic passing tone in measure 15, but a chord tone in measure 16. If we feel that these leadings should be satisfied, we must show the overlap by resolving the passing tone on its own manual. Still more important is the overlapping in measures 20 and 21, where the tendencies of the passing tones are greatly strengthened by chromatic alteration. Here the overlapping should certainly be shown, and consistency would suggest that the other cases be treated the same way.

Another solution, which the author favors, is suggested by noting the ending of the last echo of each phrase, and assuming that its predecessors end at the corresponding point. According to this plan the manual changes occur as follows: In measure 11 the tenor goes to Manual III on the last beat (F); in measure 14 the alto changes on the last beat (e^1), and again at the corresponding point (second beat) in measure 16; after the fifth phrase, the tenor and alto change on the last beat of measure 19, and on the second beat of measure 21. This method seems to be the most consistent, but it involves a careful manipulation of the swells in order to preserve the balance when the moving parts are transferred to a softer manual. Incidentally, if the alto melody beginning at measure 26, and the tenor two measures later, are treated as solos, the overlappings must be clearly shown by playing the common tone on both key-boards.[22]

More varied transition problems are encountered in Brahms's setting of 'O Gott, du frommer Gott'. The scheme of this work is as follows: The melody is treated as a cantus firmus, each phrase being preceded by a twofold introduction of which the first part is forte and the second is piano. Each section of each introduction develops as a melodic figure the initial motive of the phrase which it precedes, using it in diminution or double-diminution, forming a variation of the entire phrase. The last two phrases of the chorale melody being similar to the first two, Brahms cast his prelude in a ternary mold. In the first and last parts the antici-patory melodic material appears chiefly in an inner voice, the fragments are used in double-diminution, and eighth-note motion prevails; in the middle part the derived melody is always in the upper voice, and there is more quarter-note motion. In the first and last parts the second (softer) portion of each introduction is at a lower pitch than the first, and the cantus firmus is in the soprano; in the middle part the softer portion is higher than the first, and the cantus is in a lower voice.

The continuous motion of the first and last parts calls for a fluent combination based on eight- and four-foot diapasons, the balance being adjusted to the pitch and dynamic level. In the middle section the ele-ment of pitch contrast is essential, and it should be emphasized in the registration. The forte low sections should be rich in absorbed partials, effecting the aural domination of the notated pitch. The combination for the piano high sections can be based on eight- and four-foot flutes. These passages suggest the contrast between men's and women's voices. Except for the final phrase, the cantus firmus should always be played as a solo. This is most easily and effectively done by playing it with the feet, using a good manual or pedal reed at four-foot pitch. The last phrase demands a very rich and full ensemble.

It remains to determine the precise points where we will change manu-als, in accordance with the principles stated above. In measure 3 the A on the third beat is common to both sections, and it must be played on both manuals. Otherwise the changes in the first part can follow the dynamic indications. At the beginning of the middle part (measure 22) the first e^1 must be played on both manuals, unless the new combination includes the practical equivalent of the preceding. In measure 26 the notated overlap must give way to the piano indication. The change might even be made two notes earlier, showing the new entry by a phrase break. In measure 31 the tenor G on the last beat should be played on

[22] For the choice of stops, see pp. 163-4.

both manuals, unless Manual I includes the equivalent of the previous
combination. In measure 35 the alto goes to Manual II after the e^1, or
possibly after the A. Overlapping on the a^1 at the end of this measure
would be logical, but it would cover the entrance of the melody on Manual II. In the third part the changes again follow the dynamic indications, with the possible exception of measure 54. Here the $d\sharp^1$ tends
strongly to the e^1, but the latter must be heard as a definite, though
unaccented, beginning. We may change manuals, or reduce Manual I,
after the first note of the measure, showing the entrance of the new section by a phrase break. The author inclines, in spite of the tendency
of the $d\sharp^1$, toward leaving it in the air, following the composer's indications. It will be noted that these problems are all concerned with reductions where the composer's manual changes involve the interruption of a
melodic unit. If these indicate that Brahms was not completely at home
with the organ, still the organist can only regret that his preoccupation
with other media prevented him from writing more extensively for his instrument.

Concluding Example of Chorale Treatment

We will now conclude our study of chorale preludes with an analysis
of Bach's setting of Luther's Communion hymn, 'Jesus Christus, unser
Heiland, der von uns . . .' — the first version in the collection of *Achtzehn
Choräle*. The registration of this work involves an unusual combination
of formal, textural, and emotional considerations. In design it unites the
fugal elements of the "Pachelbel form"[23] and the sectional differentiation of Buxtehude's fantasias; but it is much more than a skillful blending of methods. Among all instrumental hymn settings this work is
unique for its perfect architectural symmetry and superb logic, contributing to a faithful and fervent interpretation of the text.

The four sections, treating the four phrases of the chorale, are approximately equal in length; the third section, like the third phrase of
the hymn, is slightly shorter, and the fourth section is extended, lending
significance to the conclusion. There is no overlapping at the division
points, save for the first note of the last section. Within the sections
the sequence of the entries of the theme is invariable: theme in the
tenor, fugal answer in the alto, theme in the pedal, theme in the soprano.
Except for a pedal point at the end of the third section, and the conclusion of the last section, the pedals are used only for the third entry
in each part. This entry is never ornamented; it functions as the
cantus firmus, which is repeated in the soprano. Within this frame

[23]Willi Apel calls it a "chorale motet." — Bibl. 137, p. 534.

the sections are differentiated in material and in mood, forming a progressive sequence.

In general there are three simultaneous voices throughout, so that
occasional additions lend special intensification. At the beginning, the
third voice does not enter until the second appearance of the theme. At
the end of the first section a fourth voice is added, the bass immediately
becoming a pedal point. For the final cadence of the second section
there are four moving parts. The third section introduces a fourth voice
(three moving parts above a pedal point) at the beginning of the fourth
entry, a fifth voice being added at the very end. In the last section there
are four moving parts beginning with the last entrance of the theme, a
fifth and sixth being added after the arrival of the final tonic pedal point.

A similar progressiveness characterizes the use of subordinate material. The first phrase is always accompanied by a countersubject, but
the third voice is a free counterpoint. The second phrase is accompanied
by two countersubjects, one of which is invariable throughout the section,
while the other is modified for the third and fourth entries. Each of the
last two sections employs two countersubjects, both of which appear unaltered with each statement of the theme.

The consistent progressiveness of the design parallels the mood development suggested by the text. This is the only chorale prelude in
which Bach interprets each line of an entire stanza.[24] The first phrase,
"Jesus Christ, our Saviour," is somber and tender, suggesting a contemplation of man's need and the redemption symbolized in the Communion. The countersubjects in the second section, "Who turned from us
the wrath of God," are characterized by rocking skips which represent,
according to Schweitzer, the "strokes of God's wrath."[25] The third section, "By his bitter sorrow," develops chromatic motives of grief, until at
the end they are heard in four voices at once, moving in similar and contrary motion. This emotional climax is interrupted by the last phrase,
"He hath saved us from the pains of hell." Immediately a joyful motive
which Schweitzer associates with the resurrection takes possession of
the mood, and the prelude ends in an ecstacy of rejoicing.[26]

All of the foregoing must be appreciated in order to give an adequate
interpretation of this work in performance. The registration must show
the horizontal and vertical elements of the design, the differentiation in

[24]In the last verse of the triple setting of 'O Lamm Gottes unschuldig', in *Achtzehn
Choräle*, he follows the text beginning with the fifth line.

[25]Compare the description of the scourging of Christ in the *Saint Matthew Passion*,
'Erbarm es Gott!', and particularly in the *Saint John Passion*, 'Barrabas aber war ein
Mörder'.

[26]See Bibl. 156, Vol. II, pp. 73-4.

thematic material and mood, and the cumulative development of texture and emotional intensity. The sections will be clearly set off by the process of fitting the combination to the material and mood, but attention must be given to the relation between the qualities and dynamic levels at the division points. Beyond that, the organist will follow the development within each section, keeping in mind its place in the structural and emotional sequence. The following general plan is suggested:

Let the first section be moderately quiet, the tone somber and warm, rich in upper partials, but with sparing use of upper ranks. At the same time there must be enough clarity to show the movement of the countersubject, whose leaning suspensions suggest the longing of the soul for redemption. The second section will probably be slightly louder. It will have more four-foot tone, and perhaps less string, because of the importance of the melodic motion of the countersubjects. The third section may be still louder, but it should be more differentiated in quality. The tone will be more complex, with a considerable proportion of mutations, but not extending too high. The quality should be intense, carrying out the mood of the grief motive. The last section will be considerably louder, and much brighter, increasing to a triumphant close.

The layout of the material favors bringing out all entries clearly, and building up somewhat toward the end of each section. The first two entries of the first phrase, being in the highest voice, are easily heard. When the pedal enters, the manual part should be subordinate, so that the theme may be prominent without being heavy. In measure 8 the hands go to a louder manual — the soprano with the entrance of the theme, the tenor with the beginning of the countersubject, and the alto on the last note of the measure. In both the second and third sections the first two entries of the theme may be played with the feet, using eight-foot or eight- and four-foot stops of diapason quality, in addition to couplers from the manuals. The hands will transfer to a louder manual, one voice at a time, with the last entrances of the theme and countersubjects. On some organs it may be advisable to make this change with the entrances of the countersubjects which accompany the pedal entry, adding to the combination with the first note of the last statement of the theme. If the resources of the secondary manuals are sufficient, it is desirable to play the third section on the Swell and Choir, so that the overlapping entry of the last phrase (at the beginning of the last section) may be brought out on a brilliant Great combination. If this is not practicable, the new Great combination must be added precisely at the beginning of the measure, in which case the B and g^1 might possibly be played on the Choir. Synchronized with the release of the chord a brilliant Swell or Choir combination (including a quint mixture and perhaps a four-foot reed) may be added. The right hand may then play on the Choir with the Swell coupled; at the end of the phrase the left hand also goes to the Choir. The right hand takes the next entrance on the Great, the left hand following at the beginning of the countersubject. It may be possible to show the crossing of parts in the succeeding measure by playing the middle voice on the Choir with a superoctave coupler. If the dynamic relation of the manuals permits, the hands can return to the Choir at the end of the phrase, so that the Great may be reinforced for the pedal entry and the beginning of the accompanying countersubjects. If the secondary manuals are too weak for this procedure, the Pedal will be reinforced, and the addition to the Great (which must come at the beginning of the first countersubject) will either be inconspicuous, or be accomplished with a superoctave coupler, so that it will not be heard in the pedal. Another addition should be made with the soprano entry of the theme, with a further build-up toward the end, if possible.

The problems presented by the various chorale settings which we have studied are typical of those to be encountered in other forms. There will always be concurrent and successive elements to be set in correct perspective, and the variations in their mutual relationship will be analogous to those we have seen exemplified in the works just discussed. We have worked out the interpretation of these pieces in minute detail, hoping that this demonstration of our manner of approach and our methods of realizing the results which we seek may be suggestive and helpful to less experienced organists.

Differentiation of Sections by Texture and Dynamics

The dovetailed sectional structure which we saw in Titelouze's 'Ave maris stella' verset is characteristic of the ricercare and fantasia, which were progenitors of the fugue. In these forms, as in the chorale settings which we have studied, each new section usually develops a new melodic phrase. In the mature fugues of Bach the differentiation of sections by thematic material gives place to differentiation by texture and dynamic plane; the distinguishing characteristics are synchronous rather than melodic.[27] This change shows a growing consciousness of the importance of vertical effects, and their structural value. From the psychological standpoint this is an advance. The introduction of new melodic themes provides new interest if they are heard, but their appreciation depends on attentive and analytical listening. On the other hand, a change in texture, in pitch level, or in dynamic plane, attracts the

---

[27] This, of course, does not apply to double fugues, or to such exceptional examples as the 'Fugue in E minor' ("Wedge").

attention of the listener and provides immediate relief without the inter-
vention of an intellectual process.

The Passacaglia

The variations of a passacaglia are differentiated by both thematic
material and texture, and to a certain extent by dynamic plane also.
Since one of the essentials of the form is to secure variety within the
limits imposed by the theme, the accompanying parts differ not only in
melodic outline, but in rhythmic character, in phrase lengths, in degree
of continuity, and in all that goes to make up the textural pattern. All
of these qualities affect the immediate impression on the listener and
assist in the recognition of thematic differentiation. At the same time,
the passacaglia is more than just a set of variations; it is a consistent
whole in which all the elements contribute to the overall design.

The supreme example, of course, is Bach's 'Passacaglia in C minor'.
We must resist the temptation to examine this work in detail, for we are
now primarily concerned with sectional structure. In general there is a
crescendo from beginning to end, with occasional respite, the dynamic
progress being completely interrupted by an episode-like section which
includes the thirteenth, fourteenth, and fifteenth variations. Corresponding to this crescendo there is a prevailing increase in the vitality of the
material, effected by the rate of motion, the range of movement, textural
intricacy, the number of voices, rhythmic emphasis, etc. Continuity is
provided by the dovetailing of nearly all division points.

This presents a difficult problem in registration. The combinations
should be adapted to the materials of the individual variations, and at
the same time provide for the general dynamic progress of the movement.
A method should also be devised for overlapping at the division points.
This can be done in the following manner: Alternate two secondary
manuals for the first five variations, increasing one while playing on the
other; Variation 6 is played on the Great with one or both secondary
manuals coupled; at the beginning of measure 57[28] an addition is made
in a closed, or partially closed, swell box, which opens during the first
two beats of the measure; an audible addition can be made at the entrance of the theme for Variation 8; Variation 9 is played on a secondary
manual; in the mean time the Great is reinforced for Variation 10; Variation 11 may possibly be played on a bright secondary manual, the right
hand changing with the entrance of the theme, and the left with the skip
in the following measure; Variation 12 is played on the Great, again

[28]For convenience we are following the numbering in the Schirmer Edition, which
begins with the initial incomplete measure.

reinforced, the left hand making the change after the rest in measure 98; Variation 13 is played on a secondary manual, with lighter registration; a still lighter combination is used for Variation 14, in which the initial five-note figure is differentiated from the ascending arpeggios, being played, perhaps, on a single eight-foot flute or a light reed;[29] two manuals are used also for Variation 15, providing a lighter combination (without two-foot tone) for the last beat than for the long arpeggios in the first part of each measure; with Variation 16 the general crescendo is suddenly resumed on a plane at least equal to that of Variation 12; an increase for Variation 17 can be effected in the same manner as for Variation 7; the addition for Variation 18 comes on the third beat of measure 145; the pedal reeds are added for Variation 19, and perhaps a superoctave manual coupler on the last eighth of measure 153; the same method can be employed for Variation 20 if another suitable coupler is available, or an addition can be made coincident with the entry of the theme.

Mention should be made, in passing, of the transition to the fugue. If it is played exactly as written, the first note of the theme is lost. Many organists make a complete break, repeating the c^1 to start the fugue. This forfeits the continuity which Bach evidently intended. The most satisfactory solution is to release everything *except* the c^1 on the last eighth of the measure (reducing the value of the last chord to an eighth). Synchronized with this release, the registration is reduced to the combination with which the fugue is to begin. It is essential that this be accompanied by a skillfully managed retard which gives a sense of finality to the conclusion of the passacaglia without breaking the rhythmic continuity. The retard should be gradual and increasing in rate throughout the measure, and sufficient to make the last eighth a little longer than a normal quarter. Strict tempo is, of course, resumed at the beginning of the fugue.

An interesting variation of the passacaglia scheme appears in Buxtehude's 'Passacaglio in D minor'. The theme is treated in a movement of four sections, connected by interludes, each containing seven statements. The first section is in D minor, the second is in F (the relative major), the third is in A minor (the dominant), and the last is again in D minor. Each section is more exciting than the preceding, and there is the usual increase within each section; so we have a general crescendo throughout the piece, marked by definite stages. The registration should be planned primarily to differentiate the main divisions, the progress within each section being related to its particular level.

---

[29] Adjacent manuals are necessary to keep it independent at the end of the variation.

Principal and Subordinate Sections

Most of Bach's music in extended forms is conceived in planes.[30] Principal sections alternate with episodes or secondary sections. In the freer forms the secondary sections use different material, but in his fugues (except, of course, double and triple fugues) the principal theme dominates the subordinate sections also, though its development is less concentrated; the entrances are more separated, and the intervening material is less restricted. This contrast in texture is usually accompanied by a lightening of the ensemble; the pedal drops out, and the spacing is more transparent. A softer dynamic level is implied, suggesting a change to a secondary manual. Indeed, Schweitzer and Widor have contended, with *almost* complete justification, that the manual parts should be played on the Great when there is a pedal part, and on a secondary manual when there is no pedal. There are numerous exceptions to this, but in general it is a sound principle; it means that we give the principal sections dynamic emphasis, and make the secondary sections subordinate.

The registration for the interpretation of such music requires (1) that the organist distinguish accurately between the principal and subordinate sections; (2) that he select tone combinations for the different planes in accordance with the material and the dynamic level, and with reference to the whole composition; and (3) that he determine the most effective transition from one manual to another, or the most advantageous point to change the combination. This procedure involves no new problems; it is merely another application of the processes described in the course of our study of choral preludes. An example will be examined at the end of this chapter.

Homophonic Formal Features

The music of Bach, with its dependence on vertical effects, leads us into the field of homophonic music. This need not detain us long. There is nothing in the later forms which was not foreshadowed by Bach. The smaller forms are not essentially different from the chorale; the larger ternary form is but a conventionalization of the scheme followed in the fugues in C minor and E minor, already cited. The principle of recurrence after contrast, which, combined with the processes of variation and development, forms the basis of almost all musical organization, is worked into a convincing and cumulative movement, 'Prelude in E flat', which introduces the so-called "Catechism Chorales" of the

---

[30] A common feature of Baroque music, which was particularly characteristic of Bach's musical conceptions.

Clavierübung.   Using letters to represent thematic material, and indicating the prevailing keys of the sections in parentheses, the plan is
as follows:

A (E♭), B (E♭-B♭), A (B♭-c), C (c), A (A♭), B (A♭-e♭), C (E♭), A (E♭)
A is massive, in five parts, essentially harmonic, and characterized by
a strong dotted rhythm. B is light, in three parts, practically without
pedal, beginning with antiphonal phrases and continuing with gentle
fluency.   C is fugal, combining fluency with vigor; its first appearance
is in three parts without pedal, and its second is in four, sometimes five,
parts with pedal. The superb logic of this scheme has never been excelled in any work based on a succession of recurring themes. Bach's
successors, using other instrumental media, adopted more stereotyped
forms, which later yielded to the demands of romanticism.   Thus the
forms were modified to allow freedom of expression – but Bach used his
form as a *means* of expression.

The 'Prelude in E flat' is a particularly clear example of Bach's
method of building a logical whole of differentiated sections. No less
convincing are the 'Toccata in F', the 'Fantasia in G minor', and the
'Prelude in B minor'. In all such works the organist will follow the
procedures already suggested. The details will vary with every composition, but the general principles remain the same. Moreover, there is
no need to carry this study on to later composers; he who can effectively
present the design of Bach's organ music will encounter no difficulty in
other forms and styles.

Even the sonata form does not involve essentially new procedures.
The differentiation of the themes, the continuity of the transitions, the
varied and sometimes cumulative presentation of the materials of the development, the adjustment of proportions, and the maintenance of the
integrity of the whole – all these are familiar processes combined in one
composite interpretation. Incidentally, it may be observed that the number of significant organ compositions which are cast in the sonata form
is very small.[31]

Often the interpretation of the formal design is influenced by other
considerations.   The relation of the various factors of interpretative
registration, including the sequence of movements in a cyclical work,
will be taken up in the next chapter. We will now conclude our study of
the use of registration to clarify the structure of individual movements
by examining what the author regards as the noblest work in the entire
realm of organ literature: Bach's 'Toccata and Fugue in F major'.
There is no other composition which, to the writer, so strongly suggests

[31]Cf. pp. 286-7.

the idea of eternity. It is doubtful if it could have been composed by a nonreligious person.

Bach's 'Toccata and Fugue in F major'

The material of which the toccata is constructed is all derived from the following elements:

A, the principal toccata theme
B, the chord cadence at the end of the first section

These materials appear in the following modified forms:

C, an expansion of B, involving the development of its first two chords above a pedal point
D, a four-measure cadence formula, developing a motive derived from A, and ending in B
E, an extension of C, using figures from D and A against detached chords
F, a section in triple counterpoint, introduced by B, developing the first four measures of A, dropping the strict canon, and adding a third imitating voice

In the first section, A is developed into a two-part canon over a pedal point, followed by a pedal solo treating the same material, ending with the cadence, B, in the dominant. Essentially the same thing is repeated in the key of C, ending with the extended cadence, C, in the same key. Then a modulating series of phrases, D, leads to the key of D minor, which is confirmed by C and E. F follows in D minor. Another modulating series of cadence phrases, D, leads to the key of A minor, confirmed by C only. F is now heard in A minor, with a shift of parts: the former soprano part is transferred to the alto, the alto to the bass, and the bass to the soprano. Again a modulating series of cadence phrases, D, leads to the key of G minor, the arrival being confirmed by both C and E. F now appears a third time, with the parts again rotated as before. The cadence phrases, D, now lead to the key of B flat, the final cadence of the last phrase being extended, and the key further confirmed by C. Two more D-phrases, extended to six measures, lead to a pedal point on CC, above which the toccata material rolls on to the final, climactic statement of C and E. The effect of the deceptive cadence is enormously strengthened by the preceding thirty-measure pedal point.

In planning the registration we must first determine the principal sections. These are identified by (1) the use of the toccata material as a theme, as distinct from the development of small fragments, and (2) stability of key. We find these conditions in the canons and pedal solos, A, of the first two sections, and in the triple counterpoint sections, F. The C and E combination assumes considerable importance, because of the massive chords and the strong tonal definition; its function, however, is to confirm the key at which the wandering episode has arrived, in preparation for the entrance of F. The final episode broadens out into a coda which is essentially one magnificent extended cadence.

The next step is to establish the dynamic scheme. The principal sections will presumably be louder than the subordinate ones. On an organ with limited resources, the determination of these two levels may suffice. It is better for the performance to lack variety than impressiveness, since the development of the music itself will carry conviction. If additional levels can be provided without sacrificing tone quality, C and E should be louder than D, and there should be a telling climax at the final entrance of C in the coda. When played on a large instrument, the organist can effect a general build-up from the beginning to the end. In that case, each section can be somewhat stronger than the preceding corresponding section – i.e., each principal section would be louder than the preceding principal section, and each episode louder than the preceding episode. However, the effective dynamic range can be increased by making the second episode, and the second triple counterpoint section to which it leads, somewhat less loud than the first. This reduction is almost implicit in the omission of E from the second episode.

The third step is to assign a suitable tone quality to each section, adjusting the combination to the dynamic level already established. Above all, the majesty of the music and the superb continuity of its movement must be faithfully presented. The beginning ensemble will be composed largely of diapason tone, the eight-foot pitch seeming to predominate. The proportion of upper work must be adjusted to provide fluency at a moderate pace, and vitality without heaviness; it must not be sufficient to impair the independence of the two voices of the canon. The pedal must not be heavy, and it should contain enough upper ranks to relate it to the manual ensemble. It may be reinforced, and the Great to Pedal added, at the beginning of the pedal solo. The vertical texture and the strong attacks on the chords of B call for reeds. That they should be added at the beginning of the measure is proven by C. The section in the key of C should be somewhat brighter, so that it will not be sluggish or indefinite in the lower range.

The registration for D should, like its material, combine the elements of A and B. Reeds may be present if covered. If possible, a suitable pedal combination should be provided without using couplers from all the manual divisions included in the ensemble, in order that the left hand may be heard when it enters on a note which a foot is playing. If the pedal can be completely independent (as Bach intended), so much the better. Schweitzer deprecates the antiphonal treatment of the D-phrases: the author does not find it objectionable provided two suitable ensembles can be devised. They would be differentiated by altering the proportion of reeds (if any), or of mixtures, or both. In any event, the reeds should be more prominent when C enters again; but there must be enough flue work to carry the sixteenth-note movement in E.

F calls for a larger proportion of flue tone, because of the polyphonic nature of the material. On that account it may be difficult to make it louder than the preceding E. It may be possible to maintain approximately the same dynamic level, identifying the new, principal section by a change of quality. Another method is to reinforce the ensemble at the very beginning of the section, reducing the reeds by partially closing the swell box when the chords give way to polyphony. If we choose to lighten the second entry of F, it is possible on a large organ to show the crossing of parts by playing the upper voices on the Choir (with the Swell coupled), while the left hand plays the tenor on the Great. The soprano goes over to the Great in measure 275, where it takes up the imitation.

Beginning with the final D section there should be a general crescendo to the end, with additions at suitable points. The climax at the last appearance of C (measure 417) can be enhanced by adding the Tuba for the inverted pedal point on c^2 (later, c^1). This would be done by coupling it to the Choir, so that all the other parts could continue on the Great without the Tuba.

The fine double fugue which follows is a worthy companion to the toccata, popular opinion notwithstanding. It gives the impression of a large ternary form, the *manualiter* development of the second theme forming the middle section. The reprise comes with the entry of the first theme in the alto, in measure 128. Beginning with the following answer (measure 134), the second theme is substituted for the original countersubject with every entry, save for a single omission of three measures.

The registration should conform to the simple scheme of the fugue. The slow theme and the moderate pace of the counterpoints call for solidity, dominant eight-foot pitch, and enough upper work to avoid heaviness. If any modification is made in the first section, there may be a slight reduction (perhaps only with the swell pedal) when the pedal drops out in measure 44, a reinforcement of the pedal for the succeeding entry, and an addition to the manual combination for the entry of the soprano at measure 56.

In spite of the fact that the second theme begins on the first beat of measure 70, the manual change should take place on the last beat.[32] The transparent texture and fluent motion of this section call for a fairly

[32]See p. 194.

light combination with few mutations. By making clever use of the silent pedal, all entries in the lower and middle voices can be brought out, using quiet eight- and four-foot diapasons added to the general ensemble. There can be a slight build-up during this section, particularly as the reprise is approached.

On the third beat of measure 128 the alto and tenor are conspicuously reinforced, by adding stops if they are already on the Great, or by changing to the Great if they are still on a secondary manual. If the balance permits, the soprano may continue on the Choir until the entry of the answer in measure 134. Except for the surreptitious entry in measure 142, which should remain subordinate, all the succeeding statements of the principal theme can be brought out. In measures 153 and 158 it enters in the highest voice, and can be emphasized by an addition to the manual combination. The pedal is reinforced for the entries in measures 147 and 163, the latter addition including telling reeds.

The satisfaction of planning a registration which sets forth clearly and in just proportion the various elements which enter into the design of such architectural masterpieces is an experience which is unparalleled in any other field of musical interpretation. The organist not only controls dynamic and temporal values in accordance with his conception of the composition, but he determines the nature of the tonal fabric, and thus shares in the creative process. This privilege imposes a corresponding obligation. If the performer is to participate in the composer's work he must completely understand the composer's purpose, and plan his interpretation for the fullest possible realization of that purpose.

CHAPTER NINE
SEQUENTIAL DESIGN
Cyclical Works

The study of a paired prelude and fugue at the conclusion of the last chapter leads us to the consideration of the succession of associated movements found in cyclical forms. In spite of the many suites, sonatas, and concertos of various types which were composed for the harpsichord and for sundry groups of instruments, very few cyclical works were written for the organ before the nineteenth century. Sets of versets,[1] which the early organ composers provided in profusion, were intended for antiphonal liturgical use, not for consecutive performance. Although the Italian canzonas, Buxtehude's sectional fugues, and Georg Muffat's toccatas present some of the features of cyclical works, their parts are not sufficiently independent to place them in that category. Some of the "suites des pièces" of the French composers of the seventeenth and eighteenth centuries may have been intended for sequential performance, but others are merely miscellaneous collections of pieces, grouped according to key or mode. Bach's Trio Sonatas may be considered the real ancestors of the organ sonata, while his 'Toccata, Adagio, and Fugue in C' is a typical three-movement composition,[2] having a slow movement between two allegro movements, the first of which is the more solid, and the last the more lively. Later eighteenth century experiments are now forgotten; the modern organist's repertoire of sonatas, symphonies, etc., begins with the works of Mendelssohn.

Obviously the treatment of an individual movement of a cyclical work does not differ from that of a similar independent piece, except as it may be influenced by its association with the other movements. The problem of sequential interpretation is always present, whether we are concerned with sections of a single piece, with movements of a sonata, with numbers in a group, or even with a whole program. In all cases we should study the interrelation of the parts and the balance of the whole.

Successive Materials

The registration of successive materials is governed by considerations of change and consistency — change to avoid monotony and fatigue, and consistency to avoid shock. In general (unless contrast is an inherent feature of the musical material) the proportion of these two

[1] See Chap. X, pp. 235, 240, 243 (fn. 69), 244-5.

[2] Two other preludes and fugues were intended to be provided with middle movements. See Bibl. 156, Vol. I, p. 278, and Bibl. 87, pp. 175-6.

quasi-contradictory elements is determined by the length and completeness of the differentiated units. Ordinarily there is less contrast between successive sections of a movement than between successive
movements of a cyclical work. The short sections do not cause fatigue,
and their incompleteness — the fact that they lead on instead of coming to
a conclusion — suggests a degree of continuity. On the other hand, after
a fairly long movement the mind is ready for a change; contrast is
needed to provide relief. The fact that the movement is complete permits contrast without shock. The movement ends, and there is usually a
slight pause before the new material is attacked. In combining cyclical
works or groups in a program we are dealing with still larger units,
separated by longer pauses, or even intermissions. Then still greater
contrast is not only suitable but desirable.

When the break between movements is slight, much importance attaches
to the relation of the end of one to the beginning of the next. Composers
usually provide a contrast in material and dynamics, to arrest the attention of the listener, to set the new mood, and to mark the formal change.
If they fail to do that, the organist should provide a change of color,
even though it is not indicated. A couple of examples will serve to
illustrate this:

In his *Grande Pièce Symphonique* Franck specifies that the end of the
first movement be played on the foundation stops and Oboe of the Récit
(Swell). He then indicates that the next movement begin with foundation
stops and reeds on the Récit to accompany a solo to be played on the
Cromorne and eight-foot flutes of the Positif (Choir). Obviously loud
reeds cannot be included in this accompaniment, so the combination is
essentially the same as that specified for the end of the first movement,
with the addition of the Cromorne solo. The organist will modify this,
guided by the change of mood: the second movement is much more placid
than the first. The first movement may therefore conclude with a more
complex tone, including eight- and four-foot strings and perhaps the
Oboe — possibly even a soft mixture if it is completely absorbed. At the
beginning of the second movement the left hand may use a Gemshorn, or
a Quintadena combined with a four-foot flute — assuming that on an
American organ a Clarinet will replace the Cromorne. Of course if the
second movement is played without the first, the question of change does
not arise. In that case a warmer quality may be used for the accompaniment.

In Widor's *Symphony in A minor*, Number 7, he specifies an eight-foot
flute on the Récit for the coda of the second movement, and an eight-
foot flute on the Grand Orgue (Great) for the beginning of the third. Here
again the organist must modify the composer's registration. He can take

his cue from the fact that the left hand part at the end of the second movement is too low for the flute anyway. It may be played on a combination which is slightly stringy — perhaps a Gemshorn, or a mild string combined with a Quintadena. In the next to the last score a soft four-foot flute may be included in the right hand combination, but it should be removed for the last score, where the upper part has more the nature of a solo. The mood of the third movement is considerably brighter. The use of eight- and four-foot flutes in the introduction provides a change in the right direction, after which the slight texture and the entrance of a contrasting solo alter the color still further. It must be admitted, however, that the sequence of these movements is not ideal.[3]

It happens less frequently that composers end one movement and begin the next on a loud plane. When they do, there is usually a definite contrast in texture which naturally suggests a corresponding change in the character of the registration. There should also be a change in dynamic level, even though the composer's indications do not show it. Often this will be suggested by the form: for example, the fact that the normal development of a fugue implies a crescendo makes it undesirable to begin the movement fortissimo.

The nature of the change made between movements, however, is but a detail in the larger conception of the relation of individual movements to one another and to the whole cycle. They are usually contrasted in form, tempo, dynamics, mood, texture, and other features. If the registration is adapted to these characteristics a contrast will be inevitable; at the same time the registration scheme itself should be studied in its relation to the whole structure, as well as to the individual, contrasted movements. Any attempt to treat this subject exhaustively would be futile, but in concluding our discussion of registration and musical design we will study two examples which will serve to illustrate the problems involved and the methods which may be employed.

Sonata in F minor, Number 1, by Mendelssohn-Bartholdy

The four movements of Mendelssohn's *First Sonata* present, respectively: i. a modified fugue, with chorale; ii. a sectional development of a song theme; iii. an antiphonal recitative; iv. a continuous toccata. They are contrasted in material, pace, dynamics, form, and in the nature, amount, frequency, and abruptness of internal change.

---

[3]A defect in Widor's symphonies as cyclical works is the frequent lack of contrast between successive movements. It is partly for this reason that complete performances have seldom been included on recital programs. Notable exceptions are the *Fourth Symphony* (which, however, is inferior to his later works), the *Sixth Symphony*, and the *Symphonie Gothique*.

The first movement alternates, and sometimes combines, harmonic texture with polyphony. The fortissimo introduction calls for a rich, cohesive, solid ensemble, which becomes less complex with the entry of the fugue theme. As the pace is only moderately animated, great fluency is not required. There should be sufficient fundamental to avoid thinness, and to preserve the seriousness of the mood. The registration of the chorale has already been discussed in Chapter VI.[4] The combination assigned to the fugal material should be reduced for the fragments interpolated between the phrases of the chorale. The indicated fortissimo is too loud: it produces too violent a contrast to the chorale, and it is inconsistent with the subordinate character of the entire section, which must be made clear in order that the listener may gain a perspective of the whole movement. The original fugal registration will be resumed with the entrance of the theme in inversion, which marks the second principal section. The following appearance of the chorale is less subordinate. There is more movement in its accompanying harmonization, and the fugue theme which had previously entered timidly in the tenor in the third phrase of the chorale, now asserts itself in the soprano before the first phrase is concluded. The interpolations between the phrases are short and exclamatory. The whole section is restless, becoming more and more excited as it leads to the climactic entry of the fugue theme, in both its direct and inverted forms, over a pedal point. This forward urge, which prevents a relaxation into the tranquil mood of the chorale, is expressed by greater intensity in the ensemble, and a somewhat higher dynamic plane than was used for the first subordinate section. The interpolated fragments can be almost fortissimo this time, anticipating the drive to the final climax. After the dramatic arrival on the German sixth, the calm submission of the chorale, "What my God wills", returns — quiet, in retrospect; then in a sudden burst of confidence the second phrase declares: "His will is best!" Probably Mendelssohn had no programmatic intentions, but this conception is consistent with the emotional development of the music. The quiet phrase should be warm, without reeds (except perhaps an Oboe), and with a considerable string content on account of the low pitch. The last phrase requires a full, rich ensemble.

Unlike the first movement with its abrupt changes and wide dynamic range, and its exploitation of two contrasting materials in a framework which involves the alternation and final merging of principal and subordinate sections, the second movement is homogeneous in substance, uniform in dynamics, and divided into sections which offer no contrast,

[4]P. 139.

but vary the material by changes of range and color and, with the addition of the pedals and the separation of the melody, of tonal texture. This little piece offers considerable opportunity to the imaginative organist to vary his registration in such a way as to bring out the development of the material. The lower phrases will be played on a mild string combination, and the higher phrases on a single flute or gedeckt. When the antiphonal use of high and low pitch ceases, the tone may become slightly more complex; at any rate, the *direction* of the manual changes indicated by the composer cannot be strictly followed. The solo which comes with the entrance of the pedal should be played on a quiet reed, on the manual *next above* the accompanying manual, so that the alto can still be played on the lower manual in the seventh and eighth measures of this section. In the ninth measure the manuals are reversed (possibly with some change), as the left hand has the melody. In the fifth and fourth measures from the end, the sixteenth-note melody continues on the solo stop, the sustained tones being played on the accompanying manual. The left hand may even follow up the chord, as shown in Example 14. It is evident that all these changes are designed to bring

Example 14. Mendelssohn: First Sonata—ii. Adagio

out what is actually in the music. If discreetly and skillfully done they do not interfere with the continuity of the movement.

The Recitative offers a startling contrast to the placidity and uniform dynamics of the second movement, featuring an alternation of pianissimo and fortissimo, and opposing textural characteristics. In its contrasts it is reminiscent of the first movement, but its form and development are radically different. The dynamic relation of the two materials is reversed, and the contrast is much greater; instead of the broad outlines with large subordinate sections found in the first movement, there is a continuous antiphonal, phrase by phrase alternation, which gives a fragmentary effect; at the same time there is overall progress in the development of the recitative material which lends unity to the movement: The first entry is in a single voice; the second, two answering voices; the third, one against two; the fourth and fifth, two against two; the sixth and seventh build up extended chords in slow arpeggios. The climax thus reached is marked by antiphonal fragments, diminishing to the return, pianissimo, of the original recitative theme in canon against a gradually disappearing background; then one more chorale fragment which is imitated and extended on a pianissimo plane, leading to the finale.

The design of this third movement is so inseparably identified with the treatment of the material itself that it is best revealed by the registration which most clearly shows that development. By the exercise of some ingenuity the reciprocal relationship of the two hands can be shown by playing on two manuals. A Clarinet in the left hand against a single flute in the right will serve the purpose, preserving the clarity of the voice leading and providing differentiation without tonal incompatibility. The build-up beginning with the sixth phrase calls for a single ensemble of increasing complexity and vitality. The canon can be played by the right hand and feet, the left hand sustaining the background on another manual. The connection with the following phrase involves practical difficulties which are not insoluble. The chorale fragments throughout this movement demand a rich ensemble, amply furnished with reeds and mixtures, and containing a considerable amount of sixteen-foot tone — unless the organist chooses to fill in the harmonies with the left hand. A full Swell combination, perhaps with octave couplers,[5] provides a suitable ensemble, and enables the organist to produce a swell on each phrase — a procedure which is effective, but more romantic than Mendelssohn probably intended.

The finale, with its continuity, fluency, and exuberant animation, balances the fragmentary recitative, and also contrasts with the more serious first movement. In spite of the definite recurrence of the initial theme and the extensive development of a second, the motion is incessant and invariable until near the end; the form is cursive, with the minimum of sectionalism. The registration suggested in Chapter V[6] is designed to bring out these distinctive qualities which both differentiate it from the other movements and provide the consummation of the entire work.

One is reluctant to conclude the discussion of this sonata without calling attention to the ingenious and subtle relation of the thematic material of the different movements — in spite of the fact that it is completely irrelevant to our primary purpose. The first three notes of the second phrase of the chorale provide the material for the introduction; the inverted fugue theme is essentially the same as the first phrase of the chorale, with the omission of the second note; the first phrase of the

[5]Suggested by the late Dr. T. Tertius Noble.
[6]P. 109

second movement is a coloratura variation of the chorale; the characteristic drop in the fugue theme is found at the beginning and end of the
recitative theme, while other melodic details parallel fragments of the
chorale; the massive chords in the recitative movement are an abridgment
of the first phrase of the chorale, and the later arpeggiated chords
anticipate the material of the finale; the first four measures of the finale
outline the inverted fugue theme in major, taking the first manual note,
and the highest chord tones in each measure; the second theme of this
movement uses the first five notes of the chorale in retrogression, with a
single interchange. Even if some of these coincidences are accidental,
the composer may have been unconsciously influenced by previous
material.

Symphonie Gothique, by Widor

For our second example of a cyclical work we have chosen Widor's
Symphonie Gothique, which, in the mind of the author, is one of the
masterpieces of modern organ literature. It owes its title to the fact that
it was inspired by the Gothic Church of St. Ouen in Rouen. The introit
for the third Mass on Christmas day, 'Puer natus est nobis',[7] is introduced in the third movement and forms the basis of the fourth. Its characteristic initial skip, sometimes inverted, often reduced to a fourth, is
a conspicuous feature of all the movements. It is doubtful that the composer had any other church themes in mind; although it is possible to relate other material to fragments of various melodies proper to the Christmas season, the resemblances are probably fortuitous, or at least,
unconscious.

The four movements provide variety and contrast in an effective psychological sequence. The first is a continuous movement, elaborately
constructed of two melodic fragments, possibly derived from the antiphon,
'Tecum principium'.[8] It is richly somber, sedate in pace, and builds up
to an impressive climax. The second movement is a song in ternary form,
developed from a single melodic phrase. The third is a sprightly fugue,
bright, and fairly loud, in which the plainsong is introduced as a cantus
firmus in the bass. The fourth movement is sectional and exceedingly
varied, beginning with a theme and variations and ending with a brilliant
toccata.

Some have imagined that the contour of the themes of the first movement was suggested by the lines of Gothic architecture — a theory which
could conceivably apply to the other movements as well. A much stronger

[7]Bibl. 187, p. 374.
[8]Bibl. 187, p. 378.

formal resemblance is in the overall design of the first movement. It is composed of a series of climaxes of varying intensity, always followed by relaxation and (except at the end) a renewal of the crescendo. The whole is governed by a general, but not consistent, dynamic increase leading to an imposing climax, suggesting the culminating heights of the vaulting. Such a conception may assist the imagination of the interpreter as well as the listener, but for the composer the architectural influence was probably subjective, rather than literal.

The indicated registration for this movement, which has been discussed from the standpoint of weight,[9] serves also to interpret the somber mood of the music. The pitch level is kept down by the inclusion of sixteen-foot stops, and the avoidance of ranks above four-foot pitch except at the climax. In general, save for occasional respite, the spacing remains close throughout, and suboctave couplers may be assumed when the full organ is introduced at the high climax. The reedy combination lends intensity to the mood and provides a wide dynamic range. There should be no color contrasts — only the slight dilution of the reed tone where the Positif or Grand Orgue is indicated. For its best effect this movement needs a French organ in a large, "resonant" room.

The placidity of the second movement comes as a welcome contrast. This quality is emphasized by the composer's indicated registration. It is advantageous, however, to use two manuals, playing the accompaniment on light eight- and four-foot flutes: the eight-foot alone is too heavy and vague in that range.[10] The pedal flute (if used) must be light, and the string which is coupled to it not too thin. The pedal part should show against the flutes, but not quarrel with them.

Contrasting with the cool transparency of the first section, the middle part is warm and rich. The general pitch level is lower, the number of voices is increased, and the texture is close. The tonal ensemble accordingly becomes more complex by the addition of strings and light diapasons, perhaps omitting the flutes. One must not be conscious of any upper pitches, but their presence in the tone is essential. The problems are: (1) to bring out the pedal without making it heavy when the double pedaling begins, and (2) to find a quality for the soprano melody which will not be thick when the other parts go over to the same manual. Sometimes a broad céleste is the best solution for the pedal, the box being partially closed when the left foot enters. The Great combination may include an eight-foot flute which will be thrown off when the other parts are transferred to that manual. The placid mood and

[9]Pp. 146-7.

[10]The composer instructed his pupils to play the first half-measure twice, in order to provide a longer introduction.

transparent color return in the last section, the registration for which was discussed under spacing, in Chapter VI.[11]

After the continuous solemnity of the first movement and the tranquillity (giving way to fervor in the middle section) of the second, the jolly polyphony of the fugue is delightfully refreshing. The composer has indicated different dynamic levels by his assignment of manuals, but the movement is uninterrupted, division points are dovetailed, and the eager progress and high spirits of the music are continuous. The specified "Cornets et mixtures" are right. There should be just enough fundamental to define the voice leading. The pedal is designed to balance the combined ensemble of the three manuals, but heavy stops should be avoided. When it is played against the Récit alone it is somewhat prominent, serving to bring out the plainsong theme. When the cantus firmus is heard against the full combination, reeds are added to the pedals.

These three movements constitute about half of the symphony. Although strongly contrasted in mood, color, and dynamics, they are all continuous — the first, an intricate development of short motives; the second, a succession of connected phrases; and the third, a polyphonic form. The fourth movement provides immediate formal contrast by beginning with a series of separated sections. The theme itself is divided in the middle, and it is followed by two variations and three other independent sections before the toccata, which is the real finale, begins. Thus we have what amounts to six short, contrasting movements. They afford relief from the previous continuity, so that the more cursive development of the toccata comes as a welcome return. They also serve to familiarize the listener with the two themes which dominate the symphony, beginning with the third movement.

The plainsong melody, already heard in the pedals in the preceding fugue, is presented in simple, chorale style. The accompanying counterpoint of the first variation immediately introduces the second theme, which is related to the fugue theme of the preceding movement, and may be derived from the last phrase of the introit. The oscillation between neighboring tones, which characterizes the accompaniment of the second variation, is borrowed from the plainsong itself. A change of form, as well as material, is provided by the merry little canon developed from the second theme, against which the pedals imply the initial fifth-skip of the plainsong. The next section introduces new material, taking up the third phrase of the plainsong which has not yet been heard. The three-part canon which follows returns to the melody and binary division of the original theme. The composer later decided that this section was

[11]Pp. 149-50.

superfluous and instructed his pupils to omit it, going directly from the preceding cadence on E (half cadence in A minor) to the toccata. There follows an exciting development of the two themes, leading to the triumphant delivery of the plainsong in pedal octaves, and subsiding to a tranquil close.

The registration of this movement need not detain us long. The composer's indications are specific, and the reader who has followed our methods thus far will recognize their suitability, if not their inevitability. Their relation to the form is obvious, since the differentiation of the musical material is so clear that the organist has only to give it a faithful presentation. A few suggestions concerning their adaptation to American organs may be helpful.

In the second variation the pedal reed should have relatively less fundamental than the one for the right hand. The upper melody can be played on a rather smooth trumpet — possibly a small or enclosed Tuba, while the lower part calls for a bright trumpet, perhaps clarified by the addition of a Clarion. The accompaniment on the Great may be too heavy. If suitable eight- and four-foot diapasons are not available on the Choir, it may be possible to use the Great Octave and Fifteenth, playing an octave lower than written. For the Allegro canon care must be taken to avoid heaviness in the pedals; the prescribed flute is doubtful. For the Moderato section the sixteen-foot diapason on the Great will probably be found too heavy. It may be possible to use the Choir diapason, coupled at the suboctave pitch. The same problem arises at the end of page 29.

The omission of the mixtures at the beginning of the toccata actually clarifies the motion at the high pitch used, and enhances the festive character of the music, *provided* the flue stops are light and the reeds bright. On many organs the flue stops should be omitted from the swell; and sometimes it is advantageous to add a mixture. Pedal reeds, though not specified, are assumed at the *fff*. At the end the listener should hear pure, warm, eight-foot diapason quality. American diapasons are usually either too heavy or too hard. The organist should select his best enclosed diapason and experiment with the addition of mild strings, very delicate four-foot and mutation ranks, and possibly a soft Oboe.

This work has been chosen for discussion, not because of the problems which it presents, but because of the ease and naturalness with which the obvious registration sets off its formal characteristics. It is a remarkable example of the successful adaptation of the musical material and tone qualities to the design.

Relativity

We have studied the principles of interpretative registration with reference to the nature of the musical material – its texture, pitch, pace, continuity, rhythm, and weight; the mood, and the structural design, including the grouping of formal units in a larger scheme. We have observed that in many cases the various musical elements serve the same purpose, and so corroborate one another. For example, high pitch, rapid pace, and light weight, all imply the use of high flutes, and all suggest the bright mood which the high flutes express. Again, a change in texture, reducing the number of parts and dropping out the pedal for a subordinate section of a fugue, serves to clarify the design; and the adaptation of the registration to the same change of material fulfills the same purpose.

Such agreement in the adaptation of the registration to various characteristics of the music is not, however, universal. Sometimes the organist is confronted with conflicting desiderata, and is obliged to effect some sort of reconciliation among them. The following are typical problems:

The variety in the musical material may invite frequent and striking changes in tone quality where greater continuity in the musical impression is desirable.

Devices for bringing out the entrances of themes, or calling attention to imitation, may interfere with the general progress of the music.

Anything which calls special attention to details tends to impair the fluency. This effect is both psychological and technical. Not only is the mind less able to take in the whole when it is concentrated on details, but often registration which is in itself effective is impracticable from the technical standpoint, and so affects the fluency of the execution.

Sometimes there is a conflict between the desired color and the requirements of the texture. A somber or intense mood is suggested by an ensemble which does not favor clarity of voice leading. Any music which combines harmonic color with polyphonic texture demands cohesion for the one and separate audibility for the other. Weight also tends to obscure the voice leading, presenting a problem when both factors are important – as in Bach's great setting of 'Aus tiefer Not' in the *Clavierübung*.

Without pausing to list further examples, we will try to establish certain general principles which may guide us in solving such problems:

The first task is to evaluate the conflicting effects and determine their relative importance. Then we will judge the degree of their incompatibility, and try to discover if there is any way of resolving the problem by devising a registration which will serve all purposes reasonably well, though it may not be ideal for each.

If the conflict is absolute, a compromise must be effected in which the various features of the music are presented in proportion to their importance.[12] At the same time we should take into consideration the extent to which the music depends on its registration for the desired effects. For example, Bach's 'Aus tiefer Not', referred to above, is massive and intense, while the texture is highly polyphonic. In spite of the complexity of the texture and the interest in the individual voices, they seem incidental, contributing to an ensemble which is essentially heavy and somber, suggesting the depths ("De profundis") from which the soul cries to the Lord. At first thought, then, it would appear that the registration should be planned primarily with reference to the considerations of mood and weight. On the other hand, the six-part writing itself is heavy, and its thick texture produces a somber impression with any registration which does not actually transpose the music to a higher pitch. It is not necessary to strengthen that impression with the registration; in fact, too much fundamental would exaggerate the weight and thickness of the ensemble. But the fact remains that the general tonal effect is more important than the clarity of the horizontal elements in the texture. We need, therefore, a complex ensemble, providing cohesion and synthetic fundamental, with just enough emphasis on individual pitches to enable the voice leading to be heard.[13]

Guiding Principles

There is no need to multiply examples, for every composition presents a different problem, and the organist is dependent on his judgment and ingenuity for its solution. We may, however, propose a few guiding principles:

1. The general effect is more important than details. If the details can be brought out without diverting the attention of the listener from the essential impression of the music, or impairing the fluency of the execution, it is advantageous to do so; but the greater should not be sacrificed for the lesser.[14]

2. Components of the musical material should be presented in accordance with their relative importance. Principal themes should be more prominent than accessory material, considering both dynamic and color

[12]Cf. pp. 92-3.

[13]Cf. p. 147

[14]Compare the discussion of possible complex registration schemes for two canonic settings in Bach's *Orgelbüchlein* on page 185.

effects. The melodic and harmonic textural elements should be carefully proportioned.

3. The major features of design should be clearly set forth, the lesser elements taking their place on a proportionate scale.

4. The relation of the formal and expressive elements in the music should be faithfully maintained. In interpreting compositions of the classic style, in which the emotional element is subordinate to the design, the registration should be planned primarily to show the formal elements in just proportion. Music, like that of Bach, in which the design is used as a means of expression, requires a convincing presentation of the essential structural features with an equally valid interpretation of the mood. On the other hand, music of the romantic school, in which the form is merely a frame for emotional portrayal, should be registered with primary attention to the mood and to the effective exposition of the material through which it is expressed.

5. The relation between the nature of the musical material and the emotion which it conveys is analogous to that existing between the larger formal and expressive elements, and calls for similar adaptation.

6. The problem of program music, though rarely encountered in the standard organ literature, cannot be completely ignored. It involves the subordination of both formal and textural considerations to specific expression. In addition to the procedures mentioned under 4 and 5, the use of exotic colors for specific effects, sometimes involving actual imitation, has its place.

7. There is a distinction between sacred and secular style which, though sometimes difficult to define, is valid, and should be reflected in the registration. Religious emotions range from intense sadness to ecstatic joy, but they are expressed with a certain amount of reserve. Passion, sentimentality, frivolity, and virtuosity are secular characteristics which should not be evident in religious music. In its registration exotic colors and highly characteristic individual stops should be sparingly used. Extremely thin strings and such effects at the Voix Céleste and the tremolo savor of sentimentalism and should be used, if at all, with great restraint. Again, an exaggerated proportion of high pitches, which in the softer dynamic range tends toward levity or exoticism, and in the louder range becomes harsh or exciting, is unsuited to normal religious expression. Of course such high pitches as are needed to express joy are entirely justified when the music itself is joyful. The use of such music will naturally depend on the occasion. Technical display and its concomitant registration are inappropriate in a religious setting, except in so far as they contribute to a legitimate religious mood. In a word, any excess should be avoided in the interpretation

of sacred music, and of course only such music should be played for a church service.

Summary

The axiom, "the whole is greater than any of its parts," is basic in all musical interpretation. The performer should envisage the entire composition, judging the relation of the main sections to the whole and to one another; he should then consider the smaller divisions in relation to the larger ones, and so on to the minutest details. The interpretation of details may affect the procedure with reference to the larger units, but they should never be allowed to disturb their essential balance and proportion. It is like a tree, the large branches of which proceed from the stem, while smaller branches and twigs in turn spring from the larger ones. The beauty and form of the whole depends on the subordination of the smaller to the larger, each unit functioning in relation to the complete design.

This conception of interpretation should control the registration. The main sections will be differentiated by combinations and registration processes suited to the material, the degree of contrast and the suddenness of its realization corresponding to the changes in the music itself. The return of the same material, as in a rondo, ternary form, or sonata, generally involves a return of similar registration. It may be varied, as the composer himself may vary his material, but the registration should assist the listener in recognizing the return. Similarly, unless contrast is an inherent characteristic of the material, subordinate differentiation is effected by correspondingly less striking contrasts in the tone combination.

At the same time we have observed that the parts of a composition are differentiated not only by the nature of their material but by the manner of its development. The movements of a cyclical work are usually cast in different forms; as a rule a prelude is more obviously sectional than the fugue which follows it; the middle part of a ternary form and the episodes of a rondo are generally less regularly constructed than the principal sections, just as the development of a sonata opposes a free fantasia to the clear, balanced organization of the exposition and reprise. Such characteristics are reflected in the registration. The differentiation is not only, and need not be primarily, between different kinds of ensemble or different dynamic levels: it may be between continuity and variation, or between subtle development and sharp contrasts.

It is obvious that the practical working out of this correspondence between musical structure and material, and the registration, has unlimited ramifications. The organist must study every conceivable aspect of the music, evaluate all the factors, and devise a registration which will preserve their essential relationship. A work of art is a composite whole.

Part IV

MEDIA OF PERFORMANCE

CHAPTER TEN

HISTORICAL SURVEY – TO 1750
LATIN COUNTRIES

The Composer's Medium

Our exposition of the theory of registration is done. On the basis of the principles set forth in the foregoing chapters the organist can, within the limits of his ingenuity and resourcefulness and of the resources of his instrument, devise an effective interpretation of what he finds on the printed page. But what does the printed page reveal?

In the chapter on 'Color and Mood' we stressed the inadequacy of a mere faithful presentation of the notated music. The interpreter should employ every possible means of understanding the composer's original conception, make that conception his own, and seek to convey it to his audience. To this end he should supplement his study of the music itself by acquiring a knowledge of the composer as revealed in his entire output, and of his historical and national setting. It is particularly important to know something about the medium for which the music was conceived. It is impossible to understand the composer's intentions without having some idea of the effect of the music as played by the composer and his contemporaries.

In these chapters we can do no more than sketch the essential facts concerning the organs and registration practices of the past, and suggest their suitable influence on our own interpretations. Even in this restricted area we must resist the temptation to go too much into detail, lest our study become unduly expanded, and lest the interest in collateral information divert our attention from our main objective.

The Earliest Organ Music

The fascinating story of the development of organs and organ music begins with the invention (or perfection) of the *hydraulos* by the Greek inventor, Ktesibios, who lived in Alexandria in the third century, B.C. This little instrument had nineteen finger keys and three ranks of pipes with stop action. Willi Apel contends that it is unreasonable to suppose that no attempt was made to play two-part music on such a keyboard.[1] He further suggests that when, perhaps about the sixth century, the increased size and power of organs led to the substitution of slides for keys, two-part music was still played by two performers on a single instrument.[2]

[1] Bibl. 51, pp. 207-8.
[2] Bibl. 51, pp. 210-12.

Hinged keys did not reappear until about the tenth century,[3] and it was perhaps three hundred years later that the mechanism was sufficiently perfected to make it possible to play with the fingers.[4] Obviously no real organ literature could exist until this condition was achieved.

Until about the fifth century the organ was apparently used solely for secular functions.[5] When it entered the service of the church it presumably supported or substituted for the voices in the rendition of plainsong. It is generally supposed that with the introduction of part singing the organ played the cantus firmus with, or against, the voices; but some contend that it was used for the *vox organalis*. This could have been true only of the note-against-note type of organum until the action was light and responsive enough to permit the execution of melismatic melodies.[6]

There is equal uncertainty concerning the independent use of the organ, and its available repertoire. According to Raugel,[7] the organist alternated with the singers in the rendition of sequences as early as the eleventh century. He also maintains that Pérotin (11..-1236) wrote *triples* (trios) to be played on two or three portable instruments, or on an organ with more than one keyboard.[8] However, these works are more generally considered vocal organa in which the organ shared by supporting the long notes of the cantus firmus.

There is similar disagreement about the mode of performance of the more advanced compositions of the Burgundian and Flemish composers of the fifteenth and early sixteenth centuries. Schering contends that much of this music was intended to be played on the organ.[9] In support of this opinion he and Hans Klotz edited collections of such compositions

[3] Bibl. 51, p. 215.

[4] Bibl. 51, p. 208. Records are meager and conflicting, and new evidence is constantly being uncovered. Thus in Bibl. 137, p. 530, Apel states that the hydraulos "had a loud and penetrating tone, noisy rather than musical"; but four years later, in Bibl. 51, pp. 196-7, he quotes such contemporary characterizations as "delectable", "sweet", "beautiful".

[5] Bibl. 147, Vol. III, p. 737. The magrepha (hydraulos) was used in the Jewish temple service, however, at the beginning of the Christian era. See Bibl. 145, p. 13; also Bibl. 137, pp. 421, 530.

[6] See Bibl. 99, pp. 7-8; Bibl. 51, pp. 213-15; Bibl. 113, p. 560. Yvonne Rokseth gives a summary of what is known about the use of the organ in the church service before 1531 and explains the confusion arising from the ambiguity of such terms as 'organum', 'vox organalis', etc. See Bibl. 117, Chap. IV.

[7] Bibl. 113, p. 560.

[8] Bibl. 113, p. 561. This view is shared by Gastoué (Bibl. 83, pp. 54-5) and Bonnet (Bibl. 167, p. 1). On the other hand Raugel himself, in *Les Organistes*, published two years before his article in the *Musical Quarterly*, seems to regard them as vocal works. Bibl. 115, p. 26.

[9] Bibl. 119.

adapted to solo organ performance.[10] This theory has been challenged by such musicologists as Raugel and Yvonne Rokseth.[11]

These differences of opinion serve to emphasize the lack of evidence that there was any definite assignment of medium. The whole problem can be summarized in the following sentences culled from Yvonne Rokseth's book: "Until the end of the fifteenth century, aside from the clearly defined types of solo *chanson* and Gregorian chant, no music is expressly intended for a fixed group of instruments or voices." "Even in the sixteenth [century] books of music are published 'to sing or play on all sorts of instruments'." "Let us beware, above all, when we consider the music of the fifteenth century, of too definitely specifying the medium and determining the manner of interpretation of a piece; it always remained more or less indefinite, and varied with the convenience of the time."[12]

Even after composers generally differentiated between vocal and instrumental music, compositions were written to be played either on a keyboard instrument or on a group of orchestral instruments,[13] while the practice of writing music for optional performance on any keyboard instrument was common until the time of Bach.[14]

In interpreting music intended for optional media the organist should bear in mind the possibilities which the composer anticipated. Music written with view to vocal performance calls for polyphonic clarity and tonal simplicity. Works which might have been played by a group of instrumentalists involve similar considerations, plus adaptation to the the graces and more florid style of the small instruments. Music intended for the harpsichord was usually less polyphonic, abounding in ornaments and rapid passages, demanding lightness, agility, and clarity of attack.[15]

We may assume that keyboard music which was written for the church service was primarily intended for the organ. In such compositions the

[10]Bibl. 197 and 185.

[11]Bibl. 115, pp. 37-8; Bibl. 117, pp. 179 ff.

[12]Yvonne Rokseth, *La Musique d'orgue au XVe siècle et au début du XVIe*, pp. 149-50, 151, 181; by kind permission of the publishers, Librairie E. Droz, Geneva.

[13]Such as the eight 'Ricercari sopra li Tuoni' attributed to Palestrina.

[14]A few examples, chosen almost at random, will indicate the prevalence of this practice:
> Frescobaldi, *Toccate d'intavolatura di cimbalo et organo*, 1637
> Martini, *Sonate d'intavolatura per l'organo ed il cembalo*, 1741
> Pachelbel, *Magnificat-Fugen*
> Handel, *Six Fugues or Voluntarys for the Organ or Harpsichord*, 1720
> Bach, *Sechs Sonaten für zwei Claviere und Pedal*

[15]Klotz suggests that, in the interpretation of Bach's Trio-Sonatas, "the thin, clear tone of the cembalo" be somewhat imitated, particularly in the first and last movements, using "overtone-rich" diapasons and combinations amply provided with high ranks. Bibl. 99, p. 290.

organ idiom, derived from plainsong and vocal polyphony, tended to become differentiated from that of other instruments. The influence of this style permanently affected the development of organ music. This is generally attributed to the restraining influence of its church associations. It might be more accurate to say that the organ has continued to be associated with the church service because of the qualities which render it uniquely suited to this type of music.

Earliest Keyboard Tablatures

The earliest music now extant which is generally conceded to have been written for a keyboard instrument is contained in the *Robertsbridge Codex* – a manuscript in the British Museum, dating from about 1325. Willi Apel suggests that the source of the music may have been Italian.[16] There is a gap of a hundred years between this codex and two manuscripts reported by Leo Schrade, which contain organ masses: a Sagan manuscript, c. 1425, and a Winsem manuscript, 1430-31.[17]

The next example is the tablature of Adam Ileborgh, rector of the monastery at Stendall, in northwest Germany. This manuscript, dated 1448, contains five independent preludes which are unique for their time, and three cantus firmus settings of a secular song. The preludes are particularly notable as the earliest known attempts at real organ music, and for their specific use of the pedal – even double pedaling.

More important are Paumann's *Fundamentum organisandi*, 1452, and the *Buxheimer Orgelbuch*, c. 1470. The former collection contains (1) examples of the method of constructing a *duplum* (a second voice, or counterpoint) above a cantus firmus, using arbitrary interval progressions in the lower voice; (2) independent preludes; and (3) organ settings of plainsong melodies and folk songs. The *Buxheimer Orgelbuch* contains a further development of Paumann's *Fundamentum*; independent preludes, somewhat more mature than those of Ileborgh; organ transcriptions of polyphonic vocal works, and original organ compositions in a similar style.

These collections exemplify the three types of organ music which existed in the fifteenth century:

1. Settings of plainsong and other existing vocal melodies by the method known as *organizare*, adding one or two accompanying melodies to the cantus firmus.

2. Keyboard adaptations of polyphonic vocal compositions through the process of *intabulare*, which consisted in a reduction to a keyboard score

---

[16]Bibl. 53, p. 21; Bibl. 137, p. 535. Compare Bibl. 127, p. 12.
[17]Bibl. 122, Part I.

with certain adaptations to the keyboard idiom, particularly the addition of ornamental variation in the upper voice.

3. Independent preludes, which represent the earliest attempt at organ music composed without reference to any vocal source, and a search for a keyboard style.

Although these fifteenth century collections are all German, they are widely separated geographically. Moreover there was much inter-communication and cultural interchange among the various countries of Europe, and we can assume a parallel development in England, France, Italy, and Spain. Evidence of this appears in various manuscript and published collections of the sixteenth century.[18]

In these compositions national differences become apparent, which are conditioned by the liturgical function of the organ as well as by the taste of the people. Corresponding national characteristics existed in the organs themselves, determined by the musical conceptions of the composers and the organists. The instruments, in turn, tended to perpetuate the conditions which produced them. Thus separate lines of evolution were established in different countries, so that, even down to the present century, there has been a distinct national differentiation in the tonal and mechanical appointments of organs. It will therefore be advantageous to take up the story, beginning with the sixteenth century, by countries.

The Organ at the Beginning of the Sixteenth Century

Before proceeding, however, we must know something about the prevailing characteristics of the organs at the beginning of this period. In general the larger instruments had two manuals and pedals and were equipped with stops and couplers.

The principal manual consisted of one large quint mixture, whose individual ranks were not available separately. In France this mixture was called *Grand Jeu*; in Holland, *Blokwerk*; in Germany, *Werck*, or *Hintersatz*.

---

[18]The most important of these collections are the following:

Germany:
    Arnolt Schlick, *Tabulaturen etlicher lobgesang und lidlein uff die Orgeln und Lauten*, 1512
    Hans Buchner, *Fundamentum sive ratio vera . . .* , early 16th century
    Also tablature books by Hans Kotter (c. 1513), Leonhard Kleber (1520-24), and Fridolin Sicher (c. 1525)

England:
    The Mulliner Book, c.1545-c.1570 (?), including music by John Redford (c.1485-c.1545), John Taverner (c.1495-1545), and William Blitheman (?-1591)

France:
    Tablatures published by Pierre Attaingnant in 1531

Italy:
    Frottole intabulare da sonare organi, published by Andrea Antico da Montona, 1517
    Marco Antonio (Cavazzoni) da Bologna, *Recerchari, Motetti, Canzoni*, 1523

Occasionally there were single ranks in addition. Praetorius gives the following typical composition of this large mixture: [19]

2 ranks of 8' pitch
3-4 ranks of 4' pitch
4-5 ranks of 2 2/3' pitch
6 ranks of 2' pitch
7 ranks of 1 1/3' pitch
8 ranks of 1' pitch
10 ranks of 1/2' pitch

Total: 40-42 ranks

The *positive organ*,[20] which had been introduced as an auxiliary instrument, was connected with the main console and constituted the second manual. Its resources were controlled by separate stops.

The pedals operated a portion of the principal manual. Independent pedal stops were rare before the sixteenth century.

The principal chorus was composed of open cylindrical pipes, relatively wider in scale for the upper pitches than for the lower. There were also wide scale separate ranks, particularly on the *Positiv*, the basic pitch of which was usually higher than that of the principal manual. Conical and stopped pipes also existed, and occasionally reeds with short resonators.[21]

The means of achieving variety in voicing had not been developed. Indeed there was little incentive to differentiate the individual voices until the stop system, which made them singly available, was generally established. The tonal resources were thought of in groups, or choruses, distinguished by the scales of the pipes, which determined the proportion of upper partials.[22] Thus a basic feature of organ design and registration methods was the contrast between the *narrow chorus* (composed of "German Principal" pipes – so-called because they were particularly characteristic of the organs of north Germany) and the *wide chorus* (composed of flute or "Italian Principal" pipes – so-called because of the generally accepted view that the Italian diapasons were particularly wide[23]). Thus until after the Baroque period tonal resources were grouped in these three categories: narrow chorus, wide chorus, and reeds.

[19] Bibl. 112, p. 102.

[20] Information concerning *positive* and *portative* organs can be found in any standard reference work.

[21] Bibl. 99, p. 12.

[22] See pp. 36-7.

[23] But see p. 232.

Italian Organs

Against this background we will now trace briefly the development of
organs and organ music in different countries. We begin with Italy because, after her early invasion by Belgian musicians, she exerted more
influence on other countries than they did on her.

The Italian organs were very small and seemingly insignificant compared with those of other continental countries. They had only one manual, and they lacked the large mixture which was the cardinal feature of,
for example, the German organs. In the fifteenth century the number of
stops ranged from three to the exceptional magnitude of nine. During the
sixteenth century the size of organs increased so that, by the end of the
century, specifications of twelve stops were not unusual. In spite of a
few extravagant experiments and occasional attempts to imitate other instruments and natural sounds, Italian organs remained essentially the
same until the middle of the eighteenth century.[24]

However, though these instruments were inferior in size, they excelled
in quality. They realized a refinement of tone consistent with the Italian
vocal ideal, and commanded the admiration of foreigners as well as local
musicians.[25]

The resources of the Italian organ included:

1. A series of diapason ranks, varying from three or four foundation
stops (16', 8', 4', 2') in the smallest organs to a full complement of
octave- and fifth-sounding ranks (extending from 16' to 1/2') in the largest. There were no duplications except, perhaps, a second *Principale*
(or *tenore* – the fundamental pitch, 16' or 8').

2. From one to three flutes (8', 4', 2').

3. A rudimentary pedal, comprising from three to seven keys[26] which
were connected with the lower notes of the manual, or with the lower section (possibly extended) of the second *Principale*.

The foregoing may be considered standard equipment. In addition some
organs possessed a *Voce umana*, or *Fiffaro*, which recent scholars have
interpreted as a beating stop, producing a céleste with the Principal.[27]
This opinion is borne out by Antegnati's statement that it "must be
played only in combination with the *Principale*; no other register should
be added, for then all would sound out of tune; and one must play slowly

[24]Bibl. 94, pp. 40-46.

[25]Bibl. 94, pp. 25, 35, 36, 51; Bibl. 84, p. 12.

[26]Bibl. 94, p. 37. But Pirro states that the organ in the Church of the Annunciation in
Florence had twelve keys "pro tastando cum pedibus" as early as 1379. Bibl. 151, p. 150.

[27]Bibl. 99, p. 94; Bibl. 84, p. 10.

and more legato than with the full organ, which is used for the beginning and end of the service."[28]

Reeds were introduced about the middle of the sixteenth century and are occasionally found in subsequent specifications. Divided manuals (enabling the organist to use different combinations for the right and left hands) and even two-manual organs are mentioned later, but they were altogether exceptional.

It is generally believed that the Italian Principal was flute-like, so that the ensemble was that of a wide chorus. On this assumption Klotz interprets the flutes in the Italian specifications as gedeckts. Refuting this conception Jeppesen cites measurements which indicate "rather that the Principal chorus at this time was quite narrow." He also quotes Renato Lunelli to the effect that the classic Italian Principal "was by no means wide scale, but rather it possessed a touch of keenness."[29] We may perhaps assume that, although the Italian diapason was less narrow than the north German type, it possessed sufficient harmonic development to provide a rich ensemble, and at the same time individual ranks would make an effective contribution to the synthetic color. This is consistent with Jeppesen's characterization of the ensemble as having a 'bright, silvery color . . . whose most beautiful characteristic comes from simple nobility."

Italian Registration Practices

These organs were less powerful than the instruments of western Europe, and the tone was less solid; on the other hand the individual control of a complete series of pitches afforded greater variety and subtlety of coloring. Such effects were clearly heard because they could only be presented singly and successively, it being impossible on a single manual to play one quality against another. That such successive changes were made, even while playing, is evidenced by Costanzo Antegnati's summary of the registration practices of his time in his *L'Arte organica*.[31]

[28]Bibl. 49, p. 72/3. In connection with this early use of the céleste principle it is interesting to note an analogous procedure in a less sophisticated society. Santha Rama Rau tells us that the Balinese "had a rather clever trick of tuning one instrument about a sixteenth of a tone higher than another which is playing the same notes because, they said, this gave the music resonance. If you play exactly the same note exactly together you get a 'dead sound'." — Bibl. 210, pp. 257-8.

[29]Bibl. 94, pp. 49-50; also Renato Lunelli, Introduction to Bibl. 49, p. 14/15.

[30]Bibl. 94, p. 51.

[31]Bibl. 94, p. 51; Bibl. 49, pp. 66/7-68/9. Compare also examples from Adriano Banchieri, *L'Organo suonarino*, in Bibl. 206, pp. 360, 364.

Costanzo Antegnati was the last representative of a famous family of organists and organ builders who lived in Brescia, and who, during the late fifteenth and the sixteenth centuries, installed more than four hundred instruments in various parts of the country. As a basis for his discussion of registration Costanzo uses his own organ in the Brescia Cathedral, which contained the following:

1. Principale	16'	
2. Principale spezzato	16'	(Divided Principal — upper section in manual, bass in pedal)
3. Ottaua	8'	(Octave)
4. Quintadecima	4'	(Fifteenth)
5. Decima nona	2 2/3'	(Nineteenth)
6. Vigesima seconda	2'	(Twenty-second)
7. Vigesima sesta	1 1/3'	(Twenty-sixth)
8. Vigesima nona	1'	(Twenty-ninth)
9. Trigesima terza	2/3'	(Thirty-third)
10. Altra Vigesima seconda	2'	("per concerto". Another Twenty-second [flute] "for concertizing")
11. Flauto in quintadecima	4'	(Flute fifteenth)
12. Flauto in ottaua	8'	(Flute octave)

Antegnati lists twelve different combinations and comments on their uses:

1. Ripieno (Full Organ): All stops except the Divided Principal and the flutes. This was used for preludes, toccatas, etc.
2. Mezzo ripieno (Medium Organ): Principal 16', Octave 8', Twenty-ninth 1', Thirty-third 2/3', Flute 8'.
3. Principal 16', Octave 8', Flute 8'.
4. Principal 16', Flute 8'.
5. Octave 8', Nineteenth 2 2/3', Flute 8', Flute 2'. This was intended to give the effect of a Cornet.
6. Octave 8', Flute 8'. This was considered good for melodic clarity, and therefore adapted to polyphony and ornamentation.
7. Same as Number 6, with tremolo added. Since the tremolo impaired the clarity this was reserved for sustained music.
8. Principal 16' alone. A very delicate effect, suitable for the elevation in the Mass.
9. The two Principals 16'.
10. Flute 8' alone.
11. Flute 8', Divided Principal 16' (treble only) — for dialogue.
12. Principal 16', Flute 4'. This was thought particularly suited to ornamentation. The addition of the Octave 8' to this combination was also considered effective.[32]

Further light on the registration practices of the Italians of this period is provided by Girolamo Diruta, a pupil of Merulo, in the second part of

[32]Bibl. 49, pp. 62/3-66/7.

Il Transilvano.[33]   He assigns specific combinations to the different church modes in accordance with the character which he attributes to each:

> Mode 1 (dignified): Principal 16', Octave 8', with the possible addition of the Fifteenth 4' and Flute 4'.
> Mode 2 (melancholy): Principal 16' with tremolo.[34]
> Mode 3 (plaintive): Principal 16', Flute 8'.
> Mode 4 (sad): Same as for Mode 2.
> Mode 5 (cheerful): Octave 8', Flute 4', Twenty-second 2'.
> Mode 6 (devotional): Principal 16', Octave 8', Flute 4'.
> Mode 7 (bright): Octave 8', Fifteenth 4', Twenty-second 2'.
> Mode 8 (pleasant): Flute 8'; or
>   Octave 8', Flute 8'; or
>   Flute 8', Twenty-second 2'.
> Mode 9 (similar): Principal 16', Fifteenth 4', Twenty-second 2'.
> Mode 10 (gloomy): Principal 16', Octave 8'; or
>   Principal 16', Flute 8'.
> Modes 11 and 12 (happy —pleasant and animated): Flute 8'; or
>   Flute 8', Twenty-second 2'; or
>   Flute 8', Twenty-second 2', Twenty-ninth 1'; or
>   Octave 8', Fifteenth 4', Twenty-second 2'; or
>   Flute 8', Octave 8', Fifteenth 4'.
> Mode 12: Particularly Flute 8', or the last combination.[35]

It is interesting not only to observe Diruta's characterization of the different modes, but to study his interpretation of the various moods in the light of the principles expounded in Chapter VII.

In Banchieri's *Organo suonarino* we find specific registration indicated for individual compositions, with changes in the course of the pieces. 'La Battaglia' and 'Dialogo per organo' are both available in modern collections.[36]

It should be noted that the *ripieno* (Antegnati's first combination) contains no flutes, and no duplication at any pitch —a condition which makes for the utmost richness, transparency, and refinement. We observe, however, that in small combinations the Italians did not hesitate to use a

---

[33]Bibl. 73.

[34]Klotz interprets this as a céleste. Bibl. 99, p. 131.

[35]These suggestions are reported in the following: Bibl. 116, Vol. I, pp. 15-16; Bibl. 135, pp. 46-50; Bibl. 78, pp. 127-8; Bibl. 99, pp. 129-33; Bibl. 94, pp. 51-5; Bibl. 60, pp. 72-3; Bibl. 84, pp. 10-11. There is some disagreement concerning the pitch of some of the ranks.

[36]See footnote 31. 'La Battaglia' is also reprinted in Bibl. 161, Vol. I, p. 27; 'Dialogo' in Bibl. 183, Vol. IV, p. 24. It is interesting to note that the manuscript of Monteverdi's *Magnificat* contains instructions for the registration of the various movements: For the first movement a combination similar to Diruta's registration for the first mode was suggested; for 'Quia fecit' the *voce umana* (diapason céleste) was specified; the *principale* alone was indicated for 'Et exsultavit' "because the tenors here perform rapid runs." See Bibl. 152, p. 121.

diapason and a flute at the same pitch – a practice which we will not find approved in northern Germany.

Italian Organ Music

The earliest known Italian organ music, found in the collection of 1517,[37] consists entirely of intabulations – keyboard reductions of vocal compositions. The music of Marco Antonio da Bologna, published six years later, has real instrumental significance and musical interest. It includes the earliest surviving examples of the organ *ricercare* – not of the imitative type, but toccata-like movements which have no relation to vocal polyphony. Each of these ricercari serves as an introduction to a following motet transcription, anticipating the prelude and fugue relationship. The motets and canzonas are free, idiomatic keyboard paraphrases which are effective as pure instrumental music.[38]

Our next example of Italian organ music is the product of one of the most remarkable prodigies in the history of music. The composer was Marco Antonio's son, Girolamo Cavazzoni, who was not more than eighteen years old when the music was published.[39] He did not merely exhibit facility in the use of familiar techniques; the music is highly original, employing forms and devices of which we know no previous examples in keyboard music. At the same time there is no evidence of experimentation; the music is mature in conception and perfectly adapted to its medium. Here we find ricercari which are legitimate forerunners of the fugue; here we find polyphonic canzonas which, though derived from vocal works, foreshadow the independent instrumental form; here we find complete sets of versets[40] for the Mass and for the Magnificat, as well as settings of hymn melodies in which the plainsong is developed with unprecedented ingenuity, skill, taste, and fidelity of expression, and in which the motet treatment and *Vorimitation*[41] are employed – not experimentally, but with complete mastery.

Development of Instrumental Forms

It was sixty-five years later that Frescobaldi's first collection of fantasias appeared. During those years, through the work of such men of

[37]See p. 229, fn. 18.

[38]Bibl. 94, 'Musikalische Transkriptionen', pp. 35-82.

[39]Jeppesen establishes that he was born between 1524 and 1526; the collection was published in 1542. Bibl. 94, p. 92.

[40]*Versets* are short interludes, usually plainsong settings, which are substituted for the singing of alternate verses of the Psalms, the 'Magnificat', and other liturgical numbers.

[41]See p. 191.

genius as Andrea Gabrieli (c.1510-1586), Annibale Padovano (1527-1575), Claudio Merulo (1533-1604), and Giovanni Gabrieli (1557-c.1612), instrumental forms were increasing and developing. There emerged the four ancestors of the fugue — ricercare, canzona, fantasia, capriccio — and the toccata. The polyphonic forms, of which melodic imitation was a common basic element, were not always clearly differentiated, but certain distinguishing characteristics were fairly usual:

The *ricercare*, originally closely related to the overlapping sectional motet, was the most compact, and contained the most varied and ingenious thematic development. The principal theme tended to dominate the composition; or successive themes were elaborately developed in successive large sections. A ricercare which was strictly monothematic might closely resemble a fugue.[42]

The *canzona*, evolved from the French *chanson*, was less compact, freer, and more animated than the ricercare. The form usually consisted of several sections, each developing its own theme. With Frescobaldi the themes of the later sections were usually variations of the first theme — a practice which was followed by others, including Zipoli and Bach.

The *fantasia* can be characterized as a free ricercare. Here too Frescobaldi varied the first theme in the succeeding sections. He also wrote fantasias on from two to four themes, all of which were introduced in the first few measures and developed with amazing skill and ingenuity. In these the *recherché* character of the ricercare was intensified, rather than relaxed.[43]

The *capriccio* was, as its name implies subject to the caprice of the composer. It might be essentially a canzona or ricercare in which he had taken some liberty. In Frescobaldi's capriccios his whim is revealed in the selection of arbitrary or borrowed themes, or even, in one case, by the suggestion that the theme be sung, cantus firmus fashion, at suitable places not designated by the composer.[44]

The *toccata* (*toccare* = to touch, or play) suggests a composition whose character is identified with the action of the fingers on the keys. It is, above all, idiomatic keyboard music, unrelated to any style which is associated with groups of performers; accordingly it is not essentially polyphonic. The toccatas of Andrea Gabrieli and many of his contemporaries

---

[42]See, for example, the Ricercari in the 1st, 2nd, 9th, and 11th modes by Gabrieli in Bibl. 212, Vol. II, pp. 3, 8, 12, 28, and 33. An abridged version of the 'Ricercare del primo tono alla quarta alta' is found in Bibl. 177, p. 1. The eight ricercari attributed to Palestrina are clear examples of the overlapping sectional motet type. See Bibl. 213.

[43]Cf. Sweelinck, pp. 251-2.

[44]The same device appears in a ricercare in the third part of his *Fiori musicali*.

consisted largely of scale passages above, below, and crossing sustained chords. Merulo expanded this scheme, sometimes replacing the scale passages with the ornamentation of individual voices of the chord progressions, and alternating these toccata sections with polyphonic interludes. With Frescobaldi the florid work becomes an integral part of the texture, adding greatly to the complexity and musical interest. In his *Fiori musicali* — an incomparable collection of three organ masses — he applies the term to short preludes, suggesting perhaps that they are conceived in the spirit of improvisations.

In the field of organ music Frescobaldi was Italy's Bach, who took the forms which had been developed by his predecessors, brought them to a point of perfection, and used them as a vehicle for musical expression. We know also from the introductions to some of his published collections that his style of playing was sensitive and flexible. [45]

Although none of his successors equaled him in skill, resourcefulness, or inspiration, Frescobaldi's music set the standard in form and style for Italian organ music until activity in that field gave way to the almost universal preoccupation with opera. Moreover, there is no evidence of any radical change in the character of Italian organs during this period. The music could be played on a single manual with the restricted pedal described above. [46] The transparent texture of the polyphonic compositions was effectively revealed by the clear ensemble of unduplicated pitches. In the toccatas the florid movement was rendered distinct from the accompanying chords by the contrast of material.

In playing this music on a modern organ the performer should avoid overelaboration, using, in general, as few stops as possible. Small combinations are best for the polyphonic movements, while the more complex ensembles should include the minimum of duplication of pitches. Different manuals may be used to set off the sections of polyphonic forms and to throw the scale passages of the toccatas into relief, provided the essential homogeneity of the music is not impaired. Contrasting qualities should be strictly avoided.

The pedal should be employed with extreme caution. Its use by the Italians was confined to essential bass notes, serving either as a pedal point or as occasional support to the harmony. It never shared in the

---

[45]See Bibl. 144, pp. 4 ff.; and 60, pp. 126-7. The instructions mentioned are found in Frescobaldi's *Primo libro di capricci* . . . , 1626; *Toccate d'intavolatura* . . . , 1637; and *Fiori musicali* . . . , 1635. Fortunately Frescobaldi's complete keyboard works are soon to be available.

[46]Only three of Frescobaldi's organ works call for the use of the pedal: two toccatas and the 'Capriccio pastorale' (all in the 1637 collection) contain long pedal points. A similar procedure occurs in Zipoli's 'Pastorale in C'. See also the crude pedal indications in the 'Sonata in F' by Giovanni Battista Bassani (c. 1650-1715), in Bibl. 116, Vol. II, p. 38.

polyphony. The modern organist should avoid giving weight to the bass which will distort the balance or obscure the transparency of the texture. The interpretation of Italian music should always be characterized by refinement and reserve.

Spanish Organs

"Organ building in Spain," observes Emile Rupp, "developed from a directly opposite point of view. The Spanish type of organ is the sharpest imaginable antithesis, the most remote antipole, of the old Italian."[47] Whereas the Italian organs were small, refined, silvery, lending themselves primarily to subtle tone shading, the Spanish organs were large, harsh, and noisy. They lacked the wide range of separate ranks, but they achieved brilliance by means of a large proportion of mixtures and an extraordinary number of reeds. These reeds were present at all pitches from thirty-two foot to two-foot; even mutation reeds (twelfth and seventeenth) were not unknown.[48] Many reeds were *en chamade*, i.e., projecting horizontally from the organ case, so that the sound was directed toward the center of the church. This not only made them sound louder to the listener but increased the brilliance of their quality.[49]

These characteristics are exemplified in the specifications of the famous Imperial Organ in the Cathedral of Toledo, built in the time of Cabezón. This instrument had two manuals of fifty-seven keys each, and two sets of thirteen pedals, the second set consisting of round pegs located behind the first set. All the manual stops were divided into bass and treble sections — a usual practice in Spain until modern times. The distribution of stops was as follows:[50]

Lower Manual

Diapasons 16', 8', 4'	Gedeckt 16'	Trumpets (*en chamade*) 16' (treble only) 8', 4', 4', 2'

[47] Bibl. 118, p. 445.

[48] Bibl. 99, p. 37.

[49] Since short waves do not diverge from their direct path so much as long waves (cf. p. 26), a larger proportion of upper partials is heard in the line of the axis of a reed pipe than in any other location. This has been demonstrated by actual analysis.

[50] In the specifications presented in these chapters the stops are grouped, whenever practicable, in the three categories mentioned on page 230.

Upper Manual

Diapasons
  16', 8', 4', 2'
Mixtures viii, v
Lleno viii[51]

Gedeckts 8', 4'
Twelfth and Fifteenth
  2 2/3' & 2'[52]
Cornet vii-xiii
Flute Celeste 8'
  (treble only)

Trumpets (in chamber)
  16' (treble only)
  8', 8' & 4' (together)
Violetas 8'[53]

Pedal

Front keys

Diapasons
  32', 16', 8', 4'

Wood Diapason 16'

Rear keys

Diapasons 2', 1'   Trumpets 16', 8', 2'

This scheme was enlarged and modified in later instruments, but its essential features – the domination of mixtures and reeds (many of the latter being *en chamade*) and the division of the manuals – were the rule. It was common practice to differentiate somewhat the assortment of stops assigned to the bass and treble sections, including more high ranks in the bass and more low ranks in the treble; likewise certain special stops, such as a Cornet or a céleste, were confined to the treble section.

It is interesting to note that the "Great Organ" in the Toledo Cathedral, built in the second half of the seventeenth century, included an enclosed section, although the invention of the swell pedal is generally attributed to the English builder, Abraham Jordan, in 1712.[54] This organ was also equipped with manual couplers and both strong and weak tremolos.[55]

Spanish Organ Music

These organs were admirably adapted to the performance of the florid compositions which made up a considerable portion of the repertoire of the early Spanish organist. Brilliant passages executed on the noisy reeds and mixtures against a background of sustained chords were much

[51]Scharf (high mixture).

[52]A two-rank stop, known in Germany as *Quarte* or *Rauschquinte*.

[53]Presumably a reed with short resonator. Klotz (Bibl. 99, p. 36) suggests a Krumm-horn; Rupp (Bibl. 118, p. 447) suggests a Vox Humana. Cf. early French organ described on pp. 242-3, and fn. 68.

[54]See p. 279.

[55]The principal sources of the above information are Bibl. 118, pp. 445 ff.; and Bibl. 99, pp. 36-8, 91-2. See also Bibl. 84, pp. 147-9, 165; Bibl. 72; and Bibl. 190, Introduction.

admired.[56]   They were extensively employed in improvisation and are
frequently encountered in written compositions of this period.   At the
same time the individual stops provided the combinations needed for
polyphony and other pieces in a more restrained style.

If Pedrell is correct in his interpretation of the pedal parts, the old
Spanish organists must have acquired a phenomenal facility on their
crude pedal board.[57]   It seems more likely that Ritter is right in sup-
posing that they played only the principal bass tones with the feet.[58]
However, the presence of a two-foot reed in the pedal and the assignment
of the high flue stops to the rear keys suggest that they were used for
the cantus firmus in plainsong settings.

The earliest Spanish organ composer known to us, and by far the
greatest of all, was the blind organist, Antonio de Cabezón (1510-1566).
His works were collected and published after his death by his son,
Hernando.   Antonio was an exact contemporary of Andrea Gabrieli, and
was in his prime when Cavazzoni's music was published.   Like Cavazzoni he wrote a large number of versets.[59]   In some of these the melody
is developed in fugal imitation; in others it appears as a cantus firmus in
the various voices, accompanied by imitative counterpoints; still others
are treated as variations, or *glosas*, in which a simple harmonization is
ornamented or accompanied by scale passages.

All of these devices he combined in his sets of larger variations
(*diferencias*), which were based on popular melodies of the time.   So far
as we know he was the first to write in this form for the organ.[60]   He also
composed *fugas* (canons) and many *tientos* — pieces combining the keyboard idiom of the toccata with the structural characteristics of the
ricercare.   In all this music he showed himself a superb master of all the
resources of composition known at that time.   Willi Apel rates his tientos
"high above all works created in the field of free instrumental composition up to the time of Frescobaldi," and goes on to say: "I know of no
one among the clavier and organ composers of all time who, by reason
of musical spirituality, profundity and exalted seriousness of purpose —

[56]A contemporary comment on the playing of Francisco Peraza, a celebrated Spanish
organist of the sixteenth century, reads: "he had an angel in each finger; ... so perfectly
did he play two thousand flowers which he invented that it is to him alone that Spain owes
the grace and the beauties of the organ."   Quoted by Felipe Pedrell, Bibl. 193, Vol. III,
p. xli.

[57]See his transcriptions of the five- and six-part compositions. Bibl. 193, Vol. III.

[58]Bibl. 116, Vol. I, p. 70. This opinion is confirmed by Muset, Bibl. 190.

[59]See p. 235, fn. 40.

[60]Concerning variations on church themes cf. Bibl. 101, Part II, pp. 549, 551-3. It must
be taken into account, however, that the exact dates of the compositions discussed by
Lowinsky are not known.

complete contrapuntal mastery, more properly belongs in [Bach's] company."[61]

A contemporary of Cabezón, Tomás de Santa María (?-1579?), wrote a treatise entitled *Libro llamado arte de tañer fantasia*, 1565, which includes a set of exquisite miniatures of the ricercare type. Many lesser composers followed Cabezón, and it is possible that an important literature has been lost through neglect and destruction.[62] The one organ composer who stands out in the succeeding centuries is Juan José Cabanilles (1644-1712).[63]

The amount of available Spanish organ music is very limited; the larger collections are not accessible to the average organist. A few isolated pieces are scattered through various miscellaneous collections, and others have been assembled in small publications devoted exclusively to Spanish music.[64]

Unlike Italian organ music, many Spanish compositions were intended to be performed on two manuals, or on differentiated sections of a divided manual. This is particularly true of the brilliant *glosas*. The modern organist who wishes to approximate the original effect may use a large proportion of reeds and mixtures for the florid melody, probably omitting all flue stops below the Octave, and perhaps adding a superoctave coupler. Pirro reports that Correa de Araujo (1581?-1663?) recommended the use of two manuals for certain polyphonic compositions in order to clarify the voice leading.[65] Such pieces would not, of course, call for a reedy ensemble.

The fantasias by Santa María and many of the compositions of Cabezón should be played with the same transparency and refinement that is

---

[61]Bibl. 52, pp. 297-8.

[62]See Bibl. 169, p. v.

[63]His complete organ works have been edited by Hyginii Anglès. Three small folios of his music are available to the organist in the Peters edition.

[64]Of the collections listed below the first three are rarely available outside of large libraries:

Felipe Pedrell, *Hispaniae schola musica sacra*, 1894-8.
Felipe Pedrell, *Antologia de organistas clásicos españoles*, 1908
L. V. Muñoz, *Antologia de organistas clásicos españoles*, 1914
Ernst Kaller *et al.*, *Liber Organi*, Vol. III, 1933
Joseph Bonnet, *Historical Organ Recitals*, Vol. VI, 1940
Joseph Muset, *Early Spanish Organ Music*, 1948

[65]Bibl. 110, p. 1211. Pirro is referring to Francisco Correa de Araujo, *Tientos y discursos musicos, y facultad organica*, 1626. Correa, who lived in Spain, and Manuel Rodrigues Coelho (five of whose 'Tentos' for organ are available in the Schott edition) were the most important Portuguese organ composers.

demanded by the old Italian music.[66] Moreover, the same discretion
should be used in the employment of the pedal. The pedal mechanism of
the old Spanish organs was clumsy and ill-suited to anything but slow
movement. The polyphonic ensemble was conceived for the manuals, and
any addition of sixteen-foot tone to the lowest voice would, in most
cases, distort the balance.

Influence of Geographical Location

Our study of Spanish organs and organ music has been in a sense a
digression. While the music itself has much in common with that of the
Italians, the Spanish organs are outside the general European picture.
We will find as we travel north that the character of the instruments
changes as we get farther from the influence of Italy. In northern Germany
the organs are larger, the diapasons narrower and more brilliant, the mixtures fuller, the resources more varied; plurality of manuals is general
and the pedal is more developed, serving both as a cantus firmus keyboard and as the foundation of the ensemble. In intermediate localities
certain characteristics of the northern and southern organs are combined.

French Organs in the Sixteenth Century

France, on the other hand, was between Spain and the general European
current. So French organs show some Spanish influence, particularly in
the inclusion of reeds in the ensemble, which was alien to the ideals of
Italy and the countries farther north. A typical large French organ of the
early sixteenth century might include the following:[67]

Grand Orgue

Grand Jeu	A series of flute stops	Régale, or
of which from one to	Cornet	Voix humaine[68]
three ranks might be		Trumpet
available separately		Rossignol
Cymbale		

[66]Fernando Germani gives the specifications of an organ built for the Lerida Cathedral
in 1624, and quotes in full a set of instructions for its use. Here are 119 different combinations which presumably represent the registration practices of that time. This unique
document merits extended study by organists wishing to present an authentic interpretation
of old Spanish music. See Bibl. 84, pp. 149-63.

[67]Yvonne Rokseth, in Bibl. 117, pp. 343 ff., gives a few specifications, but as the
interpretation of some of the details is uncertain it seems advantageous to generalize,
rather than to quote individual schemes. Since the lowest note of these organs was often
FF, the original specifications would identify the stop pitches as 12', 6', 3', etc., instead
of 16', 8', 4', etc.

[68]Christhard Mahrenholz, in Bibl. 102, p. 171, says: "This form of Regal, in all
probability developed in France, was the first Vox Humana." Sumner (Bibl. 128, pp. 61,
65, 74) tells us that it was introduced in the fifteenth century, and that experiments were
made with various types of resonators in an attempt to imitate different vowel sounds. It

Positif

Similar resources, reduced, the basic pitch an octave higher; or
Some of the special stops might be assigned to this manual

Pédale

Very small range, duplicating manual keys
Independent 32' rank (rare)

Thus the French organist of this period may have had at his disposal a large and small ensemble (low and high) which he could use selectively for a homogeneous texture, while duos and important melodies could be kept separate by using the two manuals simultaneously. The organ music of the Attaingnant collections[69] was intended for such an instrument, but the use of two manuals is nowhere implied, nor does it provide any occasion for the use of pedals. From that standpoint this music differs little from the early Italian organ music.

The Time of Titelouze

Jean Titelouze (1563-1633), organist of the Cathedral of Rouen, was perhaps the greatest of all French organ composers. In his day French organs began to show the direction which their later development was to take. We do not know the specifications of Titelouze's own organ, but a design which he prepared for the Church of St. Godard in Rouen shows the resources which he expected.[70] It specified two manuals of forty-eight notes each ($CC - c^3$, lacking CC♯) and a pedal keyboard of twenty-eight notes ($CC - f^1$, lacking CC♯ and $c\sharp^1$), with the following stops:

Grand Orgue

Diapasons	Flutes	Trumpets 8', 4'
16', 4', 2'	8', 4', 2 2/3',	Régale 8'
Fourniture iv[71]	2', 1 1/3', 1'	
Cymbale iii	Cornet v[71]	

is interesting to note the early appearance of this ubiquitous stop, of which individual specimens have been famous, even down to comparatively recent times. Burney, in his musical journey through Europe in 1772, was particularly interested in the effect of the Vox Humana in the various organs which he heard, although his comment (almost equally pertinent today!) scarcely vindicates his interest: "I must confess," he writes, "that of all the stops I have yet heard, which have been honoured with the appellation vox humana, no one, in the treble part, has ever reminded me of anything human, so much as the cracked voice of an old woman of ninety, or, in the lower parts, of Punch singing through a comb." Bibl. 140, Vol. II, p. 305.

[69]Consisting of transcriptions of vocal works, plainsong versets, and three preludes. See p. 229, fn. 18.

[70]Given by Pirro in Bibl. 205, p. xiv, and by Klotz in Bibl. 99, p. 59. Klotz states that the pedal stops were borrowed from the Grand Orgue.

[71]The Fourniture was a full quint mixture; the Cymbale was a high quint mixture; the Cornet was a wide scale mixture containing a tierce. See pp. 46-7, 248.

Positif

Diapasons 8', 4', 2'   Flute 2 2/3'   Cromorne 8'
Fourniture iii
Cymbale ii

Pédale

Flutes 8', 4'   Trumpet 8'

Coupler: Positif to Grand Orgue

It will be observed that this scheme provides a sixteen-foot diapason chorus on the Grand Orgue and an eight-foot chorus on the Positif, each including two mixtures. The Grand Orgue contains a complete series of separate octave- and fifth-sounding flute ranks above an eight-foot fundamental, extending to one-foot pitch, and a solo mixture; while the Positif has a single flute mutation. The Grand Orgue is equipped with eight- and four-foot chorus reeds, and each manual has a solo reed. The pedal is designed to carry a melodic line — either a cantus firmus or a single voice of the polyphony, but not to serve as a supporting bass. It is notable that the only separate mutations are of flute quality, suitable to lend color to a single melody, rather than to share in the composition of a cohesive mass.

Such an organ is capable of considerable variety in ensemble, as well as the differentiation of individual voices and the separation of solo parts. Titelouze himself commented on its adaptability to the performance of polyphonic music:

"Moreover we have further increased its perfection in recent years, having them [organs] in several places in France constructed with two separate keyboards for the hands, and a pedal keyboard in unison with the eight-foot stops, containing twenty-eight or thirty keys, to play the bass separately, without playing it with the hand, the tenor on the second keyboard, the alto and soprano on the third. By this means can be shown the unison, the crossing of parts, and a thousand kinds of musical figures which would otherwise be impossible [to hear]."[72]

This procedure was of course susceptible of modification according to the layout of the music. If independence of the soprano was called for, the two middle parts could be played with the left hand. Again, the bass could be played with the left hand and the tenor with the feet.

Such a presentation was beautifully adapted to show the pure polyphony of Titelouze's versets. We know nothing of the composers who

[72]Jean Titelouze, *Hymnes de l'Église* . . . , 1623, "Au Lecteur," reproduced in Bibl. 205, p. 5.

came between the Attaingnant publications and Titelouze, but it is evident that his music must represent the culmination of a long period, during which the art of the instrumental polyphonic treatment of plainsong was developed and refined. It combines fidelity to the tonality and spirit of the church melodies with technical resourcefulness and ideal religious expression, to a degree unequaled by any later French composer.

Developments in the Seventeenth Century

The general plan of the organs of the following generations did not differ essentially from the scheme devised by Titelouze. Resources were expanded, more stops were provided in each section, and the number of manuals was increased to four, or even five – but there was no fundamental change in the design. The Grand Orgue still contained a complete diapason chorus, including the Fourniture and the Cymbale; a complete series of separate flute ranks (open and stopped); a Cornet; Trumpets 8' and 4', and one or two solo stops. The composition of the Positif was similar, but less complete, and it was higher in pitch: whereas the Grand Orgue usually included one or two sixteen-foot stops, the ensemble of the Positif (*Petit Orgue*) ordinarily began with the eight-foot pitch.

Other manuals were added for special effects, and often had no more than two stops each. The *Récit*, primarily intended for solo melodies, was usually provided with a Cornet and a Trumpet 8'. The *Écho* was located in the lower part of the chamber, underneath the main chests, so that the tone was somewhat confined, giving the impression of remoteness. Its resources might include a Cornet and a Trumpet, Flute, or other solo stop. If there was a fifth manual it would be a *Bombarde*, containing a sixteen-foot chorus reed, and perhaps other reeds to go with it.[73]

The pedal section remained meager: often it had only two or three stops, capable of outlining the bass or tenor melody. Even in larger schemes which provided a fuller pedal ensemble the basic pitch was the same as that of the manuals, sometimes even without the sixteen-foot pitch which was represented on the Grand Orgue. Moreover, the manual to pedal coupler (*tirasse*[74]) seems to have disappeared when independent pedal stops were introduced, so that the pedal was not added to the manual, but substituted for it – unless, of course, the pedal part was duplicated by the left hand. The French composers wrote no monumental fugues; there was little organ music which required a deep, solid tonal

---

[73]According to Dufourcq the earliest known Récit was installed in the seventh decade of the 17th century; the earliest known Écho in 1647; and the earliest known Bombarde in 1733. Bibl. 75, table at the end of the volume.

[74]From *tirer* (= to pull). The term is derived from the original function of the pedals, which was to pull down the corresponding manual keys.

foundation: so the pedal section was not designed to support the ensemble, but to participate in it.

The manuals were located in the following order, beginning with the
lowest: Positif, Grand Orgue, [Bombarde,] Récit, Écho. Dom Bédos[75]
describes a method of coupling the Positif to the Grand Orgue by sliding
the lower manual in so that projections affixed to the keys would coincide. Similarly the Grand Orgue would be coupled to the Bombarde by
pulling the latter manual out. Obviously this coupling could not be done
while playing.

As an example of a large French organ of the latter part of the seventeenth century we give below the specifications of the instrument built
between 1679 and 1686 by Alexandre Thierry, under the direction of
Nicolas Le Bègue, for the church of Saint-Louis des Invalides in Paris.[76]
It is interesting to note that the organ in the Cathedral of Rouen, where
Titelouze had played, was rebuilt in 1689 to specifications very similar
to these.[77]

Grand Orgue (CC, DD $-$ c^3)

Diapasons	Bourdons 16', 8'	Trumpets 8', 4'
16', 8', 4', 2'	Flutes	Voix humaine 8'
Fourniture v	8' (treble), 3 1/5',	
Cymbale v	2 2/3', 2', 1 3/5'	

Positif (CC, DD $-$ c^3)

Diapasons 8', 4', 2'	Bourdons 8', 4'	Cromorne 8'
Fourniture iv	Flutes 2 2/3', 1 3/5',	Petite voix humaine 8'
Cymbale iii	1 1/3'	

Récit (c^1 $-$ c^3)

Cornet v	Petite trompette 8'

Écho (c^1 $-$ c^3)

Cymbale iii	Bourdon 8'	Cromorne 8'
	Cornet v	

Pédales (AAA, CC, DD$-$f^1)

Flute 8'	Trumpet 8'

---

[75]Bibl. 61, Vol. I, pp. 107-10.

[76]From Félix Raugel, *Les Grandes Orgues des Églises de Paris* . . . , (Paris: Librairie
Fischbacher), p. 57; by kind permission of the publishers.

[77]See Bibl. 75, p. 337

French Organ Music — Seventeenth and Eighteenth Centuries

The practice, which had been recommended by Titelouze, of clarifying the movement of the individual voices of a polyphonic ensemble by the use of different manuals, influenced the writing of later composers. Even quartets were devised so that they could be played on four different keyboards. This rendered the voice leading clearly audible, but it imposed practical limitations on the melodic motion and the dynamic range. Trios and duos increased in favor, since they were easier to play, allowed greater freedom in voice leading, and demanded less attention from the listener. The taste was for clarity, simplicity, and color.

This tendency was further encouraged by the fact that organists were equally concerned with the harpsichord, and by the popularity of Italian opera. In this music a more harmonic idiom was employed, prominence was given to a single melody, and various devices for ornamentation were exploited. Moreover, the increased color resources of the organ made it natural for the organist to appropriate this style. Instrumental effects superseded interest in the weaving of the voices. A popular form was the dialogue, in which similar phrases were played on alternate manuals, giving an antiphonal or echo effect. This procedure was extended to include even four manuals. Above all, the dominance of a single melody, either as the upper voice of the ensemble or as a voice made prominent by solo treatment, was characteristic of the French organ music of the period following Titelouze. However, polyphonic writing was not completely abandoned, and around the turn of the century (1690-1711) the genius of Couperin and de Grigny produced works in which the new melodic freedom served to enrich the polyphonic texture and to enhance the expressiveness of serious compositions.[78]

French Registration Practices

Throughout this period procedures became conventionalized, and composers wrote with specific registration in mind. So definitely was the manner of performance a part of the musical conception that it was included in the titles of the compositions, such as: 'Plein Jeu', 'Récit de tierce en taille', etc. Since an intelligent interpretation of such music requires an understanding of these indications an explanation of their meaning is important in this connection. The following definitions and

[78]François Couperin, *Pièces d'Orgue*, 1690. These masses, long thought to have been composed by his uncle, are now believed to be the work of Couperin "le Grand" himself.
Nicolas de Grigny, *Livre d'Orgue*, 1711.
Both of these collections are reprinted in Bibl. 182, Vol. V.

descriptions of registration practices are derived from contemporary sources.[79]

Definitions and Equivalents

Grand Orgue = Great
Positif = Choir, or Positiv
Récit = Swell, or small Solo
Écho = Echo
Bombarde = Bombarde, or Solo
Fonds = Foundation stops[80]
Anches = Reeds
Montre ("to show" —display pipes) = Diapason
Prestant ("standing in front") = Principal 4', or Octave
Cornet = Cornet —a five-rank mixture, consisting of wide scale pipes of unison, octave, twelfth, fifteenth, and seventeenth pitches, without break. Usually only in the upper part of the keyboard. Sometimes placed on a separate, raised chest, when it is called *Cornet séparé* (= Mounted Cornet).
Dessus = Soprano, or Treble
Haute-contre = Alto (cf. 'contralto')
Taille = Tenor
Basse = Bass, or lower section (of a stop)
Récit = Solo melody
Example: *Récit de Tierce en Taille* = Melody played on a Tierce combination in the tenor range

Description of Combinations

Plein Jeu du Grande Orgue: Foundation stops of all pitches, diapason mixtures, Trumpets 8' and 4' (Cornet and flute mutations omitted)

Plein Jeu du Positif, or *Petit Plein Jeu*: Foundation stops and mixtures, Trumpets (if available), and possibly Cromorne

Grand Jeu (Grand Orgue): Bourdons and flutes of all pitches except 16', including mutations; Prestant 4', Cornet, Trumpets 8' and 4'

Petit Jeu (Positif): Bourdons and flutes of all pitches, Cromorne (?)

Cornet: Cornet alone, or in combination with foundation stops

Petit Cornet (Positif): Foundation stops 8'—1' (without duplication) and mutations, including Tierce

Grande Tierce (Grand Orgue): Foundation stops (especially bourdons and flutes) of all pitches and mutations, including 16' and Tierce

Petite Tierce (Grand Orgue or Positif): Bourdon 8', diapasons or flutes 4' and 2', Nasard, Tierce

Tierce en Taille, or *Basse de Tierce*: Petite Tierce plus Larigot

Nasard: Similar to Tierce combinations, omitting the Tierce itself

---

[79]Marin Mersenne, *Harmonicorum libri XII*, c. 1625 (about the time of the publication of Titelouze's organ collections), and Mersenne, *L'Harmonie universelle*, Vol. II, 1637 (embodying the practices of Claude Raquette). We have drawn freely from Gastoué's summary in Bibl. 83, pp. 82-5, with the kind permission of the publishers, Éditions Musicales de la Schola Cantorum et de la Procure Générale de Musique, Paris.

Nicolas Le Bègue, *Les Pièces d'Orgue*, 1676, and André Raison, *Livre d'Orgue*, 1687. These are reprinted in Bibl. 182, Vols. IX and II, respectively.

Dom Bédos, Bibl. 61, Vol. III, pp. 523-36.

[80]See pp. 45-6.

Trompette: Trompette alone, or in combination with one or two foundation stops

Trompette en Taille, or *Basse de Trompette*: Trompette with Prestant and/or Clarion 4'

Cromorne: Cromorne alone, or in combination with Bourdon 8', a 4' stop, and (possibly) Nasard

Cromorne en Taille: Cromorne and Prestant, perhaps with Bourdon 8', possibly with Nasard

Voix Humaine: Vox Humana, Bourdon 8', Prestant or Flute 4', Nasard (?), Tremolo

Various special combinations are mentioned for quiet movements or for the accompaniment of solo qualities described above. Among these are the following:

1. Bourdon 8', Flute 4'

2. Bourdon 8', Prestant 4'

3. Bourdon 8', Flageolet 2', with or without Nasard

To the first two combinations were occasionally added a sixteen-foot stop, a two-foot stop, and/or a single mutation. The eight-foot diapason was rarely included without at least two stops above it. Dom Bédos, writing at the very end of the period under consideration, favored combining different eight-foot stops for accompaniments, and suggested several four-foot or two-foot stops to imitate high flutes. This indicates a tendency, which we will find paralleled in the late eighteenth century in Germany, which finally led to the romantic registration of more recent times.

Choice of Combination

Serious fugue: Dom Bédos recommends eight- and four-foot reeds with Prestant. This recalls Couperin's famous *Kyrie* verset which is entitled, 'Fugue sur les jeux d'anches'.

Lively fugue: Dom Bédos suggests the Grand Jeu or a Tierce combination.

Dialogue: Usually played on the Grand Jeu and the Petit Jeu. Additional planes, if required, were provided by the Cornet séparé (Récit) and the Écho.

Duo: Many pairs of combinations were available, the left hand playing on the louder manual. The most common procedures were (1) to use two Tierce combinations, or (2) to play the upper part on a Cornet or Tierce and the lower part on a Trompette. The registration was often specified in the title.

Trio, on two manuals:
1. Upper two parts on the Cromorne alone, or with the addition of a four-foot stop or an eight-foot bourdon; lower part on a Tierce
2. Upper two parts on a Tierce or Cornet; lower part on a Trompette
3. Other Duo combinations

Trio, on three keyboards:
Duo combinations with Pedal bourdons, or Tierce (if available)

Quatuor, on three keyboards:
Soprano: Récit — Cornet
Alto: With the soprano or tenor, according to the material
Tenor: Positif — Cromorne, with Prestant or other high stop
Bass: Pédale — Bourdons or Tierce

Quatuor, on four keyboards — Combination I:
Soprano: Récit — Trompette
Alto: Grand Orgue — Tierce
Tenor: Positif — Cromorne and Prestant
Bass: Pédale — Bourdons or Tierce

Quatuor, on four keyboards — Combination II:
Soprano: Récit — Cornet
Alto: Grand Orgue — Trompette
Tenor: Positif — Tierce
Bass: Pédale — Bourdons

Plainsong: If the cantus firmus was in the bass or tenor it would presumably be played on the pedal reeds.[81]

Style of Playing for Various Combinations

Plein Jeu du Grand Orgue: Slowly, stately, legato

Plein Jeu du Positif: Lightly, fluently

Duo: Fast, definitely, cleanly, lightly (but some Duos are slow and serious)

Cromorne: Sweetly, tenderly, in a singing style

Cornet: Definitely, fast, gaily, fluently

Tierce en Taille: In a smooth, singing style; not fast

Basse de Trompette, *de Cromorne*, or *de Tierce*: Definitely, cleanly, animated

Voix Humaine: Slowly, expressively, legato, in a singing style

To realize the effect of these combinations we must bear in mind that the wind pressures were low and the voicing was mild. There were no strings; diapasons were unforced: flutes and gedeckts (bourdons), for the most part, were of metal, and they lacked the assertiveness of many modern examples; the reeds doubtless mixed well with the flues.[82] There was less contrast in the tonal pallette than our present organs provide.

We have more exact information about the registration practices of the French organists of the seventeenth and eighteenth centuries than about those of any other organists before modern times. No other composers left such specific directions. In no other country was the registration so essential a part of the original musical conception. It follows that in no other organ music is the registration so important a part of the interpretation.

---

[81] The above list is by no means exhaustive. See the registrations indicated in the original scores, and Klotz, Bibl. 99, pp. 210-20.

[82] Dom Bédos speaks of the "edge" and "sweetness" (*douceur*) of the Trompettes, which the addition of a Cornet would destroy; but he suggests adding a Prestant if the Trompette is not "harmonious". Bibl. 61, Vol. III, pp. 525, 527.

CHAPTER ELEVEN

HISTORICAL SURVEY – TO 1750
NORTHERN COUNTRIES

Organ Music of the Low Countries

As we pass over into Germany by way of the low countries we notice in Belgian music certain traces of methods which were employed in France. The 'Salve Regina' versets of Pieter Cornet (c.1562-1626),[1] although freer in their development, suggest the motet organization which was characteristic of Titelouze. Likewise the compositions of Abraham van den Kerckhoven (1627?-post 1673)[2] remind us of the music of his French contemporaries, both in their texture and in the occasional registration indications. Nevertheless, the Italian influence was stronger; it is particularly evident in the extended fantasias of these composers.

Sweelinck

The most important link between Italy and Germany, however, was Jan Pieterszoon Sweelinck (1562-1621). Because of his general historical significance and his unique place in the history of Dutch music our interest in the organs of Holland centers in his work. It has been supposed that he was a pupil of Zarlino in Venice, where he at least became acquainted with the music of Merulo and the Gabrielis. Bernard van den Sigtenhorst Meyer insists, however, that he was never absent from Amsterdam for more than a few days at a time;[3] but it is evident that he was thoroughly imbued with Italian traditions, and on them he laid the foundation for that incomparable development which we know as the "organ Baroque". With Sweelinck the rambling passage work which had characterized the older toccatas became controlled by a logical harmonic design; his fantasias were no mere adaptations of vocal forms, embellished with instrumental flourishes. He established a real organ idiom, different from the vocal style, distinct even from the idiom of the harpsichord and of instrumental ensembles. This was not a matter of exploiting various gadgets with which the organ was equipped, but of composing music which the organ was preëminently suited to interpret. It is true that five of his fourteen fantasias featured echo effects, but in all save the shortest one Sweelinck confined the obvious echo treatment to the middle section of a ternary form. Even here musical interest predominates

[1]The set is printed in Bibl. 168.
[2]See Bibl. 184.
[3]Bibl. 148, Vol. VIII, p. 201.

(unlike the dialogues of his French imitators); while in the other nine fantasias, combining elements of the Italian canzona and ricercare,[4] instrumental polyphony is developed into a logical, extended form which points to the architectural masterpieces of Bach.

Of the ten compositions based on church melodies only two sets of variations now exist. These suggest the road which his pupil, Samuel Scheidt, was to follow. His folk song variations, which, though classed as harpsichord music, may have been intended for optional performance on the organ, represent the highest development of the variation form before Bach.

Dutch Organs

All this music appeals through its inherent qualities; it does not depend on any special tone effects. Still, a study of Sweelinck's organs will contribute much to an intelligent interpretation of his music. Until recently our principal sources of information about sixteenth and seventeenth century organs were the works of Italian, French, and German authors, such as Antegnati, Diruta, Mersenne, Schlick, and Praetorius, who paid little attention to foreign instruments. The only comparable Dutch source was a pair of works written in the latter part of the eighteenth century by Joachim Hess,[5] whose information concerning alterations in older instruments was not always complete. Recent research, however, has thrown considerable light on the characteristics of the organs which were familiar to Sweelinck.[6]

We are not surprised to find that the Dutch organs possessed certain elements in common with those of France and various parts of Germany, depending somewhat on the geographical location. Except in the extreme north the pedal department, as in France, served only a melodic function. Large organs in Groningen, the northernmost province, had a fully developed pedal which provided a foundation for the ensemble. In the southern and central parts of the country the manual equipment was similar to that found in France. On the larger instruments the wide chorus of the principal manual was assigned to a separate keyboard. The Positif usually contained a Quintadena and one or two other wide-scale stops, but no flute mutation. In the northern provinces the specifications were more complete, and more like those of northern Germany.

---

[4]See Max Seiffert's commentary in Bibl. 202, Vol. I, p. xix (German text, p. xvii).

[5]Bibl. 90 and 89.

[6]Particularly informing are the books by Floris van der Mueren (Bibl. 103) and M. A. Vente (Bibl. 131). We are indebted to the latter work for most of the information presented here, including specifications which are reproduced with the kind permission of the author and the publisher, H. J. Paris.

Differentiation of Manuals

In France, before the middle of the seventeenth century, no organ possessed more than two manuals. When others were added, they were characterized by their function. In Holland, as in Germany, the different manual departments were identified, and their characteristics somewhat determined, by their location.

The *Hoofdwerk* (German, *Hauptwerk*; French, *Grand Orgue*; English, *Great*) was the original large organ, to which other manuals were added as accessories. It inherited the great diapason chorus which composed the *Blokwerk*.[7] This indivisible ensemble gave way, around the middle of the sixteenth century, to individual stops and smaller mixture groups.

The *Bovenwerk* (*Oberwerk* = upper organ) was located on a chest above the Hoofdwerk. It usually contained a complete series of wide labial stops, beginning at eight-foot pitch, and one or two reeds. On large organs one or two diapason ranks would be included. On small organs this division was controlled by the Hoofdwerk manual.

The *Rugwerk* (*Rückpositiv*; *Positif de dos* = back Choir) was an annexed positive organ, placed behind the player, between him and the congregation. Originally a separate instrument, it became playable from a second manual of the main organ, both in France and in Holland, early in the fifteenth century. Its fundamental pitch was usually an octave above that of the Hoofdwerk. Its resources included a diapason chorus, supplemented by a few wide scale flue stops, and from one to three solo reeds.

The *Borstwerk* (*Brustwerk* = breast, or front organ) was located in the front of the organ chamber. Here the height was insufficient for open eight-foot pipes, so that the eight-foot pitch had to be provided by stopped pipes, or by reeds with short resonators. This manual was often substituted for the Bovenwerk, and/or (in small organs) the Rugwerk. Four-manual organs were not known until the latter half of the seventeenth century.[8]

Characteristics of Sweelinck's Organs

Against this background we can study the instrument for which Sweelinck's music was written. Two organs were installed in the Oude Kerk (Old Church), Amsterdam, of which he was organist, shortly before the middle of the sixteenth century, and may be assumed to have remained in service in Sweelinck's time. The smaller organ, built in 1544,

---

[7] See pp. 229-30.

[8] The earliest of which we find record are in the churches of Saint Germain des Prés, Paris (1667), and St. Katharine, Hamburg (1670).

possessed the following resources:[9]

' Hoofdwerk

Hoofdlade (main chest)

Prestant 4'
Superoctaaf 2',
Mixtuur (full mixture)
Scherp (high mixture)

Bovenlade (upper chest)

Terscimbel [10]

Roerfluit 8'   Schalmei 4' [11]
Quintadeen 8'
Gemshoorn 2'

Borstwerk

Roerfluit 4'   Regaal 8' [11]
Sifflet 1-1/3'

Pedaal

Trompet 8'

Thus the Hoofdwerk contained on the main chest a full diapason chorus, depending on the Roerfluit and Quintadeen for the fundamental, and on the upper chest a series of wider scale stops and solo effects. The Borstwerk provided additional color resources; both the Borstwerk and Pedaal were useful for single voices.

A somewhat larger organ was installed in Breda in 1534 with the following specifications:

Rugwerk

Prestant 4'   Roerfluit 8'   Kromhoorn 16'
                                              Regaal 8'
                                              Schalmei 4'

Hoofdwerk

Prestant 8'
Prestant 4'
Mixtuur
Scherp

---

[9] Because of the similarity of the Dutch stop nomenclature to that with which we are familiar, it has been thought unnecessary to translate the names of the stops.

[10] A high mixture containing a tierce. Presumably its chief function was to color small combinations.

[11] A solo reed with a short resonator, which tended to exaggerate certain upper partials.

Bovenwerk

Terscimbel	Roerfluit 8'	Trompet 8'
	Fluit 4'	
	Gemshoorn 2'	
	Sifflet 1 1/3'	

Pedaal

Prestant 16'		Trompet 8'

The conception of this larger scheme is similar to that of the small organ in the Oude Kerk. The Hoofdwerk is identical with the Hoofdlade section of the smaller instrument except that the foundation stops are an octave lower, providing a diapason fundamental. Presumably this was balanced by greater brightness in the mixtures. The Bovenwerk omits the Quintadeen which is not needed for the principal chorus, and takes over the four-foot flute and high mutation from the Borstwerk of the smaller organ; it also substitutes a trumpet for the Schalmei 4', which is here assigned to the Rugwerk. The latter has two foundation stops and three solo reeds — sixteen-, eight-, and four-foot, affording color possibilities which suggest the later German Rückpositiv. The sixteen-foot diapason in the pedal is exceptional.

The large organ in the Oude Kerk in Amsterdam was built between 1539 and 1543 by Hendrik Nijhoff, of Amsterdam and 's-Hertogenbosch, and was restored in 1567 by Peter Jans of Utrecht. There is no question that Sweelinck played this organ; there is a record of repairs made to it under his direction in 1595.[12] The discovery of the specifications of this instrument, in 1953, is an event of major importance to organists. The stop-list follows:[13]

Rugpositief

Prestant 8'	Quintadeen 8'	Baarpijp (Regaal) 8'
Octaaf 4'	Holpijp 4'	Kromhoorn 8'
Mixtuur	Sifflet 1 1/3'	Schalmei 4'
Scherp		

Hoofdwerk

Prestant 16'
Octaaf 8'
Mixtuur
Scherp

[12]Sweelinck was an organ building expert as well as an organist. Vente lists seven jobs for which he was responsible. Bibl. 131, p. 76.

[13]For this information we are indebted to Dr. M. A. Vente.

Bovenwerk

Prestant 8'	Holpijp 8'	Zink 8'
Terscimbel	Openfluit 4'	Trompet 8'
	Nasard 2 2/3'	
	Gemshoorn 2'	
	Sifflet 1 1/3'	

Pedaal

Nachthoorn 2'   Trompet 8'

Coupler: Hoofdwerk to Pedaal

Range of manuals: FF, GG, AA $- g^2$, a^2
Range of pedals: FF, GG, AA $- c^1$

This is a natural expansion of the scheme of the Breda organ. The most significant differences are (1) a sixteen-foot chorus on the Hoofd-werk; (2) the enlargement of the Rugwerk, which has become a fully developed Rückpositiv, containing a complete diapason chorus which could be set off against the Hoofdwerk, and three wide scale stops; and (3) the omission of the pedal sixteen-foot diapason.

The manual and pedal keyboards of these three instruments were almost identical in range. Such a range was usual in Dutch organs of Sweelinck's time, but there were exceptional instruments one or more of whose manuals descended to CC. The extended pedal range seems to have been more unusual until near the time of Sweelinck's death.[14] It is interesting to note that some of Sweelinck's music calls for the greater manual compass.

Shortly after the death of Sweelinck his pupil, Samuel Scheidt (1587-1654), supervised the building of an organ in the Church of St. Moritz in Halle, which may reflect the taste of his teacher. The resources of this organ were as follows:

Hauptwerk

Prinzipal 8'	Quintadena 16'	Trompete 8'
Oktave 4'	Gedackt 8'	
Oktave 2'	Gedackt 4'	
Mixtur iii	Nasat 2 2/3' (tapering?)	

---

[14]An example of a Dutch organ whose manual range extended below that of the pedals is the instrument built by Lampeler van Mill for the Church of St. Lambert in Münster (over the border in Germany) in 1573-9. Its specifications are very similar to those of Sweelinck's large organ; the manuals, however, extended to CC, while the pedals stopped at FF. It was in cages hung from the tower of this church that the bodies of John of Leiden, Dutch Anabaptist fanatic, and his companions were exposed after their execution in 1635.

Rückpositiv

Oktave 4'	Quintadena 8'	Krummhorn 8'
Oktave 2'	Gedackt 8'	Schalmei 4'
Mixtur iii	Gedackt 4'	
	Gemshorn 2'	
	Sifflöte 1 1/3'	
	Spitzflöte 1'	

Pedal

Subbass 16'	Spitzflöte 1'	Posaune 16'
Oktave 8'		Cornett 2'[15]
Oktave 4'		

The use of the Quintadena as the lowest rank of a principal chorus has been observed in the small Amsterdam organ. The new features of this scheme are the reduction in the range of the mixtures and the provision of a pedal foundation for the ensemble. We have seen that such a pedal, conforming to the north German tradition, existed in Groningen, but we have no reason to believe that Sweelinck had access to such an instrument.

Registration of Sweelinck's Music

Sweelinck provided no registration indications other than *piano* and *forte* to show the change of manuals in his echo fantasias. For further suggestions we are dependent on the internal evidence of the music itself, the specifications of instruments such as he probably had in mind, and our knowledge of Italian registration practices.

For his fantasias and toccatas we may surmise that he used a diapason ensemble, varying it to suit the material. Italian tradition would indicate that foundation stops were used for the more polyphonic movements; however, the architectural build-up of his large fantasias suggests the possibility of a more imposing presentation. It is not likely that reeds were included in the ensemble, for the organs lacked the four-foot chorus reeds which were essential to the French *grand choeur*, and neither the Italian nor the German organists made such use of reeds until a considerably later date.

The fact that Sweelinck carefully indicated the changes of manual in his echo fantasias would lead us to believe that he did not intend such changes where they were not indicated. If he made them at all it was undoubtedly at division points where there was a change of material — agreeing with the contemporary Italian practice. An examination of these works also shows that, except for single voice echo effects, he did not play simultaneously on two manuals. Evidences of this are (1) the fact

---

[15] A reed stop, doubtless used for the cantus firmus in the soprano.

that chords and individual notes are often shortened in order to show an entrance, or to make way for a scale coming into their range, in cases where the conflict might have been avoided by the use of another manual; (2) the constant shifting of the textural elements – such as florid passages and accompanying chords, making a consistent division on two manuals impracticable; and (3) the unified texture which prevails elsewhere.

For the antiphonal effects called for in his echo fantasias, his organ provided such possibilities as the following: (1) He could alternate the principal choruses of the Hoofdwerk and Rugwerk, or more colorful combinations on the Bovenwerk and Rugwerk, giving a contrast of location; (2) he could set off a combination of narrow-scale stops on one manual against wide-scale stops on another; (3) one combination could include mutations and the other consist mainly of foundation stops; (4) in the case of single melody echoes a reed could contribute its characteristic color to one or both combinations, or be used alone.

In playing variations Sweelinck probably distinguished between the principal melody and the accompanying parts by playing the tune on a solo reed, or on a small flue combination colored by mutations. If he played on an organ whose pedal had a high-pitched reed, we may assume that he used it for the cantus firmus – a procedure which Scheidt specifically recommends in his *Tabulatura Nova*.[16] Sweelinck's own pedal Nachthoorn doubtless served a similar function.

A special problem in the interpretation of Sweelinck's organ music concerns the use of the pedals; moreover it is here that the organist is in particular danger of being led astray by modern editors. We read in *Grove's Dictionary of Music and Musicians* that Sweelinck was the first composer to write an independent pedal part.[17] Robert Eitner, who edited the first publication of these works, assumed the almost continuous use of the pedal, and marveled at the virtuosity of the old organists.[18] Eitner's enthusiasm distorted his judgment, and later editors have been influenced by his interpretations.

An examination of all the organ compositions in the collected works of Sweelinck[19] fails to reveal any evidence of an *obbligato* pedal part. On

[16]Bibl. 195, pp. 223-4. See also Bibl. 135, p. 99.

[17]Bibl. 147, Vol. V, p. 197, in the article on 'Sweelinck' by Reginald Poole. The statement is repeated in Percy Scholes's *The Oxford Companion to Music* and in Oscar Thompson's *The International Cyclopedia of Music and Musicians*. This error does not appear, however, in the 1954 edition of *Grove's Dictionary*. See Vol. VIII, p. 201.

[18]Bibl. 203, p. v.

[19]Bibl. 202, Vols. I & IX. C. F. Peters Corporation announces the publication of a complete edition of Sweelinck's organ works, edited by Flor Peeters.

the contrary, there are definite indications that the music was conceived
for manuals only, except for the variations referred to above. It is so
written that the bass can always be played with the left hand — even at
the occasional expense of natural voice leading and effective spacing.
Also, the bass is often interrupted for passage work and melodic figures
in a way that makes the use of the pedal quite illogical. Furthermore,
one finds fingering indications where the use of the pedals would be expected, if it were intended at all.[20] These considerations led Max
Seiffert to contend that the composer had in mind "no obbligato treatment
of the pedal, but he employed it only here and there, perhaps to give more
emphasis to a fugue theme appearing in the bass, or more support for
heavy chords."[21] But even Seiffert was not aware of the characteristics
of the organs for which Sweelinck's music was written. When we realize
that his pedal section contained only an eight-foot reed and a two-foot
flute, and that his music often extended below the range of the pedals,
we are forced to the conclusion that the pedal was *never* intended to
reinforce the bass of the ensemble.

Organ Music in Germany

Except for Frescobaldi, who was twenty-one years his junior, Sweelinck
was the most famous organist of his time and attracted pupils from various parts of northern Europe. Indeed he was described as the "German
organist maker". Having absorbed the Italian tradition and revitalized it
with his own genius, he transmitted it through Heinrich Scheidemann and
Jacob Praetorius to northern Germany, and through Samuel Scheidt to
central Germany — not to mention many other disciples who carried his
influence over a wide area, extending as far as Danzig and Stockholm.
To southern Germany and Austria the Italian tradition came directly
through Hans Leo Hassler (pupil of Andrea Gabrieli), Johann Jacob
Froberger (pupil of Frescobaldi), Johann Kaspar Kerll (pupil of Carissimi,
and perhaps of Frescobaldi), and others.

But before we trace this interesting development we must go back and
study the indigenous characteristics of the German school. We already
know that the earliest development of organ music of which we have
record took place in Germany.[22] Following the composers of the *Buxheimer Orgelbuch* the most important instrumental figures of the German
Renaissance are Arnolt Schlick (c.1450?-*post* 1517) and Paul Hofhaimer

[20]See, for example, Bibl. 202, Vol. I, p. 81, measure 25.

[21]Paraphrase of the words of Max Seiffert in Bibl. 157, p. 33. He goes on to discuss
the unsuitability of Eitner's pedal assignments. See also the same author's remarks in
his introduction to Bibl. 202, Vol. I, pp. xv, xvi.

[22]Pp. 228-9.

(1459-1537).   The latter was probably the most brilliant organist of his time, and led a group of composers whose works are preserved in the German tablatures (excepting that of Schlick) mentioned in footnote 18 on page 229.[23]

Arnolt Schlick

For our purpose, however, the work of the blind organist, Arnolt Schlick, was far more important. He was the author of two publications, each of which was unique in its field: *Spiegel der Orgelmacher und Organisten* ("Mirror of the organ makers and organists"), 1511, and *Tabulaturen etlicher lobgesang und lidlein uff die Orgeln und Lauten* ("Tablatures of several songs of praise and little songs for the organ and lute"), 1512.[24]

The first book gives instructions for building an organ, including specifications and suggestions for voicing, together with brief observations concerning the use of stops. His design for an organ is as follows, some of the stop names being susceptible of conflicting interpretations:

Hauptwerk

Prinzipal 8' (two ranks —   Gemshorn 4' (cylindrical)   Regal
    narrow and wide)   [Gemshorn 2' — for large   Rauschpfeife (reed
Oktave 4'   organ]   or solo mixture)
[Oktave 2' — for large organ]   Zink (Sesquialtera
Hintersatz xvi-xviii   or reed)
Zymbel v   Hölzern Glechter[25]

Rückpositiv

Prinzipal 4'[26]   Gemshorn 2'
    (flute-like — wood
    or metal)
Hintersätzlein
    (small Hintersatz)
Zymbel

Pedal

Prinzipal 16'[26]   Posaune 8'
Oktave 8'
Hintersatz

[23]An admirable selection from these collections, edited by H. J. Moser and Fritz Heitmann, is published in Bibl. 188.

[24]Modern reprints of these works are noted in the Bibliography, Nos. 120 and 198.

[25]Mahrenholz believes that all these effects were produced synthetically, by compound stops (Bibl. 102, pp. 236, 241, 245). The *Hölzern Glechter*, which Schlick himself likened, *in gravibus*, to playing on a pot with a spoon (Bibl. 120, p. 24), has been variously interpreted as a high mixture (Mahrenholz), a mechanical xylophone (Apel, Bibl. 137, p. 819; Frotscher, Bibl. 81, p. 111; and Klotz, Bibl. 99, p. 29), a wood flute (Sumner, Bibl. 128, p. 67), and a tremolo (Rupp, Bibl. 118, p. 12).

[26]Gottlieb Harms, editor of the modern reprint of Schlick's *Tabulaturen*, believes that the Rückpositiv Prinzipal was of eight-foot pitch, and that the Pedal foundation stops were eight- and four-foot, respectively. The last is consistent with Schlick's expressed preference for an eight-foot pedal. See Bibl. 120, p. 25.

Comparing these specifications with the description of a typical organ at the beginning of the sixteenth century, given in the last chapter,[27] one notices (1) the reduction in the size of the Hintersatz and the addition of a solo mixture, (2) an increase in the number of single stops in the Hauptwerk, (3) the inclusion of three or four solo or imitative stops, (4) a second principal chorus on the Rückpositiv, and (5) an independent pedal with a full ensemble and a reed stop.

Schlick expressed a preference for a small organ with well differentiated stops which would be effective both singly and in combination. He insisted that the mixtures be made of narrow pipes, voiced bright, so that the individual ranks would not be heard. He revealed a taste for small combinations, or single stops heard one against another. He specifically suggested playing the Hauptwerk Oktave against the Rückpositiv Prinzipal; any single stop against one or two foundation stops an octave apart (two stops of the same pitch were not combined); the Zimbel (presumably combined with a foundation stop) against a single stop; the Hintersatz against the Posaune. Preludes were always played on the full principal chorus; a cantus firmus could be brought out by playing it on the Hauptwerk chorus, while the accompanying parts were played on the Rückpositiv chorus. The pedal participated in the polyphony, so that the voice-leading could be kept clear.

Schlick's Music

These ideals are beautifully exemplified in the fourteen organ pieces included in the *Tabulaturen*. Their purity, freshness, spontaneity, artfulness, and expressiveness, revealed in a polyphonic but instrumental idiom, were unprecedented. The number of parts ranges from three to six, but all the settings are designed to be played on two manuals, so that the crossings of parts can be heard, and the cantus firmus kept distinct.

Thus Schlick anticipates the ideal of polyphonic clarity which Titelouze expressed a century later. Schlick's music is more naïve and less influenced by the vocal idiom. About the cantus firmus, itself sometimes embroidered, he weaves a lacy pattern of melodic threads whose varied rhythms demand the utmost flexibility and grace of execution, as well as transparency and fluency in the registration. In general these qualities, though less exquisitely displayed, are characteristic of German organ music until the time of Hassler, Praetorius, and Scheidt. Large forms were lacking; for the most part the literature consisted of polyphonic settings of plainsong, chorales, and other vocal melodies. Their appreciation

[27]Pp. 229-30.

depends on a clear presentation of what Moser calls "the filigree of their tracery." [28]

Considerations of Pitch

In his reprint of Schlick's *Tabulaturen* Harms has transposed all the organ pieces down a fourth, to coincide with the pitch for which he supposes them to have been written. There is much disagreement concerning the interpretation of Schlick's instructions. Raymond Kendall's argument, which seems convincing, would make his pitch only about a quarter of a step below our present standard. [29] Harms's most significant contention is that the notation does not imply any specific fundamental pitch, since "all octaves are equally valid." He continues: "I might emphasize that all organ music, until the seventeenth century, indicated the keys [to be played] rather than the pitch, so that adherence to the eight-foot pitch is not only unbeautiful, unimaginative, but false." [30]

Italian Influence

These works of Schlick and the achievements of the Hofhaimer group of composers show that, in the early sixteenth century, southern Germany was far in advance of any other locality, both in the development of the organ as an instrument and in the maturity and refinement of its organ music. Soon, however, it yielded its leadership to Italy, where, under the influence of vocal polyphony, a new instrumental style was being developed. South German organists who studied in Italy brought back a new conception of organ music, based on the logical, imitative development of melodic phrases, possessing cumulative, structural interest, providing successional, as well as immediate, satisfaction. They imported the toccata, the canzona, the ricercare, and the fantasia — forms which were capable of extensive development independent of any textual associations.

These compositions appealed through their intrinsic musical and structural qualities. They did not call for variety of tone quality or any simultaneous color differentiation. They were designed to be performed on a single, uniform ensemble. For this the Italian organs were not only sufficient; from the standpoint of the period they were ideal. So the adoption of Italian methods and musical forms resulted in a more limited

[28] Bibl. 188, Vorwort.

[29] Bibl. 96. This article was reprinted with modifications and additions in Bibl. 97. The interested reader should also study Bibl. 26, as well as A. J. Ellis, 'The History of Musical Pitch', which is printed in Bibl. 16, App. xx, Sec. H, pp. 493-513. It is this last-mentioned work to which later writers have taken exception.

[30] Bibl. 198, p. 59. This idea has been carried out by Karl Straube in some of the registrations suggested in Bibl. 200.

instrument. By the time of Hassler, only the largest organs in southern Germany had two manuals. For the most part there was only one manual and a pedal keyboard of short compass, restricted to the essential bass function; the diapason chorus was composed largely of single ranks, with perhaps one small mixture; the differentiation between the diapasons and the flutes was rather scant, and reeds had little place in the scheme.

In north Germany, through the influence of Sweelinck, the Italian tradition did not supplant the German characteristics, but supplemented them. The northern organists absorbed what Sweelinck offered, but used it in their own imaginative and brilliant fashion. The result was a stupendous development which differentiated German organ music from that of all other countries. Forms were expanded, elaborated, and unified; processes of thematic development were multiplied and related; all the elements were proportioned and fitted into a logical scheme which constituted a consistently designed, cumulative tonal structure. Unity and variety were combined in large forms by the application of architectural principles.

Thus the fantasia and ricercare developed into the more coherent and unified fugue. The canzona found its counterpart in the sectional fugues of the great Danish composer, Dietrich Buxtehude (1637-1707), while his toccatas and chorale fantasias were controlled by an overall design, combining freedom and order.

At the same time the variation form was enriched by the use of methods of figuration which Sweelinck learned from the English virginal composers, and an adaptation of the imitative texture derived from the motet. Coloratura treatment became less conventionalized; the cantus firmus provided only the germ of new melodies which were expressive in themselves. These procedures stimulated the melodic imagination of the composers, affecting their invention of original melodies.

Into central Germany flowed these three currents: the direct stream from Italy through south Germany; the Sweelinck branch, carried by Samuel Scheidt; and the flood from the north, which also was fed by the influence of Sweelinck. Thus was the soil prepared which was to bear the fruit of Bach's genius.

German and Dutch Organ Building

But the development of organ building shows an interchange between Germany and Holland long before the German organists began their pilgrimage to Amsterdam's Oude Kerk. In 1549 an organ was installed in Johanniskirche in Lüneburg by Jasper Johansen, of s'Hertogenbosch, with specifications very similar to those of Sweelinck's large organ.[31] The only important differences were in the pedal which contained Diapasons 16' and 8' (borrowed from the Hauptwerk), an independent Metallgedackt 16', and, for solo purposes, Trompete 4', Nachthorn 2', and Bauernflöte 1'.

As an example of the work of German builders operating in Holland we note the extraordinary instrument built for the Schlosskirche in Groningen by David Beck, of Halberstadt, 1592-6. The Hauptwerk of this organ had nineteen stops on two chests, the Rückpositiv had fourteen, and the Pedal controlled twenty-six stops, distributed among the side towers, the upper chest, and the front chest. The pipes were voiced on a wind pressure of about two and three-quarters inches, supplied by eight oaken bellows, each eight by four feet. The resonators of the reeds were made of brass. The specifications follow:[32]

Hauptwerk

Prinzipal 8'	Quintadena 16'	B Rankett 8'
Oktave 4'	Gemshorn 8'	B Grobregal 8'
Quinte 2 2/3'	Querflöte 8'[33]	B Zimbelregal 2', 4', 8'[34]
B Oktave 1'	Gedackt 8'	
Mixtur vi-viii	Nachthorn 4'	
B Mixtur iii	Querflöte 4'	
Zimbel ii	Hohlflöte 2'	
B Zimbel ii	B Kleingedackt 2'	

Rückpositiv

Prinzipal 4'	Quintadena 8'	Sordun 16'
Oktave 2'	Gemshorn 4'	Trompete 8'
Quinte 1 1/3'	Rohrflöte 4'	Krummhorn 8'
Mixtur iv	Spitzflöte 2'	Singendregal 4'
Zimbel iii	Sifflöte 1'	

[31]See pp. 255-6. The specifications of the Lüneburg organ are given by Klotz in Bibl. 99, pp. 68-9. Vente, Bibl. 131, p. 63, omits the bass function pedal stops and substitutes Trompet 8' for Trompet 4'.

[32]We are indebted to Professor Dr. Hans Klotz for his revision of the specifications previously given, resulting from his recent studies. In the stop-list the distribution of the pipes is indicated as follows:
B = Brustlade (front chest)
O = Oberlade (upper chest)
T = Seitentürmen (side towers)
In Bibl. 99, pp. 58 and 410, Professor Klotz refers to this as Praetorius' organ. Groningen was the residence of the prince whom Praetorius served.

[33]An overblown cylindrical Gedeckt. Bibl. 99, p. 58.

[34]A "repeating" Regal, starting at two-foot pitch in the lower octave, breaking back to four-foot in the second octave, and eight-foot from middle C.

Pedal

T Prinzipal 16'	T Gemshorn 16'	T Posaune 16'
O Oktave 8'	O Untersatz 16'	T Sordun 16'
O Oktave 4'	O Quintadena 16'	T Trompete 8'
O Quinte 2 2/3'	T Gemshorn 8'	B Rankett 8'
O Mixtur v	O Quintadena 8'	B Krummhorn 8'
B Zimbel iii	T Querflöte 8'	T Schalmei 4'
	O Hohlflöte 4'	B Kleinregal 2'
	O Nachthorn 4'	
	T Kleingedackt 4'	
	O Hohlquinte 2 2/3'	
	T Gedacktquinte 2 2/3'	
	B Gedacktquinte 1 1/3'	
	B Bauernflöte 1'	

Coupler: Rückpositiv to Hauptwerk

Early Baroque Characteristics

The more complete choruses, the richer quota of reeds, and the amazing pedal which this last scheme provides, represent not only the ideas of the north, but half a century of development toward the definitive Baroque organ. The usual features of the seventeenth century German organ were as follows:

The Hauptwerk contained a full principal chorus with from two to four foundation stops, a large full mixture, and usually a second, high mixture; a wide chorus, largely made up of single ranks; reeds and other solo stops — especially the Zimbel.

The Rückpositiv also contained both narrow and wide choruses, and a particularly varied representation of reeds, so that this was often the most colorful division of the organ.

Since the Brustwerk usually had to depend on stopped pipes and short resonator reeds for its eight-foot pitch, it favored the wide chorus and solo stops. Sometimes a narrow chorus was included which used a Gedeckt or a Quintadena for its fundamental.

The Oberwerk also had a series of wide-scale stops, with trumpets and other solo effects, including the Zimbel. Sometimes there were one or two diapason ranks, perhaps intended to combine with the Zimbel for solo effects.

In general the Pedal stops were of wider scale than those of the manual ensemble. They included diapasons, bourdons, etc., of various pitches from sixteen-foot (later thirty-two) up to two-foot, with mutations and mixtures. Reeds were provided at octave pitches throughout the same range; also two- and one-foot flutes, and sometimes a small Zimbel. The pedal sounded the bass of a polyphonic ensemble (usually a distinct melodic line) and also served to bring out the cantus firmus, not only in the lower range but in the upper voices as well.

The high pitched stops which did not form a part of a chorus seem to have been specifically intended for treble melodies.

The High Baroque Organ

During the seventeenth century there was a gradual expansion of the resources of the individual manuals, and a corresponding reduction of their individuality. Toward the end of the century the Baroque organ found its finest and most characteristic realization in the work of Arp Schnitger. The new developments may be briefly summarized as follows:

Each chest had its own keyboard; so the large organs possessed four manuals and pedals.

Each keyboard had its own principal chorus, providing an independent full combination. These choruses differed in pitch and also in quality, since the fundamental rank was not necessarily a diapason. Thus on a large four-manual organ the basic pitch of the Hauptwerk and Rückpositiv might be sixteen-foot (represented by a diapason in the Hauptwerk, and by a Dulzian and perhaps a bourdon in the Rückpositiv), the mixture ranks beginning at 1 1/3'; the lowest pitch of the Oberwerk and Brustwerk was eight-foot, the mixture ranks probably beginning respectively at 1', and 2/3'. The Pedal usually included a diapason and a reed of 32' pitch.

The mixtures of the Brustwerk and Oberwerk took over the function of the Scharf which was found on the Hauptwerk of the earlier organs, couplers being installed so that the resources of the manuals could be combined. This provided greater variety in the composition of full combinations. Moreover, single mutations were introduced in the narrow group as well as in the wide, adding subtlety to the shading of the principal ensemble. Likewise third-sounding ranks were more common, and the Sesquialtera was no longer restricted to the wide group.

As heard by the congregation the principal choruses of the individual, uncoupled manuals sounded about equally loud, except that the Brustwerk was perhaps somewhat softer, and the Rückpositiv, because of its location, tended to be more prominent.

New qualities, such as strings, began to be introduced; but the basic grouping into three categories — narrow chorus, wide chorus, and reeds — persisted. All groups were found on each manual, and the number and variety of reeds greatly increased. Reeds as well as flutes could share in the ensemble at foundation pitches. As a general rule reeds with a stronger fundamental were found in the Hauptwerk and Oberwerk, and those with a weaker fundamental in the Rückpositiv and Brustwerk.[35]

---

[35]Klotz gives a very interesting comparison of the specifications of the organ in the Marienkirche in Bernau as originally built by Hans Scherer, 1572-3, as rebuilt by Paul

A Schnitger Masterpiece

Perhaps the most famous example of Schnitger's work is the organ which he rebuilt for the Jakobikirche in Hamburg, 1688-93, and which is still in use. This organ dates from 1512-16, when it had one manual and pedals. It had already been rebuilt several times and gradually enlarged to four manuals before Schnitger began his work. As completed by Schnitger its specifications were as follows:[36]

Hauptwerk

Prinzipal 16'	Quintadena 16'	Trompete 16'
Oktave 8'	Spitzflöte 8'	
Oktave 4'	Gedackt 8'	
Oktave 2'	Rohrflöte 4'	
Rauschpfeife ii	Flachflöte 2'	
Mixtur viii-x		

Rückpositiv

*Prinzipal 8'	Gedackt 8'	Dulzian 16'
*Oktave 4'	Quintadena 8'	Bärpfeife 8'
*Oktave 2'	Blockflöte 4'	Schalmei 4'
*Quinte 1 1/3'	Querflöte 4'	
Sesquialtera ii		
Scharf vi-viii		

*Upper octaves very wide, like flutes

Oberwerk

Prinzipal 8'	Holzflöte 8' (much tapered)	Trompete 8'
Oktave 4'	Rohrflöte 8'	Vox humana 8'
Oktave 2'	Spitzflöte 4' (moderately tapered)	Schalmei 4'
Scharf iv-vi	Nasard 2 2/3' (slightly tapered)	
Zimbel iii	Gemshorn 2' (cylindrical)	

Brustwerk

Prinzipal 8'	Holzprinzipal 8' (wood)	Dulzian 8'
Sesquialtera ii	Rohrflöte 4'	Trichterregel 8'[37]
Scharf iv-vi	Waldflöte 2'	

Lindemann in 1626, and as rebuilt again by Arp Schnitger in 1710. This comparison exemplifies some of the developments noted above, and also shows a tendency to lighten the lower pitches and render the ensemble more transparent. Bibl. 99, pp. 72-4, 172-7.

[36] Again we are indebted to Professor Dr. Hans Klotz for communicating his latest findings. In 1720 Bach sought the appointment as organist at this church, but finally declined it. After giving a recital on this organ Schweitzer wrote to Widor: "Great fatigue for the hands . . But what nobility, what blending of sound . . and what a lesson for the organist!" — Bibl. 134, p. 13.

[37] A trumpet type of reed with short resonators:

Pedal

Prinzipal 32'	Subbass 16'	Posaune 32'
Oktave 16'	Nachthorn 2'	Posaune 16'
Oktave 8'		Dulzian 16'
Oktave 4'		Trompete 8'
Rauschpfeife ii		Trompete 4'
Mixtur vi-viii		Kornett 2'

Couplers: Rückpositiv to Hauptwerk; Oberwerk to Hauptwerk

Organs Played by Buxtehude and Pachelbel

The Jakobikirche organ represents the peak of the development of the north German organ.   Buxtehude's organs at Lübeck belong to an earlier stage. The resources of his larger instrument are summarized below:[38]

Hauptwerk
   Principal chorus: 22 ranks, from 16'
   Wide chorus: 8 ranks, from 16'
   Reeds: Trompeten 16', 8'; Zink 8'

Brustwerk
   Principal chorus: 10 ranks, from 8'
   Wide chorus: 6 ranks, from 8'
   Reeds: Krummhorn 8'; Regal 8'
   Special stops: Schweizerpfeife 2': Zimbel iii

Rückpositiv
   Principal chorus: 12 ranks, from 8' (plus Bordun 16')
   Wide chorus: 7 ranks (including Bordun 16')
   Reeds: Dulzian 16'; Trichterregal 8'; Bärpfeife 8'; Vox Humana 8'

Pedal
   Principal chorus: 10 ranks, from 32'
   Wide stops: Subbass 16'; Gedackt 8'
   Reeds: one 32'; two 16'; two 8'; one 2' (solo)
   Solo flutes: Nachthorn 2'; Bauernflöte 1'

In the organs of central Germany the brilliance of the northern instruments and the refinement of the south appear in varying proportions. Pachelbel's organ in Erfurt, built by Ludwig Compenius in 1647, contained the following:[39]

Hauptwerk
   Principal chorus: 10 ranks, from 8'
   Wide chorus: 5 ranks, from 16'

Rückpositiv
   Principal chorus: 5 ranks, from 4'
   Wide chorus: 6 ranks, from 8'
   Reeds: Trompete 8'; Schalmei 4'

[38] From Bibl. 99, p. 159, and Bibl. 142, pp. 119-20.
[39] From Bibl. 76, p. 82.

Pedal

>   Flue stops: Prinzipal 16'; Subbass 16'; Gemshorn 8'
>   Reeds: Posaune 16'; Trompete 8'; Schalmei 4'; Kornett 2'

Again we see the principal chorus dependent on the wide chorus to provide its lowest rank. The paucity of pedal flues and the full complement of pedal reeds are significant in view of the characteristics of Pachelbel's organ music. He was a pupil of Kerll and strongly influenced by the Italian tradition. Nowhere does his music call for the pedal reinforcement of the lowest voice of a polyphonic ensemble. The flue stops were adequate for the long pedal points and occasional slow moving bass of his toccatas. More than a quarter of his chorale settings are purely *manualiter*.[40] The remainder include cantus firmus treatment in which the melody would naturally be played by the feet. In more than half of these the chorale is assigned to the soprano and was presumably played on the pedal two-foot reed. In most of the twenty-five settings in which the cantus firmus appears in the bass it is accompanied by brilliant manual counterpoints. The use of the pedal reed chorus against the Hauptwerk principal chorus was doubtless assumed.

Gottfried Silbermann

The greatest organ builder following Schnitger was Bach's Saxon contemporary, Gottfried Silbermann. Although a follower of the north German tradition he was also familiar with the work of the Italians and the French and incorporated some of the features of their organs in his own instruments. The principal changes which he introduced were as follows:

He omitted the Rückpositiv, never building an organ with more than three manuals. Thus the different departments contributed to a total ensemble, with no division standing apart. The organ gained integrity at the expense of differentiation.

He greatly reduced the diversity of solo effects, omitting the treble reeds in the pedal and most of the exotic manual reeds. He also discarded the Zimbel, but he introduced the French Cornet, which he sometimes called "Sesquialtera", and even mounted it on a separate chest, behind the diapason.[41]

He reduced the range of the wide scale group, avoiding the largest scales and the harmonic pipes, and confining the wide scale mutations to the twelfth and seventeenth.

Working at a time when the purity of tonal design was beginning to deteriorate, when the narrow chorus was becoming adulterated and the wide

[40]Based on a study of Bibl. 191.
[41]Bibl. 76, p. 146.

chorus disintegrated, when stops were valued for their characteristic individual color rather than for their contribution to the ensemble, Silbermann maintained the integrity and balance of the groups, and he designed the manual ensembles in relation to one another and to the entire organ. The reeds were intended to share in the full chorus.

These German Baroque organs produced a rich, homogeneous ensemble in which the upper ranks contributed to the quality and power without asserting their own pitches. If the Schnitger organs were perhaps more varied and more subtle, Silbermann's instruments were particularly admired for their beauty of tone. Such adjectives as "charming", "singing", "murmuring", "ravishing", "lovely", "sweet", "delightful", "clear", "delicate", "refreshing", were applied to various stops; and the full combinations were characterized as "splendid, solemn, silvery."[42] These organs, according to Albert Schweitzer, "attained to a beauty and richness of tone . . . which have not been surpassed since." Later he observes:

> "on such an instrument the diapasons and mixtures give a *forte* so rich, intense, full-coloured, and yet in no wise fatiguing, that we can, if need be, preserve it unchanged throughout a prelude or a fugue. . . . moreover, both the inner parts and the pedal come out clearly."[43]

German Registration Practices

Contemporary records of the German registration practices during the period which we have been discussing — from the end of the sixteenth to the middle of the eighteenth century — are rather meager and not very specific. Indeed, writers seemed more interested in the possible permutations of various registration factors than in the artistic value of the resulting combinations.[44] Nevertheless, we find evidence of certain fairly consistent practices which prevailed, only slightly relaxed as the instruments became more flexible and less conventionalized.

The distinction between the narrow and wide choruses was basic. In the narrow chorus the upper ranks had, in general, a higher overtone content than the lower ranks; indeed wide scale stops could be substituted for the fundamental and octave pitches. This made for a cohesive ensemble suited to the performance of several parts on one manual. In the wide chorus the fundamental had a higher overtone content than the upper

[42]Anonymous, *Einige Discurse zweier Orgelfreunde* (Greiz, 1742), as quoted in Bibl. 99, p. 239.

[43]Albert Schweitzer, *J. S. Bach* (London: A. & C. Black; New York: The Macmillan Company), Vol. I, pp. 200, 296-7. Quoted by kind permission of the publishers.

[44]See Bibl. 99, pp. 43, 98.

ranks.   This enhanced the color function of the mutations.   The wide
chorus was used primarily for single melodies as solos or as parts of a
duo or a trio.

The registration of music played on a single manual depended on the
character of the material.   Before the fugue form was established it was
the custom (as we found in Italy) to play brilliant toccatas on full ensemble combinations, and to use small octave combinations or single
stops for vocal transcriptions and polyphonic pieces in vocal style.
Organists realized the value of brilliant, complex combinations in giving
clarity to rapid movement, and the effectiveness of small combinations
in keeping the voices of a polyphonic ensemble distinct.   As instrumental
forms developed, and the more characteristic instrumental figures invaded polyphony, full combinations were used for brilliant fugues and
other pieces suggesting the toccata style.

The original full organ was the diapason chorus of the Hauptwerk.   As
the resources of the different divisions became more complete and varied,
a full ensemble could be produced by many different combinations of
foundation stops, mutations and mixtures.   Variations in the character of
the ensemble resulted from the alteration of one or more of the following
factors: (1) the pitch of the fundamental; (2) the relative strength of the
fundamental (in comparison with the upper ranks); (3) the pitch range of
the components of the ensemble; (4) the pitch spacing (close or dis-
parate).   Assigning two values to each factor would provide sixteen
possible permutations, while other values would greatly increase the
available number of differences.[45]

The full combinations of the different manuals were used independently
and in contrast.   They alternated in dialogue and echo effects, and they
set off successive parts of sectional compositions.   They were not
coupled together until the Brustwerk and Oberwerk were specifically designed to supplement the Hauptwerk.[46]

The diapason chorus of the Pedal was complete and independent of
the manual divisions, and also differentiated in quality.   Thus the entrance of a manual part on a note already held by the pedal (as occurs
repeatedly in Bach's 'Toccata in F') was perfectly clear.

Single stops and octave combinations were used for soft movements,
pieces in vocal style, and accompanying.   The eight-foot diapason was
particularly recommended to accompany singers because its pitch corre-
sponded with the vocal range.   Two stops of the same pitch were never
combined except in a complex ensemble.   The common practice was to

[45]Bibl. 99, pp. 203-5
[46]See p. 266.

use two stops an octave apart, the upper rank having a wider scale (less overtones) than the lower. Later two stops of similar quality were combined at the octave, but in small combinations the upper rank was never, except in the pedal, narrower than the lower. Examples mentioned in the seventeenth century are:[47]

> Dulzian with a higher flute
> Quintadena 8', Gedackt 4', Gemshorn 2'
> Quintadena 8', Rohrflöte 4'

The choice of registration for single melodies, though fairly clearly defined, permitted a wide range of effect. Full combinations were available when consistent with the character of the music. Moreover almost all single stops were usable. For this purpose foundation stops were not combined at adjacent octaves, but they were used at a distance of two octaves (16' and 4'; 8' and 2'). Unlimited variety of color was provided by the use of a reed or flue stop for the fundamental, coloring it with a selection of overtone stops from the wide or the narrow group, and varying the number, pitch, and spacing of the component ranks. Particularly valued for this purpose was the Zimbel — a repeating, high pitched, narrow scale solo mixture. Originally used with a foundation stop of the narrow group, in seventeenth century practice it was combined with either narrow or wide stops, or with reeds — often with the addition of other overtone ranks. In none of these combinations, of course, was there any duplication of the same pitch.

There was very little reference to the selection of combinations for duo and trio playing. Presumably all solo combinations were available for this purpose. A principal chorus was sometimes set off against a wide chorus combination. Where more vitality was called for, the full principal chorus of two manuals could be used. This was particularly effective if one of the manuals was the Ruckpositiv, whose tone was distinguished by its location.

In the late Baroque period the greater flexibility of the instruments and the increased freedom of tone mixing provided additional variety in the composition and color of ensemble-combinations. Organists planned their registration with more specific regard to the desired tonal effect. Not only wide scale stops but reeds could be substituted for the fundamental and octave ranks of the diapason chorus. In the eighteenth century different qualities were combined at the same pitch; even a reed was "covered" with a flue stop, such as a gedeckt or a diapason. But this may be regarded as the beginning of an era of decadence.

[47] Bibl. 99, p. 107

Throughout the Baroque period stop changes were rarely made in the course of a composition; sections were differentiated and dialogue effects were produced by the use of combinations already set on the different manuals. Except in trios, accompanied solos, and other types specifically designed to show the individuality of one or more voices, two manuals were not used simultaneously. One mass combination heard against another was not thought effective. In this connection we may profitably read the comment of Hans Klotz on the interpretation of Bach's music on the old organs:

> "Never should a manual change or the use of two manuals be adopted in order to bring out an inner voice. This must be clearly understood. The parts sounded perfectly clear on the old organs when played on only one manual. The individual manuals did not differ in loudness but in placement, tone quality, and pitch. On such organs any effort to bring out an inner voice by playing on two manuals (with full combinations) will in most cases not only be quite unnecessary, but will produce a truly ugly tone effect. ... But on most of the organs at our disposal today one must frequently resort to playing on more than one manual at a time, to secure clarity; in such cases, however, it is assumed that an essentially uniform quality will prevail in all voices."[48]

Special Effects

Many organs of this time contained stops imitating birds, bells, and other extraneous sounds, which of course have no importance in the interpretation of the music which has survived. For the rebuilding of the organ at Mühlhausen Bach specified for the pedal a Glockenspiel of twenty-six bells at four-foot pitch. Pirro suggests that he may have had them in mind for the pedal figure in his setting of 'In dir ist Freude'. It is perhaps significant, however, that they were "desired by the parishioners".[49] Organs were also provided with tremolos of varying degrees of effectiveness.

In addition to the manual couplers already noted, a Hauptwerk to Pedal coupler made it possible to join the manual ensemble to the pedal. It should be noted that these couplers were used only for full combinations; small groups of stops were not coupled.

Since crescendos and diminuendos were impossible on German organs before the latter part of the eighteenth century,[50] composers anticipated

---

[48]Klotz, *Über die Orgelkunst* . . . (Kassel: Bärenreiter Verlag), p. 255. Quoted by kind permission of the author and publisher.

[49]Bibl. 111, pp. 74, 77; also Bibl. 143, p. 59.

[50]A swell pedal is said to have been introduced in Leipzig eight years before the death of Bach, but there is no evidence that he took any notice of it. See Bibl. 69, p. 78; also Bibl. 134, p. 9, fn. 2.

an invariable dynamic level, modified only at division points or between phrases, where an abrupt change was suggested by the music. Gradual dynamic variation was rare. A possible example occurs in the bridge between the 'Adagio' and the 'Fugue' of Bach's 'Toccata, Adagio, and Fugue in C'. It is conceivable that (as Widor has suggested) Bach used the single melody leading to the massive six-part chorus as an opportunity to add stops, building up to the full ensemble needed for the attack on the diminished seventh chord against the dissonant pedal.

Interpretation of German Baroque Music

In general — summarizing the foregoing account — organists who wish to present the German music of the seventeenth and eighteenth centuries in its original garb will build their ensembles of many ranks, with the minimum of duplication of individual pitches. The fundamental will be felt as the pitch center to which the upper work contributes, but it will not be emphasized by dominating eight-foot ranks. In these combinations flutes or reeds may occasionally be substituted for, and rarely flutes may be added to, unison and octave ranks; but the mutations and mixtures will always be of diapason or Geigen quality. In registration for a solo melody and other small combinations duplication at the same pitch will be avoided, and the upper ranks will normally be less rich in overtones than the lower ones. For solo purposes a reed *may*, for eighteenth century music, be combined with a flue stop of the same pitch.

Fidelity to the Baroque conception involves the avoidance of romantic treatment. Modern strings and imitative reeds will not be used. Color will be produced synthetically, rather than by employing characteristically voiced stops, except for solo reeds of the Baroque type. If any use is made of the swell pedal, it will be within the limits of clearly defined dynamic planes, since the music of this period achieved dynamic variety by changes of level rather than slopes. The expression of mood through color and shading need not be excluded, but it will be subordinate to a clear presentation of the material and a logical interpretation of the design.

Early English Organs and Organ Music

The progress of organ building, composition, and registration in Germany, which we have briefly outlined, overshadows anything that took place in other countries — although it was influenced by the developments in Holland, Italy, and France, and perhaps indirectly by the practices in Spain. England was outside this sphere, and her organs and organ music followed a different pattern.

The famous Winchester Cathedral organ, with its two sets of twenty sliders, each controlling ten pipes, shows that in the tenth century the English could make as much noise as anyone.[51] Moreover, the organ pieces in the Robertsbridge Codex indicate a genuine, if primitive, artistic development early in the fourteenth century, which antedates any known keyboard music on the continent.[52] Two hundred years later John Redford (c.1485-c.1545), Thomas Tallis (c.1505-1585), and William Blitheman (?-1591) wrote organ motets which were unsurpassed by any of their continental contemporaries.[53]

The cathedral and parish records in England contain much information concerning the costs of various organs, and there are many references in contemporary literature to their effect on the hearers, but little is known about the specifications of the early instruments. Rimbault quotes a contract for an organ to be installed in Allhallows' Church, Barking, dated 1519, and gives Hopkins' interpretation of the details.[54] Hopkins states that two stops are mentioned; Charles W. Pearce speaks of it as a "three stop organ",[55] while Margaret Glyn says it was "an organ of one stop".[56]

Reasoning from internal evidence, Pfatteicher believes that the music of Redford was written for a two-manual organ, of which one manual was of eight-foot pitch (but extending to AAA) and the other of four-foot pitch.[57] Whatever may have been the specific resources of these sixteenth century organs, we may be sure that they were very small and possessed neither reeds, mixtures, nor pedals.

The organ did not play so important a part in the church service in England as on the continent—particularly in France and Germany; so there was less stimulus to the production of organ music. Moreover, after the separation from Rome in 1534, its composition was less influenced by plainsong melodies and the vocal polyphony of the church. As Margaret Glyn says: "Later organ music lost the purely religious ritual character of the earlier, and about the middle of the century a gradual secularization took place, which is exemplified in the work of Tallis

[51]A description of this instrument may be found in any history of the organ.

[52]See p. 228.

[53]The richest source is *The Mulliner Book*, Bibl. 181. Other examples may be found in Bibl. 179, 109, and 204. For additional commentaries see Bibl. 127 and 101.

[54]Bibl. 91, Part I, pp. 56-7.

[55]Bibl. 107, p. 156. See also Bibl. 128, p. 102.

[56]Bibl. 179, Preface.

[57]Bibl. 109, pp. 36-7. Pfatteicher infers this from the actual pitches indicated. On this assumption the composer must, contrary to the practice in Germany, have notated the *pitches* desired; rather than the keys to be played. Cf. p. 262.

himself."[58]   The growing popularity of the virginal and the existence of many small organs outside the churches[59] led to the indiscriminate composition of keyboard pieces in which the style was largely determined by the more common virginal.   Secular forms, such as the pavane and galliard, were common.   A few polyphonic fantasias ("fancies") and voluntaries, apparently conceived primarily for the organ, are found among the works of William Byrd (1543?-1623), Thomas Weelkes (1577?-1623), and Orlando Gibbons (c.1570-c.1650).[60]

Early English Organ Specifications

The earliest English organ specifications which have come to us are for the organ built by Thomas Dallam in 1613 for the Cathedral Church of Worcester, which contained the following stops:[61]

Great Organ

Two Diapasons 8'	Recorder (metal Gedeckt) 8'?
Two Principals 4'	
Twelfth 2 2/3'	
Two Fifteenths 2'	

Chaire Organ[62]

Wood Diapason 8'	Wood Flute 8'?
Principal 4'	
Fifteenth 2'	
Twenty-second 1'	

[58] Bibl. 179, Preface.

[59] The inventory of Henry VIII's collection of musical instruments contained 28 organs, 32 virginals, and 3 combinations of the two. See Bibl. 154, p. 303.

[60] The chief sources of Elizabethan organ music are the following:

The Byrd Organ Book, ed. Margaret Glyn (London: William Reeves, c. 1923)
William Byrd, *Fourteen Pieces for Keyed Instruments*, ed. J. A. Fuller Maitland and W. Barclay Squire (London: Stainer and Bell, 1923)
The Collected Works of William Byrd, ed. E. H. Fellowes (London: Stainer and Bell, 1950), Vols. XVIII-XX.   Now that a complete collection of the known keyboard works of Byrd has at last appeared, it is a disappointment to discover that the editor has revised them for performance on a modern piano.
Orlando Gibbons, *Ten Pieces from the Virginal Book of Benjamin Cosyn*, ed. J. A. Fuller Maitland (London: J. & W. Chester, 1925)
Thomas Weelkes, *Pieces for Keyed Instruments*, ed. Margaret Glyn (London: Stainer and Bell, 1924)
Twenty-five Pieces for Keyed Instruments from Benjamin Cosyn's Virginal Book, ed. J. A. Fuller Maitland and W. Barclay Squire (London: J. and W. Chester, 1923)
Old English Organ Music, ed. John E. West (London: Novello and Co., n.d.).   A series of sheet music items which, unfortunately, seem to be going out of print.

[61] From Sumner, *The Organ* . . . (London: Macdonald & Co., Ltd.), p. 112.   Quoted by kind permission of the publisher.

[62] See Bibl. 128, pp. 154-6, for an excellent discussion of the meaning of *Chaire Organ*, of which the modern term 'Choir' is a misleading corruption. Chaire = char = chare = chore (cf. charwoman). It was an adjunct or alternative organ, like the Positif of the continental instruments.

In 1632 the contract was signed for the famous organ in York Minster, which was built by Thomas Dallam's son, Robert, to the following specifications:

Great Organ

Two Diapasons 8'   Wood Diapason 8'
Two Principals 4'   Recorder 2'
Twelfth 2 2/3'
Fifteenth 2'
Twenty-second 1'

Chaire Organ

Wood Diapason 8'   Wood Flute 8'?
Principal 4'   Recorder 8'
Fifteenth 2'

These two instruments may be considered typical of the more important installations between the establishment of the Church of England and the Revolution. From them and from other specifications of the period we learn that the English organs still had only one or two manuals and no pedals. "Short octaves" made it possible to reach wide intervals in the lower part of the keyboard which would now require the assistance of the feet. When the lower octave was complete AAA was substituted for CC♯, and GGG was sometimes added, providing notes below the normal range of the keyboard.[63] As yet there were no reeds or mixtures, and only an occasional mutation; so the instruments must have lacked color;[64] moreover, the duplication of stops, shown in the specifications given above, would tend to make the tone heavy. Contemporary comments, however, included such adjectives as "sweet", "rich", "deep", "delicate", "fair".[65]

English Organs after the Restoration

The almost complete destruction of organs under Cromwell, following their previous neglect and deterioration under Puritan influence, was perhaps a blessing in disguise. In order to supply the demand for new organs after the Restoration, Bernhard Schmidt (who became known as "Father Smith") was brought from Germany, and Thomas and Renatus Harris returned from France, where they had lived during the period of the

[63]See, for example, Gibbons' 'Voluntary in A minor' in John E. West's series of *Old English Organ Music*.

[64]Gibbons' 'Fantasia in A minor' (No. 7 in Fuller Maitland's collection) is in the style of a 'cornet voluntary', but we do not know of that stop being introduced in an English organ before the Restoration.

[65]Bibl. 91, Part I, p. 72.

Commonwealth. These builders brought with them continental ideas of organ design. Immediately mixtures and reeds appear in the specifications, and there is less duplication. A third manual, an Echo, was often added.

The famous organ built by Father Smith for the Temple Church in London, in 1684, shows the progress which had already been made.[66] The specifications follow:

Great Organ

Prestand 8'	Holflute 8'	Trumpett 8'
Principall 4'	(wood and metal)	
Quinta 2 2/3'	Gedackt 4' (wood)	
Super octavo 2'	Cornett ii	
Mixture iv	Sesquialtera iii	

Choir Organ

	Gedackt 8' (wood)	Violl and Violin 8'
	Holflute 4'	
	Sadt 4'[67]	Voice humane 8'
	Spitts Flute 2'	

Ecchos

Super octavo 2'	Gedackt 4' (wood)	*Trumpett 8'
	*Gedackt 8'? (wood)	
	*Flute 4'?	
	*Cornett iii	
	*Sesquialtera iv	

*Half stop, beginning at middle C

The range of the keyboards extended from FFF to c^3, semitones beginning at BBBb. Except in the lowest octave, separate keys were provided for D♯ and E♭, and for G♯ and A♭, making it possible to play in keys which would otherwise have been unusable with the unequal temperament used at that time. This device was already known on the continent, but it had never been commonly adopted.[68] The "Ecchos" "consisted in a duplicate of the treble portion of some of the stops enclosed in a wooden box, which rendered the sound softer and more distant."[69]

The most important English organ composers of the half century following the Restoration were John Blow (1648-1708), Henry Purcell (c.1658-1695), and William Croft (1677-1727), all of whom were organists at

[66]The famous competition between Father Smith and Renatus Harris, known as the "battle of the organs", is related in the histories of English organs. In our specifications we have followed Charles W. Pearce's interpretation of the mixtures. Bibl. 107, p. 2.

[67]A kind of Gemshorn.

[68]Bibl. 136, pp. 64-7.

[69]Bibl. 91, Part I, pp. 136-7.

Westminster Abbey. Nothing is known about the instrument which they played except that it cost £120 (to build or repair), and that Samuel Pepys heard it on November 4, 1660.[70] We may surmise that it had only one manual from the fact that, in the next to the last year of Purcell's incumbency, Father Smith was engaged to "add a double sett of keys and four new stops", as follows:[71]

Principal 4'	Stop[ped] Diapason 8' (wood)
Fifteenth 2'	Nason 4' (wood Gedeckt)

With the possible addition of a Cremona (= Cromorne), these stops would constitute a typical Choir organ of the period.

Eighteenth Century Developments — The Swell Pedal

It is obvious that the chamber which housed the "Ecchos" of the Temple organ was essentially a swell box which was permanently closed. In 1712 Abraham Jordan built an organ for St. Magnus Church, London Bridge, in which he equipped the echo box with a sliding shutter, operated by a pedal. This is generally considered the birth of the swell pedal. We have seen, however, that this invention was anticipated by José Verdalonga, who built the "Great Organ" in the cathedral of Toledo, Spain.[72] Indeed, the Spanish installation was more significant, for its enclosed division contained a brilliant ensemble of twenty stops, including many ranks of mixtures and a telling array of reeds — such an ensemble as provides the maximum degree of effectiveness in the operation of the swell.[73] Jordan's innovation won immediate popularity in England, but the "smothered fire" of the modern swell came from Spain, through the nineteenth century French and English builders, Cavaillé-Coll and Henry Willis.[74]

In the eighteenth century the improvements which were exemplified in the Temple organ became more generally adopted; mixtures and reeds were commonly included on the Great, and gradually they found their way to the secondary manuals. The art of voicing was developed; solo stops were introduced — and exploited, as they were in France.[75] But in spite of improvements, the English organ was an insignificant affair compared

[70]Bibl. 108, p. 13; Bibl. 209, Vol. I, p. 186.

[71]Bibl. 108, p. 22. It is a curious coincidence that Purcell died the very day that the final payment was due. See Bibl. 108, pp. 22, 24.

[72]P. 239.

[73]See Bibl. 118, pp. 449-51.

[74]See Bibl. 128, pp. 95-6.

[75]Notably by Maurice Greene (1696-1755). See Bibl. 135, p. 203.

with the complete and balanced instruments of Germany. Moreover, the pedal was still lacking.

The Introduction of Pedals

Sumner quotes an entry in the "Wages Book" of St. Paul's Cathedral for the year 1720-21 which includes "Adding six large Trumpet Pipes down to 16 foot tone to be used with a pedal or without" and "the Pedal and its movements".[76] The next mention of pedals tells of the addition of nineteen pull-down pedals, from FFF to C, to the organ built by John Snetzler for the German Lutheran chapel in the Savoy, sometime between 1766 and 1780.[77]   Charles W. Pearce quotes Samuel Wesley (1766-1837) to the effect that he could "well remember the time when the only organ in London to which pedals were affixed was that in the German church in the Savoy." He also cites a 'Voluntary in F' by C. F. Baumgarten, organist at this German chapel, as probably "the first *complete* three-staved organ piece printed in this country [England]."[78] The organ in Westminster Abbey acquired an octave of pedal pipes about 1778,[79] and other installations are recorded at around that time. In the nineteenth century pedals were commonly included in the specifications for new organs and were frequently added to old ones, but there were comparatively few instruments in England on which the works of Bach could be played before the middle of the century.

English Organ Music

The lack of pedals restricted the range and texture of the organ music, and the differentiation between organ and harpsichord music was slight. Even Handel (except for one or two examples) wrote for an organ without pedals, and in a style suited to the harpsichord. Later English composers gradually developed an organ idiom, but the influence of Handel persisted until the middle of the nineteenth century. Samuel Wesley, an ardent admirer of Bach, favored a more solid style of fugal writing and exerted a salutary influence on the design of organs. On the other hand, the insignificant tunes which Maurice Greene (c.1695-1755) played on the cornet and other solo stops contributed to the development of a superficial taste from which English and American organ music has not yet completely recovered.

[76] Bibl. 128, p. 173.

[77] Bibl. 106, p. 30. Sumner states that they were installed when the organ was built, in 1757, Bibl. 128, p. 174.

[78] Bibl. 106, pp. 30-31.

[79] Bibl. 108, p. 35.

Performance of English Organ Music

To realize the effect of the old English organ music players should strive for simplicity. They should bear in mind that all music written before the Restoration was intended to be played on an instrument without mixtures, reeds, sixteen-foot stops, or pedals—although AAA and GGG existed on some organs. Even in the eighteenth century few organs possessed more than one full ensemble, while pedals were not considered essential until the beginning of what, for our purpose, may be called the modern period. The music did not call for different planes or contrasting masses of tone. Such color differentiation as the instruments afforded was largely confined to small combinations.

In playing this music the pedals should be used with extreme discretion. In general, the bass was not intended to be different from the other voices, and should not be weighted with sixteen-foot tone. Where the texture is essentially harmonic, or the bass functions as a *basso continuo*, a sixteen-foot pedal may sometimes be included. Such a situation commonly occurs in the *tutti* sections of Handel's concertos, when played without orchestra; for the sixteen-foot pitch of the contrabasses was a part of the original conception. More often, however, it is better to omit the sixteen-foot stops, unless the style and texture permit their inclusion in the entire ensemble.

It is sometimes convenient to use the pedal keyboard, with the manual combination coupled or duplicated, to extend the reach of the left hand — particularly where the composer has assumed the contraction of the keyboard resulting from a short lower octave. Moreover, the sixteen-foot pedal may provide the AAA and GGG which do not exist on our manuals; but care must be taken to match the manual quality as closely as possible at the lower pitch. In order to avoid a change of quality for single notes, it is sometimes better to play the bass of an entire section or phrase on a sixteen-foot pedal combination — of course playing an octave higher than the part is notated.

Summary of Chapters X and XI

In concluding this brief survey of the organs previous to 1750 it may be helpful to set down, for comparison, the most essential facts concerning the instruments and registration practices of each country.[80]

Italian organs for the most part had only one manual, which contained a complete diapason chorus beginning with the sixteen-foot pitch, of which

---

[80] Germani concludes his comprehensive treatise with a summary of the characteristics of Italian, French, German, Spanish, and English organs in each century, from the 16th to the present, with comparative tables showing the number of manuals, their range, the compass of the pedals, and the stops which might be included. See Bibl. 84, pp. 191-200.

all, or nearly all, the ranks were controlled separately. It is generally
thought that the scales were moderately wide, producing a rather round
tone which enabled each rank to make its characteristic contribution to
the tone quality.   Flutes existed only at eight-, four-, and two-foot
pitches. The octave of pedals controlled only low-pitched pipes, suitable
for pedal points and for giving occasional support to the harmonies. Stops
were combined with considerable freedom, full combinations being used
for brilliant toccatas and mass effects, and small combinations for polyphonic music. There was no objection to combining two stops of the same
pitch, but the specifications provided little duplication. The upper flutes
were sometimes combined with mutations to produce the effect of a
Cornet.   On most organs a solo could not be separated out, and reeds
were not available.

The Spanish organs were larger and more complete, and provided
greater variety. The principal chorus was rich in overtones, being composed of many ranks of narrow scale pipes.[81] A large number of reeds of
many pitches lent brilliance to music of a florid or imposing character,
while the foundation stops provided suitable combinations for polyphonic
movements.   The variety available on different manuals enabled the
organist to set one quality against another; and the resources of the
pedals, including a large range of both diapason and trumpet ranks, made
it possible for the feet to play independent melodies in any part. They
could bring out solo melodies or a single line of a polyphonic ensemble,
or they could provide a solid foundation for the harmonies.

In France plurality of manuals was early established. The Grand Orgue
possessed a fairly narrow principal chorus with mixtures, a series of
separate flute ranks and a Cornet, perhaps two chorus reeds and a solo
reed. The Positif was similar but smaller; its basic pitch was an octave
higher, and chorus reeds were generally lacking. Other manuals were
added for special purposes: a Récit to provide independent solo stops;
an Écho (under the main chest) to give the effect of distance; a Bombarde to add a reedy ensemble. The pedal department was intended for
single melodies (either a cantus firmus or a part of the polyphony), rather
than to support the tonal mass. These organs were designed primarily for
a clear differentiation of simultaneously sounding melodies or of successively sounding ensembles. The wide scale mutations were used for
single melodies, while the narrow scale chorus provided a homogeneous
ensemble. There were few rules for combining stops, but combinations
tended to be stereotyped, and composers wrote with specific registration
in mind.

[81]Bibl. 99, p. 44.

In Holland and Germany the various divisions of the organ were differentiated, and their characteristics determined, by their location. Contrasting ensembles were provided on the different manuals, and a few solo stops. In general the pedal of Dutch organs served only to bring out a cantus firmus and perhaps, through the Hoofdwerk to Pedaal coupler, to supplement the reach of the hands. In the extreme north, however, Dutch organs were very much like those of northern Germany.

From the organ of Schlick with its three independent divisions, each provided with a principal chorus and stops suitable for solos and trio combinations, to the architectural masterpieces of Schnitger and Silbermann, German organs show a consistent evolution. The resources became increasingly varied; the different divisions, while preserving their individual characteristics, became more and more related to one another; and the whole scheme was adapted to the effective presentation of the various forms which composers were developing.

Aside from the logic and completeness of their design, these instruments were noteworthy for the range and diversity of their pitch components, shown both in the profusion of mixtures and mutations and in the rich overtone content of the individual ranks. The scale of the pipes of the principal chorus was narrower than in other countries, and the mouth was low cut, giving the tone a bold, bright quality.[82] For the wide chorus partially stopped pipes (of the Gemshorn and Rohrflöte types) or overblown pipes (Quintadena and Querflöte) were often used instead of the more fundamental flutes and gedeckts.

The taste was for richness and vitality with the avoidance of heaviness. The same ideal was served by the registration practices: in small combinations duplication at the same pitch was not permitted, and octave combinations were not used in which the lower rank had a stronger fundamental than the upper one. In full combinations, on the other hand, cohesiveness was achieved by the inclusion of a large proportion of small scale, high pitched ranks.

In England the more important organs apparently had two manuals at an early date, but their resources were insignificant compared with contemporary continental instruments. There were no pedals until comparatively modern times; and organs built before the Restoration lacked mixtures, reeds, and sixteen-foot stops, and possessed only an occasional mutation. There was apparently no conception of tonal architecture, and reinforcement was sought by duplication. The influence of French and German ideas after the Restoration was beneficial, but the overemphasis of the fundamental, both in the specifications and in the voicing, persisted. At

[82]Bibl. 102, p. 43.

the same time, in spite of the genius of Redford, Tallis, Blitheman,
Gibbons, and Purcell, English organ composers can scarcely be said to
have shared in the development of organ music which culminated in the
work of Bach, and on which all later progress has been based. Still,
there is a considerable quantity of English music which is worthy to be
included in the organist's repertoire, and which can be completely understood only in the light of a knowledge of the instruments for which it was
written.

The Interpretation of Old Music

There remains the practical question, regarding all organ music prior to
the nineteenth century: To what extent should the modern interpreter be
guided by the conception of the composer, the characteristics of the instruments with which he was familiar, and the registration practices of
his time and country? Only the extreme purist would insist on an exact
duplication of the original effect, which, in fact, could rarely be realized
on a modern instrument. Only the most unscrupulous romanticist or
radical would ignore all evidence concerning the way the composer expected his music to sound.

It was suggested at the beginning of this survey that the organist
should try to make the composer's conception his own, and to convey it
to his audience. Just how this will be done will depend upon the characteristics of the instrument which the organist plays, the occasion at
which the music is performed, and the psychology of the listeners. This
is a special case in the whole problem of conformity to the composer's
indications, which will be discussed at the end of the next chapter. For
the present we will simply state the principle that the essential qualities
of the music, as revealed by both internal and external evidence, should
be preserved.

CHAPTER   TWELVE

HISTORICAL   SURVEY

LATER   DEVELOPMENTS

The Decline of Polyphony

For more than a century following the death of Bach organ music suffered from the decline of polyphony. The great composers of this period were concerned with the development of new forms which were imperfectly suited to the organ. Haydn left us nothing for the instrument. Mozart, though a master of fugal writing, used the organ only as a member of an ensemble — unless we take into account his three compositions for clockwork instruments, which are ill adapted to keyboard performance. Beethoven's organ music is negligible; Schubert's, nil.

The immediate pupils of Bach, some of whom were musicians of exceptional talent, were overshadowed by their great teacher whom they assiduously imitated. The following generation of organ composers paid homage to Bach, but their idiom was affected by the music of their contemporaries. Fugal movements were less consistently developed; harmonic figuration often replaced polyphonic treatment in chorale variations; much organ music was written frankly in the new homophonic idiom. For example, Johann Christian Rinck, who was born in the same year as Beethoven, and who studied with Bach's pupil, Johann Christian Kittel, wrote a great number of chorale preludes and variations and many fugues, but the homophonic conception dominated his music. His *Praktische Orgelschule*, 1818, included a "flute concerto" which may have been the first real organ sonata. It follows clearly the form of the classical concerto, beginning with a sonata movement and ending with a rondo, including the usual modifications for the alternation of *tutti* and solo effects. These effects themselves suggest an orchestral conception which is characteristic of a much later period.

The music of Rinck, as well as that of his contemporaries and immediate successors in the field of organ composition, is now forgotten. Even the present interest in neglected music of the past is not sufficient to resuscitate it. These men had neither the genius nor the background to carry on the traditions of Bach, and they were equally incompetent to adapt homophonic and essentially secular forms to an instrument which was by its nature polyphonic, and by its associations religious.

Mendelssohn

Not until the revival of interest in the music of Bach, which took place in the second quarter of the nineteenth century,[1] did composers of real genius again apply themselves to writing for the organ. Mendelssohn's labors for the appreciation of Bach and his centennial performance of the *Saint Matthew Passion* are well known. A few years later he was inspired to write organ music himself. His three Preludes and Fugues, 1837, and six Sonatas, 1844-5, were the most significant addition to organ literature in the entire century following the death of Bach.[2] Schumann also fell under the spell and wrote, in 1845, *Sechs Fugen über B-A-C-H*. Even Liszt paid effective, if not idiomatic, tribute.

Mendelssohn's preludes and fugues are in the tradition of Bach. The basic harmonies are more obvious, and the balance between the polyphonic and homophonic elements has shifted somewhat to the homophonic side, but the kinship of these works with the older models is unmistakable. At the same time they do not represent a reversion to an obsolete style; they are no mere *"homage à J. S. Bach"*. They are the fresh fruit of a great genius, whose roots, reaching with the strength of complete technical mastery, drank from springs coming from the distant height, while he breathed the warm air of early nineteenth century romanticism.

Mendelssohn's sonatas are the first successful attempt[3] to write cyclical works for the organ corresponding to the sonatas of Haydn, Mozart, and Beethoven. It is significant that not a single movement of these sonatas is in the classical first movement form — although the pigeon-hole analyst might force the first movement of the *Sonata in F minor* into that category. Sensing the natural unsuitability of the conventional sonata form to the organ, Mendelssohn adapted polyphonic forms: The movement from the First Sonata, just mentioned, contains elements of both the fugue and sonata forms; some of the larger movements, as in the Second, Fourth, and Sixth Sonatas, are real fugues; the middle section of the principal movement of the Third Sonata is a double fugue, against which the pedals enunciate the phrases of the chorale, 'Aus tiefer Not'; other movements are developed along individual lines.

[1] Forkel's biography, *Über Johann Sebastian Bachs Leben, Kunst und Kunstwerke*, was written in 1802; others also were trying to promote interest in his music, but the movement did not gather much momentum until after Mendelssohn's performance of the *St. Matthew Passion*.

[2] He also wrote a number of short pieces for the organ, only four of which have ever been published:
   Fugue in F minor (Stanley Lucas, Weber & Co., 1885 — now out of print)
   Prelude in C minor (Paterson & Co., n.d.)
   Andante with Variations in D; Finale in B flat (Novello & Co., 1898)

[3] Unless we except Rinck's *Flute Concerto*.

Mendelssohn's solution of the problem of the organ sonata pointed the way for succeeding generations. Other trends appeared, and later works sometimes included one or more movements in the sonata form; but that form is usually modified — adapted to the organ idiom. In the best examples the composer has managed to employ polyphonic procedures within the framework of the classical form.

Romanticism

The influence of the Romantic movement was soon to be felt in organ music. Liszt was the first to write significant romantic music for the organ, but the sole surviving work of his pupil, Julius Reubke (1834-58), is far more important. Reubke was perhaps the only composer ever to achieve immortality through a single composition; his *Ninety-fourth Psalm* is the most isolated work in the whole realm of organ literature. He appropriated the romanticism of Liszt's orchestral music, borrowing also from Wagner, and applied it to organ composition more completely and effectively than Liszt himself; and he accomplished this without doing violence to the essential organ idiom. This sonata was the first program work of the nineteenth century type to be written for the organ, and it remains unmatched.[4]

In general the romantic influence affected the material and the spirit, rather than the forms and methods of organ composition. Harmonies became richer and more chromatic, both harmonic and tone color were exploited, and emotional expression was less restrained. Because of the nature of the instrument and its religious associations, these developments were later and less pronounced than in secular music; but while composers were writing and people were hearing orchestral music and opera of the Wagnerian style, it was inevitable that the organ, with its varied color possibilities, should follow the general trend. In spite of such would-be reactionaries as Max Reger,[5] the orchestral conception became more and more evident until the recent neoclassic reaction of J. N. David, Paul Hindemith, and others, who have led a wholesome return to polyphony.

Tonal Changes in the Organ

All of these changes — the neglect of polyphonic writing after the death of Bach, the growing interest in orchestral music, and the effect of romanticism — are reflected in contemporary organ building. Balanced ensembles with a high mixture content, which were essential to the clarity

[4]In the consideration of serious music we may disregard the pictorial performances by Vogler, Knecht, and others.

[5]Some of Reger's organ music is as romantic and orchestral as that of Franck or Vierne.

of polyphonic texture and characteristic of the German Baroque organs, were often lost in the rebuilding of old organs and disregarded in the design of new. At the same time more attention was given to variety and distinctive quality in the voicing of individual stops, and to the color effect of mutations; the tonal differentiation of the manuals became more pronounced; and the swell box was established as an essential feature of the instrument. Altogether the evolution of the organ, like that of music generally, was directed toward romanticism.

These developments were anticipated even in the lifetime of Bach. The most sensational contributor, however, was the theorist, composer, teacher, organist, organ builder, abbé, Georg Joseph Vogler (1749-1814). As a student he was impatient of traditional discipline; as a teacher he promised quick results by new methods; as a theorist he expanded the recognition of vertical relationships — tending away from polyphony toward harmonic color; as an organist he played to the gallery with sensational success, imitating thunder storms, 'The Fall of the Walls of Jericho', 'The Last Judgment according to Rubens', etc.; as an organ builder and designer he was a worthy predecessor of Hope-Jones.

Posing as an acoustician he worked for "simplification", greatly reducing the cost and space required for the organ. He substituted resultants produced by quints for the low fundamental pipes; he eliminated the multi-rank mixtures, leaving only a few single mutations to color the tone; he substituted free reeds for reed pipes. He devised a portable organ embodying these principles, and entirely enclosed, which he called the "orchestrion"; with this he toured Europe. His use of free reeds doubtless pointed the way to the eventual development of the harmonium and the American cabinet organ.[6]

The characteristics of the organs in common use at the time Mendelssohn gave impetus to the revival of organ music are suggested in the "prefatorial note" to his Six Sonatas. After commenting that every organ requires "its own particular treatment, owing to the fact that the like-named stops on different instruments do not always produce uniform effects," he makes certain specific recommendations. His warning that, while "it is essential to take care that in combining two manuals the one manual shall be distinct from the other," a "harsh contrast" should be avoided; his suggestion that "several 8-foot stops" be combined for

---

[6]For a fuller description of the developments of this period, see Bibl. 118, Chap. V: 'Die Zeiten des Verfalls'. Vogler's career is adequately described in Bibl. 147, Vol. V, pp. 559-66. On the other hand there were many notable organs built in this period, which preserved the old ensemble as well as adding new resources. See the specifications in Bibl. 91 and 128.

piano, and the specific indications in the last sonata[7] – all these things show how far organ design and registration practices had departed from the Baroque ideal.

Nineteenth Century Developments

However, a reform was already under way. Its champion was Eberhard Friedrich Walcker (1794-1872) – builder of many remarkable instruments, including the famous Boston Music Hall organ. His specifications included complete ensembles with many ranks of mixtures and mutations, as well as a wide variety in individual stops. He also introduced important mechanical improvements for ease of control.

These instruments mark the beginning of modern organ building in Germany, but they had little immediate influence on organ composition. The only important German organ composers between Reubke and Reger were the prolific Josef Rheinberger (1839-1901), and Johannes Brahms (1833-97), who wrote thirteen masterpieces,[8] ranging from an exquisite miniature of a single page to the superb 'Fugue in A flat minor'. This music is independent of any particular type of organ; as Harvey Grace suggests, it is effective even on an instrument of very meager resources.[9] Brahms, who was not an organist, omitted registration indications; Rheinberger, the virtuoso, suggested only the following:

ff = Full organ
f = Full organ without mixtures
mf = Principal 8', or 8' & 4' stops; or full second manual
p = Several soft stops
pp = Salicional, or similar soft 8' stop alone
ppp = Softest 8' stop
       Pedal in corresponding strength

Before considering the characteristics of the modern German organ as it finally evolved, let us pause to see what was taking place in France and England.

Developments in France

We have already carried our study of French registration practices into the second half of the eighteenth century, quoting from the famous work of Dom Bédos.[10] His suggestions assumed the tonal characteristics of

---

[7]Note, in the first variation, the specification of a lifeless eight-foot tone for the fluent accompaniment, and the assignment of eight- and four-foot stops (presumably flues) to the chorale melody.

[8]Excluding his two early preludes and fugues.

[9]Bibl. 88, p. viii.

[10]See p. 248, fn. 80.

the organs of François Henri Cliquot (1728-91), who stands out as by far
the greatest French organ builder of his century. His refined, unforced
diapasons; his rich mixtures merging in a homogeneous ensemble; his
prompt, gentle reeds which blended perfectly with the flue work – these
characteristics invited duplication in the stop combinations which would
have sounded heavy in more aggressively voiced instruments. These
organs preserved the primary and secondary choruses of the Grand Orgue
and Positif, respectively, and also provided ample opportunity for the
variety of color and solo effects which the taste of the time demanded.
They were not suited to the brilliant toccatas and elaborately developed
fugues of the German masters, and the pedals were not adapted, either
tonally or mechanically, to the independent role assigned to them by the
northern composers.

Much of the music played by the organists of this period was unworthy
of the instruments. Even in the seventeenth century composers and
organists began to yield to a taste for contrasting sonorities and pretty
tunes, and thus "entered upon the facile descent of virtuosity, of para-
sitic ornamentation, and the exclusive and wholly material search after
tone effects."[11] Gathering impetus in the eighteenth century, this tendency continued until the middle of the nineteenth, when the acme of degeneration was reached in the frivolities of Lefébure-Wely and Edouard
Batiste.[12]

Boëly

In France, as in Germany, reform in organ music was stimulated by interest in the music of Bach. According to Widor it was Charles V. Alkan
(1813-88) who first introduced the organ works of Bach in Paris, playing
them on a pedal piano made for him by Érard, since none of the French
organs possessed suitable pedal boards.[13] More important was Alexandre
François Boëly (1785-1858), who was organist at Saint-Germain-
l'Auxerrois from 1840 to 1851. When the rebuilding of this organ was
undertaken in 1838, Boëly had stipulated that it be provided with a pedal
board "à l'allemande". There he gathered about him a group of admirers
whom "he taught above all to know and love the living beauty of the

[11]Bibl. 113, p. 571.

[12]In Bibl. 69, pp. 173-8, we find a vivid description of the organ playing in the first
half of the nineteenth century, with quotations from contemporary writers.
   Henry F. Chorley, in Bibl. 141, Vol. III, p. 246, speaks of "The old ferocious and
tinkling organs, as devoid of any real devotional tone as a dowager in the days of the
Regency, . . . and the old players, whose evolutions used to remind me of nothing so much
as a game of hunt-the-slipper played by a party sitting on all the four ranges of keys."
He was much impressed with the theatrical character of French church music.

[13]Bibl. 134, p. 7.

works of Johann Sebastian Bach, at that time almost unknown in France."[14] Among these disciples was Camille Saint-Saëns, who acknowledged his debt by an extravagant appreciation of the compositions of Boëly, claiming that in his *Recueil de Noëls* "J. S. Bach's pupil has equaled his model."[15]

Although we cannot fully accept Saint-Saëns' evaluation of the intrinsic merit of Boëly's compositions, we must admit that his place in the history of French organ music is unique. At a time when his compatriots had descended to the nadir of triviality and poor taste, he maintained high ideals, following the polyphonic methods of the German tradition without sacrificing the lucidity which is characteristic of the French. Above all, in promoting familiarity with the works of Bach he gave impetus to the French school of organ playing and composition which became preëminent in the late nineteenth and early twentieth centuries.

Cavaillé-Coll

Another stimulus to French organ music is to be found in the instruments built by Aristide Cavaillé-Coll (1811-99). Having learned his trade from his father who was an organ builder in southern France, he had had experience with Spanish organs. He was also an acoustician and was skilled in engineering. His first masterpiece was the organ in the Basilica of Saint-Denis, completed in 1841. This organ, then the largest in France, marked an epoch. In addition to the perfection of the workmanship and the unusual completeness of its specifications it included important innovations, the most notable of which were the first use of the Barker lever,[16] and variation in wind pressure to suit the requirements of different pipes.

No other organ of comparable tonal resources was constructed in France until the rebuilding of the organ at Saint-Sulpice in 1862. At first, however, like other French organs of the time, the instrument at Saint-Denis possessed an inadequate pedal board on which the music of Bach could not be performed. In 1851 Cavaillé-Coll installed in the church of Saint-Vincent de Paul an organ with two octaves of pedals, beginning at CC (16' = CCC). On this organ the Belgian, Jacques Lemmens (1823-81), was heard, astonishing his hearers with his artistry and the quality of his repertoire. His playing of Bach was a revelation. In the words of Widor:

[14]Bibl. 115, p. 110

[15]Preface to Bibl. 166.

[16]An English invention, spurned by English organ builders, which was the first application of the principle of using the force of the compressed air to overcome the resistance of the pallets. It was the first step in the development of the modern action.

"For Cavaillé it was [a burst of] light. From this master virtuoso he discovered the directives which he had previously lacked — the controlling principles. After that Saint-Sulpice, Notre Dame, Saint-Ouen (at Rouen) . . . For the artists it was a revelation.

"They began to write . . . . In half a century France had regained its lost ground: no country possesses a richer literature."[17]

Like Walcker in Germany, Cavaillé-Coll designed a complete ensemble on each manual, including a full array of mutations and mixtures. His ensembles, however, were more perfectly balanced and differentiated. Emile Rupp, an Alsation writing for German readers, says of his mutations and mixtures: "These voices are handled in France with the discretion and subtle silvery brightness of our old Silbermann school."[18] Thus were determined the characteristics of the modern French organs which have prevailed until the recent, tardy application of the electric action, which was deplored by some of the older French organists.

The first significant compositions written for these instruments were César Franck's *Six Pièces*, 1862. When Liszt said of them: "These poems have their place beside the masterpieces of Sebastian Bach!"[19] his exaggeration was pardonable. These were the first important organ works of large dimensions to be written by any French composer; they contained, in the first movement of the *Grande Pièce Symphonique*, 'Prière', and 'Final', the first successful adaptation of the sonata form to the organ idiom;[20] they were the first significant French romantic works for the organ; they were the first music employing as an essential feature the color resources of the modern organ;[21] the *Grande Pièce Symphonique* was the first organ composition of symphonic type, anticipating the symphonies of Widor, Vierne, and others. If these compositions are deficient in polyphonic interest and occasionally unidiomatic, it must be remembered that the composer was blazing a new trail. Even without making such allowances they should be rated among the finest organ works of the nineteenth century.

Developments in England

The degeneration in organ music which we have observed on the continent, after the death of Bach, is less evident in England. This was due to several causes: English organ music had never achieved a height

[17] Bibl. 134, pp. 11-12.

[18] Bibl. 118, p. 293.

[19] Bibl. 149, p. 137.

[20] Excepting Gustav Merkel's *First Sonata* — long since forgotten.

[21] Perhaps we should except Saint-Saëns' 'Fantaisie in E flat', 1856, the first part of which makes effective use of the alternating colors of three manuals.

comparable to that attained in Germany, or even in France, from which to fall. The efforts made to recover from the almost complete destruction suffered under the Commonwealth gave impetus to further development, so there is a rather consistent improvement in the instruments from the time of the Restoration. Moreover, music having been almost completely obliterated in the middle of the seventeenth century, it was rising from practically nothing; so it possessed characteristics of youth, rather than decadence. Again, while Bach was being forgotten in Germany the influence of Handel persisted in England, providing a worthy model, although retarding the development of a national school. Perhaps the most important advantage to English organ music was the fact that it was not overshadowed by other forms, and some of the nation's best talent was devoted to its interests. So the organ music produced in England during this period has more vitality than that of contemporary German and French composers; but its merits are not sufficient to give it a significant place, either in the total history of organ literature or in the repertoire of the modern player.

In England, as in France and Germany, the greatest stimulus to the improvement of organ music was acquaintance with the works of Bach. It was in 1784 that Augustus Frederic Christopher Kollmann went to London and began his labors to promote interest in Bach's music, and, incidentally, his efforts for the adoption of the pedal keyboard. More effective, however, were the efforts of Samuel Wesley (son of the hymn writer, Charles Wesley, and father of Samuel Sebastian Wesley) and his contemporaries, Carl Friedrich Horn and Benjamin Jacob. Wesley was instrumental in the publication of the first English translation of Forkel's biography of Bach, which was projected in 1808, but finally realized in 1820.[22] He also edited some of Bach's music for publication, performed his organ works, urged the installation of pedals, and labored in every way to promote the recognition of Bach's greatness in England.

Wesley's own compositions, conceived in the spirit of Bach, set a worthy example which, unfortunately, later nineteenth century English composers did not follow. The instruments continued to improve in variety of resource and convenience of control, but they were used for the effective expression of insignificant ideas. Not until Stanford and Parry began to write, at the end of the century, do we find any English organ music worthy of our study.[23]

[22]This translation is reprinted in David and Mendel, *The Bach Reader*, Section VI. The activities of Wesley are reported in the same work, Section VII, pp. 363-9.

[23]This whole period is effectively discussed by A. C. Delacour De Brisay in Bibl. 71, Chap. III: 'The Romantic Revival'. For the story of the revival of Bach, see Bibl. 156, Chap. XII: 'Death and Resurrection', and Bibl. 143, Sec. VII: 'The Rediscovery of Bach'.

Modern Conditions

This brief survey brings us down to our own era, when composers have spoken in the idiom most familiar to the present generation. This includes German music beginning with Rheinberger, French music beginning with Franck and Saint-Saëns, English music beginning with Stanford, and practically all American music. National characteristics still distinguish the product of different countries: German music tends toward complexity of polyphony and harmony; French music is more colorful and brilliant; English music is more restrained, with a predilection, among the best composers, for diatonic movement; the most significant American music combines a certain amount of the German intellectual quality with the French feeling for immediate effect, often introducing tonal complexities which are practicable only with our superior mechanical resources.[24]

In spite of these differences there is nothing remote about the music of foreign schools. There is so much interchange among the different countries that we are almost equally at home in all styles. This is particularly true in England and America, where French and German music is frequently performed, and where foreign study is encouraged. Moreover, the differences which are due to the characteristics of the instruments are incidental. It is not necessary, therefore, to devote much time to the study of modern foreign organs in order to know the proper interpretation of the music written for them. It is always helpful, even in playing American music, to have a general idea of the tonal resources which the composer had in mind, and it is essential that we be able to interpret his specific indications for the registration. For this we need (1) an elementary knowledge of the language used; (2) an understanding of the more common technical terms and the meaning of various foreign stop names;[25] and (3) information concerning the usual console appointments.

German Organs

Taking up first the organs in Germany, we find a considerable variation in tonal design, so that certain individual instruments may be quite similar to certain organs built in this country. In general (ignoring the present "Baroque" movement) the German organs have a smaller proportion of fundamental tone than ours, and a more complete array of upper

---

[24]We would not forget the contributions of Belgium — particularly Joseph Jongen, Paul de Maleingreau, and Flor Peeters — Holland, the Scandinavian countries, Italy, and Spain. However, neither in quantity of output nor in national differentiation do they call for separate consideration.

[25]The reader is referred to the various dictionaries of organ stops, listed in the bibliography, and to Bibl. 128, pp. 276-307. All have their limitations; probably the best for handy reference, for one who reads German, is Smets, *Die Orgelregister* . . . . For French organs the best source of information is Wallace Goodrich, *The Organ in France*.

work, affording a fuller, more cohesive, and more varied ensemble. The practice of providing additional eight-foot diapasons on large organs, which prevailed in England and America until recently, is not followed; on the contrary, power is sought through the addition of more upper ranks. The presence of different qualities at various pitches, supplemented by many single mutations, affords a rich palette for synthetic colors. These principles control the design of each department, so the individual manuals are more independent and less sharply differentiated than in the American organ. Orchestral imitation and other special colors are rare, except in large instruments where they can be included without the loss of stops which are essential to the ensemble.

The foregoing applies to the best German organs, and more especially to those built after the first world war. Many of the instruments of the late nineteenth and early twentieth centuries shared some of the defects of American organs of the same period. Schweitzer comments:

"Our registers are all voiced too loudly or too softly . . . . The lighter manuals are weak in comparison with the great organ; they usually lack the necessary mixtures. Our pedals are coarse and clumsy and also poor in mixtures, as well as in four-feet stops."[26]

Of such an organ in the church of St. Andreas in Brunswick, Ellerhorst remarks: "The inherently dark, thick quality is brightened by loud mixtures and trumpets."[27] Thus one defect is used to compensate for another, with the result that the ensemble lacks balance, refinement, and cohesion.[28]

Console Appointments

The following is an attempt to describe the appointments of a modern German console, ignoring recent developments which have not been

[26] Albert Schweitzer, *J. S. Bach* (London: A. & C. Black; New York: The Macmillan Company), Vol. I, p. 296. Quoted by kind permission of the publishers. For a fuller discussion see Bibl. 123. From this booklet, originally written in 1906, are culled the following pertinent quotations:

"A fat person is neither beautiful nor strong." – P. 23.

"Our voicing of the foundation stops, which is not directed toward the ensemble, has the result that the mixtures do not mix with it but only make it loud." – P. 27.

"Our pedals are too loud and at the same time too weak, since the tone is uncharacteristic and vague. If one hears a pedal solo on one of our organs, one has the impression that a dragon's body is wallowing in the rear of the church with a wild, sluggish twisting." – P. 29.

From Albert Schweitzer, *Deutsche und Französische Orgelbaukunst und Orgelkunst* (Leipzig: Breitkopf & Härtel Musikverlag); by kind permission of the publishers.

[27] Bibl. 77, p. 558.

[28] One may wonder if their habituation to this type of ensemble might be in part responsible for the thickness and heaviness of some of the writing of Reger and Karg-Elert. Cf. p. 149.

Karg-Elert, more than Reger, employed a thick texture for its own color, rather than for dynamic effect, often producing it, or enhancing it, by means of his indicated registration. One may question his taste, but the effect is obviously intentional.

reflected in the music or the printed registration indications.

The arrangement of the manuals is not absolutely standardized, but they commonly appear in the following order: I. Hauptwerk (Great); II. Positiv (Choir); III. Schwellwerk (Swell); IV. Fernwerk (Echo). They are often identified by number rather than by name. The action is electro-pneumatic, as in American organs. The stops are usually controlled by tilting tablets or stop keys, located in receding jambs, or arranged in a quasi-semiellipse. Frequently there is one row of tilting tablets on each side of the console for each manual, with an additional row for the pedal; the foundation stops are located at the left, and the mutations, mixtures, and reeds at the right of the keyboard. The normal couplers are controlled by pedals, often duplicated by thumb pistons.

Usually there are no pistons between the manuals. This enables the keyboards to be closer together,[29] but it limits the number of Spielhilfen ("playing aids" – mechanical accessories). The effect of this limitation is to restrict the number of combination pistons; but the foreign organist is impressed with the ingenious array of different gadgets, operating on the 'blind' principle. These devices do not move the stop registers, or other affected controls, but operate invisibly until released.[30]

The principal accessories with which the German console is commonly equipped are:

1. Freie Kombinationen ("free combinations"): From one to four (often three) adjustable combination pistons affecting all stops and couplers. These are adjusted by means of pins – miniature draw stops – located over the stop tablets. Each stop has one of these pins for each combination piston, sometimes identified by color. When, for example, the red piston is in, all the stops whose red combination pins are out, will sound. At the same time all other stops whose tablets are in the 'on' position will also sound unless they are cancelled by the operation of the piston. Usually this cancellation is adjustable for each piston.

So the organist may find at the beginning of a printed piece several lists of stops for the registration. The first, labeled Handregister, indicates the stop registers to be drawn ('on'); the others indicate the stops and controls to be set on the respective pistons. The point where a piston is intended to be operated is shown by printing its name in a box,

[29]Ellerhorst, Bibl. 77, pp. 547 & 550, gives the difference in level between adjacent manuals as 55 mm., or about 2 1/6", as against our practice of 2 1/2". Incidentally, the placement of the pistons under the lowest manual has a disadvantage from the standpoint of visibility, which is of practical importance in the case of locking pistons without indicators. The Setzerregistratur, similar to our system of adjustable pistons under each manual, is occasionally found on later instruments.

[30]In principle this method is like the 'blind' combination pistons which were common in this country some years ago. They still persist in our 'Tutti' ("Sforzando") and 'Crescendo' pedals.

thus: 2.Komb. ; the release of the piston is indicated by the same symbol crossed out, thus: 2.Komb. . If the American organist finds it desirable to duplicate the printed plan of registration he can set up his general pistons to correspond to the *freie Kombinationen*, noting that for any combination which does not include the *Handregister ab* (register cancel) he should see that all the stops indicated for the Handregister are included. The Handregister list will be set on an additional piston, which will be operated whenever the cancellation of any piston is indicated. If there are changes in the hand registration in the course of a movement, additional pistons will have to be used, unless the music allows time to make such changes by hand when required.

2. *Rollschweller, Registerschweller,* or *Walze* ("roll-swell", "register-swell", or "cylinder"): This device differs from our 'crescendo pedal' only in the method of control. Instead of a balanced lever there is a horizontal, rotating cylinder, mounted with its side toward the player. The surface is roughened, so that the cylinder can be turned by a rubbing motion of the foot — forward for 'on' and backward for 'off'.

The effect of the Rollschweller can be modified by other gadgets, such as the following: (1) The *Walze ab* is a piston which silences the Rollschweller without the position of the control being changed; it immediately becomes effective again, as adjusted, when the piston is canceled. (2) The *Pedalmoderator* is an auxiliary cylinder which reduces the pedal combination which has been brought on by the main cylinder. (3) Sometimes there are piston-operated *Auslöser* which prevent the Rollschweller from acting on the couplers.

The abuse of the Rollschweller has perhaps even exceeded that of its American counterpart. Composers indicate long and sometimes rapid general crescendos, assuming its use, and sometimes even specifying the various stages of its range by means of numbers, thus: W 5, W 6, etc. The organists, finding it a very convenient *Nothilfe* ("help in need"), have used it as a panacea for difficulties of registration. This condition is not unfamiliar to Americans and will be discussed in Chapter XIV.

3. The console is sometimes provided with a series of blind pistons which are not adjustable, but control combinations differentiated dynamically or on the basis of classification. The latter sometimes select from stops already in operation: four group pistons (wide chorus, narrow chorus, mixtures, reeds) act on the stops already drawn through the registers or otherwise, allowing only the stops of their respective groups to speak. These devices are not standardized.

The mechanical differences between German and American organs do not present any problem. In planning his tone combinations the organist needs to bear in mind that the German instruments provide relatively less

fundamental, and that color is produced synthetically, rather than through
the characteristic voicing of individual stops.

French Organs

French organs, on the other hand, are so unlike ours in design and
methods of control that they call for an entirely different approach. Since
French composers usually indicate specific registration their intentions
cannot be understood without a knowledge of the characteristics and
equipment of the instrument. Fortunately this problem has been adequately explained to the American organist by Wallace Goodrich, [31] so we
need only summarize the most essential information in this connection.

The French organ is designed for ensemble. Both the specifications
and the voicing of the individual stops are planned with reference to the
effectiveness and variety of combinations. Solo stops are an added
luxury. In large instruments each division contains a complete ensemble.
The differentiation among the manuals is less marked than in American
organs, but in general the Grand Orgue has a large diapason chorus,
topped by telling reeds; the Positif serves as a secondary Grand Orgue;
the Récit is rich and fiery with brilliant reeds and mixtures; the Solo or
Bombarde adds a telling reed ensemble, enriched with mixtures and mutations, intended to serve as a climax to the full organ, rather than for
solo use against it. The Pédale also is complete and without duplications, often functioning uncoupled.

The *montres* are less heavy and aggressive than our diapasons, having
some of the warmth but not the thinness of string quality. The *gambes*
(strings[32]) are mild and effective in combination. The flutes, commonly
made of metal, are brighter than ours. The *bourdons* (generic term for
gedeckts) are often brightened by the addition of a chimney without its
being indicated in the name; overblown bourdons (*Quintatons*) are also
common.[33] The *anches* (reeds) are brilliant, having a comparatively weak
fundamental and a high development of upper partials.[34] The mixtures
are so designed and balanced that they merge with the other stops, contributing to the quality without thickening the ensemble or protruding
above it.

---

[31]Bibl. 85.

[32]*Gambe* is also used instead of *Viole de Gambe* as the name of a specific stop. Cf.
'Gamba'.

[33]Concerning the small proportion of wood pipes in French organs, see Bibl. 85, p. 22, fn.

[34]Compare the analyses of the Austin and Cavaillé-Coll Trompettes, Graphs XX &
XXI. But until recently American builders rarely made reeds as brilliant as this Austin
Trompette.

In general, the foundation stops provide a placid, normal tone, susceptible of variation from sonorous to fairly bright; mutations and mixtures
add richness and brilliance, and reeds are used for power. The full organ
is dominated by the reeds, enriched by many mixtures, producing a
brilliant, solid tone which is concentrated in the fundamental without
giving any impression of heaviness. Sixteen-foot stops may be included
more freely than we would expect; even suboctave couplers are commonly
used, while superoctave couplers are rare. The concentration of the ensemble in the fundamental makes it possible to play high on the keyboard
(as required in many modern French compositions) without screechiness,
while the suboctave couplers bridge the gap between the manual and
pedal parts.

Mechanical Control

The ensemble conception which is evident in the tonal design of the
French organ has also determined the means of mechanical control. No
conveniences are provided for making intricate changes in the stops, but
the console affords great flexibility in the selection, addition, and sub-
traction of various groups of stops. The following is a brief description
of the mechanical equipment of the organ as developed by Cavaillé-Coll
and adopted generally in France until the recent trend toward electrifica-
tion.

The established order of the manuals is: I. Grand Orgue (Great);
II. Positif (Choir); III. Récit (Swell); IV. Solo or Echo. Sometimes the
Solo is replaced by a Bombarde, located next above the Grand Orgue,
which differs from the Solo (if at all) in being designed and voiced for
greater cohesion. In the organs at Saint-Sulpice and Notre Dame in Paris
the Grand Orgue is divided, the reeds and mixtures being played from the
Grand Choeur, below the Grand Orgue. The registers of the French organ
are controlled by draw stops located in receding jambs which continue
the approximate levels of the keyboards. On large organs they are semicircular in shape.

The action is tracker-pneumatic, providing direct mechanical connection from the key to the chest, where a pneumatic lever overcomes the
resistance of the pallet, so that the touch remains approximately as light
as that of an electric action. There are no combination pistons or pedals,
but various stop groups are controlled by unison and suboctave couplers
and *appels* (ventils), which are operated by locking pedals.

The division of the stops of each department into two groups, *jeux de
fond* and *jeux de combinaison*, was explained in Chapter II.[35] The ventil

[35]P. 46.

pedals control the admission of the air to the chest of the *jeux de com-binaison* of each division.   When the pedal is up these stops are silent
even though the registers are drawn; when the pedal is depressed the air
is admitted to the chest under its control, and the stops belonging to that
chest are immediately effective.   Thus the reeds and mixtures of any key-board can be drawn in advance, and added by means of the ventil pedal
when needed.   Such a procedure is indicated in the printed registration by
Anches préparées, or a similar expression. [36]

The coupler pedals include not only the interkeyboard couplers, but
also the connection of the lowest manual, and sometimes the pedal, to its
own action, serving the function of our 'unison release'.   Thus the lowest
manual is a sort of master keyboard to which can be connected at will, by
means of foot-operated ventils and couplers, the stops of any manual,
with or without its *jeux de combinaison*, in combinations determined by
the stop registers.

The French organist, therefore, makes little change in the stop regis-ters in the course of a movement.   He draws at the beginning all the
stops which he plans to use, controlling their selection during the com-position by his choice of manual and the adjustment of the coupler and
ventil pedals.   The equipment seems crude to an American, accustomed
to many adjustable pistons giving instantly any desired combination; but
the skillful French organist produces results which are far from crude. [37]
These organs, with their easy control of various dynamic planes, are
particularly suited to the interpretation of the larger works of Bach —
although the Baroque enthusiast may find their upper work insufficiently
brilliant.   Apparently Schweitzer had them in mind when he prepared his
suggestions for the registration of these works in the Schirmer edition. [38]

In addition to the control of predetermined groups by means of couplers
and ventils, certain large organs are equipped with another means of
effecting an instantaneous change of combination, called *Registres de*

[36]A special use of this device is indicated in the introduction to the first movement of
Guilmant's *First Sonata*, and in the last section of his 'Grand Choeur Triomphal' in A,
where the reeds are added for occasional chords, producing the effect of the entrance of
the brass of the orchestra.

[37]How often have we marveled at the effect of continuous crescendo produced by Widor
at Saint-Sulpice — far smoother than any crescendo pedal could effect although only the
Récit was enclosed, and the opening was controlled by a locking lever pedal which could
be left only in the closed, half open, or open position. See Bibl. 85, p. 60.

[38]See Albert Schweitzer, *J. S. Bach*, Chap. XIV; also the introductions to the various
volumes of the Schirmer edition of Bach's *Organ Works*. These notes are not, as is gen-erally supposed (see Bibl. 85, p. 73, fn.), translated from French notes in which Widor and
Schweitzer collaborated; they are translated from the German of Schweitzer. In spite of his
admiration for Schweitzer, Widor disagreed with him in many details and wrote a different
set of notes for the French edition — at least, he declared his intention of doing so. I have
not had an opportunity to see the French edition.

combinaison. These are in the form of stop-knobs (two for each department — one on each side of the console), and operate as follows: So long
as these combination stops are *in*, no change in the speaking registers
will have any effect. A new stop combination is effective immediately,
and only, when the corresponding combination stop(s) is drawn. Thus
the organist can prepare a new combination in advance, when his hands
are free, and later, at the proper instant, bring it into operation with a
single motion. The combination stops being pushed in again, another
change can be prepared in advance at the convenience of the performer,
to be brought into effect later by the operation of the combination stop(s).

In printed French organ music the indication of keyboards and couplers
is simple and uniform. G.O. or G. = Grand Orgue; P. = Positif; R. =
Récit; Péd. = Pédale. Couplers are indicated by specifying all the participating keyboards, beginning with the one on which the music is
played. Thus G.P.R. means to play on the Grand Orgue with the Positif
and Récit coupled; Péd.R. indicates the Pédale with the Récit coupled;
etc.

Adaptation to American Organs

The registration process determined by these mechanical characteristics necessitates some adaptation on the part of the organist seeking to
interpret it on an American console. Instead of thinking in terms of
equivalent procedures he must consider the *effect* which the original
registration was intended to produce, and translate that into the idiom
of the American organ.

A simple example is afforded by the 'Adagio' from Widor's *Fifth
Symphony*. The following registration is indicated:

R: Gambe[39] et Voix-Céleste
G: Fonds 8, 16
Péd: Flûte 4

The hands play on the Récit and the Pedale is indicated *Solo* (uncoupled). At the beginning of the next to the last score the Récit is
coupled to the Pédale; three measures later the Grand Orgue is also
coupled to the Pédale. The intention of these indications is to provide
throughout the greater part of the movement a pedal solo at four-foot
pitch against the Voix Céleste.[40] Where the left foot part becomes the

[39]It should be noted that on foreign organs the Voix Céleste stop draws only the out-of-
tune rank; it is therefore necessary to draw another string with it.

[40]The flute was chosen for its separating contrast to the Voix Céleste, and because
there was no other four-foot stop on Widor's pedal which was usable for this movement.
The melody lies below the most effective range of a flute, unless its quality approaches
that of a diapason. The author sometimes uses a French Horn, coupled at four-foot pitch
from the Solo.

bass of the ensemble the Récit coupler adds the eight-foot pitch which is needed; the later coupling of the Grand Orgue, after the conclusion of the double pedaling, adds the weight of its sixteen- and eight-foot stops to the concluding measures. The American organist can realize the composer's conception, but he will employ different mechanical means. For the pedal solo he will probably couple a manual stop, which will provide a more suitable quality than any available pedal stop, and may even have the advantage of swell-box expression. At the next to the last score he may couple the Swell to the Pedal as indicated, or he may substitute a broad eight-foot string without the céleste, which is offensive with the four-foot solo stop. For the end his Great stops would certainly be too heavy; so he will add a fairly soft Pedal combination, or possibly select his material from the Choir.

The mechanical adaptation of the registration process offers little difficulty to the intelligent organist who takes the trouble to discover what the composer intended; the real problems result from the tonal dissimilarity of the French and American organs. The prominence of our unabsorbed upper ranks, the heaviness and frequent hardness of our diapasons, and the dullness of our reeds, make it often impossible to realize the effect intended. For example, the beginning of Widor's *Symphony in G minor*, Number 6, calls for a rich, solid, telling ensemble. On a French organ the reeds and mixtures provide the necessary brilliance and solidity, while the foundation stops and sixteen-foot ranks add richness and cohesion. On the average American organ the mixtures which are needed for brilliance stick out; the diapasons and reeds stand against them instead of absorbing them; the sixteen-foot stops make for heaviness, rather than richness. The whole is an irreconcilable combination of screechiness, assertiveness, and muddiness. The effect may be improved by a judicious deletion of the heavier eight- and sixteen-foot stops, relying on reeds, broad strings, and the lightest diapasons for the lower pitches, and taking pains to keep the four-foot brilliant. Sometimes it is advantageous to omit the sixteen-foot stops and all heavy eight-foot stops, adding suboctave couplers.

The octave passage at the beginning of page 4 presents another problem. The composer wants the sixteen-foot pitch to be heard, but our heavy diapasons and reeds sound clumsy, our bourdons and gedeckts are too vague, while a sixteen-foot Dulciana would be almost inaudible. We cannot reproduce the effect of the warm, singing *montre* of the French organ. If the organ possesses a Contrafagotto which is both mild and prompt in speech, it may lend definition to the other soft sixteen-foot stops. If experiment and ingenuity fail to discover a satisfactory balance, it may be necessary to omit the sixteen-foot pitch.

Such problems presented by the specification, "Fonds 4, 8, 16", are encountered fairly frequently.   A different example occurs in Widor's *Symphony in A minor*, Number 7, at the beginning of the 'Lento'.   The combination is intended to be loud and rich, but on most American organs it sounds hard and heavy.   Probably the composer did not intend the *ff* to be interpreted too literally; the quality is more important.   The problem is to combine stops which will blend, avoiding those which are too aggressive.   Often the Choir Diapason 8', coupled at the suboctave pitch, is preferable to the Great Diapason 16'.   Sometimes it is effective to use the Great soft eight-foot stops (including a Gemshorn or a mild string), Octave, and Fifteenth, playing an octave lower than written, or transposing down with the unison off and suboctave couplers.[41]

Electrification

In 1927 Bonnet's organ at Saint-Eustache was rebuilt, provided with an electro-pneumatic action, and equipped with mechanical accessories similar to those found on a modern American console, at the same time retaining the pedal control of couplers, duplicated by manual control.[42] This gave impetus to the adoption of the electric action in France. Mechanically French organs are becoming more like ours; let us hope that they will not lose their fine tonal ensemble.

English Organs

The organs in England are so much like our own that we can pass over them very briefly.   Both in their specifications and in their voicing the English, like us, have been inclined to give too much prominence to the fundamental pitch, but they never abandoned the ensemble conception of tonal design so completely as we did in the early part of this century.   Of course Hope-Jones was an Englishman, but his greatest success was in this country.   The best English builders have made consistent progress and have built some magnificent instruments.   Two differences between typical English and American organs are worthy of mention:

1. The English Choir has retained its function as a secondary Great. This is so definitely a part of the design that the Choir is often unenclosed, and the Choir to Great coupler is frequently lacking.   The organist chooses between these two similar manuals, but does not combine them.

2. The fourth manual is in fact as well as name, a Solo.   It is not intended to combine with the other manuals but to stand apart from them.

[41]For other suggestions, see p. 350.

[42]The builder was Joseph Rinkenbach of Ammerschwihr, Alsace.   Details are given in Bibl. 114, pp. 200-203, and in Bibl. 118, pp. 343-5.

In addition to small solo stops, some of which imitate orchestral instruments, the Tuba is designed to be heard against the full organ. This conception is characteristically British, and a considerable number of English compositions demand such a Tuba. American organs, even though similarly designed, seldom have a Tuba which is adequate for the purpose. In playing such compositions the American organist is frequently obliged to modify his ensemble and add other stops or an octave coupler to the Tuba, thereby reducing the separateness of the solo and marring the effect.

Both the English Solo and the French Bombarde are valuable resources. Ideally the Solo should provide the characteristics of each: a fiery, reedy ensemble, and a number of solo stops, including a Tuba which can stand out against the full organ.

The Harmonium

Another instrument, whose literature is appropriated by the organist, is the *harmonium*. Many compositions, like Vierne's *24 Pièces en style libre*, are written for optional performance on the organ or harmonium. They differ from organ music in their simple registration requirements, the absence of an obbligato pedal part, and the fact that they are printed on two staves. They present no special problem to the organist except in cases where the composer has been restricted by the limited reach of the hands. For example, the space between the right and left hands, as conceived for the harmonium, often needs to be filled in when the lower part is played with the feet. This is illustrated by the 'Carillon in B flat' from Vierne's *24 Pièces*, which on the organ should be played somewhat as shown in Example 15. Other compositions, however, are definitely

Example 15. Vierne: Carillon in B flat[43]

written for the harmonium, exploiting its special features. Such pieces can be effectively played on the organ, but in order to interpret them correctly the organist should know how they were intended to sound on the harmonium.

[43]From *24 Pièces en style libre*. Permission for reprint granted by Durand & Cie., Paris, France, copyright owners; Elkan-Vogel Co., Inc., Philadelphia, Penna., agents.

Although the harmonium may be considered the European equivalent of
the American cabinet organ, it is quite a different instrument. Both employ free reeds without pipes; both are 'blown' by the feet of the player,
who thus can control the air pressure to a certain extent; both have divided stops and some half stops, so that the quality and relative pitch of
the upper and lower part of the keyboard can be differentiated, giving the
effect of two short manuals; both have knee swells which alter the loudness. The American cabinet organ operates on suction, while the harmonium operates on pressure, which provides greater flexibility and better
control of the air force.[44] Altogether the harmonium is more artistically
conceived and is worthy of consideration on its own merits, and not
merely as a substitute for the organ. Indeed it has its own literature, to
which such composers as César Franck, Charles Tournemire, and Sigfrid
Karg-Elert have contributed. It is sufficiently standardized so that the
composer can indicate the exact registration with confidence that it will
sound as he intends it. The following paragraphs describe the resources
of the instruments made by Mustel, which are recognized as superior.

Description of the Harmonium

The range of the harmonium is the same as that of the organ: CC to
c^4 — five octaves, divided between e^1 and f^1. The bass stops therefore
extend from CC to e^1, and the treble stops from f^1 to c^4. The stops are
identified by numbers, although they also have names which, for the most
part, are devoid of significance.

There are four complete sets of reeds which, though the bass and
treble sections are separately controlled, are continuous throughout the
range of the keyboard. Specifically, the stops are as follows:

1 (bass). Cor anglais   1 (treble). Flûte

    An eight-foot stop with a fairly pure tone, serving the function of the
    Diapason 8' of the organ.

1^P (bass). Percussion 1^P (treble). Percussion

    A stop which adds to '1' a percussive attack and prompt speech by
    causing little hammers to strike the reeds.

2 (bass). Bourdon   2 (treble). Clarinette

    A sixteen-foot stop, somewhat thinner and more somber than '1'. It is
    useful both in combination and as a solo stop.

---

[44]It might be noted that some of Karg-Elert's harmonium pieces were written for a
suction instrument.

3 (bass). Clairon   3 (treble). Fifre

A four-foot stop, fairly intense, serving the function of the organ Octave. The bass section is useful as a solo stop.

4 (bass). Basson   4 (treble). Hautbois

An eight-foot stop of penetrating quality, serving the function of an organ reed. It contributes vitality to the ensemble and is also effective as a solo stop.

These four ranks constitute the full organ of the harmonium. They can all be drawn by means of a single stop:

G. Grand jeu

Controlled by a draw stop or by   a device operated by the heel.

The foregoing represent the minimum tonal resources of the harmonium. Large instruments possess, in addition, certain half stops which provide further variety of tone color and increased flexibility in two-manual effects. It will be noted that here there is no relation between the bass and treble stops of the same number. Details follow:

5 (bass). Harpe éolienne

A 2' two-rank beating stop, combining the richness of an organ Voix Céleste with the delicacy of an Unda Maris.

5 (treble). Musette

A 16' stop suggesting the quality of an English horn, primarily useful as a solo stop.

6 (treble). Voix céleste

A 16' two-rank beating stop, analogous to the Voix Céleste of the organ.

7 (treble). Baryton

A 32' stop, ranging from a delicate pp to a sonorous mf.

8 (treble). Harpe éolienne

An 8' stop similar to '5' (bass).

In addition to the foregoing speaking stops there are a number of mechanical devices for increasing the expressive resources of the instrument, as follows:

E. Expression simple, or Expression pédale

A stop conveniently located above the center of the keyboard, which enables the player to control the air pressure by his operation of the pedals. Normally the air chamber communicates with a reservoir where the pressure is regulated by the constant action of springs. This stop closes the passage from the chamber to the reservoir, so that the pressure responds directly to the force of the "pumping."

Thus the player can vary the dynamics through his control of the air pressure.[45] Because of this possibility the harmonium is sometimes called *l'orgue expressif*.

F (bass). Forte fixe   F (treble). Forte fixe

Draw stops which increase the loudness by opening swell boxes. Since the two sections are controlled separately, the balance between the treble and bass stops can thus be altered.

O (bass). Forte expressif   O (treble). Forte expressif

A stop which connects the operation of the swells of the *Forte fixe* with 'E', so that they respond, in proportion, to the variations in the air pressure.

Met (bass). Métaphone   Met (treble). Métaphone

A device which causes Nos. 3, 4, 5, 7, and 8 to speak into a sound chamber, instead of out into the open, thus softening the tone and filtering out some of the upper partials.

Pr or R. Prolongement

A stop located in the left key-cheek which causes any key in the lowest octave, when depressed, to remain down until it is released by striking another key in the same octave, or by operating a heel release on the left pedal. This device serves somewhat as a substitute for the organ pedals.

Double expression (bass)   Double expression (treble)

This is an invention of Victor Mustel which provides independent, flexible dynamic control of the treble and bass. It consists of two knee-swells which, operating like water faucets, regulate the amount of air which passes through the reeds.

Thus the instrument provides three different methods of dynamic control: (1) by means of swell boxes – F; (2) by varying the air pressure – E; (3) by varying the volume of air – *Double expression*. (1) and (2) may be coupled – O; (3) is independent of the others, and itself operates separately on the two halves of the keyboard. It is obvious that great skill in coordination is necessary for the full realization of the possibilities of these resources.[46]

In the printed score of harmonium music the registration is indicated by a method similar to the German combination piston indications. The number or sign representing the stop or mechanical device to be used is

[45]The pitch of a free reed is practically independent of the air pressure.

[46]For a fuller description of the harmonium, see the following: Bibl. 62, pp. 97-117; Bibl. 68, pp. 113-28; Bibl. 93, pp. 191-8; Bibl. 105.

placed in a square ($\boxed{2}$) or a circle ($\textcircled{4}$) to show that it is 'on' or added
at a certain point; the same sign crossed by a line ($\boxed{\not{2}}$ or $\not\textcircled{4}$) indicates
that the stop or control is to be put 'off'. In some editions the letter
signs are not enclosed.

Harmonium Music on the Organ

By studying the registration indications in the light of the information
given above, an accurate conception of the composer's intention can be
formed. If the registration is the same for the treble and bass (shown by
the use of the same numbers below 5), no differentiation between the two
hands is intended, and the organist will presumably play on one manual.
If half stops or different numbers are indicated for the two hands, different qualities and perhaps different relative pitches are intended, and the
organist will play on two manuals.

One must be careful not to overlook the specification of sixteen- and
four-foot stops, which may be used not only for their special qualities,
but often to enable the two hands to overlap in pitch. As a general rule,
if the music is intended for optional performance on the organ the actual
notation shows the intended pitch, and the transposition necessary on the
harmonium is indicated by *8va* lines. In music specifically written for
the harmonium, however, the notation usually shows the actual keys to
be played: then the organist, if he is using eight-foot stops, must transpose the music to produce the pitch intended. Thus, in Examples 16 and
17 a four-foot stop is assigned to the bass and a sixteen-foot stop to the
treble.   Everything from e[1] down, therefore, must be transposed *up* an
octave, and everything from f[1] (e$\sharp$[1]) up must be transposed *down* an
octave.

Example 16. Franck: Andantino (canon) in D flat, from *L'Organiste*

In addition to an accurate interpretation of the notation, the organist
may wish to approximate the free reed quality of the harmonium. This

Example 17. Franck: Quasi Marcia

can sometimes be done with a fair degree of success by combining a warm string with a light flute, possibly adding a very small diapason or Geigen. Light solo reeds, perhaps modified, may be used for solo voices. As a rule combinations should be confined to the pitches specified. The *Grand jeu* can be represented by sixteen-, eight-, and four-foot stops which are rich in upper partials. Mutations can be used only if completely absorbed. A complex ensemble, synthetic color, audible high pitches, any heavy stops, a sixteen-foot pedal not matched in the manual combination — all these must be avoided if the original effect is to be preserved.

Summary

This concludes our survey of the various instruments for which the music of the organist's repertoire has been written. We have compared the organs of Gabrieli and Frescobaldi with those of Cabezón and Cabanilles; we have followed the development in France from the composers who contributed to the Attaingnant collections to the time of Couperin *le Grand*; after a brief consideration of the music of Sweelinck and the organs for which it was written we turned to Germany, tracing the evolution of its organs and registration practices from Schlick to the great achievements of the Baroque period; we then observed the vicissitudes of English organs and organ music from the time of Redford and Tallis to the slow recovery following the Restoration. Reviewing briefly the period of decadence after the death of Bach, and the reawakening in all countries which was stimulated by the revival of interest in his music, we then studied the characteristics of more recent German, French, and English organs in their bearing on the interpretation of modern music, finally taking up the humble harmonium.

Practical Application of Foregoing Information

We have assumed that all this information is of practical value to the modern organist. We have even paused from time to time to suggest how the effect which the composer had in mind might be realized, or approximated, on the American organs of today. Does that mean that a legitimate interpretation of music written for instruments which are unlike ours involves the reproduction of the original registration, regardless of changes in taste and environment?

Such an attitude is consistent with contemporary ideas. There is now a very keen interest in the music and media of the past. Musicologists have uncovered many works which had been gathering dust in libraries and museums for centuries, and have studied their authentic interpretation. Many of these works have been performed and have shown that their interest is not confined to the antiquarian, but they have an appeal to modern ears. Artists and groups of artists are playing obsolete instruments. The clavier music of Bach, Couperin, and others is more and more performed on the harpsichord instead of the modern piano.

In the organ field there is a lively interest in the Baroque instruments. In 1921 an organ was installed in the University of Freiburg, built by Walcker under the supervision of the musicologist, Willibald Gurlitt, according to specifications given by Praetorius in his *De Organographia*.[47] Karl Straube, who gave the opening recital, was so impressed with the effectiveness of Baroque music played on such an instrument that his whole conception of its interpretation was changed. A few years later he brought out his collection, *Alte Meister, Neue Folge*, in which he indicated registration for the organ in the Jakobikirche in Hamburg.[48] This new conception is revealed in the following excerpts, themselves somewhat condensed, from his Foreword to this collection:

"Every musical period has its own organic character from which result certain laws of form and expression, and the wish of today, rightly to comprehend these factors, is greatly furthering the growth of musical understanding. The realization that perfection is self-contained in any great art has led to the desire to try and reproduce it in all sincerity as it was originally conceived, and, in so doing, only to make use of means strictly in accordance with the conditions of its time. Considering the matter from this point of view, we can no longer accept the opinion . . . that all the means of expression available in a modern instrument should be employed to obtain an interpretation calculated to make a strong emotional impression . . . .

[47] Bibl. 107, p. 191, specifications 2.
[48] See pp. 267-8.

"Every organist who aspires to something higher than indulging the senses in a mere mass of sound effects, must wish to express as truly as possible the genuine character inherent in the works belonging to the great period of organ composition . . . .

"The aim of an organist can no longer be to give a subjective interpretation, but to render faithfully the given work as it presents itself in its own architecture. Subjective interpretation belongs to the period after 1750, and only by discarding it can the organist hope that the deeper sense of eternal significance, embodied in those early works of art, may be revealed.

". . . The idea is not to suppress [the individuality of the interpreter] altogether, but merely to liberate the mainspring of his energy from the prejudices and limitations of his own period and personality, so that . . . all his faculties may be devoted to serving a great work of art in humbleness of spirit . . . .

"In 1904[49] the devices of the 'modern organ' held full sway: today there has arisen a young generation of organists animated by the desire to do the fullest justice to every artistic style according to the precepts decreed by its period."[50]

Problems Encountered

Although these remarks refer primarily to music written before 1750, the principle of subordinating the personal prejudice of the performer to the conception of the composer is equally applicable to any music written for a medium, or in an idiom, which is foreign to the interpreter's more intimate experience. If we assume that Straube's contention is valid we are confronted with certain practical problems. It is often impossible for the American organist to duplicate, or even to approach the registration intended by a Baroque or a modern French composer. It may be impracticable not only because of the characteristics of his instrument, but because of the acoustics of the auditorium, or the different circumstances under which the music is played.

If the original effect cannot be reproduced, the organist must choose between approximating it as closely as possible and substituting an entirely different registration. The different possibilities will be appraised on their own merits. The result should be consistent with the composer's musical conception, but nothing is gained by imitating the original registration if the result is ineffective.

[49]The date of Straube's previous collection, *Alte Meister.*

[50]Condensed version of the 'Foreword' by Karl Straube to his collection, *Alte Meister des Orgelspiels, Neue Folge* (Peters Edition No. 4301 A & B); quoted with the kind permission of the publishers, C. F. Peters Corporation, New York.

Modification of the Composer's Indications

Modifications may be necessitated not only by the limitations of the conditions under which the music is played, but by special characteristics of the composer's own resources. Organists often compose for their own instruments, indicating registration which is unavailable or ineffective on the average organ. In this connection Alexandre Cellier calls attention to the specification *Trompette du Récit* for the middle section of Franck's 'Pastorale in E', saying:

> "Now it is undeniable that on most instruments this registration is disagreeable; the Sainte-Clotilde organ has on the Récit a small trumpet, almost an oboe, of great refinement and flexibility, which justifies a registration possible on the author's organ but dangerous elsewhere."[51]

The same fact may explain Franck's frequent indication of a combination of eight-foot foundation stops with the trumpet and oboe for solos which should normally be played on a single reed.[52]

Every organist is familiar with the problem of reducing the composer's plan in order to adapt it to a small instrument. It is equally proper, within limits, to expand the original scheme in order to take advantage of resources which the composer did not envisage. This is particularly true for music written for optional performance on a harmonium. For example, the effectiveness of the 'Arabesque' from Vierne's *24 Pièces en style libre* can be greatly enhanced by a somewhat orchestral differentiation of the phrases of the middle section. To adopt a similar procedure in the interpretation of old music, on the ground that the composers themselves would have used the modern resources if they had been available, is more questionable. If the composers had had such resources in mind they would have written different music.

Sometimes there is an actual conflict between the composer's intentions and the artistic convictions of the performer. The player is under no obligation to reproduce the defects in the composer's registration. It is not necessary, for example, to employ the muddy combinations sometimes indicated by Karg-Elert, or to use the Vox Humana and the Voix Céleste every time such stops are specified by French composers. Indeed, many good composers have been quite ignorant of the art of registration.

The music of composers who are not organists often shows an imperfect understanding of the instrument, not only in the registration but in the actual writing. Such composers are apt to think orchestrally, and

---

[51] Bibl. 68, p. 74, fn.; quoted with the kind permission of the author.

[52] For example, 'Cantabile in B' and the middle sections of the first and third Chorals.

sometimes they seem to believe that, because they have written notes which can be played on the organ, they have written organ music. Some such works tax the ingenuity of the organist to the point of being impracticable. On the other hand there are fine, idiomatic organ pieces which in one detail or another show a lack of perfect familiarity with the medium. An example is Honegger's beautiful 'Fugue in C sharp minor'. Knowing that the normal pitch of the pedals is an octave lower than that of the manuals, he assigned to the pedals the bass of his polyphony, notating it an octave higher than he wished it to sound. Apparently he did not realize that it is usually impossible to devise a sixteen-foot pedal ensemble which will match the quality of the manuals, so that a literal interpretation of his notation does not produce the effect intended. On most organs the first pedal entry should be played an octave lower than written, without sixteen-foot stops, and with the manual combination coupled. The companion 'Choral' is perfectly written for the instrument, but its orchestral conception demands a varied and sensitive registration, with special regard to the implications of pitch, texture, and harmonic color.[53]

In considering modifications of the composer's indications the performer must decide what features are essential to the musical conception. In general, the assignment of different manuals to the two hands, and perhaps an independent combination for the pedals, indicates that the composer specifically intended differentiation in tone quality. A change of manuals usually shows that the composer wanted a change of color or of dynamic plane: the choice of color may be free, but the fact of change is a part of the design. If the score calls for a specific fundamental pitch, that is as definite as the notation itself. To substitute an eight-foot stop for an indicated four-foot stop (playing as notated) actually transposes the music down an octave. Carelessness about pitch indications may so distort the effect as to destroy the sense of the music.[54]

Fidelity to the Composer's Basic Conception

If the organist finds it impracticable or undesirable to follow the registration of the composer, he can determine its aesthetic and interpretative purpose and plan his own combinations to serve the same end. If the composer's qualities are bright or somber, clear or rich, light or heavy, separate or fused, contrasted or homogeneous, Baroque or romantic — whatever their characteristics, they will be studied in their relation to

[53] Arthur Honegger, *Two Pieces for Organ* (London: J. & W. Chester, Ltd., 1920).

[54] The writer has actually heard the 'Adagio' from Widor's *Fifth Symphony*, discussed on pp. 301-2, played with an eight-foot, and even a sixteen-foot pedal, by organists who ought to know better.

the musical material and the style of composition. Then the organist can plan his own registration so as to bring out the same elements in the music which the composer intended to reveal. A literal reproduction of the original registration may be ineffective, and thus defeat its purpose; to understand the effect which the composer wished to produce, whether or not he chose the best means of indicating it, and to find a means of giving that impression to the listener — this is genuine fidelity to the intentions of the composer.

So we return to the principle enunciated at the beginning of our discussion of interpretative registration: "The function of registration is to enhance what is inherent in the music, and to make it clear to the listener."[55] To this end the organist should employ every possible means of acquiring a complete understanding of the music as originally conceived. He should adjust his own mind to the composer's conception and make it his own as fully as possible. Then his task is to convey that conception to his audience.

In the earlier chapters we proposed a theory of tone combination and endeavored to show how the organist could, through his registration, present the various elements of a musical composition in just proportion to his hearers. We have now concluded an investigation of media and practices which is intended to shed some light on the composer's own conception of his music. The ambitious organist will go much further in his own studies. His success in realizing an ideal registration will depend on the justness of his appraisal of the music itself and the resourcefulness, skill, sensitivity, and imagination with which he plans his tonal interpretation.

[55]P. 122.

CHAPTER THIRTEEN

RELATION OF THE ORGAN
TO OTHER MEDIA

Relation of Style to Medium

"All music which is worthy of the name must in the nature of things be written to be performed by instruments or voices; and they all have their particular idiosyncracies. Organs have their special aptitudes and their special inaptitudes; and the music which is written for them, if it is to attain to any degree of artistic perfection, must be based upon a recognition of the fact. Violins have their special powers of expression and effect, and their special limitations; horns have theirs, and trombones theirs. Voices can do certain things that instruments cannot do, and all instruments can do things which voices cannot do. There is, as it were, a dialect appropriate to each instrument and each class of voice; and there are even ideas which can be better expressed in one dialect than another; and the employment of any particular means of utterance, whether violins, pianofortes, organs, hautboys, bassoons, voices, harps, or trumpets, is only justified when they are used for passages which can be given with fullest effect by them.

". . . any one who has any sense of the adequate adaptation of technique to material or means of performance realizes the absurdity of choral music written in the style of a brass band or organ music which is mere pianoforte music or orchestral music in disguise. But the hurry and lack of concentration of modern life, and the desire of purveyors of music to ingratiate a public which has neither discrimination nor education, and the habit of playing such a vast amount of arrangements, all tend to dull people's sense of the essential meaning of musical style, and to make composers miss the higher artistic opportunities in the urgent desire to gratify the ephemeral whims of fashion."

These words were spoken by C. Hubert H. Parry on the occasion of his inauguration as Professor of Music at Oxford University in 1900, and were later incorporated in his significant book, *Style in Musical Art.*[1] The validity of his contention is incontestable. All must admit with him that "the most perfect style is that which is most perfectly adapted to all the conditions of presentment."[2] But it often happens that performers are

[1] C. H. H. Parry, *Style in Musical Art* (Copyright 1911, 1932), pp. 3, 4. Quoted by kind permission of The Macmillan Company, New York.

[2] *Ibid.*, p. 2.

impelled, from one motive or another, to forego the perfect adaptation to
the medium in order to gain some other value which seems more important. Before the days of radio concerts many organists played transcriptions of orchestral works which their public had no other opportunity to
hear, believing that an imperfect presentation was better than none. Performers from Liszt to Stokowski have yielded to the craving to adapt to
their own medium music in other styles which they particularly admired.
Church organists are obliged to play many accompaniments originally
conceived for orchestra or piano, or, even if ostensibly intended for the
organ, written in a pianistic idiom. To avoid such transcriptions would
deprive congregations of some of the most inspiring music which their
choirs can offer.

As in all questions of conflicting desiderata, the different values must
be weighed and a decision made accordingly. We are not here concerned
with the propriety of the transcription, but with its effective registration.

Differences between the Organ and Other Media

Any successful adaptation to the organ of music otherwise conceived
must take into account certain inherent differences between the organ
and other media. In the first place, the organ possesses certain unique
qualities which are not found elsewhere: Its resources are vastly greater
than those of any other medium controlled by a single performer. A large
instrument provides a greater range of dynamic intensity, of pitch, and of
tone color, than a full orchestra. Most significant is the fact that the
organ alone has the power of sustaining tones indefinitely.

But since we are interested in performing the music of other media on
the organ, we are more concerned with the characteristics found in them
which the organ lacks. The most important are the following:

1. All other instruments and voices are capable of a more or less accented attack, which differs from the continuation of the sound. The
tone of wind instruments may begin with a slight explosion; that of
stringed instruments with a "bite", due to the initial exaggeration of the
relation of the pressure to the speed of the bow. The strength of these
accents can be controlled by the player. On the other hand, the percussive attack of the piano (which is greater than the listener realizes)
and the plucking attack of the harp are inevitably proportioned to the
loudness of the tone which follows. In contrast to these the tone of the
organ merely starts, with the same characteristics which will continue.
Crude accents can occasionally be produced by the swell pedal, but they
do not modify the *quality* of the attack.

2. The organ lacks dynamic flexibility. The contrast between the enclosed Aeoline and the full organ is impressive, but it is impossible to

obtain a perfectly continuous gradation from the softest to the loudest tone. The range of the swell shades is limited, and their operation is clumsy; their inertia prevents the quick changes of direction which are necessary for elasticity. The restricted control which they provide is applied alike to the entire ensemble, or such portion of it as is included in the swell box. Independent dynamic expression may be given to two combinations if both feet are free, but more than that is impossible. Even a pianist can apply a certain independence of touch to the different parts, while the orchestra and other ensemble groups can provide an almost infinite subtlety of nuance through the independent control of the individual voices.

3. The same holds true for flexibility of timbre. The continual shifting of colors resulting from the polyphonic interweavings of contrasting voices is impossible on the organ for more than three parts. Even there it is limited by the continuity of the same three colors and their lack of independent dynamic control. The color range of the organ is comparable to that of the orchestra, but the relation of the constituent elements is more fixed. The tone color comes in blocks which may be fitted into a design suggestive of plaid, while the various threads of the orchestra are woven into a tapestry.

Imitation of the Original Effect

It is obvious that the sensitive listener cannot be deceived by any attempt to make the organ sound like what it by nature cannot be. The success of a transcription depends not on reproducing the effect of the original, but on making it effective as organ music. This does not mean that no attempt should ever be made to imitate the color which the composer intended. If a certain orchestral quality suits the musical material, the same interpretative purpose *may* be served by the nearest organ equivalent to that quality. This will usually hold from the standpoint of color and mood, but the success of the substitution depends on the adaptability of the organ stop or combination to the *style* of the material. For example, in Bach's *Magnificat* the oboe d'amore solo which accompanies the soprano aria, 'Quia respexit', may be effectively rendered on a good Orchestral Oboe or English Horn stop, but to employ an imitative string combination to represent the violins in the tenor aria, 'Deposuit potentes', would be absurd.

Except for the use of chorus reeds to represent the orchestral brass, the effective imitation of orchestral color is largely confined to a relatively soft dynamic level. Most imitative stops are weaker than their orchestral prototypes; otherwise they sound coarse or heavy because of their inflexibly sustained tone. Even the

English Horn, suggested above, *may* need to be reinforced by a keen
string.

Controlling Considerations

All adaptations of foreign material to the organ must, regardless of
other considerations, satisfy the requirements of interpretative registration. The organist should study the relation between the composer's
medium and his material, and try to effect a corresponding relationship
between the registration and the material, treating the music as an organ
composition. If imitation of the effect of the original medium is consistent with this interpretation, its use is desirable; if not, it should
usually be foregone. The application of this principle can be clarified
by a few further examples:

Bach's setting of 'Wer nur den lieben Gott lässt walten' in the collection of *Sechs Choräle* (Schübler) is a transcription of the fourth stanza of
the cantata of the same name, Number 93. The original is a duet for
soprano and alto, accompanied by strings and *continuo*, the strings playing the chorale melody. It is obviously impossible to imitate the quality
of the singers; their parts may be played on a quasi-solo combination
suited to the varied contour and fluent movement of the melodies —
perhaps flutes colored by one or two mutations. The slowly moving
chorale in the tenor range is effectively brought out by a rich céleste
combination, imitating the original strings, while the bass, both in quality
and phrasing, can suggest the traditional *basso continuo*, even including
a light sixteen-foot stop.[3]

The last of the *Sechs Choräle*, 'Kommst du nun, Jesu, vom Himmel
herunter', presents a very different situation. This was originally set to
the second stanza of 'Lobe den Herren' in Cantata 137. The chorale was
sung in unison to the accompaniment of a solo violin and *continuo*. We
may be sure that Bach did not choose his solo instrument for its color,
but rather for its style. The facility and grace with which this agile and
discursive melody can be executed on the violin, together with its subtle
phrasing and flexible nuance, make it the ideal medium. Indeed, the
melody is so clearly conceived for the violin that one wonders that Bach
should have wished to transcribe it. Any effort on the part of the organist to imitate the color of the violin tone will result in a caricature. He
should seek to duplicate the agility and flexibility of the violin, rather
than its quality.

---

[3]This *basso continuo* is rather charming heard on a single unimitative English Horn,
played detached throughout, suggesting the effect of a bassoon, which often formed a part
of the *continuo*.

Concerning Orchestral Strings

The strings are the most versatile section of the orchestra and are used for many different types of material. This may be illustrated by citing a few examples in well-known works. In Mozart's *Requiem*: the vigorous but not too detached rhythm in 'Rex tremendae';[4] the ominous figure in 'Confutatis', the contrasting grace and placidity of the melody which accompanies "Voca me", and the gentle repeated notes in the last section of the movement; the graceful couplets and easy detached chords of 'Lacrymosa'; the gracious, expressive melody of the 'Benedictus'. In Mendelssohn's *Elijah*: the sweeping arpeggios suggesting the rushing waters in 'Thanks be to God'; the quiet syncopation in the first section of 'Hear ye, Israel'; the peaceful undulation accompanying the chorus, 'He, watching over Israel'. In Brahms's *Ein deutsches Requiem*, the expressive melodic contour of the upper strings at the beginning of 'Ihr habt nun Traurigkeit'. In all these cases the choice of the orchestral strings was inevitable, not so much because of their color as because of other characteristics, such as flexible continuity, dynamic subtlety, elastic phrasing, melodic range, etc. Sometimes strings are used, because of their lack of exotic color, for material which is primarily formal, rather than expressive. Examples are the fugue section of the overture to Handel's *The Messiah*, and the countersubjects in the fugal sections of the third and sixth choruses of Brahms's *Ein deutsches Requiem*.

Of all the foregoing examples there are only two in which the organist might advantageously imitate the quality of the orchestral strings: Mozart's (Süssmayer's) 'Benedictus' and Brahms's 'Ihr habt nun Traurigkeit'. Even these exceptions are questionable, while all the other passages cited can be more effectively presented by the use of normal registration procedures.

In cases where the color of the orchestral strings is an essential part of the musical conception it is often desirable to try to reproduce that effect on the organ. Thus, in Mendelssohn's *Elijah*, the 'cello melody which accompanies the baritone aria, 'It is enough', should, if possible, be assigned to a similar quality on the organ; but the accompanying detached chords (also played by the orchestral strings) require greater clarity and differentiation from the 'cello melody than the organ strings can provide. The 'cello quintet which introduces the tenor aria, 'Urbs Syon aurea', of Horatio Parker's *Hora Novissima* calls for imitative treatment; moreover such familiar excerpts as the introduction to 'Lovely

---

[4]Compare the dotted sixteenths and thirty-seconds of the strings, suggesting continuity and couplet phrasing, with the more separate and heavy dotted eighths and sixteenths of the wind instruments.

appear', from Gounod's *The Redemption*, afford ample opportunity for orchestral registration.

Other Orchestral Instruments

The use of wind instruments is more frequently dictated by considerations of color which may, if possible, be imitated in transcription for the organ. But even these instruments are often used because of other characteristics than their timbre, such as the marcato effect of their attack, the clarity in low range of the bassoon, the extreme agility of the flute, the fortissimo of the brass, etc. Here again the organist will consider what is the essential purpose of the orchestration, whether it be color, rhythm, clarity, phrasing, or what not.

It is obviously impossible for the organ to approximate the tone of instruments in which the sound is produced by percussion or plucking. There is nothing on the organ to approach the attack, which is the most essential feature of such instruments. The organist can only hope to simulate their clarity and prompt speech by using high ranks — perhaps flutes, if the material permits — with mutations for color and definition. Of course the organ Celesta is practically the equivalent of the orchestral instrument, and it can occasionally be used to reproduce the original effect — as in the concluding movement, 'In paradisum', of Fauré's *Requiem*.[5]

The reader is referred to Appendix II for a table of registration for specific orchestral effects.

Adaptation of the Music

It should be remembered that the success of a transcription depends as much on the skillful adaptation of the music as on the choice of registration. Many transcriptions are too literal; orchestral works are ineffective because the arranger has tried to include everything which he found in the score. It is important that the music sound idiomatic to the medium used. To achieve that, music which is conceived for orchestra must, in most cases, be considerably simplified.

On the other hand, it is frequently advantageous for the organist to elaborate the tonal effects of music written for a monochromatic medium, such as the piano or a string ensemble. He cannot reproduce the subtle shades of color which even such media can create, or their dynamic flexibility; so he is obliged to resort to greater color differentiation in

---

[5]The manipulation requires some ingenuity. A harmonic background can be sustained on the Swell, using mild strings 8' and perhaps 4', transposed down by the use of the unison off and suboctave coupler, in order to bring the hand high on the keyboard, so that it can at the same time touch the Célesta notes on the Great. The other hand plays the arpeggio figures on the Choir, while the pedal plays the bass, without 16'.

order to bring out elements which the other instruments can make clear within a more limited tonal range. He may occasionally allow his imagination to carry him beyond the possibilities of the original medium, so long as he remains within the limits of fidelity to the spirit of the composition. Such a treatment is invited by the nature of the accompaniments to Dvořák's *Biblical Songs*. Indeed, the composer himself orchestrated the first set. We will take, for example, Number 4, which is a setting of the first four verses of the Twenty-third Psalm.

The single note at the beginning certainly represents the shepherd's horn. A good French Horn is ideal; a Flügel Horn or Oboe with soft flute will serve. It should be given a sharp accent with the swell pedal. The repetition an octave higher will probably be played on a flute — at least in the soprano key. It is perfectly feasible to repeat this horn effect whenever it appears (measures 5, 6, 7, 14, 15, 27, 28, and 31), playing the supporting chords on a mild string combination. The melodic phrase which appears in the first and second interludes and at the end will, in the soprano key, be played on a harmonic flute, the left hand remaining on the accompanying combination. In the contralto key a Clarinet (or *possibly* a soft Orchestral Oboe) may be used for the upper voice alone, the alto remaining with the lower voices. Eight- and four-foot reinforcements will be necessary for the louder phrases, the nature of which will depend on the pitch: more flute tone will be used in the soprano key, while very light eight- and four-foot diapasons may be used in the low key. In measure 24 the imitation can be brought out on a different manual, but it should not be too much emphasized. The suggestion of the "valley of the shadow of death" in measure 21 can be enhanced as follows: Measures 19 and 20 are rather placid, the quality tending toward richness; then a dark quality[6] is immediately substituted in measure 21. In the middle of measure 22 the hopefulness of the next line is suggested by a brighter color, which carries on to the climax.

The Organ Combined with Other Media

The reader has observed that the constant aim of these suggestions has been to determine the essential significance of the music and to plan a registration which will show the various elements in just proportion. In order to avoid what might be considered debatable ground our examples have been selected chiefly from the accompaniments to works which might reasonably be used in the church service. This involves

[6]Preferably a light, warm reed. The Contrafagotto 16' (transposed to eight-foot pitch, of course) may be excellent; an Oboe may be used, or, if necessary, a broad string. It should be noted that the English translation destroys the connection between the music and the text. The line should read: And though my steps must wander in death's dark valley.

problems, which we have for the moment ignored, relating to the organ as a member of an ensemble group, or as an accompanying instrument.

The relation of various tonal characteristics to the clear presentation and interpretation of musical material is independent of medium. If the problem of organ registration differs from that of orchestration, it is because of differences in the tonal resources employed. The principles which we have applied to registration can, with equal validity, be applied to any instrument or combination of instruments. The use of other media, having different tonal characteristics, introduces new factors which must be taken into consideration, but the fundamental principles remain the same. In discussing the registration of music in which the organ is associated with other media, then, we need only call attention to a few practical problems resulting from the addition of these new characteristics.

Whenever the organ is played in combination with other media it must be remembered that its tendency, because of the insistent continuity of its tone, is to absorb other tones. Stringed and wind instruments (including the voice) are apt to diminish as the end of the bow or breath approaches, while the piano, with its very sudden drop from its initial loudness, disappears completely, so that only the attack is heard. Reed instruments, because of the small volume of air which they consume, suffer less handicap; but they do not have the unlimited tonal duration of the organ.

In all ensemble performance, therefore, the organist must take pains to avoid too large a proportion of fundamental, both in the quality of individual stops and in the balance of the ensemble. The less differentiation there is in the material assigned to the different media, the greater is the danger of absorption. If the composer has been so indiscreet as to make the organ part duplicate the others, the fundamental should be extremely slight.[7] If the organ part includes a melody which needs to be brought out, it should be made prominent by its quality, rather than its loudness.

Organ and Piano

Of all instrumental combinations in actual use that of the organ and piano is perhaps the least grateful. If skillfully handled, however, it can be made effective, and it has practical value. In the absence of an orchestra the organ may be preferable to a second piano for the accompaniment of a piano concerto; or the two instruments combined may be a more satisfactory substitute for an accompanying orchestra than either alone.

[7] As a general rule, if the organ has nothing independent to contribute, either it or the other medium should be silent.

The following suggestions may assist in assigning material to the two instruments:

1. The organ may provide a sustained background against which a moving piano part is heard. For this purpose the organ combination should be cohesive and spread, lacking concentration on individual pitches.

2. The percussion of the piano may serve to lend accent, rhythmic definition, or clarity of movement in the lower range. For this the piano may sometimes play the bass line only, presumably in octaves.

3. The piano may add decoration, florid figures, and passage work to the more slowly moving, essential progressions of the organ.

4. The two instruments may be used antiphonally, alternating complete ensembles, single melodies, or other phrases. It is important to preserve the balance between them, avoiding too much weight in the organ tone. The registration should provide a complex ensemble, with light fundamental; single melodies may use flutes or refined solo stops, but not trumpets or diapasons.

The accepted principle of orchestration that the choirs should be independent is many times more important in combining these almost incompatible instruments. Above all, they must not play exactly the same notes; and an ensemble which is a musical unit may not effectively be divided between them. One of them (preferably the piano) may present a single line if it is added to a complete ensemble in the other part, but it is seldom satisfactory to play a solo melody on one instrument and its accompaniment on the other. Franck made such a division of material in his arrangement for piano and harmonium of his *Prélude, Fugue et Variation*, but the tone of free reeds is less positive than that of pipes, and it blends better with the piano. If the harmonium part is played on the organ the effect is greatly improved by sustaining the harmonies on a delicate string or Dulciana. Even if the background is almost inaudible it will render the instruments more congenial.

In Chapter III we discovered that a wide distribution of pitches, without emphasis on any one, favored cohesion. This is a general principle which holds for all tones, regardless of their source. So the tones of the organ and piano can be somewhat reconciled by the use of many pitches in both instruments. Given a wide spread of pitches in the organ, without too much fundamental, the piano may punctuate with dispersed chords; or the distributed pitches may be heard successively in arpeggios and passage work. If the piano plays a single melody against the organ, it is usually more effective played in octaves.

The effect of the combination of these two instruments is much influenced by their relative range. If the piano part is above the organ, it is easily heard. It brightens and colors the ensemble, lending clarity to the movement by its percussive emphasis of high pitches. It need not be played loudly in order to be heard, yet it blends well with a rich ensemble.

If the two instruments are played in the same range, the piano is easily covered. The tone itself is absorbed by the organ, leaving only the attack to contribute to the ensemble. If the piano duplicates the organ part, it lends weight rather than brilliance. If it plays florid passages against the organ, it is necessary to exaggerate the percussiveness of each tone, avoiding the natural elasticity which is habitual with a good pianist.

If the piano part is below the organ, extreme care must be taken to keep the organ combination light, and the bass should usually be duplicated by the organ. The lower tones of the piano lack fundamental, and their rapid diminuendo allows their upper partials to be absorbed.

In this connection Dupré's *Sinfonia for Piano and Organ* may be studied with profit. The writing for the two instruments is impeccable until just before the last movement (bottom of page 35), where the composer made the mistake of duplicating a series of chords in the two instruments. (Compare the much more brilliant treatment on pages 11 and 12.) A similar procedure mars pages 41 and 43, while less literal duplications elsewhere in this finale impair the vivacity of the movement. But it is an effective work, and these small blemishes enhance its value for our study.[8]

By observing carefully such matters as have been discussed, and listening critically to the result, the combination of organ and piano can provide a useful additional interpretative resource.

The Organ with Plucked Strings

The combination of the organ with the harp, which was popular a few years ago, presents a similar but simpler problem. The harp has an even more rapid diminuendo than the piano, but for that very reason its idiom is so different from that of the organ that there is no question of duplicating or sharing similar material. Arpeggios (notated or in the form of rolled chords), which are characteristic of the harp, are the most effective type of material to combine with the organ ensemble. At the same time the harp tone is more easily heard against the organ, partly because its larger proportion of fundamental is less absorbed, and partly because its accented attack is practically all tone, while much of what we hear in the piano attack is merely noise, which is made up of high frequencies

[8]Marcel Dupré, *Sinfonia for Piano and Organ,* Op. 42 (New York: The H. W. Gray Co., 1947).

which are lost against the organ. Nevertheless, the harp is a comparatively feeble instrument, and cannot compete with a heavy ensemble.

The harpsichord and organ are more congenial. The harpsichord attack, like that of the harp, is nearly all tone, and, being more incisive, it is more clearly heard against a discreet organ combination. Moreover, the harpsichord tone has a smaller fundamental and a wider distribution of partials than that of the piano — a condition which favors blend with a complex organ ensemble. As harpsichords become more commonly available, the potentialities of this combination should be more fully explored.

Organ and Orchestra

When an organist plays with an orchestra he adapts his registration to another complex ensemble. The qualitative relation is similar to that which obtains between two sections of the organ, but the problem is again complicated by the greater sustaining power and the lack of dynamic flexibility of the organ. Here again the organist must be on his guard against too large a proportion of low pitches. In general, the ensemble will be rich in upper partials, or bright with upper ranks, according as the organ part is intended to fuse with the orchestral ensemble or stand out against it. Important works for organ and orchestra have been written by Rheinberger, Saint-Saëns, Widor, Horatio Parker, Sowerby, Casella, Dupré, Hindemith, *et al.*, in which the role of the organ has ranged from a subordinate place in the orchestra to that of a solo instrument. The division of the material between the two media presents an enormous variety of new problems which differ in detail, but not in principle, from those which we have already discussed.

Handel's Concertos

Of all the works of this class the most famous are, of course, the sixteen concertos of Handel.[9] For the most part these were intended for optional performance on the harpsichord; Number 6 is specifically for harp, and Number 7 has indications for the use of pedals. Throughout these compositions the transparent texture, the florid material, the conventional figuration, and the lack of polyphony — all suggest the harpsichord rather than the organ. The music itself invites a light registration, such as is best suited to the combination of media.

The sections of these works offer variations in the assignment of material which may be considered typical of the treatment of ensemble groups. These assignments fall into five categories:

[9]Excluding duplications and spurious arrangements, this is the number contained in the collected works of Handel, edited for the German Handel Society by Chrysander.

1. Tutti passages in which the organ and orchestra share on equal terms. If, as is usually the case with Handel, there is little differentiation in the material, the organ should reinforce the orchestra without being separately heard. Fusion is, as always, effected by a rich, wide spread combination of pitches, the details being determined by the dynamic level, the orchestration, and the nature of the material. If the organ part contains independent material, as in the second half of the last movement of the *First Concerto*, the registration should make it audible by imperfect blending, emphasizing the fundamental or octave pitches in a proportion suited to the range and character of the music.

2. Solo passages, in which the orchestra is silent. Here the registration is determined as for any other organ music of the same type, adapted to the implications of its optional performance on the harpsichord and the original function for which it was written,[10] as well as the dynamics and other tonal characteristics of the movement as a whole. As a general rule the quality will be quite transparent, octave pitches lightening the effect and clarifying the figuration.

3. Sections in which the organ is a solo instrument accompanied by the orchestra. The principal methods of treatment are as follows: (1) Two different types of material are combined, as at the beginning of the second half of the last movement of the *Second Concerto*. This differs from the second case under '1' in the relative importance of the two media; here the organ part should be more than clearly audible; it should be prominent. Not only will fusion be avoided, but the registration will provide a more characteristic color which will attract the attention of the listener. The difference is relative: real contrast will be avoided. (2) The organ may have a solo melody, whose accompaniment it shares with the orchestra, as in the third movement of the *Fifth Concerto*. Here the melody should be brought out by a suitable solo stop or solo combination, while the accompaniment merges with the tone of the orchestra — its function being to provide fusion rather than reinforcement. The solo should not contrast too sharply with the accompaniment, lest it seem foreign to the ensemble. On the other hand, an isolated melody, such as the one which introduces the last movement of the *Second Concerto*, should have a more characteristic quality: its recitative character is best interpreted by a single stop.

4. Sections played by the orchestra alone.

5. Sections in which the organ serves as an accompaniment to the orchestra, as in the first movement of the *Third Concerto*. Except for the

---

[10]Handel's concertos were intended for performance between the parts of an oratorio, to rest the listeners from the more serious music.

fact that the organ bass is reinforced by the contrabass of the orchestra (which thus serves the function of the sixteen-foot pedal which the English organs of Handel's time lacked), this is a simple example of the use of the organ as an accompanying instrument. It is with this re- lation of the organ to other media that the average organist is most com- monly concerned.

The Organ as an Accompanying Instrument

There is no clear line of demarcation among the three categories (1, 3, 5, above) which involve the combination of the organ with other media. Their differentiation is based on the mutual relation of the materials assigned to the two media — a relation which is susceptible of unlimited gradation and variation which must be reflected in a finely adjusted registration. Although the designation "accompaniment" implies a certain degree of subordination to the solo medium, such subordination is by no means universal, and it is rarely continuous. The relation be- tween the media is always flexible, and the terms 'solo' and 'accompani- ment', if justified at all, signify nothing more than a general prevalence of primary and secondary function in the ensemble. There are, however, certain practical considerations in playing organ "accompaniments" which merit our specific attention.

If the organ serves as an accompaniment to the melody of the solo medium, the acoustical relation between the two is as explained in Chapter IV.[11] In this case the registration must be adapted to an un- alterable solo quality. The combination will be determined by the nature of the musical material, the degree of contrast necessary to allow the clear separation of the solo without impairing the general ensemble, and an adjustment of the balance to the relative importance of the parts. Care must be taken to avoid qualities which will absorb the tone of the solo.

The balance between the solo and accompaniment is greatly affected by their relative range. If the solo is above the accompaniment it is easily heard, because it is nearer to the region of greatest sensitivity of the ear, and because it is an outside voice. Moreover, many instru- ments and almost all voices are louder in the upper part of their range. In accompanying singers, particularly, adjustment is often necessary to avoid covering their low tones, or to give sufficient support for their high ones. Again, while too much fundamental will tend to absorb or mask the tone of the solo, prominent upper ranks may compete too strongly with the solo part. Usually it is desirable, from the dynamic

[11]Pp. 95-8.

standpoint, to have many upper pitches which are not separately heard.[12]

When the organist is called upon to play accompaniments which were originally written for the orchestra, the problems of transcription and ensemble playing are combined. To the question of the general desirability of orchestral imitation is added that of its suitability to combination with the other medium. Imitative effects which would be satisfactory in themselves are often too soft for this purpose, because of the usual dynamic inferiority of imitative stops. In such cases it may be necessary to substitute a normal organ registration.

A general orchestral impression may sometimes be given by using a noncohesive combination of pitches covering a wide range. Care must be taken to avoid heaviness in the lower ranks, and to prevent any single pitch of the ensemble from protruding. Such a combination reproduces the principal characteristics of an orchestral ensemble, which is extensive in range and, excepting the strings, lacking in cohesion, and most of whose voices are comparatively weak in fundamental and, in general, unduplicated.

Accompaniment of Voices

A considerable proportion of the playing of the average church organist is devoted to the accompaniment of voices, especially choruses. This involves the following functions: (1) to furnish a background; (2) to give support; (3) to reinforce; (4) to present independent material heard against, or in alternation with, the vocal parts.

1. The background is, as usual, provided by a spread, cohesive ensemble. Dulcianas and other mild strings may be used for soft effects, adding pitches and increasing to a diapason chorus (with the minimum of duplication) as more power is needed. Flutes should usually be avoided

---

[12]The amazing amount of upper work which can be used with light fundamentals, even for the accompaniment of a single violin, is exemplified in a registration worked out for a student performance of T. A. Vitali's 'Ciaconna' for violin and figured bass. On an organ voiced somewhat as a chamber instrument and entirely enclosed, so that the player had immediate control of the dynamic balance, the following combination proved perfectly adapted to the fortissimo parts, providing vitality and support without overpowering the violin:

Great	Choir	Swell	Pedal
Octave 4'	Diapason 8'	Rohrflöte 8'	Contrabass 16'
Twelfth 2 2/3'	Chimney Flute 4'	Salicional 8'	Gemshorn 16', 8'
Fifteenth 2'	Nasard 2 2/3'	Flute 4'	Gedeckt 16', 8', 4'
*Mixture V	Flautino 2'	Piccolo 2'	'Cello 8'
		Mixture V	

Couplers: Gt. to Ped., Sw. to Ped., Ch. to Ped.
            Sw. to Gt. 8', 4'; Ch. to Gt.; Sw. to Ch.
*15-17-19-21-22

because of their imperfect fusion; reeds, because their intensity tends to make them prominent.

2. The use of the organ for support involves two different functions: First, to supply the underlying harmonic basis of a solo part. If the solo melody lies largely above the accompaniment, it may be considered an addition to the ensemble, and the organ combination will not offer too much contrast in quality. If the solo melody lies within the range of the accompaniment, greater contrast is desirable, and it is still more important to avoid heaviness, so that the solo may be heard in relief.

The second supporting function of the organ is to assist the intonation of the singers. It must be admitted that this use is a concession to their incompetence. On the other hand, in many installations the organ cannot be made clearly audible to the singer without sounding too loud to the congregation. From the practical standpoint, therefore, such support is sometimes necessary, and its effectiveness depends much on the registration.

Singers are unconsciously affected by their tonal surroundings. A dull registration encourages a dull production, which is conducive to flatting, while a bright organ tone encourages a brighter vocal quality, which favors better intonation. Moreover, a large proportion of upper ranks, particularly octave pitches, is more audible to the singers, and also makes it possible for the accompaniment to be louder without overpowering them. So it is often helpful, when singers are tending to flat, to make the four-foot pitch abnormally prominent.

3. The use of the organ to reinforce a choral ensemble calls for a registration which will increase the dynamic efficiency of the whole,[13] and not merely add power. The organ must supplement, not cover, the voices. Heaviness should be avoided and high pitches stressed without the use of conspicuous high ranks, so that the organ will blend with the voices, intensifying them without overtopping them.

In certain cases the organ may compensate for deficiencies in the choral ensemble. Lower pitches may be emphasized in accompanying women's voices, depending on synthetic tone rather than strong fundamentals, so as to weld the vocal and instrumental tone as effectively as possible. Similarly a more brilliant combination may be used with a men's chorus, compensating for their naturally dark color. Here also there should be ample overlapping of pitch to integrate the ensemble.[14]

A chorus singing in unison or octaves will tolerate a much more massive, as well as a more brilliant, accompaniment than a similar group

[13]See p. 65 ff.

[14]It is an error for composers and arrangers to rely on the organ to supply the missing parts of a choral ensemble. It is impossible to effect a sufficiently good match.

divided in parts. This is due not only to the distribution of forces in
part singing, but also to the fact that tonal complexity of any kind favors
a blending of the components.

4. The use of independent material in the accompaniment – which
greatly increases the musical interest – introduces the mutual relationships of ensemble music in addition to the more characteristically ac-
companimental functions of the organ.

In this field, as in all branches of musical interpretation, the various
elements which have been discussed separately rarely occur as isolated
conditions. The problem is a complex mixture of many considerations
which must enter into the solution, each contributing to the result in
proportion to its importance.

The Accompaniment of Congregational Singing

The use of the organ with congregational singing is in quite another
category. Unless a large, well-trained choir is present, the function of
the organ is to lead, rather than to accompany. For this purpose the
organ must be heard by the congregation: indeed, except in hymns in a
meditative mood, the organ should be loud and brilliant enough to stimulate enthusiasm, without making the singers feel overpowered. All of
this requires a large proportion of upper pitches, although the fact that
most of the congregation sing the melody makes it advisable to avoid a
thin or top-heavy ensemble. In hymns of a majestic type it is often effective to include light or bright sixteen-foot manual stops.

It is a mistake to use the same registration for all hymns, regardless
of their style or mood. Such a procedure encourages perfunctoriness and
indifference to the text on the part of the singers. It is equally errone-
ous to make frequent changes in the tone quality which have no relation
to the music or to the sense of the words.[15] In playing hymns and accompanying chants the function of the registration is, as always, interpretation – not decoration. If the text is suitably set, the music will indicate the general mood and style; variations will be suggested by the
words. Limits are imposed by the necessity of leading the congregation
and the desirability of maintaining continuity in a small form, but within
these limits the organist should seek to interpret the text throughout.

There is much difference of opinion as to the most effective transition
from one stanza of a hymn to the next. The essential considerations are
these: No artist would play a composition twice without a slight pause

---

[15]Standing beside a distinguished English organist during a service we have marveled
at the skill and ingenuity with which a new combination was introduced with each new
line of a hymn or psalm. It seemed to be a matter of conscience to avoid playing two successive phrases alike; but it was never possible to discover any relation between the tone
quality and the text.

before the repetition. The piece comes to a conclusion and stops; a moment of adjustment is necessary before starting again. To this artistic consideration is added the practical necessity, to the average member of the congregation, of taking a little time to regain his breath before proceeding to the next stanza. Ideally the length of the pause should vary with the character of the hymn and the degree of continuity in the text.[16]

The organist's problem is to find a procedure which will, without any artistic offence, (1) indicate the end of the last note of the stanza, (2) prevent a sense of void during the pause, and (3) prepare the congregation for the attack on the succeeding stanza. In the opinion of the author this is best accomplished by the following method: (1) Reduce the organ at the end of the last note of the hymn; (2) sustain the last chord, with or without pedal, on the reduced combination; (3) release this chord as a signal to the congregation that the next stanza is about to begin. The length of the pause should be felt, rather than computed; the organist should imagine that he is singing. An extra measure, or less, may be interpolated. The release signal normally allows about one beat before the new attack – often a little more, because of the psychological advantage of delaying beyond the expected time. Of course the congregation does not realize the purpose of this maneuver, but when it is consistently adopted the people come to feel it and attack the new stanzas with greater confidence and unanimity.

Aural Judgment

All that has been said concerning the importance of listening from the standpoint of the audience, imagining what they hear, and securing criticism and advice from trusted listeners located where the effect will most nearly approach that heard by the majority of the auditors, must be doubly emphasized in regard to the performance of any type of ensemble music. If it is difficult for the organist to know the effect of his own instrument in the auditorium, it is impossible for him to form an accurate conception of the balance and ensemble characteristics of a combination of media in which he plays a part. Even after long experience under identical conditions it is advisable to check one's judgment frequently by borrowing the ears of a non-participating listener.

---

[16]In singing such a hymn as Washington Gladden's 'O Master, let me walk with thee' to a four-line tune, the last two stanzas should ideally be run together. The hymn was originally written in eight-line stanzas. Again, if the imitation is brought out in 'Tallis' Canon', there should be no pause between the stanzas.

Part V

PRACTICAL SUGGESTIONS

CHAPTER FOURTEEN

PLANNING REGISTRATION

Preliminary Considerations

The interpretation of music through the control of the tone quality has been considered from many angles; principles have been developed and examples discussed. But an organist can no more plan a suitable registration by rule than a composer can write significant music by merely observing the conventions of harmony and counterpoint. The principles of registration can only be suggestive, and to a certain extent corrective; an artistic result still depends on the taste and judgment of the performer.

Moreover, it is not to be expected that a truly interpretative registration will result from aimless experiment; if it does, it is fortuitous. The organist who tries, largely at random, a number of combinations until he stumbles onto something which pleases him, is like the composer whose "fingers wander idly over the noisy keys" until he strikes something which he wants to write down. Interpretation, like composition, must be inwardly conceived before it can be outwardly expressed.

Imagination, therefore, should precede experiment. The organist should auralize the music with what seems to him to be an ideal quality; then try to reproduce that quality on the organ. He will first devise a combination which he expects most nearly to approach the desired quality; he will listen to it critically and analytically and make corrections until he is satisfied with the result. If he reaches an *impasse* he may be obliged to start again with another combination and repeat the process.

Practicability should be considered from the beginning. There is little advantage in planning a registration which cannot be realized. Nothing is gained by adopting a scheme which is so complex that the fluency of execution and the naturalness of interpretation are impaired. Moreover, there is always the question of what is the most profitable use of one's time. Is the advantage of a difficult procedure sufficient to justify devoting time to it which could otherwise be spent, perhaps, on some more rewarding work? This point of view offers great dangers to the indolent and easily satisfied, but it must be considered by the perfectionist. It is not a matter of saving time, but of making it count for the most in artistic achievement.

Economy of Resources

In planning combinations it is generally desirable to use as small a number of stops as will serve to produce the desired tone quality. Each rank should make a definite contribution to the total effect. The inclusion of a number of voices which are individually inaudible serves, in the aggregate, to impair the clarity, refinement, and vitality of the ensemble.[1] Their blurring tendency is sometimes useful to conceal defects in the blending of essential stops, and their inclusion may occasionally be excusable on practical grounds in a sequence of combinations designed for a general crescendo. Moreover, the effect of obscuring the tonal texture, which in most cases is a blemish, may in others serve an interpretative purpose. As a general rule, however, the practice of retaining the soft stops as part of a loud combination is to be deprecated.

Let us, therefore, begin our experimentation with the simplest combination which the imagination suggests, adding stops to modify the quality as desired, but not forgetting the possibility of some elimination. We will confine ourselves to stops which make a desirable contribution to the ensemble, and will beware of flutes, fat diapasons, and exotic registers – except that high flutes may be used for brightness and clarity of movement.

The use of "stops which make a desirable contribution to the ensemble" means that we will select those whose natural tendency is consistent with the quality desired. We will seek to avoid stops for which compensation must be made in another direction. A simple diapason is ordinarily preferable to the combination of a string and flute; these two opposite qualities do not unite to form a compromise timbre in the middle of the spectrum. Similarly the addition of screechy supers to compensate for a heavy fundamental does not produce a balanced ensemble. The constituent voices should all be related to the whole, their qualities reaching out to join the other components of the ensemble, rather than asserting their individuality.

At the same time we should remember that in the composition of our ensemble proportion and balance are as important as the quality of the individual ranks. Especially we should not neglect the medial pitches which serve to join the upper work to the fundamental.

Obviously the foregoing is an ideal which cannot always be realized on a small organ. If the right stops are not available, it is necessary to effect a compromise, which often means compensating for one defect with another. Such compensation is usually preferable to the use of an inappropriate quality without any correction.

Solo Qualities

In selecting a solo quality it is again desirable to begin with the simplest possible combination. If a suitable solo stop is available, we

[1]Compare p. 91.

may use it alone, or we may modify it with one or two other stops until we are satisfied with the color. If the type of melody invites a synthetic color, we may start with the mutation ingredients (Tierce, Nasard, or both), adding foundation ranks to define the pitch. We may arrive at some such combination as (1) Gedeckt and Tierce; (2) Flute 4', Nasard, and Tierce; (3) Dulciana and Nasard; etc.

In general, registration which relies for its tone quality on the individual colors which the voicer has produced is less interesting, less varied, and less adaptable to different types of material than that which results from an intelligent combination of ranks of various pitches. On the other hand, solo stops are usually voiced for a special effect which is best realized when they are used alone. Their distinctive timbre is lost in combination, unless the added stop produces a very subtle shading in an abnormal direction. Thus an Orchestral Oboe should almost never be combined with an eight-foot flute; but a very delicate four-foot Rohrflöte may brighten the color slightly, or perhaps even increase its acidity, without the loss of its individuality. Similarly a Clarinet should rarely be combined with a diapason, although, if it is too thin, it can be mellowed by the addition of a light gedeckt; but it may often be brightened by a soft four-foot flute or, in the tenor range, even by an Octave; or it may be colored by the addition of a Tierce or a Nasard. These are more or less random examples of the shading of solo colors.

Interrelation of Companion Combinations

If two qualities are to be used together, as in a trio or a solo with accompaniment, neither should be considered final until a satisfactory companion combination has been found. The relation between the two is often more important than the particular quality of either. The nature, range, relative importance, and degree of independence of the material will determine their tonal relationship, both as regards quality and dynamics. Sometimes great ingenuity is required to reconcile all these values.

If any use is to be made of the swells, the dynamic balance should, if possible, be right when the swell pedals are in the same position. Any discrepancy requires one shoe to be carried somewhat in advance of the other most of the time, complicating the manipulation of the pedals and reducing the total dynamic range — for one swell is never quite closed and the other is never quite open. Since the swell shades are not equally effective on all qualities,[2] the balance should be tested both with the boxes closed and with them open. The registration should then be

[2]See p. 67.

planned (if there is sufficient choice) for the most effective shading, taking into consideration the nature and relative importance of the material and the extent to which its expressive presentation is dependent on dynamic change. Often on a small organ, and sometimes on any instrument, the organist will be obliged to choose between an ideal quality and a perfect balance of the swell pedals. Sometimes he may find it advantageous to abandon all thought of dynamic expression in order to present the material in the most favorable guise and most perfect proportion.

Timing of Stop Changes

It has already been mentioned that the organ is incapable of producing a continuous dynamic gradation from the softest to the loudest tones.[3] Beyond the narrow range of the swell shades any dynamic change must be effected by adding or subtracting stops. Such changes are sudden, and they affect the quality as well as the loudness of the combination. They are more or less audible, depending on the extent to which they are covered by other stops, and must be timed so that their effect is consistent with the music, taking into consideration such matters as rhythmic stress, thematic material, phrasing, melodic contour, etc.

Audible additions should be made only at points where a definite attack or accent would be consistent with the music, as at the beginning of a phrase, at the entrance of a theme, at a point of rhythmic accent, or at a point of arrival or climax. The first case is covered by the discussion of changes at division points in Chapter VIII.[4] The second, as applied to single melodies, was illustrated earlier in the same chapter.[5] Obvious examples of opportunities to add to the general ensemble at the beginning of a theme occur in Bach's great 'Fugue in B minor' at the entrance of the theme in the soprano in measure 15, and again at the entrance of the new countersubject at the beginning of the third section of the fugue. A similar situation at the beginning of the third section of the double 'Fugue in F major' is mentioned at the end of Chapter VIII.[6]

An excellent application of the principle of reinforcement at strong rhythmic points occurs in Schweitzer's suggestions for the registration of Bach's 'Toccata in F major', where he recommends the following approach to a climax: ". . . add further reinforcements on the first beats in measures 372-375." Then again, "From measure 412 on, stops will be

[3]Pp. 316-17.
[4]Pp. 194-7.
[5]Pp. 178-9.
[6]P. 208.

drawn successively on the first beats, arriving at full organ in measure 417."[7] The last illustrates also the effectiveness of adding at a point of climax. Among innumerable other examples we may mention Bach's frequent arrival at a point of suspense, or a diverted cadence, just before a coda or conclusive cadence, as in the 'Prelude in F minor', measure 70; 'Fantasia in G minor', measure 44 and 48; 'Fugue in A minor' (the "Great"), measure 139; 'Prelude in B minor', measure 16 and corresponding points. The most thrilling examples are the famous six-four chords in the 'Fantasia in G minor', measures 21 and 36.

Concealment of Stop Changes

It often happens that reinforcement is necessary in passages where sudden, audible increases would be inconsistent with the natural interpretation. In such cases it is desirable to conceal the addition as much as possible. The following methods are suggested:

1. The change may be covered by other stops. If the addition is in a swell box, it is less noticeable if the shades are closed; if it is in an unenclosed section, any coupled enclosed sections should be open if possible. Thus it is often advantageous to add within closed boxes at the beginning of a crescendo; then, after the shades are open, to increase the unenclosed section. Sometimes it is effective to lead up to the final addition with the swells, gaining a crescendo momentum which makes the more audible change come as a natural climax.

2. When an addition is made in an enclosed section which is already open, or partly open, it is often advantageous to close the shades just before the change is made.[8] The closing should be so timed that the maximum effect synchronizes with the addition, and so gauged as to compensate exactly for the increase effected by the stops.

3. Additions can often be concealed by taking advantage of a compensating feature of the music.[9] A reduction in the number of voices has the effect of lightening the ensemble; so an increase at the moment that one or more voices drop out is less conspicuous. On the other hand, a sudden increase in the number of voices produces an accent which it may sometimes be appropriate to emphasize by the addition of stops. A melodic skip often provides an opportunity for an inconspicuous change: the addition of upper pitches when the soprano drops, or of sixteen- or

[7] Bibl. 165, Vol. IV, p. vii. This method, however, is exceptional with Schweitzer. He almost always changes registration at the beginning of the phrase, which usually occurs *after* the accent. The result is often disturbing to the rhythmic flow. In this case, however, the phrase units obviously begin at the first of the measure.

[8] "Just before" assumes that the action of the shades is not instantaneous; but one may also assume a psychological lag in the perception of the diminuendo.

[9] Compare p. 179.

eight-foot stops with an upward skip of the lowest voice, is partially concealed by the compensating change of range.

The inverse process of reduction accompanies reciprocal conditions: stops are thrown off at the conclusion of a theme or phrase, and after a point of rhythmic stress or of arrival. These changes too may be covered by other stops, or concealed by compensating conditions. Naturally the process in a decrescendo is the reverse of the crescendo: the unenclosed combinations are reduced before the shades are closed, and further reductions within the boxes are made after they are closed.[10] The opening of the swell to compensate for a reduction is seldom practicable, but it is frequently possible to take advantage of compensating features of the music itself: a reduction may coincide with an increase in the number of voices, or it may serve to emphasize the release of voices which drop out; or, again, it may be synchronized with an upward skip of the soprano, or a downward skip of the bass.

General Crescendos

It is important that an extended crescendo begin with a quality which is consistent with that which will be attained at the climax, so that the process will be one of gradual intensification without any drastic change. It is practically impossible, for example, to effect a good general crescendo if the initial combination contains a Voix Céleste: it must not be retained in the ensemble, but it is bound to be missed when it drops out. Its use is only possible when there is, in the course of the build up, a change in material which justifies an audible change in quality. Such a condition is found in Howells' 'Psalm-Prelude, Number 3', which was discussed in Chapter VII.[11] If the Voix Céleste is used, it will drop out in the third measure of page 4. In order that the new quality may not be too much out of line it must be highly complex, containing many absorbed upper ranks and a good proportion of string tone.

Certain stops which are essential to a full combination are almost impossible to add without a noticeable change of quality. This is particularly true of mixtures and reeds. It is important that they be available in enclosed sections, so that they can be added under cover of fairly bright open combinations. The introduction of the reeds is eased by adding a four-foot reed before the eight-foot. In general, a crescendo which leads to a fortissimo is more effective if there is latent vitality in the initial

[10]Of course the order of operation, both for crescendos and diminuendos, is flexible. In practice the different sections will be balanced against one another so as to avoid too much change of quality. In a decrescendo, for example, the Great may be only partly reduced before the swell begins to close; then the Swell reeds may be thrown off before the reduction of the Great is completed.

[11]Pp. 158-9.

combination. Upper work, often mixtures, should be included in an enclosed section from the start.

One of the most difficult, and most exciting, crescendos in all organ literature is in Bach's 'Fantasia in G minor', beginning at the second beat of measure 31. The procedure will depend on the resources, voicing, and balance of the individual instrument, and can be perfected only by exhaustive experimentation. The following method, suggested as a point of departure, serves to clarify the musical texture, bringing out, and taking advantage of, the imitating ascending couplets as they appear in successive voices.

At the beginning the Swell combination contains a light eight-foot diapason, judiciously enriched with upper work, perhaps including an unobtrusive Octave; the Choir is somewhat brighter; the Great has eight- and four-foot stops, mezzo forte or mezzo piano; the Pedal is always adjusted to balance the manual combination in use; the Swell and Choir are coupled to the Great, and the Swell is coupled to the Choir and to the Pedal; the swell boxes are closed.

Begin on the Swell, starting at once to open its shades; the third voice enters at the end of measure 31 on the Choir; the alto goes to the Choir at the second beat, and the soprano at the fourth beat, of measure 32; the Choir opens during measure 32, on the second beat of which the Choir to Pedal may be added; the Swell shades close just before the second beat of measure 33, so that the Swell mixtures can be added unnoticed; at that point the left hand enters on the Great, and the Swell crescendo is resumed; the Choir is reinforced on the last beat of this measure, the box having been partially closed to conceal the addition; on the second beat of measure 34 the third voice enters on the Great, and the Great to Pedal is added; the full Choir may be brought on at the same time; on the fourth beat all voices are on the Great, to which the Twelfth and Fifteenth are added on the first beat of measure 35. All this while the Swell and Choir shades have been gradually opened in such a way as to conceal the additions and effect a continuous crescendo. On the second beat of measure 35 the Swell box is partially closed, and the full Swell is added; the opening of the shades, releasing its rich, reedy ensemble, and a further addition to the Great on the last beat of the measure, lead to the fortissimo crash on the six-four chord at the beginning of measure 36.

The foregoing suggestions assume that every detail of the registration will be carefully planned with respect to tone quality, balance, and timing. Such are the requirements of perfection, but they cannot be met without ingenuity, persistent experiment, and precision in execution. The genius of the twentieth century, which has produced countless labor-saving devices in all fields of human activity, has not neglected the organist. The modern console is a marvelous machine, giving the player almost miraculous control of the complicated resources of the instrument. This mechanical equipment greatly facilitates the realization of an ideal registration, but it sometimes encourages laziness. The organist, unaccustomed to coping with the clumsy mechanism of former years, is tempted to seek the easy solution, rather than taking advantage of the means provided to eliminate the defects which were inevitable before the advent of the electric action.

The Crescendo Pedal

A common offence is the indiscriminate use of the crescendo pedal. Obviously the addition of stops in a predetermined order at fortuitous moments cannot provide the perfect adjustment to the musical material which we are seeking. At best it is a practical means of securing a general increase in power, distributed over a given expanse of time. If an organist feels obliged to resort to the use of the crescendo pedal, he should seek to mitigate its defects as much as possible. He may operate it in controlled stages at rhythmic points, so that the additions may be compatible with the sense of the music. He may conceal the changes by preceding the use of the crescendo pedal with a swell box crescendo, applied to a full, enclosed combination.[12] Owing to the sluggish response of the ear, the use of the crescendo pedal is less objectionable for rapid, than for slow increase. Moreover its use for a diminuendo is more satisfactory than for a crescendo, since the cessation of tone is less noticeable than its beginning. Thus, at the end of the middle section of Franck's 'Choral in A minor', the rapid decrescendo on the pedal E can be most effectively accomplished by means of the crescendo pedal, provided the quality of its ensemble is suited to the preceding passage. Again, the crescendo which leads to the final statement of the theme on the next to the last page may be effected by small movements of the crescendo pedal, timed to produce additions on the beats.

Many of our best organists contend that the use of the crescendo pedal is never legitimate. Ideally they are right, but practically we are again concerned with relative values. As in all problems of registration, the final criterion is the audible result. If the organist can produce a more effective increase or decrease with the crescendo pedal than he can in any other way, and if the dynamic change is essential to the interpretation of the music, there can be no question as to the legitimacy of its use. He should, however, spare no pains to avoid the defects of the crescendo pedal.

[12]Compare p. 338.

CHAPTER FIFTEEN

MECHANICAL MATTERS

Mastery of the Mechanical Process

The organ subjects the interpreter to a very special handicap in that it interposes between the performer and his effects a vast amount of arbitrarily controlled mechanism. Not only is it highly complex, but there is no inevitable psychological connection between the process and the result. For example, it is the only instrument, except perhaps the harpsichord, in which the dynamic effect is completely independent of the muscular effort of the player. It is true that the operation of the swell pedal, evolved from the old lever control, carries out the more or less intuitive principle of pushing harder to make the tone louder. Moreover, logic and convenience are consulted in planning the arrangement of the stops, couplers, and other controls. In general, however, the organist produces his effects by purely artificial movements.

This situation is inevitable, but it must be unsuspected by the lisener. The mechanism is the means; the listener should hear only the intended musical effect. The controls should be so operated that there will be no mechanical noise, and that there will be no modification of the rhythm, phrasing, or natural, plastic, fluent delivery of the music. Audible changes should be exactly synchronized with the music: this involves the perfectly timed premature operation of pistons and other devices whose effect is not instantaneous. In a word, the music should sound as natural and spontaneous as if no mechanism were involved.

In order to accomplish this the mechanical manipulation must become second nature to the organist. It is a part of his technique which must be mastered, to the point of unconscious control, by intensive practising. In addition to a general command of the console, each piece should be completely planned in advance, leaving nothing to chance. If the registration is at all complicated, any change on the spur of the moment may lead to difficulties. As a general rule, a definite time should be assigned to each operation, so that it can be associated with the note technique.[1] For example, the preparation of a pedal coupler may coincide with the

---

[1]It was said that Lynnwood Farnam, who did much practising at the piano, would place a small object, such as a penknife, on the side of the music rack. At any place in the music where he planned to make a stop change he would shift the position of the penknife, so that a mechanical adjustment would be associated with the music at that point. Such mastery of detail to the point of intuitiveness made him, perhaps, the most perfect executant that ever presided at an organ console.

release of the last note of the preceding pedal phrase. Moreover, in the
case of changes which can be made at any time in the course of a given
passage, it is frequently advantageous to make them at the first opportunity; then it is no longer on the player's mind, or, in case of failure for
any reason, the change can be made later.

Control of the Swell Pedals

It is comparatively easy to practise the notes of a composition, and
even stop changes, the operation of pistons, etc. These processes are
definitely successful or definitely not. They may be difficult, but the
problem is clear-cut. The control of the swell pedals is in a different
category. The discrepancies are subtle; often it is not a matter of right
or wrong, but of better or less good. The practising has a less definite
aim, but it is none the less important; and it is even more stimulating,
since it is directly concerned with musical expression. It calls for more
discriminative self criticism, and requires indefatigable perseverance.
The work is constantly guided by the ear, but a few mechanical suggestions may not be amiss.

The mastery of the technique of the swell pedal involves the ability
to produce a *continuous* motion at controlled speeds, ranging from very
slow to rather fast. The speed is not uniform in any one crescendo or
diminuendo. The rate of audible change needs to vary for the interpretation, and the rate of motion varies with respect to the audible change. A
quarter of an inch when the swells are closed produces more effect than
an inch when they are almost wide open. Modern mechanisms compensate
for this discrepancy to a certain extent, but by no means in proportion to
the effect. The movement of the foot, therefore, must be relatively slower
when the shades are nearly closed than when they are open.

The electro-pneumatic swell action moves the shades by predetermined
stages, the action being retarded to cover the sudden small changes and
provide continuity. Since it is impossible for the player to know the
exact location of the individual stations he must ignore them and operate
the pedal as if the action were under continuous control, as in a direct
lever connection. If the builder has provided enough stations, and the
action is well regulated, the effect will be in fact continuous. If there
are bulges, the organist must determine where they come, and try to bring
them where they will not be inconsistent with the music.

For the best control of the operation of the swell, the foot should be
securely placed on the pedal so that the axis of the ankle corresponds
with that of the pedal, exerting just enough pressure on both the heel
and the ball of the foot to overcome the resistance of friction and inertia. The motion of the pedal is then controlled by adjusting the angle

at the ankle, rather than through the amount or pressure at one end or the other.

If two pedals are to be operated with one foot, it should be placed on the crack between the pedals. The two can then be operated as one so long as no discrepancy in the adjustment is called for; but independence of control is often essential. To a limited degree the balance can be altered, even in the course of a crescendo or diminuendo, by tipping the ball of the foot in opening, or the heel in closing the shades. It is seldom practicable with one foot to open one box and close another at exactly the same time.

The simultaneous operation of two swell shoes with one foot is obviously dependent on their being adjacent. All organs with more than two swell pedals should be equipped with some sort of coupling device which makes it possible to control any two swells by adjacent pedals. If the shades cannot be connected with adjacent pedals, the organist must either resort to the use of the master shades control ("all swells to swell"), thereby forfeiting independence of operation, or he must move the swells in alternation. Such alternation should, of course, be guided by the musical material; indeed it may sometimes serve a definite interpretative purpose, as in Example 18.

Example 18. Bach: O Mensch, bewein' dein' Sünde gross

The foregoing assumes that one foot is occupied with the pedal part. If both feet are free there can, of course, be complete independence in the operation of two swell pedals. More frequently the organist has to contend with the opposite situation, where both feet are busy playing the notes. In such cases the use of the swells must be definitely planned, taking advantage of brief opportunities to change the adjustment where it is appropriate to the music. Considerable practise may be necessary in order to acquire control of the amount of change in the brief time available. A particularly difficult example is shown in Example 19, where, in order to effect the crescendo implied in the music, the organist must shorten the pedal notes to provide time to give little quick kicks to the swell pedals. Here, as often, the interpreter is obliged to choose between dynamic change and a literal execution of the notes. It should

Example 19. Widor: Symphonie Gothique—iv .... Allegro[2]

*Swell, with mixtures

always be remembered that the effect of the whole is more important than
details, but slovenly details mar the whole.

Couplers

With the exception of the swell pedals the more important mechanical
accessories of the modern console fall into two categories: (1) Couplers
—devices to make the tonal resources of one department available from
another keyboard, or at another pitch, from that with which it is normally
identified; (2) Pistons—devices to handle groups of stops with a single
movement, and to provide duplicate, convenient control of couplers which
are most frequently changed.

The primary function of unison manual couplers is to combine the
resources of two keyboards to provide greater strength, richness, complexity, or brilliance, or to complement each other. If the two combinations are sharply differentiated, a shading of tone color can be effected
by the use of the swells to alter the balance of the coupled departments.
The use of couplers also provides greater flexibility in the mixing of
small combinations, since the player can choose his ingredients from
the resources of two or more manuals.

A less common, but valuable function of intermanual couplers is to
reallocate the manual divisions of the organ. If the console provides
'unison off' couplers for all manuals, and reverse direction couplers
(Gt. to Ch., Ch. to Sw., etc.), any division can be assigned to any desired keyboard, giving complete flexibility of arrangement. The purpose
of such reallocation is to bring on adjacent keyboards combinations
which should be under the fingers of one hand, either for a close or quick
connection, or for actually playing simultaneously on both.

Such use of couplers has been suggested from time to time on these
pages.[3]   To these incidental examples we will add two specific

[2]Reproduced by kind permission of B. Schott's Söhne, Mainz.

[3]See pp. 232-3, 250, 421, fn. 5.

registration schemes for short, polyphonic works:

1. 'Liebster Jesu, wir sind hier' (distinctius), from Bach's *Orgel-büchlein*. The solo qualities are (1) an unimitative English Horn on the Solo; (2) the Swell Oboe, perhaps colored by a Quintadena or a Nasard, but in any event less penetrating than the English Horn; (3) a Swell combination based on the Viole d'Orchestre, suggesting an Orchestral Oboe, less biting than the orchestral stop, but thinner than the unimitative English Horn. During the first two phrases the soprano is played on (1) and the alto on (3); at the repeat the soprano is played on (2) and the alto on the Great, to which (1) is coupled; the original combination is resumed for the last two phrases. Thus the canonic imitation in the alto always has a slightly more incisive quality than the soprano, and is played from the manual next below the soprano manual, making it possible for the right hand to play the two melodies on different keyboards.

2. 'Quatuor sur le Kyrie, à trois Sujets' by d'Anglebert. The following registration may be prepared:

Pedal	Swell	Great	Choir	Solo
Dulcianas 8', 4'	Rohrflöte 8'	Gemshorn 8'	Clarinet 8'	English Horn 8'
Gedeckt 4'	Flute 2'		Octave 4'	
	Dolce Cornet		Nasard 2 2/3'	
		Unison off	Unison off	Unison off
Gt. to Ped.		So. to Gt.	Sw. to Ch. 16'	Ch. to So.

The right hand plays the soprano on the Great (= Solo); the left hand plays the tenor on the Solo (= Choir); the bass is played on the Pedal, which includes the Great Gemshorn; the alto is played on the Swell, divided between the left hand (reaching down from the Solo) and the right hand (reaching up from the Great); in measures 11 and 12 the right hand plays the alto on the Choir, an octave higher than written – for which the Sw. to Ch. 16' coupler was prepared. In this way the parts can be kept completely independent and can be played perfectly legato, or with any desired phrasing.[4]

Octave Couplers

The modern American organ is completely equipped with transposing couplers, except that the Great intramanual couplers are often not included. This omission is due to the prevalent notion that their principal function is to add to the ensemble, for which purpose they are but a makeshift, and are superfluous on an adequate Great division.

[4]See pp. 247, 250. Compare the registration suggested above with Combination I for a Quatuor on four keyboards, p. 250.

There are many valid objections to this use of octave couplers: (1) If the organ is artistically designed, each stop is scaled and voiced for its own pitch, in its normal relation to the ensemble; it is not equally adapted to use at other pitches. (2) The use of octave couplers in combination with the normal pitch throws the ensemble out of balance: (a) Whenever two notes an octave apart are played simultaneously there is a duplication of function, the same pipes serving at their normal pitch for one, and at the transposed pitch for the other. This results in a general weakening of the middle pitches of the ensemble, and the loss of individual voices where the octave happens to occur. (b) Since the ensemble is presumably designed to provide a proper balance without the use of such couplers, the addition of super- and suboctave transpositions overemphasizes the upper and lower pitches. This produces a spreading and dispersion of the ensemble: the top is screechy, the bottom is muddy, and the tone lacks cohesion and vitality. (3) Mutations, which are essential to the integration of the ensemble, often become shrill if they are transposed up. On the other hand, the suboctave coupler ends abruptly at "tenor" C.

These objections apply chiefly to the addition of octave couplers to an ensemble which is already fairly complete. We have noticed their usefulness in bringing certain notes within reach of a hand which is also playing another part. However, if discreetly used, they afford other, more important advantages:

1. They provide much greater flexibility in combination. Each stop becomes available at three pitches: its normal pitch, an octave above, and an octave below. Thus to the stops available at each pitch are added those which normally speak an octave higher or lower. Although this transposition is by whole divisions, it provides the possibility of considerable increase in the variety of ensemble.

2. It also makes possible a certain amount of compensation for deficiencies in the tonal resources of the instrument, due to faulty specifications or voicing. Many American organs, for example, are inadequately supplied with upper work and have too large a proportion of fundamental tone. In such cases superoctave couplers may furnish the needed upper pitches, though not in perfect balance. If the Great has a Twelfth and Fifteenth, but no mixture, the use of the superoctave coupler (probably omitting the Fifteenth) will partially fill the lack. This procedure is particularly necessary on small organs which contain no Great rank above the Octave. It is sometimes preferable, however, to couple secondary manuals to the Great at the upper octave, particularly if the upper ranks of the Great are too brilliant. But if, as often happens, the Swell is the only manual which is provided with a mixture, it is

frequently advisable to transpose only the *other* manuals, so that the mixture can be retained without screechiness.

If the organ lacks a four-foot reed, a superoctave coupler should be used to supply it. From the standpoint of the ensemble the four-foot chorus reed is the most important reed. Sometimes it may be advisable even to forego the mixture if it becomes intolerable with the coupler necessary to obtain this four-foot reed. On small organs the Sw. to Gt. 4' will be in almost constant use in full combinations.

The chief function of suboctave couplers in ensemble combinations is to provide a sixteen-foot tone when no suitable rank of that pitch is available. The usual sixteen-foot Bourdon or Gedeckt is too heavy except in large ensembles. In piano or mezzo forte combinations the Swell or Choir (having no eight-foot stops excepting mild strings) may be coupled in at suboctave pitch. In larger combinations a light diapason or a small eight-foot reed may provide the sixteen-foot tone in the same way. Since the sixteen-foot stops on American organs are almost always too heavy, this use of the suboctave coupler is a very valuable resource in playing music in which the sixteen-foot pitch is not needed in the lowest octave.

The fact that octave couplers transpose all the stops which are drawn in the coupled section makes it necessary to consider the entire combination, and sometimes to make certain modifications because of the use of the coupler. Two-foot stops should usually be absent from a division which is coupled at superoctave pitch, as well as any mixtures which do not break back enough to avoid shrillness when transposed. Sometimes even the eight- and four-foot ranks are voiced so loud that the superoctave coupler makes them too prominent.

The use of the suboctave coupler requires special care. Of course all sixteen-foot stops must be omitted from the coupled manual,[5] as well as heavy eight-foot stops. It is often advisable to omit four-foot flutes which, when transposed to eight-foot pitch, tend to fatten the ensemble. On the other hand, a combination which includes only light eight-foot tone and bright upper work is perfectly suited to be coupled at the suboctave pitch. If mutations and mixtures are included, their transposition produces a gross mixture effect which lends richness to a cohesive ensemble. Similarly a larger mass may be composed by drawing the Great Octave, Twelfth, Fifteenth, and Mixture (with perhaps a very light eight-foot stop), transposing the combination down with the suboctave coupler and unison release, and coupling in brilliant ensembles from the Swell and Choir. If the subsidiary manuals are sufficiently brilliant the effect

[5]The author finds no use whatever for a thirty-two foot manual stop.

is admirably suited to many-voiced harmony with a minimum of polyphonic interest.

Obviously the balance of the ensemble depends on the pitches sounding, regardless of whether they come through octave couplers or directly from stops speaking at their normal pitch. The tendency of transposing couplers to emphasize outer pitches can, in the case of intermanual couplers, be somewhat mitigated by adjustment in the combination of the receiving manual: if a superoctave coupler is used, there should normally be compensating emphasis on medium pitches, and perhaps on lower pitches, in the manual to which it couples; a suboctave coupler calls for an increase in the medium and upper pitches. If the tonal balance permits, the unison coupler should be omitted from any section which is coupled at octaves, in order to avoid the duplication mentioned above.

With such adjustments as have been suggested it is often possible to conceal the disadvantages of transposing couplers and to use them in the composition of an ensemble which is more perfectly balanced and better suited to the interpretation of the music in hand than any which could be devised without them. The following examples illustrate their usefulness, and may suggest other possibilities:

The Ch. to Gr. 4' may serve to provide upper work for the lighter Great combinations, or to bridge the gap between the Great "to Fifteenth" and the mixture. On some organs this coupler may be in almost constant use for ensemble combinations above a mezzo forte.

The combination of Great sixteen-, eight-, and four-foot diapasons, specified in many foreign compositions,[6] is rarely effective on American organs. In addition to the possibilities mentioned previously,[6] the following suggestions are offered: Sometimes the lightest Great diapason can be used with the Swell Diapason coupled at superoctave pitch, and the Choir Diapason at suboctave pitch. Again, the passage may be played on the Choir, its Diapason and Octave being transposed by the suboctave coupler and unison release, while the Swell [Diapason and] Octave are coupled at unison pitch. For a softer effect, the Great Gemshorn may provide the sixteen- and four-foot pitches and the Choir Diapason the eight-foot — a combination which can be brightened by the addition of the Choir Octave.

On some organs it is advantageous, for the loudest climaxes, to transpose the entire Great up by means of the superoctave coupler and unison release, the subsidiary manuals being coupled at unison, and perhaps at superoctave, pitch. Lacking intramanual couplers on the Great, the same

[6]E.g.: 'Lento' from Widor's *Seventh Symphony*; 'Prelude on Rhosymedre' by Vaughan Williams, middle section. See pp. 302-3.

effect can be obtained by playing an octave higher and substituting suboctave and unison intermanual couplers for the normal unison and superoctave couplers, respectively.

Use of Couplers for Small Combinations

In small combinations the use of octave couplers, with or without unison releases, provides a whole new series of effects in which the four-foot stops, or more rarely the sixteen-foot stops, serve as fundamentals; or the eight-foot stops can function as four- or sixteen-foot stops. In the following examples, which are merely suggestive, the transpositions are mentioned without specifying the particular couplers used:

A four-foot string can be provided by transposing a Salicional, Aeoline, or Dulciana. This combination will tie up two manuals unless the same manual has a suitable sixteen-foot stop to serve at eight-foot pitch.

The Gemshorn 8', frequently found on the Great, is often useful at four-foot pitch when the Octave would be too brilliant. Occasionally the sixteen-foot diapason is light enough to be used as the eight-foot fundamental.

Combinations based on a four-foot fundamental, transposed down, are often useful where the range of the music permits. They are apt to be brighter, lighter, and more refined than similar combinations based on eight-foot stops; they give a subtle tonal variety, and often provide a more satisfactory balance for the accompaniment of solo stops. A few examples are: the substitution of the Octave 4' for the Diapason 8' on the Swell or Choir, perhaps brightened by the addition of the two-foot (becoming four-foot) flute; the substitution of the four- and two-foot flutes for the eight- and four-foot flute combination, which usually involves a change of type and balance; the preceding substitution with the addition of a Violina 4', which takes the place of the less delicate Salicional in the normal combination; etc., etc.

Varying shades of color or balance may be effected by combining with stops normally associated with another manual. For example: The Swell may have a Gedeckt 8' and a Harmonic Flute 4', and the Choir a harmonic Concert Flute 8' and a Rohrflöte 4' or a Flûte d'Amour 4'. By coupling the two manuals the organist can secure a combination of eight- and four-foot harmonic flutes, or one of eight- and four-foot stopped flutes. Again, if the Choir Rohrflöte 4' is very soft, it may be used at eight-foot pitch with the Swell Aeoline at four-foot pitch to produce a very delicate effect. Again, if the Swell unfortunately has only a Gedeckt unit for its flute quality, an independent four-foot flute can be obtained by the use of either the eight- or four-foot flute of the Choir.

The application of octave couplers to solo stops and combinations is obvious: as a convenient means of playing a melody in octaves it is particularly useful in orchestral transcriptions; a superoctave coupler with the unison release may be used for a melody which extends beyond the range of the keyboard; a super- or suboctave coupler with the unison release can convert a sixteen- or four-foot stop, respectively, into an eight-foot solo stop; an octave coupler with unison release, or coupling to another manual, may be used to shift the location on the keyboard to facilitate playing on two manuals with one hand.[7]

It is often convenient actually to transpose the notes, instead of making use of an octave coupler. If the music is simple, even a quint mutation may thus be converted into an eight-foot stop.[8]

Pedal Couplers

The use of the pedal couplers, although obviously the same in principle as that of the intermanual couplers, is related to the special functions of the pedal keyboard and the tonal equipment of the pedal department. The addition of the manual resources to those of the pedal, through the couplers, serves the following purposes:

1. To unify the ensemble of which the pedal is a part.[9] In that function the pedal should match the other parts as closely as possible. This involves connecting the entire effective manual combination, including any superoctave couplers, to the pedals.

2. To supplement the resources of the pedal department. The average pedal section is inadequately supplied with metal stops and with upper work. The use of manual to pedal couplers can, to a certain extent, compensate for these lacks. Sometimes even sixteen-foot manual stops are useful on the pedal — not only the soft stops (which on modern organs are usually borrowed into the pedal), but a sixteen-foot diapason or reed. For example, a manual Contrafagotto 16' may be used at eight-foot pitch for somber chords, and at the same time be coupled to the pedal for a sixteen-foot bass. The same stop may supply the sixteen-foot pedal for a small complex ensemble, where the Dulciana 16' would be too small and a bourdon or diapason would be too heavy.

It is obvious that if the manual ensemble, through the pedal couplers, provides the upper work for the sixteen-foot pedal ensemble, there is a duplication of function like that which results from the simultaneous use

---

[7]See p. 347.

[8]The organ which the author played for many years contains a Gemshorn Twelfth on the Choir, which is delightful as a single stop.

[9]Compare p. 100.

of unison and octave manual couplers.[10] If the manual and pedal parts overlap they lose their independence; the pedal part is deprived of its upper work, thereby weakened and rendered dull in quality, so that it does not blend with the ensemble. This problem is encountered in music of the time of Bach, which was written for organs having a more complete pedal division than is ordinarily found on modern instruments.[11] The defect can sometimes be mitigated by omitting one manual from the general ensemble and coupling it, perhaps at both unison and superoctave pitches, to the pedal.

3. To enable the feet to use the manual resources without pedal stops. If a solo melody is to be played on the pedal keyboard (as in Brahms's second setting of 'Herzlich tut mich verlangen', or his 'Schmücke dich, o liebe Seele'[12]), a manual stop or combination is usually selected and coupled to the pedal at unison or superoctave pitch, according to the range of the solo. Again, it is often convenient to play the bass of the manual part with the feet, to supplement the grasp of the hands and provide a better legato, as in the first section of Franck's 'Choral in E'. The same method is often used in the development of a fugue, in order to free one hand to bring out the theme on another manual; or the pedal itself may play the theme. Such a procedure is greatly facilitated if the organ possesses a Pedal Unison Release, controlled by a reversible pedal and also subject to the operation of the general pistons. It is difficult to understand why this valuable device is so seldom included in organ specifications.

In general, the purpose of couplers is to make possible the combination and flexible employment of the resources of various sections of the organ. They do not alter those resources or the principles governing their use; they merely provide added means of controlling them. They are of incalculable value, but are susceptible of abuse. They should be used for a purpose, not merely from habit. Moreover, it should be remembered that the use of octave couplers together with the normal pitch of the same manual adds notes, not stops.

Pistons

The second main group of mechanical accessories, pistons, add nothing of themselves; they merely provide a convenient means of handling the resources of the instrument. Their operation is so familiar that any discussion beyond a few practical suggestions would be superfluous.

[10]See p. 348.
[11]See p. 271.
[12]See pp. 100-101.

Before presenting these suggestions, however, let us go on record concerning the equipment which ought to be provided:

In the first place, there should be more combination pistons than one usually finds. A meager supply of pistons favors stereotyped registration. Eight pistons for each department and from twelve to fifteen general pistons are not too many for an organ of fifty stops.

The pistons should be adjustable by means of a set button. The system which requires that the piston be held in while the stops are changed wastes an enormous amount of time, particularly with a large organ. Fine registration is the result of a considerable amount of experimentation, which naturally precedes the setting of pistons. With the set button system the combination can immediately be assigned to a piston as soon as it is determined. With the other system it must be written down or memorized; then when the piston is pressed the combination previously set on it appears, and stops have to be thrown off as well as added in order to set the new combination.

The manual pistons should affect the intramanual couplers, including the unison release, since they are essential parts of the manual combinations. They should not affect the intermanual couplers, as that would reduce their flexibility, either necessitating frequent changes of setting or limiting the variety of the registration. No couplers, not even the Unison Release, should be affected by the pedal pistons.

The manual pistons should control the pedal stops on a second touch. If properly adjusted the technique of this mechanism is easily acquired, and it has the preëminent advantage of being instantaneously selective. The second touch should not be arbitrarily connected with predetermined pedal combinations, but should control independent pedal combinations set by the second touch itself. If that should be prohibitively expensive with the mechanical system used by the selected builder, a switchboard should be provided whereby any pedal piston could be assigned to the second touch of any manual piston.

When playing an organ on which the control of the pedal combinations by the manual pistons is governed by 'on' and 'off' buttons, it is often advantageous, as a routine procedure, to keep the pedal combinations 'on' the Great pistons and 'off' the others. The adjustment is of course changed for specific situations.

Some of the general combinations should be controlled by toe pistons, so that they can be operated while the hands are busy. The unison manual to pedal couplers should be affected by reversible pedals and pistons. The Solo to Pedal piston control should be duplicated under the Great, since the hands are often on that manual when it needs to be used.

Assignment of Combinations to the Pistons

It is important that the setting of the combination pistons follow some logical plan, to assist the memory and to facilitate a quick adjustment to unanticipated situations. Most of the manual and pedal combinations and, if possible, some of the general combinations (usually those which are controlled by toe pistons) should remain approximately the same. When these combinations are changed, the new combinations should be assigned to those pistons whose usual setting they most nearly resemble. This reduces the danger and seriousness of error, and is particularly necessary when two or more organists play the same instrument. If a special situation (such as the necessity of bringing a combination within reach of a hand which is busy with notes) requires a departure from this practice, a normal setting should immediately be restored as soon as the piston has served its special purpose.

The practice of arranging ensemble combinations in ascending dynamic order is good, and there is great practical value, particularly to the organist playing on a strange console, in holding to this convention. If the number of pistons permits, a quality differentiation may be superimposed on this plan, such as, for example, assigning brighter combinations to the even-numbered pistons, or alternating cohesive and wide-scale combinations.

If possible, one or two pistons in each section, at one end of the row, should be reserved for special or solo combinations. For the Solo manual a majority of the pistons are usually used for solo effects, which, differing little in loudness, call for some other logical arrangement. An excellent plan[13] is to arrange these combinations (which are frequently imitative) in the order of the orchestral score: Flute, Oboe, English Horn, Clarinet, Bassoon, French Horn, Strings. The chorus reeds, being the loudest, are assigned to the last pistons.

It is advantageous to set ensemble combinations on the general toe pistons, since they provide changes of level which are frequently required while the hands are busy. Special combinations for specific places in particular compositions, often involving complicated changes, are more likely to occur at punctuation points where there is time to reach the thumb pistons. Such combinations are of course changed frequently and cannot follow any logical arrangement. Unless there is a practical advantage in having a certain combination in a specific location, these may well follow the order in which they are to be used on the program.

---

[13]Suggested by the late T. Tertius Noble.

Blind Pistons

It can doubtless be assumed that the system of 'blind' combinations is obsolete, except for tuttis and the crescendo pedal; but because of its rarity it may cause trouble to the organist who encounters it for the first time. Such pistons do not move the stop registers and seldom cancel stops which are drawn. Their effect, therefore, is to add their stops to those which are already on. They are released by pressing another piston in the same group, or the cancel (O) piston. This involves an entirely different approach to the use of pistons from that to which most organists are now accustomed.

The advantages and disadvantages of the system result from the fact that the stop registers and combination pistons are independent and simultaneously effective. Whatever stops are drawn remain in the combination, whether they are set on the pistons or not. This involves the following adjustments in the usual registration process:

1. In the dynamic series stops are normally drawn to provide the softest combination, which becomes effective whenever the pistons are cancelled. This softest combination can be adjusted while playing by merely changing the stop registers. It is represented by the 'O' piston; so the *second* combination of the series is set on piston 1, the third on piston 2, etc.

2. An entire series of piston combinations can be colored by drawing one or two stops which, by reason of their timbre or pitch, are sufficiently audible to affect the ensemble. A natural corollary to this is that the retaining of soft stops in loud combinations is encouraged.

3. Any combination of stops which are included in the setting of a piston which is in operation can be prepared while playing, to be instantly effective when the piston is released. Since the combination to be prepared is restricted to the stops which are sounding at the time, the possibilities of this procedure are greatest under large combinations. It is particularly convenient when a tutti or crescendo pedal is in use. Indeed, some organists have advocated the addition of blind manual tutti pistons to our present console equipment.

It is obvious from the foregoing that blind pistons are not adapted to special or solo combinations unless the stop registers are all silent. Their usefulness is largely confined to ensemble combinations.

Under this system it is usual for each manual piston to have its own pedal combination. All these pedal combinations are mutually canceling, so that the piston which is pressed *last* determines the pedal stops which will be effective. It is important to remember this when two or three pistons are used at the same time.

Recording Registration

Since a satisfactory registration is frequently the result of considerable study and experiment, it should be recorded for future reference. Moreover, the organist who does not have time to memorize his registration needs to consult his notes while playing. For this purpose the indications should be not only accurate and unmistakable, but instantly and easily understandable.

It is very important to avoid cluttering the score with unnecessary marks. To be obliged to select from profuse annotations the particular indications to be noted in an instant is confusing and diverts the attention from the music itself.[14] As far as is possible without ambiguity, the shortest and simplest abbreviations should be used. A change in practice will require a brief period of adjustment — one who is accustomed to seeing "Sw." will not so readily recognize "S" as indicating Swell — but as soon as the habit is formed, the advantage of the simplest symbol will be recognized.

Each organist should devise a method suited to his own psychology, but any system should be characterized by clarity, simplicity, consistency, and psychological naturalness. The author's plan is based on the following principles:

1. The use of the fewest possible letters. If there is no ambiguity a single letter will suffice, e.g.: 'G' = Great, 'C' = Choir. If one possible signification is more common than the others, the single letter may be used for the most common, e.g.: 'S' = Swell, 'So' = Solo; 'D' = Diapason, 'Du' = Dulciana.

2. If the name contains two separate words, it is represented by the initial letters in capitals, e.g.: 'EH' = English Horn, 'HF' = Harmonic Flute. Further identification is added only when necessary, e.g.: 'CF' = Concert Flute, 'ChF' = Chimney Flute. If the stop name consists of two words combined in one, the second word is represented by a small letter, e.g.: 'Gh' = Gemshorn, 'Rf' = Rohrflöte.

3. Further identification is made by using the most distinctive letters or syllables, taking into consideration other stops whose names begin with the same letters, e.g.: 'Clr' = Clarion, 'Clb' = Clarabella, 'Clt' or 'Ct' = Clarinet, 'Co' = Cornet, 'Cn' = Cornopean, 'Cp' = Coupler.

The further application of these principles is shown in Appendix III, where a list of abbreviations for the most common registration indications will be found.

---

[14]The same principle applies to fingering and pedaling indications.

Although the foregoing suggestions are the result of many years of experience, they are not to be regarded as final or of universal application. Each organist will work out his own system, based on his individual technique and mental approach. Whatever method will, in the long run, give him the most complete and intuitive command of his instrument is best for him. The essential requirements are an unimpeded execution and an easy control of the mechanics of the instrument, so that the interpretation will sound natural and convincing.

CHAPTER SIXTEEN

CONCLUSION

Retrospect

At the beginning of our study we noted the influence of fashion, familiarity, habit, inattention, and even sensationalism, on the registration practices of many organists. We set about to evolve a theory of registration which would give direction to the player's thinking, stimulate his imagination, and increase the sensitivity of his judgments. We examined acoustical phenomena and sought to relate them to the musical material. The results of this study were then applied to the interpretation of different types of organ composition, taking into consideration the content, the various expressive and structural elements, and the instruments for which the music was conceived.

The fundamental principles of interpretative registration are, we found, simple in themselves, but their application to specific compositions involves countless ramifications. Every aspect of the music must have its share in determining the result. Often the individual considerations are mutually corroborative, but sometimes the requirements of different features are in conflict, and a compromise in just balance has to be effected. Each piece presents a new problem which cannot be solved by rule, but must be analyzed and its elements weighed by the performer.

The Problem of the Small Organ

The application of the principles developed in the foregoing chapters is greatly complicated by the varied characteristics of the organs on which the music is to be performed — particularly faults of design and the inevitable limitations of small instruments. It must be evident to the reader who has had the patience to arrive at this point that fairly complete specifications, providing a balanced ensemble, are essential to an adequate interpretation of a large proportion of the significant organ works. It is as impossible to give a correct impression of Bach's great 'Prelude and Fugue in B minor', or Widor's *Symphonie Gothique*, on a small organ which lacks mutations and mixtures, or which depends on unification for pitch variety, as it would be to produce the effect of a Mozart or Brahms symphony with a quartet of brass instruments.

There has always been prevalent a vicious notion that the size of an organ should depend on the size of the auditorium; that an organ in a small room should have few stops. People do not realize that the need of a large number of stops is not primarily for power, but for variety and quality of ensemble. Obviously the scaling and voicing of the pipes

359

must be suited to the acoustical characteristics of the auditorium, but the number of stops, up to a point of completeness, should be limited only by the maximum amount of money and space which can be provided.[1]

All this is poor comfort to the organist who plays an instrument of fifteen or twenty stops and is baffled by the discussion of various types of ensemble and the recommendations which assume a variety and completeness of tonal resources which he does not have at his disposal. Under such conditions an ideal registration is seldom possible, but the organist can still have in mind the type of ensemble which the music calls for, and work in that direction. All instruments have their weak features, and success is a relative matter.

On a small organ the possibilities of synthetic color are very limited. If there is no mutation stop, nothing can be done about it.[2] A single Twelfth or Nasard can contribute color to various combinations. If it is in tune, the addition of a superoctave coupler will simulate a mixture. Even in the absence of any mutation stop, the organist can still control the balance of octave pitches, adjusting it to the type of material or the mood of the music.

It is a mistake to assume that the limitations of a small organ necessitate the use of all its resources, including couplers, for a fortissimo. All combinations should be selective, and it is important, even on the smallest organ, to omit undesirable elements. For example, a low flute adds bulk at the expense of vitality; its effect is particularly objectionable in a small instrument, because of the dearth of compensatory upper work. Again, the suboctave couplers often actually detract from the effective power, adding only weight and muddiness. In many cases the Great Diapason 8' and Octave alone, with the Swell Oboe and Flute 4' coupled at superoctave pitch (perhaps omitting the unison coupler) will provide a more effective full organ than the full Crescendo Pedal. If richness is desired, the Swell to Great suboctave coupler can be added, possibly substituting the Swell Salicional for the Oboe.

The superoctave couplers play a very important part in registration on a very small organ. The duplication which results from using the same stops at more than one pitch, though a defect in itself, is a lesser evil than the slighting of upper work. Moreover, a better balance can often be secured by omitting the unison coupler, which at the same time eliminates the duplication. By choosing only the qualities and pitches which contribute to the desired effect, and taking advantage of the

---

[1] Compare p. 65.

[2] Lynnwood Farnam was said to have improved the ensemble of an organ by merely shifting the pipes of a small diapason to provide a Twelfth, or converting a two-foot flute into a Nasard or Tierce. Obviously the latter would require retuning.

flexibility afforded by couplers of different pitches, a small organ can often be made to sound surprisingly well.[3]

On the other hand, the presence of a reasonable amount of upper work in the specifications does not in itself assure the ingredients needed for the composition of a good ensemble, or for varied synthetic color. Some builders, in a worthy effort to reproduce the classic instruments of the past, have occasionally stressed high ranks as a means of loudness and brilliance. The ensemble is neither balanced nor cohesive; refinement is lacking; subtlety is impossible. For richness, beauty of color, shading, and nicety of adjustment to the interpretative requirements of the music, there must be provided many voices which do not assert their own individuality, but make characteristic contributions to the composite sound. We have insisted on the imperative need of high ranks, but if they are coarse and noisy they fail to serve their purpose.

The Organist's Equipment

However valid may be the principles and methods expounded in this book, their successful application depends on the taste, skill, and resourcefulness of the organist. In addition to an adequate technique and thorough musicianship, including a complete understanding of music theory and a wide knowledge of music history, the following qualities are essential:

1. Intuition; artistic perception. The organist must be able to sense what is important in the music and to see how it can be brought out in the registration.

2. Imagination — the ability to auralize the music in its most effective tone quality, and to devise mentally a registration which will approach that quality, anticipating the various related problems.

3. A sensitive and discriminating ear, enabling him to appraise and to improve the effect produced.

4. Ingenuity — the ability to devise combinations which meet the multiple and sometimes contradictory demands of the musical material; to make stop changes natural and consistent with the musical development; to master the complex technical problems involved in combining the manipulation of stop controls with the execution of the music; to contrive practical methods of securing effects which are beyond the normal resources of the instrument.

---

[3]The author once supplied in a small church near his summer home during the vacation of the regular organist. The organ was diminutive, but amply equipped with couplers and pistons. He at once set up, according to the method suggested above, a series of routine ensemble combinations. The effect of the organ was transformed. It was interesting to return the following summer and find the pistons unchanged!

5. Versatility — the ability to adapt his methods to different styles and situations.

6. Open-mindedness. In no other field of artistic endeavor is the performer more dependent on the advice of others. The most experienced organist is susceptible to error in judging the effect of his registration on the listener. While holding uncompromisingly to his artistic convictions, his realization of them must be subject to correction.

The Organist's Procedure

Possessing these qualities, the organist will proceed first of all to study the music which he is to interpret, acquainting himself with every feature of the material and organization. If he has not already done so, he will learn all he can about the composer and his historical and national setting, and about the type of instrument for which the music was written; about the kind of occasion for which it was intended, and its function in the service or program; about the acoustical characteristics of the auditorium in which it was expected to be played, and about the style of execution with which the composer was familiar.

He will also study his own instrument, becoming thoroughly familiar with its resources and learning how to use them to the best advantage; appraising its defects and discovering how he can most effectively conceal or compensate for them. If the organ is in the early twentieth century American tradition, he will seek the best means of lightening the fundamentals, adding upper pitches, and unifying the whole. If it is a modern "Baroque" organ he has the opposite problem of providing enough fundamental and intermediate pitches to balance the upper work. In any case the most perfect solution depends on subtle adjustments which require an intimate acquaintance with the individual instrument.

To all this he will add a study of the acoustical characteristics of his auditorium in their bearing on the composition of the ensemble, the balance of the different sections of the instrument, the balance between the organ and the choir which he may be accompanying or the congregation which he may be leading, and many other matters which cannot be unerringly determined at the console.

The Function of the Music to be Played

The interpretation will also be affected by the function of the music in the service, or its place on a recital program. For example, Brahms's last chorale prelude, 'O Welt, ich muss dich lassen', will be given a quiet registration, calm and contemplative, if it is played as an offertory; if played as a postlude it will be given strength and solidity, expressive of the Christian's confidence on entering his "ewge Vaterland." Again, tonal effects may be used at a recital or concert which would not be suited to a service of worship. Handel's concertos, for example, were written for concert performance and invite a treatment which would sound trivial in the church service. The same compositions may suitably be played in church, particularly on a festive occasion, provided the registration is restrained.

In this connection it should be observed that the function of church music is to deepen the experience of worship. Anything which is purely entertaining diverts the attention of the congregation from the primary purpose of the service. This does not mean that the music should not be attractive, or that the mood should be somber. Man worships through beauty, and there is a wide range of religious moods, from the Passion of Good Friday to the triumph of Easter and the joy of Christmas. Any performance which is consistent with the spirit of the service of which it is a part and fits into the psychological sequence of the program can contribute effectively to the devotions of the congregation; but anything which suggests triviality or secularism has no place in ·a service of worship.[4]

The Plan of a Program

In planning the registration of individual works in their relation to the whole program of a recital or concert the organist is guided by considerations of sequence and balance. The psychological aspect of the registration of successive materials was discussed in connection with our study of cyclical forms.[5]

Since the registration is mainly determined by the material, an effective succession of tone qualities is dependent on the succession of musical styles, moods, etc. A program should be planned like a cyclical work. If it is arranged in groups, the relation of the individual pieces within each group should be the same as among movements of a sonata or suite, providing contrast and consistency. Each group should have its own individuality, different from all the others. The larger break between the groups provides opportunity for greater contrast than can suitably be introduced within a group. Even exotic material can thus be introduced without too much shock, while other groups provide a normal balance.[6]

In general, a program which is effectively arranged from the standpoint of musical material will provide opportunity for a suitable sequence of tone qualities, but this result is not inevitable. In planning the

[4]Compare pp. 221-2.
[5]Pp. 209 ff.
[6]See pp. 153-4.

registration of any movement it is important to keep the whole program in mind, so as to avoid monotony, too much repetition of similar sound, fatigue resulting from excessive use of exotic or harsh qualities, and the shock of the justaposition of incongruous effects. To this end the organist will take advantage of whatever latitude may be possible in the choice of registration without doing violence to the music. However, in order to avoid impairing the perfection and naturalness of the interpretation, the registration should enter into the original planning of the program.

The Effect on the Listener

It is a truism that music exists to be heard, and that the primary purpose of a musical performance is to enable the listener to hear what the composer had to say. The performance is justified, then, by its effect on the audience. Every interpretative process must be evaluated from that standpoint. This must not be interpreted as a sanction of cheap showmanship and extravagant effects: we are concerned not with the thrill which the listener may experience, but with the fidelity of the impression which he receives.

In order to adjust his playing to the reaction of the listener, the organist must take into account the difference between the effect heard by the player and that heard by an inactive hearer. The player knows the music better than the listener. He can hear every detail without its being made aurally evident. He knows the unexpected turns in the music, and his mind is ready for them when they come. He anticipates the interpretative effects which he has planned, so that they seem natural to him. He often hears what he thinks he is doing when it actually does not happen.[7]   The listener, on the other hand, needs to have important features brought to his attention; he needs time to adjust his mind to changes in the music and in the registration. It is the problem of the organist to provide this assistance to the listener without interfering with the continuity and balance of the interpretation.

It follows from this that the manner of presentation may vary with the taste and intelligence of the audience and its familiarity with the composition. It is not necessary to make concessions to vulgar taste, but the music should be made as attractive as possible without compromising artistic ideals. A more obvious interpretation may be offered to the uninitiated than to the connoisseur, but it should never do violence to the character and spirit of the music. It is better to limit the selection of music played than to give a distorted impression of great works which the audience is incapable of enjoying in a legitimate interpretation. We

---

[7]Who has not had the embarrassment of discovering that some stop which he had drawn and thought he had been hearing, actually was not working?

may lead the public partway up the mountain and reveal an inspiring, if limited, landscape; but we must not reduce the mountain to the level of the valley.

Supreme Importance of Taste

In the end we come back to the preëminent importance of the organist's own taste. This should be the object of his constant study, examining the influences which have entered into its formation, comparing it with the taste of others, and checking it with theoretical criteria.

Taste is inevitably influenced by habit: that which is familiar seems normal, and the ear becomes insensitive to its defects. If an organist has acquired the habit of exaggeration, in any direction, his point of reference shifts off center, and his whole tonal perspective becomes distorted. Thus the organist of the early twentieth century who, trying to think in orchestral terms, made constant use of highly colored stops, found the diapason quality flat and prosaic. On the other side he could not produce a special tonal effect because he was constantly using tonal superlatives. Similarly some of our "Baroque" enthusiasts seem to have become so accustomed to the sound of high pitches that their ears are insensitive to them; qualities seem normal to them which others find harsh and screechy.

There will always be conflicting tastes, and uniformity is not to be desired. The purpose of this book is not to establish a pattern into which all registration must fit, but to suggest standards of comparison; to call attention to considerations which are often overlooked; to stimulate an awareness of the complex relation of tone quality to interpretation; to encourage a sensitiveness to subtle effects; to discourage exaggeration, artificiality, and prejudice; and above all to urge the practice of attentive, discriminative, objective, critical listening. No more suitable conclusion can be found than the oft-repeated admonition of Widor: "Écoutez-vouz bien!" – to which he would usually add, "Les organistes ne s'écoutent jamais."[8]

---

[8]"Listen to yourself attentively! – Organists never listen to themselves." The last sentence is quoted from his book, *Technique de l'Orchestre Moderne*, p. 182.

APPENDIXES

APPENDIX I

DESCRIPTION OF ANALYSES

Although the actual analyses represented by the graphs in Chapter II were made in a short period of time, they were preceded by years of experiment under varying conditions. The preliminary problem was to determine how we could secure results which would most accurately and effectively represent the distinctive tonal characteristics of the different organ stops.

Measurements of the tone as picked up in the organ chamber or auditorium proved very erratic, because of standing wave resonance and phase differences. Only when the microphone was placed very near the source of sound did the results appear to possess any validity. Because of this complication the greater part of the experiments were conducted in the physics laboratory, using the sound treated room described by Paul A. Northrop in Bibl. 33. Even there the analyses were made with the microphone near the end or mouth of the pipe, in order that the relative strength of the standing waves (which the sound treatment did not completely eliminate) might be reduced to a negligible quantity. Tests made with the apparatus in different positions indicated that this result actually was attained.

Since, in general, the most characteristic qualities are found in the middle section of an eight-foot rank, nearly all our measurements were made in that range. Moreover, preliminary experiments revealed such close correspondence among the analyses of different pipes of the same set that there seemed to be no advantage in using more than one, or at most, two, pipes of each rank for the final record. Indeed, we thought it desirable to analyze the different qualities with as little time lapse as possible, so that the conditions would be identical, and comparison would have the maximum validity.

The pipes chosen for the final analyses gave a pitch near a^1 (= 440), the selection being made on the basis of dependable speech and characteristic quality. For harmonic pipes, one of the lowest double-length pipes was used. The tone was picked up by an Altec Model 21B microphone (rated flat up to 15,000 cycles), made by the Altec-Lansing Corporation. Measurements were made on a Hewlett-Packard Harmonic Wave Analyzer, Model 300A. No intermediate amplification was introduced beyond the unit belonging with the microphone. To assure clear readings for the soft pipes and avoid overloading from the loud ones, the distance from the pipe to the microphone varied with the intensity of the tone, ranging from 1/4" to 2 5/8". For the analysis of open and reed pipes the microphone was placed near the end of the pipe, in line with the axis; for stopped pipes, near the mouth, in front and slightly above; for the Rohrflöte, at the end of the chimney; and for capped reeds, near the slot.

The pipes studied were, for the most part, taken from the organ in the Vassar College chapel – a hybrid instrument originally built by Hutchings-Votey in 1904, rebuilt by the Aeolian Company, 1927-9, and partially revoiced (diapasons and chorus reeds), under the guidance of J. B. Jamison, by Austin Organs, Inc., in 1939. It may be considered a normal organ, possessing neither the tubbiness which was characteristic of American voicing in the first quarter of this century, nor the extreme brilliance of some modern "Baroque" instruments. Most of the stops analyzed were a part of the original organ, and were later revoiced; those represented by graphs IX, XXV, and XXVII were made by the Aeolian Company and never revoiced; those represented by graphs II, XX, and XXII were made by Austin Organs, Inc. The following graphs represent pipes which were loaned by Austin Organs, Inc.: XVI (Willis), XX (Austin), XXI (Cavaillé-Coll), XXII (Austin).

It is obviously impracticable to describe all the details of voicing which produced the qualities analyzed, but certain observations are recorded on pages 372 and 373. It may interest the reader to study the analyses presented on pages 50-55 with reference to these structural characteristics. Complete correlation must await more exhaustive research. Here we will call attention to only a few notable points:

Comparing graphs I and II, observe the effect of the narrow scale and spotted metal in producing a brighter tone in II.

Comparing III and IV, observe the greater prominence which the more tapered pipe gives to the second partial. This seems to corroborate Ernest M. Skinner's initial contention that his Erzähler sounded the fundamental and its octave with equal strength.

The effect of narrow scales on the strings is obvious.

It is interesting to note that the Harmonic Flute contains a weak subfundamental (which would be the fundamental if the pipe were not harmonic) with its partials.

The presence of weak even partials in the Gedeckt was mentioned on page 37.

In the Rohrflöte note the tone of the chimney between the fifth and sixth partials.

Observe the prominence of the odd partials in the Triangular Flute.

The English Horn (though unimitative) is colored by prominent second and third partials.

The Clarinet shows the expected emphasis on the odd partials, but the conical section of its resonator provides a noticeable proportion of even partials.

The following table gives a striking comparison of the analyses of the chorus reeds:

TABLE 6

COMPARISON OF EIGHT-FOOT CHORUS REEDS

Showing the relative strength of selected partials
in percent of the total sound*

PARTIALS	TRUMPET	HARMONIC TRUMPET	TROMPETTE	CAVAILLÉ-COLL TROMPETTE	BOMBARDE
Fundamental	19.5	20.25	16.1	12.45	8.4
First four partials (through 2′ pitch)	64.3	76.05	45.11	33.91	30.1
First five partials (through tierce)	78.5	87.55	52.66	39.91	38.95
First eight partials (through 1′ pitch)	93.52	95.29	76.6	64.13	64.8
Above one-foot pitch	6.48	4.71	23.4	35.87	35.2

*Computed from pressure readings

The following tables show the principal structural characteristics of the pipes analyzed:

FLUE PIPES

Graph	Pitch	Diameter	Mouth	Cut up	Material	Slotted?	Wind
I	G# (415)	1 5/8″	2/9	1/3	metal	yes	6″
II	G# (415)	1 3/8″	1/5	1/3	s m[1]	yes	6″
III	A (440)	1 7/32″[2] 11/16″	2/9	1/3[4]	s m	yes	6″
IV	A (440)	1 7/32″[2] 7/16″	1/5	1/4[4]	s m	yes	4″
V	A (440)	15/16″	2/9	1/3	s m	yes	4″
VI	A (440)	29/32″	2/9	1/3	s m	yes	4″
VII	A (440)	15/16″	2/9[3]	1/3	s m	yes	6″
VIII	G# (415)	1″	2/9[3]	1/3	s m	yes	6″
IX	A (440)	11/16″	2/9[3]	1/3	s m	yes	6″
X	A# (466)	1 11/32″[5]	1 5/32″	1/4	wood	no	6″
XI	G# (415)	1 5/32″[5]	29/32″[6]	2/7	wood	no	6″
XII	A (440) B (494)	1 11/16″ } 1 5/8″ }	2/9	1/3	metal	yes	6″
XIII	D (587)	1 1/2″	2/9	1/3	metal	yes	6″
XIV	A (440)	31/32″[5]	13/16″	1/2″	wood	no	4″
XV	A# (466)	1 2/3″	2/11+	1/3[4]	metal[7]	no	4″
XVI	C (523)	1 1/2″[5]	1 1/4″[6]	2/7	wood	no	5″
XVII	G (392)	1 1/8″	1/4[3]	2/7	metal	no	6″

[1] s m = spotted metal.
[2] Tapered pipe. Measurements show diameter at the mouth and the end, respectively.
[3] Bearded.   [4] Upper lip rounded (arched).
[5] For wood pipes the depth, or inside measurement of the sides, is given under 'Diameter'.
[6] Inverted mouth.   [7] Length of chimney = c. 2/5 length of pipe.

REED PIPES

Graph	Pitch	Diameter at top	Form of Resonator	Slotted?	Shallot	Wind
XVIII	A (440)	2 ⁹⁄₃₂″	straight taper	yes	normal	6″
XIX	D (587)	2 ⁹⁄₁₆″	straight taper double length	yes	normal	6″
XX	C (262)	1⅞″	straight taper	yes	narrow parallel [8] bevel 45°	4″
XXI	C (262)	2 ¾″	straight taper	no	narrow French [9] wide opening	4″
XXII	C (262)	3⅛″	straight taper	yes	large parallel wide opening bevel 45°	4″
XXIII	F# (370)	1 ¹⁵⁄₁₆″	broken taper slender 9 ¹¹⁄₁₆″ flare 5½″	yes	normal	6″
XXIV	F (349)	1⅜″	straight taper	yes	narrow open slight bevel	4″
XXV	A (440)	1 ¹⁵⁄₁₆″	broken taper slender 7¾″ flare 2 ⁹⁄₁₆″ capped	yes	narrow cylindrical	10″
XXVI	C# (277)	1⅛″	conical 2¾″ cylindrical 10⅝″	no	normal	4″
XXVII	F (349)	2 ¹⁄₃₂″	straight taper capped	yes	large filled in ⅜″	10″

[8] Cylindrical with parallel opening.
[9] Parallel shallot with dome (rounded) head.

APPENDIX II

ORCHESTRAL EFFECTS

Bearing in mind the observations in Chapter XIII concerning the limited effectiveness of imitative registration, the following table of orchestral qualities may be useful:

Orchestration	Organ Substitute
Flute	Harmonic Flute, or Orchestral Flute May be reinforced, if necessary, by nonimitative flutes, gedeckts, flute 4', or even French Horn; but plurality of stops impairs the imitation.
Piccolo	High flute
Oboe	Orchestral Oboe, or imitative English Horn. Oboe, or unimitative English Horn, colored by Nasard, Quintadena, or thin string Thin string with Quintadena or Nasard, possibly plus flute 4'
English Horn	Same as Oboe, perhaps modified Strings, if used, should be more mellow.
Clarinet	Clarinet, with or without Gedeckt 8' Nasard may sometimes be added. Gedeckt and mild string, with Nasard or Quintadena
Bassoon	Unimitative English Horn Oboe, colored by Nasard or Quintadena
Wood Wind (fluty)	Clarinet and/or Concert (Harmonic) Flute 8' Flute 4' may perhaps be added.
Wood Wind (reedy)	Clarinet with or without flute 4' May be colored or reinforced by Oboe, mutations, etc. Unimitative English Horn, Oboe, or similar reed, modified as may be necessary
Horn (soft)	French Horn Unimitative flute, such as Melodia Unimitative English Horn and flute
Horn (loud)	Combine above and/or use louder round reed or diapason
Trumpet	Trumpet, bright Tuba, or other clear, incisive chorus reed
Trombone (soft)	Waldhorn, or other smooth chorus reed, with swell closed Chorus reed modified by unimitative flute or round diapason, with swell closed
Trombone (loud)	Similar to preceding, using brighter reed, with swell open
Tuba	Lower range of smooth chorus reed
Brass Ensemble	Chorus reeds 8', or 8' & 16'

Orchestration	Organ Substitute
Celesta, or Glockenspiel	Celesta (Harp) Flutes 8' & 4', or 8' & 2', possibly colored by Quintadena or mutation Celesta, reinforced by light flutes and/or mutations
Single notes	Flutes 8' & 2', possibly colored by mutation or Quintadena, with tremolo, or Quintadena 8' and flute 2', with tremolo In both cases the effect is produced by playing an octave, the upper note *staccatissimo*, the lower note held. A swell pedal accent may be added.
Harp (pianissimo)	Harp, or Celesta, or both May be reinforced by soft flute 8', or 4', or both.
Harp (normal)	Substitute organ effect, probably using flutes of various pitches and mutations. Harp and Celesta may be included.
Piano	Substitute organ effect, according to material.
Harpsichord	Same as piano, keeping fundamental light and combination cohesive, except that flute 4' and/or 2' may be needed for clarity in florid style
Kettle Drum	Wood diapason or large Bourdon 16', played staccato
Roll (forte)	Same, with half-step trill, in lower octave Same, played in tremolo with upper octave Same, sustaining two or three adjacent notes in lower octave
Roll (piano)	Soft Bourdon 16', sustaining single note, or two or three adjacent notes, in lower octave
Bass Drum	Wood diapason, single low note, or two or three adjacent low notes, played staccato
Strings (for color)	
Violin solo	String céleste Same, with light Gedeckt 8', perhaps with tremolo Oboe may possibly be added.
High range	Rather thin string with tremolo (without céleste)
G string	String céleste, Gedeckt 8', Vox Humana, and tremolo
Harmonics	Flute at sounding pitch
Violins (tutti)	String célestes, soft Geigen or small diapason Light Gedeckt 8' and/or Oboe may be added or substituted for Geigen or diapason. The same, without Geigen or diapason, perhaps with tremolo, for single melody
Violins (divisi)	String céleste with sub- and superoctave couplers A 4' string may be added. A 16' string may be substituted for the suboctave coupler.
Violas	Same as Violins, using mellower strings

Orchestration   Organ Substitute

Strings (for color)

  'Cello solo   'Cello Céleste, or Gamba Céleste
                     String céleste, light Gedeckt 8', Oboe and/or Vox Humana,
                     with tremolo

  'Cellos (tutti)   Same as preceding, perhaps using a Geigen or thin dia-
                     pason, without tremolo

  String Ensemble   8' strings with célestes, Geigen or small diapason, etc.,
                     without tremolo

Strings (not for color) Organ ensemble, suited to the character of the music,
                     keeping color bright and as warm as the material will
                     permit

Strings and Wood   Include Clarinet (if suitable) and/or Oboe, or possibly un-
  Wind   imitative English Horn, and fairly prominent mutations.

Wood Wind and Brass Predominant reeds at various pitches, with flutes, muta-
                     tions, and mixtures; Clarinet may be included, and
                     possibly English Horn or Orchestral Oboe at four-foot
                     pitch.

Full Orchestra   Full organ ensemble
                     If the brass dominates the orchestra, use brilliant reeds
                     and many mutations and mixtures, avoiding too much
                     flue tone at lower pitches.

APPENDIX III

REGISTRATION ABBREVIATIONS

Suggested abbreviations and signs for use in registration indications are given below. The list is not intended to be exhaustive. The recent interest in instruments of the past and the attempt to reproduce many Baroque features in modern organs have resulted in the addition of a large number of stop names, most of which are German or French. There is no need to include all such stops, some of which may not find a permanent place in the American organ. The list provides for the most common requirements; other abbreviations can easily be devised by the method suggested on page 357.

Keyboards

G = Great   So = Solo   Rp = Ruckpositiv
S = Swell   E = Echo   Bw = Brustwerk
C = Choir   Po = Positiv   Bb = Bombarde

P = Pedal

Adjustments

At the beginning of a section or phrase:

S ◁───── = Swell open   S ─────▷ = Swell closed

S ◁─┤, S ──┤──, S ───┤▷ = Swell 1/4, 1/2, 3/4 open, respectively

The same indications preceded by 'C' or 'So' indicate the position of the Choir or Solo shades. Similar signs within a phrase signify a crescendo or diminuendo with the particular shades specified.

Combinations

Cr = Crescendo Pedal

Tt = Tutti

Sz or Sfz = Sforzando

G⑤ = Great piston, number 5

G⑤P or G⑤+ = Great piston, number 5, with its pedal combination (through second touch or 'on' button)

⑤ or Gn⑤ = General piston, number 5

Cp⑤ or K⑤ = Coupler piston, number 5

Couplers

SG = Swell to Great

CP = Choir to Pedal

SoS = Solo to Swell

CG4 or CG-sp = Choir to Great superoctave

SS4 or SS-sp = Swell to Swell superoctave

SG16 or SG-sb = Swell to Great suboctave

SU, PU, etc. = Swell unison release, Pedal unison release, etc.

Stops

A or Ae	= Aeoline		EH	= English Horn
			Ez	= Erzähler
BH	= Basset Horn			
Bs	= Bassoon		Fg	= Fagotte
Bf	= Blockflöte		Ff	= Fernflöte
Bb	= Bombarde		Fi	= Fife
B or Bd	= Bourdon		15	= Fifteenth
			Flg	= Flageolet
Car	= Carillon		Fno	= Flautino
Ca	= Celesta		FA	= Flauto d'Amore,
C	= Céleste. In combination:			Flûte d'Amour
	FC, GhC, VlC, etc.		FD	= Flauto Dolce
Vc	= 'Cello (Violoncello)		FT	= Flauto Traverso,
ChF	= Chimney Flute			Flûte Traversière
ChB	= Choral Bass		F	= Flute
Clb	= Clarabella		Fs 8, 4	= 8' and 4' Flutes
Ct, Clt, or Cnt	= Clarinet		FCh	= Flûte à Cheminée
Clr	= Clarion		FCo	= Flûte Conique
CF	= Concert Flute		FH	= Flûte Harmonique
Cb	= Contrabass		FTg	= Flûte Triangulaire
CBd	= Contra Bourdon		Fnt	= Fourniture
Cfg	= Contrafagotto		FrH	= French Horn
Cp	= Contraposaune		FrT	= French Trumpet
Cpa	= Copula		Fu	= Fugara
CA	= Cor Anglais			
CN	= Cor de Nuit		Gb	= Gamba
Co	= Cornet		Gbt	= Gambette
CnB	= Corno di Bassetto		G or Gd	= Gedeckt
Cn	= Cornopean		GP	= Gedeckt Pommer
Cp or K	= Coupler		Gg	= Geigen
Crm	= Cromorne, Cormorne		Gh	= Gemshorn
Cmb	= Cymbal		GC	= Grand Cornet
			GM	= Grave Mixture
D	= Diapason		GN, Gn	= Gros Nasard,
1D, 2D, 3D	= First, Second,			Grossnasat
	Third Diapason		Gf	= Grossflöte
Ds 8-2	= Diapason, Octave,			
	Twelfth, Fifteenth		HA	= Harmonia Aetheria
MD	= Metal Diapason		H	= Harmonic. In combina-
WD	= Wood Diapason			tion: HF, HPc, HT, etc.
Dph	= Diaphone		Hs	= Harmonics
Dcn	= Dolcan		Hp	= Harp
Dc	= Dolce		Hb	= Hautboy, Hautbois (= Ob)
DC	= Dolce Cornet		Hf	= Hohlflöte
Dpf	= Doppelflöte		Hn	= Horn
D16 or DD	= Double Diapason		HnD	= Horn Diapason
Dbt	= Doublette			
Dct	= Dulcet		Ke or Kp	= Keraulophone
Du	= Dulciana		Ki	= Kinura
			KEz	= Kleiner Erzähler
E	= Echo. In combination:		Kg or Kgd	= Kleingedeckt
	EB, ED, EV1, etc.			

Kf = Koppelflöte
Kh = Krummhorn
La, Lr, or Lg = Larigot
Lb or Lbd = Lieblichbordun
Lf = Lieblichflöte
Lg or Lgd = Lieblichgedeckt
Ml or Md = Melodia
M or Mx = Mixture
Mtr = Montre
Ms or Mus = Musette
Mu or Mt = Mutation
MuV = Muted Viol
Nh = Nachthorn
N = Nasard, Nasat
NF, Nf = Nason Flute,
Nasonflöte
O or Ob = Oboe
8v or Oc = Octave. In combina-
tion: 8vGg, OcO, etc.
8vn or Ocn = Octavin
Or = Orchestral. In com-
bination: OrF, OrHn,
OrO, etc.
Pm = Philomela
Pc = Piccolo
PJ = Plein Jeu
Ps = Posaune
Pt = Prestant
P or Pr = Principal
Q = Quint
Qd = Quintadena, Quintade
Qt = Quintaten, Quintatön
Rk = Rankett
Rq = Rauschquinte
R = Reed
Rg = Regal
Rf = Rohrflöte
Rsm = Rohrschalmei
Sct = Salicet
S, Sa, or Sl = Salicional
Sm = Schalmei
Sf = Scharf
7e, Spt, or 21 = Septième

Sq = Sesquialtera
17 = Seventeenth
Sif = Sifflöte
Spl = Spillflöte
Spz = Spitzflöte
SD = Stopped Diapason
SuF = Suabe Flute
Sb = Sub
Sp = Super
10 = Tenth
Tz = Terz
Tib = Tibia
TCl = Tibia Clausa
Ti or 17 = Tierce
TF = Traverse Flute
Tr = Tremolo
TgF = Triangular Flute
Tba = Tromba
Tbn or Tbo = Trombone
Tpe = Trompette
T or Tp = Trumpet
Tu = Tuba
TuM = Tuba Mirabilis
12 = Twelfth
UM = Unda Maris
Us = Untersatz
Vl = Viol, Viole
Va = Viola
VA or VdA = Viola d'Amore,
Viole d'Amour
VGb or Gb = Viola da Gamba
VO or VdO = Viole d'Orchestre
Vn = Violin
VD or VnD = Violin Diapason
Vna = Violina
Vc = Violoncello
Vne = Violone
VC = Voix Céleste
VA = Vox Angelica
VH = Vox Humana
Wf = Waldflöte
Wh or Whn = Waldhorn
Zf = Zauberflöte
Zb = Zimbel
Zk = Zink

BIBLIOGRAPHY

BIBLIOGRAPHY

A. Technical Works

1. Anderson, S. H., and Ostensen, F. C. 'Effect of Frequency on the End Correction of Pipes', *The Physical Review*, Feb., 1928, 267-74.

2. Bartholomew, W. T. *Acoustics of Music.* New York: Prentice-Hall, 1942.

3. Bate, A. E. 'Determination of the End Correction and Conductance at the Mouth of a Stopped Organ (Flue) Pipe', *The London, Edinburgh and Dublin Philosophical Magazine and Journal of Science*, Jan., 1930, 23-28.

4. ———. 'The End Corrections of an Open Organ Flue Pipe and the Acoustical Conductance of Orifices', *ibid.*, Oct., 1930, 617-32.

5. Boner, C. P. 'Acoustical Spectra of Organ Pipes', *The Journal of the Acoustical Society of America*, July, 1938, 32-40.

6. Brown, G. B. 'The Mechanism of Edge Tone Production', *The Proceedings of the Physical Society* (London), Sept., 1937, 508-52.

7. ———. 'Organ Pipes and Edge Tones', *Nature* (London), Jan. 1, 1938, 11-13.

8. ———. 'The Vortex Motion Causing Edge Tones', *The Proceedings of the Physical Society* (London), Sept., 1937, 493-507.

9. Culver, C. A. *Musical Acoustics.* 2nd ed. Philadelphia: The Blakiston Co., 1947.

10. Fletcher, Harvey. 'Auditory Patterns', *Reviews of Modern Physics*, Jan., 1940, 47-65.

11. ———. 'Loudness, Masking and their Relation to the Hearing Process and the Problem of Noise Measurement', *The Journal of the Acoustical Society of America*, April, 1938, 275-93. .

12. ———. 'Loudness, Pitch and the Timbre of Musical Tones and their Relation to the Intensity, the Frequency and the Overtone Structure', *ibid.*, Oct., 1934, 59-69.

13. ———. *Speech and Hearing.* With an Introduction by H. D. Arnold. New York: D. Van Nostrand Co., 1929.

14. ———. *Speech and Hearing in Communication.* New York: D. Van Nostrand Co., 1953.

15. Fletcher, Harvey, and Munson, W. A. 'Loudness, its Definition, Measurement and Calculation', *The Journal of the Acoustical Society of America*, Oct., 1933, 82-108.

16. Helmholtz, H. L. F. *On the Sensations of Tone.* Translated by A. J. Ellis. Reprint of the last English edition with an Introduction by Henry Margenau. New York: Dover Publications, 1954.

17. Ingerslev, Fritz, and Frobenius, Walther. 'Some Measurements of the End-Corrections and Acoustic Spectra of Cylindrical Open Flue Organ Pipes', *Transactions of the Danish Academy of Technical Sciences*, No. 1, 1947.

18. Jeans, James. *Science and Music.* New York: The Macmillan Co., 1937.

19. Jones, A. T. 'End Corrections of Organ Pipes', *The Journal of the Acoustical Society of America*, Jan., 1941, 387-94.

20. ———. 'Recent Investigations of Organ Pipes', *ibid.*, July, 1939, 122-8.

21. Kingsbury, B. A. 'A Direct Comparison of the Loudness of Pure Tones', *The Physical Review*, April, 1927, 588-600.

22. Knudsen, V. O. 'The Sensibility of the Ear to small Differences of Intensity and Frequency', *The Physical Review*, Jan., 1923, 84-102.

23. Kock, W. E. 'A New Interpretation of the Results of Experiments on the Differential Pitch Sensitivity of the Ear', *The Journal of the Acoustical Society of America*, Oct., 1932, 129-34.

24. Lloyd, Ll. S. *Decibels and Phons: A Musical Analogy*. London: Oxford University Press, 1938.

25. ——. *Music and Sound*. London: Oxford University Press, 1937.

26. Mendel, Arthur. 'Pitch in the 16th and 17th Centuries', *The Musical Quarterly*, 1948: I, Jan., 28-45; II, April, 199-221; III, July, 336-57; IV, Oct., 575-93.

27. Miller, D. C. *Anecdotal History of the Science of Sound*. New York: The Macmillan Co., 1935.

28. ——. *The Science of Musical Sounds*. New York: The Macmillan Co., 1916.

29. ——. *Sound Waves, their Shape and Speed*. New York: The Macmillan Co., 1937.

30. Mills, John. *A Fugue in Cycles and Bels*. New York: D. Van Nostrand Co., 1935.

31. Nolle, A. W., and Boner, C. P. 'Harmonic Relations in the Partials of Organ Pipes and of Vibrating Strings', *The Journal of the Acoustical Society of America*, Oct., 1941, 145-7.

32. ——. 'The Initial Transients of Organ Pipes', *ibid.*, 149-54.

33. Northrop, P. A. 'Problems in the Analysis of the Tone of an Open Organ Pipe', *The Journal of the Acoustical Society of America*, July, 1940, 90-94.

34. Ogden, R. M. *Hearing*. New York: Harcourt, Brace & Co., 1924.

35. Redfield, John. *Music: A Science and an Art*. New York: Alfred A. Knopf, 1928.

36. Richardson, E. G. *Acoustics of Orchestral Instruments and of the Organ*. London: Edward Arnold & Co., 1929.

37. ——. *Sound: A Physical Text Book*. London: Edward Arnold & Co., 1927.

38. Riesz, R. R. 'The Relationship between Loudness and the Minimum Perceptible Increment of Intensity', *The Journal of the Acoustical Society of America*, Jan., 1933, 211-16.

39. Sabine, W. C. *Collected Papers on Acoustics*. Cambridge: Harvard University Press, 1927.

40. Seashore, C. E. *Psychology of Music*. New York: McGraw-Hill Co., 1938.

41. Shortley, George, and Williams, Dudley. *Physics: Fundamental Principles for Students of Science and Engineering*. 2 vols. New York: Prentice-Hall, 1950.

42. Shower, E. G., and Biddulph, R. 'Differential Pitch Sensitivity of the Ear', *The Journal of the Acoustical Society of America*, Oct., 1931, 275-87.

43. Smith, Hermann. *The Making of Sound in the Organ and in the Orchestra*. New York: Charles Scribner's Sons, 1911.

44. Stewart, G. W. *Introductory Acoustics*. New York: D. Van Nostrand Co., 1933.

45. Trendelenburg, von F. 'Untersuchungen über Einschwingvorgänge an Orgelpfeifen', *Zeitschrift für technische Physik*, 17 (1936), 578-80.

46. Wachsmuth, R. 'Labialpfeifen und Lamelltöne', *Annalen der Physik*, Vierte Folge, Band 14 (1904), 469-505.

47. Watt, H. J. *The Psychology of Sound*. Cambridge, Eng.: Cambridge University Press, 1917.

48. Wood, Alexander. *The Physics of Music*. 5th ed. London: Methuen & Co., 1950.

B.   Concerning   Keyboard   Instruments
and   their   Music

49. Antegnati, Costanzo. *L'Arte organica*. Brescia: Francesco Tebaldino, 1608. Reprint with a Preface by Renato Lunelli. German translation by Paul Smets. Mainz: Rheingold-Verlag, 1938.

50. Apel, Willi. 'Early German Keyboard Music', *The Musical Quarterly*, April, 1937, 210-37.

51. ——. 'Early History of the Organ', *Speculum: A Journal of Mediaeval Studies*, April, 1948, 191-216.

52. ——. 'Early Spanish Music for Lute and Keyboard Instruments', *The Musical Quarterly*, July, 1934, 289-301.

53. ——. *Masters of the Keyboard*. Cambridge: Harvard University Press, 1947.

54. ——. 'Die Tabulatur des Adam Ileborgh', *Zeitschrift für Musikwissenschaft*, April, 1934, 193-212.

55. Arnold, Friedrich Wilhelm. 'Das Locheimer Liederbuch, nebst der Ars Organisandi von Conrad Paumann', rev. and ed. Heinrich Bellermann, in Friedrich Chrysander, *Jahrbücher für Musikalische Wissenschaft*, Band II. Leipzig: Breitkopf und Härtel, 1867, 1-234.

56. Audsley, G. A. *The Art of Organ Building*. 2 vols. New York: Dodd, Mead and Co., 1905.

57. ——. *Organ Stops and their Artistic Registration*. New York: The H. W. Gray Co., 1921.

58. Banchieri, Adriano. *Conclusioni nel suono dell' organo*. Bologna: Heredi di Giovanni Rossi, 1609. Reprint. Milan: Bollettino Bibliografico Musicale, 1934.

59. Barnes, W. H. *The Contemporary American Organ*. 5th ed. New York: J. Fischer & Bro., 1952.

60. Bedbrook, G. S. *Keyboard Music from the Middle Ages to the Beginnings of the Baroque*. London: Macmillan & Co., 1949.

61. Bédos de Celles, François. *L'Art du facteur d'orgues*. 3 vols. 1766-78. Facsimile reprint. Kassel: Bärenreiter-Verlag, 1934-6.

62. Bie, Oscar. *Klavier, Orgel und Harmonium*. 2nd ed. Leipzig: B. G. Teubner, 1921.

63. Bonavia-Hunt, N. A. *The Modern British Organ*. London: A. Weekes & Co., 1947.

64. ——. *Modern Organ Stops*. London: Musical Opinion, 1923.

65. ——. *Modern Studies in Organ Tone*. London: Musical Opinion, 1933.

66. Bonavia-Hunt, N. A., and Homer, H. W. *The Organ Reed*. New York: J. Fischer & Bro., 1950.

67. Brunold, Paul. *Le Grand Orgue de Saint-Gervais à Paris*. Paris: L'Oiseau Lyre, 1934.

68. Cellier, Alexandre. *L'Orgue moderne*. Paris: Librairie Delagrave, 1921.

69. Cellier, Alexandre, and Bachelin, Henri. *L'Orgue: Ses éléments, Son histoire, Son esthétique*. Paris: Librairie Delagrave, 1933.

70. Clutton, Cecil, and Dixon, George. *The Organ: its Tonal Structure and Registration*. London: Grenville Publishing Co., 1950.

71. De Brisay, A. C. D. *The Organ and its Music*. New York: E. P. Dutton & Co., 1935.

72. Dickinson, Helen A. and Clarence. 'A Musical Journey in Spain', *American Organ Monthly*, Jan., 1921, xxxiii-xl.

73. Diruta, Girolamo. *Il Transilvano*. Venice: Alessandro Vincenti, 1625.

74. Dufourcq, Norbert. *Documents inédits relatifs à l'orgue français*. 2 vols. Paris: Librairie E. Droz, 1934/5.

75. ——. *Esquisse d'une histoire de l'orgue en France du XIIIe au XVIIIe siècle*. Paris: Librairie E. Droz, 1935.

76. ——. *Jean-Sébastien Bach, le Maître de l'orgue*. Paris: Librairie Floury, 1948.

77. Ellerhorst, von Winfred. *Handbuch der Orgelkunde*. Einseideln: Verlagsanstalt Benziger & Co., 1936.

78. Fellerer, K. G. *Orgel und Orgelmusik.* Augsburg: Benno Filser Verlag, 1929.

79. Flade, Ernst. *Der Orgelbauer Gottfried Silbermann.* Leipzig: Kistner und Siegel, 1926.

80. Fleury, Paul de. *Dictionnaire biographique des facteurs d'orgues.* Paris: Office Général de la Musique, 1918.

81. Frotscher, Gotthold. *Die Orgel.* Leipzig: J. J. Weber, 1927.

82. Gammons, E. B. 'Some Modern Trends in the Tonal Design of the Organ', *Proceedings of the Music Teachers National Association,* 1947/8, 118-25.

83. Gastoué, Amédée. *L'Orgue en France de l'antiquité au début de la période classique.* Paris: Bureau d'Édition de la "Schola", 1921.

84. Germani, Fernando. *Method for the Organ.* 4 parts. Part IV, Book I. Rome: Edizioni de Santis, 1953.

85. Goodrich, Wallace. *The Organ in France.* Boston: The Boston Music Co., 1917.

86. Grace, Harvey. *French Organ Music.* New York: The H. W. Gray Co., 1919.

87. ——. *The Organ Works of Bach.* London: Novello & Co., 1922.

88. ——. *The Organ Works of Rheinberger.* London: Novello & Co., 1925.

89. Hess, Joachim. *Dispositien der merkwaardigste Kerkorgelen.* Gauda, .1774. Reprint, ed. Lambert Erné. Utrecht: J. A. H. Wagenaar, 1945.

90. ——. *Luister van het Orgel.* Gauda, 1772. Reprint, ed. Lambert Erné. Utrecht: J. A. H. Wagenaar, 1945.

91. Hopkins, E. J., and Rimbault, E. F. *The Organ, its History and Construction.* 3rd ed. London: Robert Cocks & Co., 1877.

92. Hull, A. E. *Organ Playing: Its Technique and Expression.* London: Augener, 1911.

93. Huré, Jean. *L'Esthétique de l'orgue.* Paris: Éditions Maurice Senart, 1923.

94. Jeppesen, Knud. *Die italienische Orgelmusik am Anfang der Cinquecento.* Copenhagen: Einar Munksgaard, 1943.

95. Keller, Hermann. *Die Orgelwerke Bachs.* Leipzig: C. F. Peters, 1948.

96. Kendall, Raymond. 'Notes on Arnolt Schlick', *Acta Musicologica* XI, 1939, 136-43.

97. ——. 'Notes on Arnolt Schlick', *Guildiana* (American Guild of Organists), Feb.-May, 1942.

98. Kinkeldey, Otto. *Orgel und Klavier in der Musik des 16. Jahrhunderts.* Leipzig: Breitkopf und Härtel, 1910.

99. Klotz, Hans. *Über die Orgelkunst der Gotik, der Renaissance und des Barock.* Kassel: Bärenreiter-Verlag, 1934.

100. Locher, Carl. *Die Orgel-Register und ihre Klangfarben.* 4th ed. Bern: Emil Baumgart, 1912.

101. Lowinsky, E. E. 'English Organ Music of the Renaissance', *The Musical Quarterly,* July, 1953, 373-95; Oct., 1953, 528-53.

102. Mahrenholz, Christhard. *Die Orgelregister, ihre Geschichte und ihr Bau.* Kassel: Bärenreiter-Verlag, 1930.

103. Mueren, Floris van der. *Het Orgel in de Nederlanden.* Leuven: Universitaire Boekhandel Uystpruyst, 1931.

104. Mulet, Henri. *Les Tendances néfastes et antireligieuses de l'orgue moderne.* Paris: Bureau d'Édition de la Schola Cantorum, 1922.

105. Mustel, Alphonse, 'L'Orgue-harmonium', *Encyclopédie de la Musique et Dictionnaire du Conservatoire,* 2e Partie. Paris: Librairie Delagrave, 1926, 1375-1400.

106. Pearce, C. W. *The Evolution of the Pedal Organ.* London: Musical Opinion, 1927.

107. ——. *Notes on Old London City Churches, their Organs, Organists, and Musical Associations.* London: The Vincent Music Co., c.1909.

108. Perkins, Jocelyn. *The Organs and Bells of Westminster Abbey*. London: Novello & Co., 1937.

109. Pfatteicher, C. F. *John Redford*. Kassel: Bärenreiter-Verlag, 1934.

110. Pirro, André. 'L'Art des organistes', *Encyclopédie de la Musique et Dictionnaire du Conservatoire*, 2ᵉ Partie. Paris: Librairie Delagrave, 1926, 1181-1374.

111. ——. *Johann Sebastian Bach: the Organist and his Works for the Organ*. Translated by Wallace Goodrich. New York: G. Schirmer, 1902.

112. Praetorius, Michael. *De Organographia* (*Syntagmatis Musici*, Tomus Secundus). Wolfenbüttel: Elias Holwein, 1619. Facsimile reprint. Kassel: Bärenreiter-Verlag, 1929.

113. Raugel, Félix. 'The Ancient French Organ School', translated by Theodore Baker, *The Musical Quarterly*, Oct., 1925, 560-71.

114. ——. *Les Grandes Orgues des Églises de Paris et du Département de la Seine*. Paris: Librairie Fischbacher, 1927.

115. ——. *Les Organistes*. Paris: Henri Laurens, 1923.

116. Ritter, A. G. *Zur Geschichte des Orgelspiels*. 2 vols. Leipzig: Max Hesse, 1884.

117. Rokseth, Yvonne. *La Musique d'orgue au XVᵉ siècle et au début du XVIᵉ*. Paris: Librairie E. Droz, 1930.

118. Rupp, Emile. *Die Entwicklungsgeschichte der Orgelbaukunst*. Einseideln: Verlagsanstalt Benziger & Co., 1929.

119. Schering, Arnold. *Die niederländische Orgelmesse im Zeitalter des Josquin*. Leipzig: Breitkopf und Härtel, 1912.

120. Schlick, Arnolt. *Spiegel der Orgelmacher und Organisten*. Mainz: Peter Schöffer, 1511. Reprint, ed. Paul Smets. Mainz: Der Rheingold-Verlag, 1937.

121. Schrade, Leo. *Die ältesten Denkmäler der Orgelmusik*. Münster: Helios-Verlag, 1928.

122. ——. 'The Organ and Organ Music in the Mass of the 15th Century', *The Musical Quarterly*, July, 1942, 329-36; Oct., 1942, 467-87.

123. Schweitzer, Albert. *Deutsche und Französische Orgelbaukunst und Orgelkunst*. Leipzig: Breitkopf und Härtel, 1927.

124. Smets, Paul. *Neuzeitlicher Orgelbau*. Mainz: Der Rheingold-Verlag, 1944.

125. ——. *Die Orgelregister, ihr Klang und Gebrauch*. Mainz: Der Rheingold-Verlag, 1943.

126. Sponsel, J. U. *Orgelhistorie*. Nuremberg: G. P. Monath, 1771. Reprint, ed. Paul Smets. Kassel: Bärenreiter-Verlag, 1931.

127. Stevens, Denis. *The Mulliner Book: A Commentary*. London: Stainer and Bell, 1952.

128. Sumner, W. L. *The Organ: Its Evolution, Principles of Construction, and Use*. London: Macdonald & Co., 1952.

129. Sutherland, Gordon. 'The Ricercari of Jacques Buus', *The Musical Quarterly*, Oct., 1945, 448-63.

130. Truette, E. E. *Organ Registration*. Boston: C. W. Thompson & Co., 1919

131. Vente, M. A. *Bouwstoffen tot de Geschiedenis van het Nederlandse Orgel in de 16ᵈᵉ Eeuw*. Amsterdam: H. J. Paris, 1942.

132. Wedgwood, J. I. *A Comprehensive Dictionary of Organ Stops*. London: The Vincent Music Co., 1905.

133. Weigl, Bruno. *Handbuch der Orgelliteratur*. Leipzig: F. E. C. Leuckart, 1931.

134. Widor, C. M. *L'Orgue Moderne*. Paris: Durand & Cie., 1928.

135. Williams, C. F. Abdy. *The Story of Organ Music.* London: The Walter Scott Publishing Co., 1905.

136. ——. *The Story of the Organ.* London: The Walter Scott Publishing Co., 1916.

C. Miscellaneous Books on Music

137. Apel, Willi. *Harvard Dictionary of Music.* Cambridge: Harvard University Press, 1944.

138. Bukofzer, M. F. *Music in the Baroque Era.* New York: W. W. Norton & Co., 1947.

139. Burney, Charles. *Continental Travels.* Abridged by C. H. Glover. London: Blackie & Son, 1927.

140. ——. *The Present State of Music in Germany, the Netherlands, and the United Provinces.* 2nd ed. 2 vols. London: T. Becket, 1775.

141. Chorley, H. F. *Music and Manners in France and Germany.* 3 vols. London: Longman, Brown, Green, and Longmans, 1844.

142. Dauriac, Lionel. *Essai sur l'esprit musical.* Paris: Félix Alcan, 1904.

143. David, H. T., and Mendel, Arthur. *The Bach Reader.* New York: W. W. Norton & Co., 1945.

144. Dolmetsch, Arnold. *The Interpretation of the Music of the XVIIth and XVIIIth Centuries.* London: Novello & Co., 1915.

145. Douglas, Winfred. *Church Music in History and Practice.* New York: Charles Scribner's Sons, 1937.

146. Geiringer, Karl. *Musical Instruments.* Translated by Bernard Miall. London: George Allen and Unwin, 1943.

147. *Grove's Dictionary of Music and Musicians.* 3rd ed., edited by H. C. Colles. 5 vols. New York: The Macmillan Co., 1927.

148. *Grove's Dictionary of Music and Musicians.* 5th ed., edited by Eric Blom. 9 vols. London: Macmillan & Co., 1954.

149. d'Indy, Vincent. *César Franck.* Translated by Rosa Newmarch. London: John Lane The Bodley Head, 1909.

150. Parry, C. H. H. *Style in Musical Art.* London: Macmillan & Co., 1911.

151. Pirro, André. *Histoire de la musique de la fin du XIVe siècle à la fin du XVIe* Paris: Librairie Renouard, 1940.

152. Prunières, Henry. *Monteverdi, his Life and Work.* Translated by Marie D. Mackie. New York: E. P. Dutton & Co., 1926.

153. *Hugo Riemanns Musiklexikon.* 11th ed., edited by Alfred Einstein. Berlin: Max Hesses Verlag, 1929.

154. Sachs, Curt. *The History of Musical Instruments.* New York: W. W. Norton & Co., 1940.

155. Scholes, Percy A. *The Oxford Companion to Music.* 8th ed. London: Oxford University Press, 1950.

156. Schweitzer, Albert. *J. S. Bach.* Translated by Ernest Newman. 2 vols. London: A. & C. Black, 1935.

157. Seiffert, Max. *J. P. Sweelinck und seine direkten Schüler.* Leipzig: Breitkopf und Härtel, 1891.

158. Thompson, Oscar. *The International Cyclopedia of Music and Musicians.* 4th ed. New York: Dodd, Mead & Co., 1946.

159. Widor, C. M. *Technique de l'orchestre moderne.* 3rd ed. Paris: Henry Lemoine & Cie., 1910.

160. Widor, C. M. *The Technique of the Modern Orchestra.* Trans. of 1st ed. of 159 by Edward Suddard. London: Joseph Williams, 1906.

D. Collections of Music

161. Apel, Willi. *Musik aus früher Zeit.* 2 vols. Mainz: B. Schott's Söhne, 1934.

162. Attaingnant, Pierre (pub.). *Deux Livres d'Orgue,* 1531. Ed. Yvonne Rokseth. Paris: Société Française de Musicologie, 1925.

163. Bach, J. S. *Johann Sebastian Bach's Werke.* Ed. Bach-Gesellschaft. Leipzig, 1851-99.

164. ———. *The Complete Organ Works.* Miniature reproductions from Gesellschaft edition. New York: Lea Pocket Scores, 1953.

165. ———. *Organ Works.* Ed. C. M. Widor and Albert Schweitzer. 5 vols. Vol. VI, ed. Albert Schweitzer and Edouard Nies-Berger. New York: G. Schirmer, 1912-13, 1954.

166. Boëly, A. P. F. *Album of Noëls.* Ed. H. A. Fricker. With a Preface by Camille Saint-Saëns. London: Breitkopf und Härtel, n.d.

167. Bonnet, Joseph. *An Anthology of Early French Organ Music.* New York: The H. W. Gray Co., 1942.

168. ———. *Forerunners of Bach.* (*Historical Organ Recitals*, Vol. I.) New York: G. Schirmer, 1917.

169. ———. *Old Spanish Masters: Cabezón to Cabanilles.* (*Historical Organ Recitals*, Vol. VI.) New York: G. Schirmer, 1940.

170. Bossi, M. E. *Sammlung von Stücken alter italienischer Meister.* Leipzig: C. F. Peters, 1908.

171. Byrd, William. *The Collected Works of William Byrd.* Ed. E. H. Fellowes. Vols. XVIII - XX. London: Stainer and Bell, 1950.

172. ———. *The Byrd Organ Book.* Ed. Margaret Glyn. London: William Reeves, c. 1923.

173. ———. *Fourteen Pieces for Keyed Instruments.* Ed. J. A. Fuller Maitland and W. Barclay Squire. London: Stainer and Bell, n.d.

174. Cosyn, Benjamin. *Twenty-five Pieces for Keyed Instruments from Benjamin Cosyn's Virginal Book.* Ed. J. A. Fuller Maitland and W. Barclay Squire. London: J. & W. Chester, 1923.

175. Couperin, François. *Pièces d'orgue,* 1690. Reprint in *Archives des maîtres de l'orgue,* Vol. V.

176. Frescobaldi, Girolamo. *Orgel- und Klavierwerke.* 6 vols. Ed. Pierre Pidoux. Kassel: Bärenreiter-Verlag, 1949 ff.

177. Gauss, Otto. *Orgelkompositionen aus alter und neuer Zeit,* Vol. I. Regensburg: Coppenrath's Verlag, 1909.

178. Gibbons, Orlando. *Ten Pieces from the Virginal Book of Benjamin Cosyn.* Ed. J. A. Fuller Maitland. London: J. & W. Chester, 1925.

179. Glyn, Margaret. *Early English Organ Music,* Vol. I. London: The Plainsong and Mediaeval Music Society, 1939.

180. de Grigny, Nicolas. *Livre d'orgue,* 1711. Reprint in *Archives des maîtres de l'orgue,* Vol. V.

181. Guilmant, Alexandre. *Concert historique.* Mainz: B. Schott's Söhne, 1889.

182. Guilmant, Alexandre, and Pirro, André. *Archives des maîtres de l'orgue.* Paris: Durand & Cie. [Mainz: B. Schott's Söhne], 1898-1910.

183. Kaller, Ernst, *et al. Liber Organi.* 8 vols. Mainz: B. Schott's Söhne, 1931-8.

184. Kerckhoven, A. *Werken voor Orgel*. Ed. J. Watelet. (*Monumenta Musicae Belgicae*, Vol. II.) Berchem-Antwerp: "Der Ring," 1933.

185. Klotz, Hans. *Orgelmeister der Gotik.* (*Liber Organi*, Vol. VIII.) Mainz: B. Schott's Söhne, 1938.

186. Le Bègue, Nicolas. *Les Pièces d'orgue*, 1676. Reprint in *Archives des maîtres de l'orgue*, Vol. IX.

187. *Liber Usualis Missae et Officii.* Tournai: Desclée & Socii, 1931.

188. Moser, H. J., and Heitmann, Fritz. *Frühmeister der deutschen Orgelkunst.* Leipzig: Breitkopf und Härtel, 1930.

189. *The Mulliner Book.* Ed. Denis Stevens. (*Musica Britannica*, Vol. I.) London: Stainer and Bell, 1951.

190. Muset, Joseph. *Early Spanish Organ Music.* New York: G. Schirmer, 1948.

191. Pachelbel, Johann. *Orgelkompositionen.* Ed. Max Seiffert. (*Denkmäler der Tonkunst in Bayern*, Vol. IV.) Leipzig: Breitkopf und Härtel, 1903.

192. ——. *Ausgewählten Orgelwerke.* 4 vols. Ed. Karl Matthaei. Kassel: Bärenreiter-Verlag, 1928-36.

193. Pedrell , Felipe. *Hispaniae schola musica sacra,* 8 vols. Leipzig: Breitkopf und Härtel, 1894-8.

194. Raison, André. *Livre d'orgue*, 1687. Reprint in *Archives des maîtres de l'orgue*, Vol. II.

195. Scheidt, Samuel. *Tabulatura nova.* Ed. Max Seiffert. (*Denkmäler deutscher Tonkunst*, Vol. I.) Leipzig: Breitkopf und Härtel, 1892.

196. ——. *Douze pièces d'orgue*, extraites de la *Tabulatura nova.* Ed. William Montillet. Paris: Éditions Maurice Senart, n.d.

197. Schering, Arnold. *Alte Meister des Orgelspiels.* Leipzig: Breitkopf und Härtel, 1913.

198. Schlick, Arnolt. *Tabulaturen etlicher lobgesang und lidlein uff die Orgeln und Lauten*, 1512. Reprint, ed. Gottlieb Harms. Klecken: Ugrino Verlag, 1924.

199. Straube, Karl. *Alte Meister des Orgelspiels.* Leipzig: C. F. Peters, 1904.

200. ——. *Alte Meister des Orgelspiels,* Neue Folge. 2 vols. Leipzig: C. F. Peters, 1929.

201. ——. *Choralvorspiele alter Meister.* Leipzig: C. F. Peters, 1907.

202. Sweelinck, J. P. *Werken van Jan Pieterszoon Sweelinck*, 9 vols. Ed. Max Seiffert. Leipzig: Breitkopf und Härtel, 1894-1901.

203. ——. *Drei Fantasien, drei Toccaten und vier Variationen.* Ed. Robert Eitner. Berlin: N. Simrock, 1870.

204. Tallis, Thomas. *Complete Keyboard Works.* Ed. Denis Stevens. London: Hinrichsen Edition, 1953.

205. Titelouze, Jean. *Oevres complètes.* Reprint in *Archives des maîtres de l'orgue*, Vol. I.

206. Torchi, Luigi. *L'Arte musicale in Italia*, Vol. III. Milan: G. Ricordi & Co., 1897.

207. Weelkes, Thomas. *Pieces for Keyed Instruments*. Ed. Margaret Glyn. London: Stainer and Bell, 1924.

208. West, John E. *Old English Organ Music.* 36 folios. London: Novello & Co.

E. Nonmusical Books and Addenda

209. Pepys, Samuel. *The Diary of Samuel Pepys.* 2 vols. Ed. H. B. Wheatley. Am. printing of ed. of 1893. New York: Random House.

210. Rau, Santha Rama. *East of Home.* New York: Harper and Brothers, 1950.

211. Reese, Gustave. *Music in the Renaissance.* New York: W. W. Norton & Co., 1954.

212. Gabrieli, Andrea. *Orgel- und Klavierwerke Andrea Gabrielis.* 4 vols.. Ed. Pierre Pidoux. Kassel: Bärenreiter-Verlag.

213. Palestrina, Giovanni Pierluigi da (?). *Ricercari sopra li tuoni a quattro voci.* Mainz: B. Schott's Söhne, 1933.

INDEXES

INDEX OF MUSIC

Cited or Discussed

INDEX OF PERSONS

See also Index of Music

GENERAL INDEX

Absorption, 23-5, 27, 28, 111, 112, 113, 114, 115
Absorption of other media, 322
Accompaniment; *see* Solo and accompaniment
Accompaniment of other media, 327-31
Acoustic tile, 24, 25
Acoustical environment, 5, 23-8, 28-9, 48, 110-17, 369
  Adaptation of registration, 113-17, 362
    Stone walls, 114-15
    Dead rooms, 115
  Appraisal, 116, 331
Acoustical research, 4-5
Adaptation to American organs
  General, 284, 294, 310-14, 350, 362
  English music, 281, 304
  French music, 147, 157, 158, 250, 301-3
  German music, 273-4, 297-8
  Italian music, 237-8, 241-2
  Spanish music, 241-2
  Harmonium music, 304, 308-9
  Transcriptions, 320-21
Additions; *see* Changes of combination, Transitions
Aeolian Company, The, 370
Agogic stress, 106, 141-3
American organs
  Characteristics, 3, 65, 100, 101, 218, 294, 295, 303, 347, 348-9, 362
  Adaptation to; *see* Adaptation
American organ music, 294
Amsterdam — Oude Kerk, 263
Analysis of tone quality, 4-5, 13, 38, 47-55, 369-73
Anches; *see* Reeds
  See also Jeux de combinaison
Architects, 117
Area of hearing, 14-16
Attack, 103, 142-4, 145, 316
  See also Speech characteristics
Audibility, 63 ff, 124, 329
Audience, Acoustical effect of, 25, 115
Auditoriums; *see* Acoustical environment
Aural additions, 20-22, 28
  Partials, 17, 20, 48
  See also Difference tones, Summation tones
Aural appraisal, 28, 63, 102, 116-17, 331, 344, 361, 365
Aural partials; *see* Aural additions
Aural response; *see* Ear
Austin Organs Inc., 54, 298 fn, 370, 373

Bach's motives, 167, 168, 198
Bach's pupils, 285
Balance
  In ensemble, 86-9, 90-91, 96, 97, 110-11, 112, 113, 114-15, 336
  Between keyboards, 110, 112-13, 114, 337-8

Balance — *Continued*
  Between media, 323-4, 325, 327-8, 329-30, 331
Bali, 231 fn
Barker lever, 291
Baroque music, 175, 203 fn, 251-2, 309, 310
  See also German organ music, Sweelinck
Baroque organs, 89 fn, 93, 100-101, 104-5 fn, 153, 230, 265-70, 310-11, 362
  See also German organs
Barye, 11-12
Basso continuo, 101, 318
Beard, 42
Beats, 21, 56, 80, 82
Beauty, 152-4
Belgian music, 251, 294 fn
  See also Peeters
Bell Telephone Company, 22
Birds, 242, 273
Blend, 71 ff, 83-4, 323
  Factors, 71-3, 74 ff, 83-4
    Coincidence of partials, 71-2
    Interspacing of partials, 72, 73
    Normal balance of pitches, 72-3
    Miscellaneous considerations, 79-83
  Tones of same pitch, 74-6, 83, 86
  Tones of different pitch, 76-9, 84, 86
  Optimum blend, 84, 85 ff
    Stops, 85-91
    Considerations of texture, 85, 91-8
  Blend between media, 323-4, 325, 326, 329
Blokwerk; *see* Hintersatz
Borrowed stops, 81, 84
Bridge; *see* Beard
Buxtehude chorale fantasia; *see* Chorale preludes

Cabinet Organ, 288, 305
Canons, 182-5, 240
  Between solo voices, 184-5
Cantus firmus, 101, 217, 226
Cantus firmus settings, 228, 240, 261
  See also Chorale preludes
Canzona, 209, 235, 236, 263
Capriccio, 236
Celesta, 57, 320
Célestes, 56, 81-2, 84, 98-9, 105, 107, 108, 126, 130-32, 136-7, 138, 160-61, 171, 174-5, 231-2, 234 fn, 301 fn, 312, 318
Chaire organ, 276, 277
Changes of combination, 122-3, 194-7, 232, 234, 257-8, 272, 330, 338-42
  Concealment, 339-40
  Timing, 338-9, 342, 343-4
  See also Contrast
Chimes, 57, 81, 82-3, 273
Chorale preludes, 182-3, 183-92, 195-200
  Simple, 186-7
  Cantus firmus, 188